Jaguar Books on Latin

Series Editors

WILLIAM H. BEEZLEY, Professor of History, University of Arizona
COLIN M. MACLACHLAN, John Christy Barr Distinguished Professor of
History, Tulane University

Volumes Published

John E. Kicza, ed., *The Indian in Latin American History: Resistance,
Resilience, and Acculturation* (1993; rev. ed., 2000).
Cloth ISBN 0-8420-2822-6 Paper ISBN 0-8420-2823-4

Susan E. Place, ed., *Tropical Rainforests: Latin American Nature and
Society in Transition* (1993). Cloth ISBN 0-8420-2423-9
Paper ISBN 0-8420-2427-1

Paul W. Drake, ed., *Money Doctors, Foreign Debts, and Economic
Reforms in Latin America from the 1890s to the Present* (1994).
Cloth ISBN 0-8420-2434-4   Paper ISBN 0-8420-2435-2

John A. Britton, ed., *Molding the Hearts and Minds: Education,
Communications, and Social Change in Latin America* (1994).
Cloth ISBN 0-8420-2489-1   Paper ISBN 0-8420-2490-5

David J. Weber and Jane M. Rausch, eds., *Where Cultures Meet: Frontiers
in Latin American History* (1994). Cloth ISBN 0-8420-2477-8
Paper ISBN 0-8420-2478-6

Gertrude M. Yeager, ed., *Confronting Change, Challenging Tradition:
Women in Latin American History* (1994). Cloth ISBN 0-8420-2479-4
Paper ISBN 0-8420-2480-8

Linda Alexander Rodríguez, ed., *Rank and Privilege: The Military and
Society in Latin America* (1994). Cloth ISBN 0-8420-2432-8
Paper ISBN 0-8420-2433-6

Darién J. Davis, ed., *Slavery and Beyond: The African Impact on Latin
America and the Caribbean* (1995). Cloth ISBN 0-8420-2484-0
Paper ISBN 0-8420-2485-9

Gilbert M. Joseph and Mark D. Szuchman, eds., *I Saw a City Invincible:
Urban Portraits of Latin America* (1996). Cloth ISBN 0-8420-2495-6
Paper ISBN 0-8420-2496-4

Roderic Ai Camp, ed., *Democracy in Latin America: Patterns and Cycles* (1996). Cloth ISBN 0-8420-2512-X   Paper ISBN 0-8420-2513-8

Oscar J. Martínez, ed., *U.S.-Mexico Borderlands: Historical and Contemporary Perspectives* (1996). Cloth ISBN 0-8420-2446-8 Paper ISBN 0-8420-2447-6

William O. Walker III, ed., *Drugs in the Western Hemisphere: An Odyssey of Cultures in Conflict* (1996). Cloth ISBN 0-8420-2422-0 Paper ISBN 0-8420-2426-3

Richard R. Cole, ed., *Communication in Latin America: Journalism, Mass Media, and Society* (1996). Cloth ISBN 0-8420-2558-8 Paper ISBN 0-8420-2559-6

David G. Gutiérrez, ed., *Between Two Worlds: Mexican Immigrants in the United States* (1996). Cloth ISBN 0-8420-2473-5 Paper ISBN 0-8420-2474-3

Lynne Phillips, ed., *The Third Wave of Modernization in Latin America: Cultural Perspectives on Neoliberalism* (1998). Cloth ISBN 0-8420-2606-1   Paper ISBN 0-8420-2608-8

Daniel Castro, ed., *Revolution and Revolutionaries: Guerrilla Movements in Latin America* (1999). Cloth ISBN 0-8420-2625-8 Paper ISBN 0-8420-2626-6

Virginia Garrard-Burnett, ed., *On Earth as It Is in Heaven: Religion in Modern Latin America* (2000). Cloth ISBN 0-8420-2584-7 Paper ISBN 0-8420-2585-5

Carlos A. Aguirre and Robert Buffington, eds., *Reconstructing Criminality in Latin America* (2000). Cloth ISBN 0-8420-2620-7 Paper ISBN 0-8420-2621-5

Christon I. Archer, ed., *The Wars of Independence in Spanish America* (2000). Cloth ISBN 0-8420-2468-9   Paper ISBN 0-8420-2469-7

John F. Schwaller, ed., *The Church in Colonial Latin America* (2000). Cloth ISBN 0-8420-2703-3   Paper ISBN 0-8420-2704-1

Ingrid E. Fey and Karen Racine, eds., *Strange Pilgrimages: Exile, Travel, and National Identity in Latin America, 1800–1990s* (2000). Cloth ISBN 0-8420-2693-2   Paper ISBN 0-8420-2694-0

The Wars
of Independence
in Spanish America

The Wars
of Independence
in Spanish America

Christon I. Archer
Editor

Jaguar Books on Latin America
Number 20

A Scholarly Resources Inc. Imprint
Wilmington, Delaware

Scholarly Resources Inc.
104 Greenhill Avenue
Wilmington, DE 19805-1897
www.scholarly.com

Library of Congress Cataloging-in-Publication Data

The Wars of Independence in Spanish America / Christon I. Archer,
editor.
    p.   cm. — (Jaguar books on Latin America ; no. 20)
    Includes bibliographical references.
    ISBN 0-8420-2468-9 (alk. paper) — ISBN 0-8420-2469-7 (pbk : alk.
paper)
    1. Latin America—History—Wars of Independence, 1806–1830.
2. Insurgency—Latin America—History—19th century. 3. Spain—
Colonies—America—Administration. I. Archer, Christon I., 1940–
II. Series.
F1412.W37   2000
980'.02—dc21   99-045128
                                                   CIP

About the Editor

Christon I. Archer is professor of history at the University of Calgary. He has written extensively on the army of New Spain and on the epoch of independence. His works include *The Army in Bourbon Mexico* (1979), which won the Bolton Prize. Archer is currently working on the insurgency and counterinsurgency during the war of independence in New Spain and on a study of Spanish oceanic exploration of the Northwest Coast (present-day California to Alaska) in the eighteenth century.

Contents

Preface

Years ago at a Southern Historical Association meeting at Atlanta, Georgia, following a panel on Spanish American independence, John TePaske of Duke University commented that he was glad to see new work being done on the period because it was so difficult to teach. Others in the discussion—mostly eighteenth-century Bourbon era specialists—noted that sometimes they spun out their colonial period lectures so that there was little time left for the chaotic post-1810 independence epoch. If there was a national period survey following, they commenced with the history of the independent nations. How things have changed! Already, the first bicentennial conferences on the independence period are being scheduled so that beginning in 2008 and 2010, we will be prepared to launch a decade and one-half of celebrations that will continue into the 2020s. One can only hope that the vision of historians in the not-too-distant future will be as clear as the numerals for perfect eyesight suggest. Likely, in part the bicentennials will be something of a hagiographer's dream and an academic historian's nightmare. Or will mature reflection produced by chronological distance from the superheated early-nineteenth-century environment of war and revolution result in new analysis and vision? And will the bicentennial era balance the glorification and national creation myths that have placed the great national heroes and founding fathers (sometimes mothers) of Spanish America in a special pantheon of glory?

In some circles, criticism of these figures is tantamount to a form of historical treason directed against the nation itself. For example, depending upon one's geographic location in the Americas, it would not be recommended to engage in public criticism of national founders and heroes such as "El Libertador" (the Liberator) Simón Bolívar, "El Protector" José de San Martín, or Father José María Morelos of New Spain. Only a few years ago, Mexico's president declared that to criticize the fathers of the nation was not only unpatriotic but also bordered on sedition. Better to repeat old views about Spanish cruelty, vice, and exploitation—or to work over the royalist army commanders and bureaucrats such as "El Pacificador" (the Pacifier), General Pablo Morillo in Nueva Granada (Venezuela and Colombia); or "El Carnicero" (the Butcher), Brigadier Félix María Calleja (New Spain). Few people today recall that the royalists described themselves as defending *la causa buena* (the good cause) against *la causa mala* (the evil cause) led by *cabecillas* of *gavillas* (wrongheaded ringleaders of gangs of thugs).

Many historians today, Spanish Americans and foreigners, have begun to strip away older views and to produce new and compelling interpretations about the nature of the insurgencies, counterinsurgencies, rebellions, guerrilla movements, civil wars, revolutions, riots, banditry, and other forms of disorder that helped to engender the new nations. The present volume includes examples of recent research, some earlier views, a number of contemporary interpretations by participants, and documents in translation from the period that illustrate major points. In this study, we emphasize the military side of the wars and the nature of insurgency, rebellion, and counterinsurgency. Many earlier studies about Spanish American independence neglected these themes in favor of diplomacy, politics, and the formation of constitutional systems.

Students will identify interesting parallels between the conflicts of Spanish American independence and twentieth-century people's revolutions and wars in Russia, China, Algeria, the Philippines, Cuba, Africa, and Southeast Asia. In all of these struggles, rebels or insurgents adopted guerrilla warfare and banditry. Their opponents—the royalists in Spanish America—in defense of the existing regime were quick to describe them as common bandits, terrorists, murderers, robbers, and thugs. We can speak of hyphenate people called guerrilla-bandits or insurgent-bandits who sometimes lost connections with major political causes espoused by the patriot leadership. These people fought for their own regions or districts, for their village-based families and clans, and often for themselves. They changed sides on one or more occasions depending upon offers of amnesty, including land, or to save themselves if they fell into the hands of their royalist opponents. It was not uncommon for insurgents to change sides several times from patriot to royalist, and in exceptional cases men switched sides back and forth as many as eight or nine times.

Historians who study Spanish American independence form an unofficial academy that has different branches according to the approaches and the regions studied. Until recently, some of the best work centered upon New Spain. There have been friendly debates and criticisms from Latin American scholars who argue that some foreign historians attempt to "reinvent the wheel" because they immerse themselves in the archives and do not give sufficient attention to published research. Historians on both sides complain that their colleagues do not read available published books and articles. Spanish American scholars wonder aloud whether highly educated and urbanized foreign historians visiting urban-based archives on brief research fellowships can comprehend accurately the complex rhythms, motivations, and rituals of eighteenth- or nineteenth-century rural and village society.

Aware of these issues concerning Mexican and U.S. historians, during the past decade Jaime E. Rodríguez O. of the University of California, Irvine, contributed an outstanding effort to promote better understanding, new research, and collaborative ties. He hosted a series of seminars at Irvine that brought together North American and other foreign Mexicanists with their Mexican counterparts and some other historians of Spanish America. Rodríguez edited several excellent bilingual volumes of essays that are listed in Suggested Readings in this volume. Colin MacLachlan and Rodríguez published the second edition of their stimulating essay on Colonial New Spain, *The Forging of the Cosmic Race: A Reinterpretation of Colonial Mexico* (1990). Moreover, Rodríguez's most recent synthesis, *The Independence of Spanish America* (1998), offers a comprehensive overview of the complex political processes and cultural continuities of Spanish American independence.

I want especially to thank those scholars who influenced my own thinking on the independence era: Jaime E. Rodríguez O., Brian R. Hamnett, Virginia Guedea, Eric Van Young, Hugh M. Hamill, John Lynch, William Taylor, Josefina Vázquez, Bill Beezley, Anne Staples, Colin MacLachlan, Asunción Lavrin, John Tutino, Peter Guardino, María del Carmen Velázquez, Timothy E. Anna, Paul Vanderwood, Mark Burkholder, Barbara Tenenbaum, Lyle N. McAlister, Juan Ortiz Escamilla, Allan Kuethe, Carlos Herrejón Peredo, John Kicza, Hira de Gortari, Anthony McFarlane, Michael P. Costeloe, and others too numerous to name. Thanks go also to my research assistant, Alex Taylor del Cid, who temporarily abandoned more recent events in Spanish America to listen to my theories about the independence era.

I

The Origins: Revolt, Insurrection, Uprising, and Reaction

Introduction: Setting the Scene for an Age of Warfare

Christon I. Archer

Writing in the 1930s, Charles E. Chapman declared that "the fundamental cause of the Spanish American wars of independence was the oppression of the colonial system and the crowning resentment of the creole class (the criollos or whites born in the Americas) against its restrictions socially, intellectually, economically, and politically."[1] Nevertheless, Chapman went on to state that the level of outright oppression was "never as great as it has often been depicted."[2] The criollos carried on for two centuries until they "awakened to the point of serious protest, and then it took yet another century to drive home the idea with sufficient force to induce them to take up arms."[3] In Chapman's view the revolutions originated from casual causes and "drifted into movements for independence almost 'in spite of themselves.' "[4] More recently, Jay Kinsbruner identified four often-cited causes of Spanish American independence: "the Enlightenment, the Bourbon reforms, the creole-peninsular controversy, and the late colonial revolts and protests."[5] John Lynch described the process as precipitated by "external shock" but as the result of "the culmination of a long process of alienation in which Spanish Americans became aware of their own identity, conscious of their own culture, jealous of their own resources."[6] Most recently, Jaime E. Rodríguez O. has presented an intriguing new interpretation of the independence epoch that emphasizes political processes and cultural continuities rather than focuses upon the rupture with Spain.[7]

While each study and interpretation has its own merits, historians today are reevaluating previously accepted causative factors. With unparalleled access to archival sources, researchers have been able to undertake regional and thematic studies that underscore the remarkable complexities of the period. Historians owe a debt of gratitude to the thousands of *escribanos* (scribes) who prepared official correspondence, kept detailed drafts and duplicates that ended up in archives, and recorded transactions from the most significant to the most mundane. Long forgotten, they continue to open windows to the past that simply are not raised elsewhere during periods of turbulence and institutional breakdown. As in the colonial era stretching back to the sixteenth-century Spanish Conquest, the use of pure rag paper gives historians of the period a tremendous advantage over those who must work with crumbling nineteenth- and twentieth-century wood-pulp paper that has not withstood the test of time. The unparalleled resources of archives such as the Archivo de Indias in Seville, the Archivo Histórico Nacional in Madrid, the Archivo General de la Nación in Mexico City, and the many other national, state, provincial, and municipal collections throughout the Americas provide the raw material for new directions and interpretations of the independence epoch.

Historians are astounded by the detail and diversity of the raw information on independence that comes alive from documents that in many instances appear to have been written only yesterday. In criminal cases involving assaults and murders, the court transcripts often include careful tracings of knives, swords, or machetes used by the perpetrators to stab, slash, or bludgeon their victims. Identity cards, passports, tax receipts, and even soiled paper icons of saints worn as talismans to protect their bearers ended up as evidence and have been preserved. Often, of course, these much-folded artifacts carried next to the skin of their wearers indicate that an insurgent suffered capture or that someone attempted to evade martial laws imposed during a period of guerrilla warfare, banditry, and counterinsurgency. During the military campaigns of the independence era in New Spain, royalist couriers—often women and children—carried dispatches written with the aid of magnifying glasses on tiny pieces of paper not more than an inch or two square. They folded and rolled these snippets into small tubes that could be hidden in body cavities as they traveled through enemy territory. Many of these people faced death before firing squads or changed sides to support those who captured them.

As is so often the case, we know much more about elite individuals and groups than we do about the thousands of *cabecillas* (rebel band leaders) and their followers who served in the *gavillas* (gangs) that infested so many regions of Spanish America. Rebels engaged in guerrilla-style warfare often took care not to keep incriminating documents that might fall into royalist hands. Moreover, these people often spent their time on the run and moved from place to place to evade the better armed royalist forces. Many rural-based insurgent chiefs and their followers were illiterate and could not afford to keep a scribe such as a priest, innkeeper, rancher, or petty bureaucrat at their sides to record their commands or their innermost thoughts. Often, the insurgents lacked both the facilities to keep archives and the printing presses to disseminate their ideas. On the royalist side, officials in major centers such as Mexico City, Guadalajara, Bogotá, Lima, and Quito maintained considerable continuity in terms of record-keeping with the established practices of the Bourbon era. Sometimes the same bureaucrats continued in their posts through independence with only minor changes in their work to recognize empire or republic in place of Spanish rule. In Buenos Aires and in some other cities of the Southern Cone, independence occurred without accompanying destruction.

The Need for Security and Armed Defenders

Throughout the eighteenth century, it was clear to Spanish imperial officials that the security of the American empire demanded much greater attention. Spain, the sick man of the Americas, was also the master of a treasurehouse of natural resources and commercial prospects desired by Britain and France. By the time of the voyage around the world of Admiral George Anson (1741–1744), it was clear to perceptive observers—and certainly to later historians—that Britain had entered a period in which it sought global domination.[8] The large-scale amphibious raid of Admiral Edward Vernon during the War of the Austrian Succession (1739–1748) against Cartagena, Nueva Granada; Guantánamo, Cuba; and Panama, while abortive, foreshadowed much more serious attacks to come.[9] When Spain entered the Seven Years' War (1756–1763) in 1762 under the Family Pact with France, the British promptly occupied Havana, the key to the Caribbean,[10] and alarmed Spanish authorities in New Granada, New Spain, and La Plata. The loss of Florida and the backhanded gift of Louisiana from France offered clear warning that the Spanish empire might well face future conflict with the expanding British commercial empire. In the immediate aftermath of the fall of Havana, the imperial government in Madrid moved to strengthen defenses and to consider controversial plans to arm Americanos of all provinces so that they could defend themselves.

Historians have made much of the military reforms that became key elements in late Bourbon efforts to shore up the empire. From this point forward the regime would mobilize criollo and *casta* (racially mixed) soldiers who might later turn their muskets and martial training against the *madre patria*.[11] The War of American Independence (1776–1783) presented Spain with a new opportunity for revenge against the British for the debacle at Havana, the loss of Florida, and many other slights. However, support for revolutionaries came at the potentially high cost of granting financial and military support to colonials who might influence Spanish Americans to do the same later against their own mother country. Itinerant American whalers, fur traders, and merchants—some of whom rounded Cape Horn and touched at Spain's Pacific Coast ports—smuggled copies of the Declaration of Independence, the *Federalist Papers*, the U.S. Constitution, pamphlets, and other so-called incendiary documents. For anyone with separatist tendencies who happened to know English or French, this documentation made fascinating reading. In fact, despite concerns by the Spanish Inquisition, which was responsible for dangerous political as well as religious materials, the model of the United States attracted relatively few Spanish Americans. The same was the case with the even more epochal French Revolution beginning in 1789, which produced agents and proselytizers who shipped propagandist literature into Spanish America. During the subsequent wars of the European coalitions against France in the 1790s, Spain and its overseas territories were unhappy participants in the struggle for Atlantic and world domination. Cut off from communications and commerce for months or even years at a time, some criollos began to consider emancipation as a means to evade economic strangulation from British naval blockades that resonated from the wars of Europe. The outbreak of the Haitian Revolution, in which black slaves fought for and attained their liberty and independence against France, shook the criollo elites and the colonial authorities from New Spain to La Plata.

Within Spanish America the Bourbon regimes of Carlos III and Carlos IV introduced reform programs designed to tighten controls over the empire and to make it yield much greater revenues for a cash-starved imperial regime. The catastrophes of 1763 following the British occupation of Havana led directly to reform initiatives that touched many different areas of colonial life. There were efforts to liberalize trade, create monopolistic companies capable of developing industries, stimulate nonproducing regions, and set up government monopolies over the production and distribution of tobacco products, alcohol, and other items. To introduce far-reaching administrative reforms, the imperial regime reestablished Nueva Granada as a viceroyalty separate from Peru and detached the great territories of La Plata by making Buenos Aires a capital city with access to trade and to the silver riches of Upper Peru. The regime carved up old provinces to create new provincial intendancies at first under a centralized bureaucracy governed by a *superintendente.* The intention was that these new bureaucrats would overcome corruption and mismanagement by the viceroys, captains general, and governors down to the level of the provincial corregidores and *alcaldes mayores.* At the regional and district level, *subdelegados* and their agents were to replace corrupt royal officials who had developed entrenched connections and relationships with the local elites.

The Impact of the Bourbon Reforms: Rebellions and Unrest

King Carlos III dispatched José de Gálvez to New Spain as *visitador general* (1765–1771). Following Gálvez, there were *visitadores* assigned to other provinces and a succession of imperial officials and scientists who toured and then recommended economic, administrative, and social reforms.[12] These metropolitan reformers were less than enthusiastic about what they encountered in the New World—tax evasion, contraband trafficking, and too much power in the hands of the criollos. Brian Hamnett illustrates many of the controversies and rivalries in Chapter 1 that continued into the insurrections in the Colombian regions. Many Bourbon reformers expressed disdain for the confused racial composition in many regions where mixed blood mestizos, *pardos* (mulattos), and *morenos* (free blacks, some of whom had other blood) played major roles, demanded greater freedoms, or simply appeared as frightening reminders of the uniqueness and complexities of the American populations. Although Spanish laws kept these *castas* under tight supervision, even prior to the Haitian Revolution their numbers and growing boldness were matters for concern. There was also an intellectual assault on the New World by philosophers and scientists of Europe that distressed criollo leaders who read the works of Georges-Louis Leclerc de Buffon and Corneille de Pauw. These writers had concluded that the animals, plants, and humans of the Americas were inferior to their European equivalents.[13] In 1767 the expulsion from Spanish America of the Jesuits, who were the educators of the criollo elites, dismayed the populace and provoked riots and minor uprisings in the provincial cities of New Spain and elsewhere. Taken together, these factors eroded old certainties and caused many observers to question the Spanish colonial regime.

As might be expected, the Bourbon reforms created hardships, exacerbated old grievances, provoked violence, and helped to spark dangerous uprisings. In Peru, a mestizo leader, José Gabriel Condorcanqui (claiming lineal descent from the Inca Túpac Amarú, executed in 1571), took the name Túpac Amarú and launched a rebellion (1780–1783) that was difficult to suppress. Tapping into reservoirs of resentment, Túpac Amarú's message triggered other uprisings and in some respects foreshadowed the contagious popularity of the 1810 Hidalgo Revolt in New Spain. In Nueva Granada, *visitador general* Juan Francisco Gutiérrez de Piñeres encountered somewhat similar resistance and violence when he attempted to enforce the Gálvez taxation program. By 1781 widespread rebellion in the Socorro region spread like wildfire until the rebels managed even to occupy Bogotá. Although Anthony McFarlane warns against any conclusions that the Comunero Rebellion was a precursor movement for the later independence struggle,[14] the defense of local autonomy and the existence of regional alliances suggest comparisons with later unraveling events in New Spain and the regionalism identified by Peter Guardino (Chapter 4). While there were no widespread rebellions in New Spain following the uprisings sparked by the exile of the Jesuits at San Luis Potosí and other cities, in 1781 Viceroy Martín de Mayorga identified parallels with the revolt of Túpac Amarú when the Indian population of Izúcar rose up against their *alcalde mayor* over fiscal concerns. In 1787 riots at Papantla and Acayucan produced a number of beatings, the stoning of gachupines (the derogatory term used in New Spain to describe

European Spaniards), and organized attacks on officials of the tobacco monopoly. Viceroy Manuel Antonio Flórez, who had held the same office in Nueva Granada during the Comunero Rebellion, took this danger seriously and fretted about the possible outbreak of a general insurrection that might be abetted by the British.[15]

In their efforts to modernize and to make the American empire profitable, the Bourbon administrators failed to deal effectively with ancient issues concerning race, class, and ethnicity. As early as the seventeenth century, Thomas Gage reported that criollos in Central America felt such disgust toward European Spaniards that they would prefer "to live with freedom and liberty under a foreign people [such as the English] rather than to be oppressed any longer by those of their own blood."[16] The great divide between the gachupines, *peninsulares* (those from the Iberian Peninsula, or Spain), *chapetones*, or *europeos*, as the European Spaniards were described, and the American-born criollos widened chronic resentments, rivalries, bad blood, and outright hatreds that would be played out in earnest during the independence wars and thereafter. In independent Mexico, this state of affairs led to expulsion orders directed against the gachupines and to a subsequent flight of capital and talent that the new nation could ill afford. In Venezuela and Colombia, the fratricidal campaigns of war to the death resulted in massacres and other atrocities that stained the reputation of Símon Bolívar, many of his associates on the patriot side, and the opposing royalist commanders. The negative criollo attitudes are not difficult to understand since the regime denied them access to appointments to senior lay and religious offices. However, the racist views of many late-eighteenth-century Bourbon reform administrators further irritated old grievances and sharpened rivalries.

The Question of Race

The division between Spanish and American whites was only one element in the complex racial mosaic. As is evident in many of the selections included in the present study—particularly in the confidential dispatch of José de Cevallos (Chapter 7)—the *castas*, including mulattos and free blacks, fought on both sides during the wars to improve their social, economic, and political status. Although the racial composition of the different Spanish American societies varied in mix according to province and region, during the independence era we must trace the activities of indigenous peoples, mestizos, mulattos, *pardos*, and *morenos*. They became the foot soldiers, cavalrymen, muleteers, pioneers, and laborers on both sides. After years of combat, many of them emerged as tough guerrilla fighters, insurgent-bandits, and sometimes royalist counterinsurgents. Without their support, Bolívar and Agustín de Iturbide could not have won independence in Venezuela, Colombia, Ecuador, Peru, Bolivia, or New Spain. One failure of José de San Martín was that he was unable to develop the broad criollo-*casta* coalition in Peru needed to overcome the royalist forces.

Fully aware of the disasters caused by Britain during Spain's short experience in the Seven Years' War, in 1764, well before any of the other Atlantic revolutions had taken place, officials in the Ministry of War initiated plans to arm and to establish military forces in the American possessions. In his instructions to Lieutenant General Juan de Villalba, charged with building fortifications and raising infantry and cavalry units in New Spain, Carlos III warned the cadre of officers commissioned for this task that they must be guided by one overarching maxim—the new defense forces must be based upon loyal inhabitants who were to be treated as true and beloved vassals of the king. Using greater or lesser firmness as prudence merited, the Spanish Americans were to be informed that "the change of times requires other approaches than the system they have experienced until now. For the security of their families and possessions, they are obliged to take steps to counter the enemies of their liberties and possessions."[17]

In New Spain the model for the projected formation of six provincial infantry regiments, two cavalry regiments, and a dragoon regiment was to follow Spanish militia ordinances or the new militia system, worked out in Cuba by the Conde de Ricla and Alejandro O'Reilly, that followed the British occupation.[18] It was based on the Prussian ideal of Frederick the Great—two battalions per regiment with one company of grenadiers and seven or eight companies of fusiliers. The imperial regime estimated that of the 500,000 suitable families in New Spain, one man should be enlisted for each twenty families to furnish a potential force of 25,000 armed and trained militiamen. The king and his advisers insisted that experienced officers, sergeants, corporals, trumpeters, and fifers would be dispatched from Spain to serve as training and operational cadres. The presence of a strong, watchful, European Spanish component was essential to keep the militias focused upon external enemies and distant from any adventures into internal politics.[19]

As might be expected, the issue of race presented the Spanish planners with some thorny problems. Following considerable reflection and deliberations, the imperial regime decided that only the blacks and Indians should be definitively exempted from military service. In reality, necessity and total confusion about racial origins soon blurred these distinctions. All other racial mixtures or *castas* who had in their veins the blood of whites or Spaniards, mestizos, mulattos, and Indians were to be admitted without distinction of color so long as no more than one-third of a company belonged to one racial type. In the event that whites took offense at having to serve alongside *castas*, the king proposed the possibility of separate regiments of whites, mulattos, and *morenos*. To make militia duty attractive to these people, they were to be awarded the honors of the *fuero militar* that granted soldiers the right to trial under the military legal system rather than in the civilian legal jurisdiction as well as other minor privileges. The costs of maintaining the militia were to be supported by new taxes established in the home jurisdiction of the individual units.[20]

Gradually, the imperial government applied this military system throughout the Spanish American provinces. Since the whites often found service shoulder to shoulder with the *castas* unacceptable, many jurisdictions in Nueva Granada and Peru where there were significant mulatto populations recruited separate regiments, battalions, and companies of *pardos* and *morenos*. In New Spain, to prevent *pardos* and *morenos* enlisted in the militias from being confused with slaves, army commanders authorized them to wear identifying red hatbands two fingers in width and tied in a bow.[21]

Early Threats of Separation

Coincident with the decision to create overseas defense forces, there were rumors in Madrid during the 1760s of grievances in the New World that might provoke the criollos to "cast off the yoke" of Spanish rule. According to a report that ended up in the hands of the Minister of Marine and the Indies Julián de Arriaga, three criollo representatives from New Spain petitioned without success to present the grievances of their province at the Spanish royal court. A French architect, Monsieur Guiller, purportedly met with two Mexican criollo merchants in Madrid while staying at the same inn. They related that in New Spain, persons who considered themselves to be nobles descended directly from *peninsular* ancestors who had first conquered their country were ineligible for government positions or special recognition of any sort. These criollos complained that they had to pay excessive taxes and suffered maltreatment by European Spaniards as if they belonged to the vilest classes. Given their debased state, even branches of their own families in Spain refused to recognize them. In the Church, European priests who had no knowledge about the Indians or their languages had been sent to replace criollos. The archbishoprics, bishoprics, canonical posts, and even the best parish curacies went to Europeans. Moreover, the complaint continued, merchants suffered a multitude of confiscatory taxes on European merchandise that drove them out of the market. Money was scarce because the imperial regime extracted too much from the local economies and charged excessive prices for mercury used by miners in the refining of silver ore.[22]

Rejected at the royal court when they attempted to present their list of grievances and threatened with punishment as traitors, the two criollo merchants declared that a general insurrection was needed to secure independence for New Spain. Prescient in their thinking, the two agents were said to inform Guiller that even people with wealth to protect who ordinarily would fear a general uprising because of the uncertain consequences of popular furor now agreed to support the cause of independence. Claiming some ignorance about what sort of regime to establish after the overthrow of the Spanish colonial regime, they recognized the need to formulate a solid plan for a government that could avoid the disturbances that so often accompanied the aftermath of revolution. They doubted that a new government could be monarchical in form since there were a great number of equally noble and powerful families in New Spain and none would be able to dominate the others.

In exchange for lending his expertise, Guiller was to be made a duke and hereditary governor of Veracruz as well as captain general of the military forces. He agreed to draft a plan for a republican government that would suit their needs and recommended that they enlist the aid of England with the promise of commercial grants and the cession of the port of Veracruz. While the two agents feared any intimate contact with British Protestantism, after numerous conferences they agreed to hand over the fortress of San Juan de Ulúa that guarded Veracruz. In exchange, Britain would recognize the "noble and powerful republic of Mexico as an independent sovereign nation and sign a perpetual offensive and defensive military alliance." A new dukedom of Orizaba was to be created with a hereditary captain general to govern the territory from the interior towns of Orizaba, Jalapa, and Córdoba down to the coast and the port city. An army of four thousand European Catholic troops supported by six thousand Mexican militiamen paid by Britain was to defend the new system. While Veracruz and San Juan de Ulúa were to be ceded, property ownership would be respected. In exchange for British assistance the new republic would agree not to import European goods except in British ships. The treaty of alliance would be signed as one of the first acts of the new Mexican republic. To accomplish the conquest, Guiller estimated that the British invasion force would need to be only one-half as large as the 1762 expeditionary force that had captured Havana.[23]

Although Arriaga dismissed the Guiller business as "*pura novela*," in New Spain, Viceroy Croix was not so sanguine. In his view the plan appeared credible and might not be difficult to execute. Even if the plot was apocryphal, the grievances expressed were common among criollos throughout the Americas. The idea of a republic (since no one family could prevail as ruling monarchs) and the fear of precipitating a social revolution (rather than confining the independence movement to politics) foreshadowed real concerns one half-century in the future. These issues returned, beginning with the Hidalgo Revolt in 1810, and continued up to the independence in 1821 won by criollo army commander Agustín de Iturbide, who became emperor. As Guiller's Mexicans had feared, Iturbide's empire collapsed amid factionalism and backbiting that divided the victors following national independence. Even with the achievement of the Mexican republic under the 1824 federalist constitution, the forces unleashed during the decade of war could not be controlled by a constitutional regime.

The Bourbons and American Realities

At the provincial and district levels the Spanish Bourbon reformers soon experienced the realities of colonial life in the Americas. Distance, slow communications, and other factors worked against efficiency and central planning. In 1762, when a British landing appeared likely at Veracruz, Viceroy Marqués de Cruillas attempted, with only limited success, to mobilize six hundred Indians to shovel sand dunes from the walls of Veracruz and strengthen defenses. One *alcalde mayor* claimed that he had lost the original order to dispatch Indians and demanded a duplicate before he sent any artisans and laborers. Towns dominated by criollo ayuntamientos (city councils) evaded financial commitments by "sleeping on their funds," and local magistrates were more interested in contributing to their own fortunes.[24] By 1771, only a few years after the creation of a system of provincial militias supposedly watched over by a strong cadre of Spanish officers and soldiers, the Provincial Legion at San Luis Potosí—nineteen cavalry and eleven infantry companies totaling 3,587 men spread over an enormous region—had only one regular army officer, one sergeant, and three corporals. Shocked by the potential danger of such a situation, Arriaga informed Viceroy Antonio María de Bucareli that "it is highly contrary to good politics to have such a numerous army unit in America whose commander, officers, and soldiers are all criollos."[25] A few years later in 1775, the *alcalde mayor* of San Luis Potosí, Antonio de Llano y Villarrutía, described the Legion of San Carlos as "not only useless and prejudicial to the public, but the cause of great disorders and frauds directed against the royal exchequer." He went on to declare that the legion "does not offer any other appearance than that of a disordered multitude that serves as refuge for the liberty of idle vagabonds and distracts hard-working and attentive men from the fulfillment of their obligations in their honest occupations." When a militiaman of the legion committed some crime or misdemeanor, invariably he pretended to be of pure Spanish origin and his officers launched grievances to have his case transferred to the military jurisdiction. In frustration, royal magistrates gave up trying to enforce the ordinary jurisdiction and some criminals evaded punishment. Llano y Villarrutía wanted the legion disbanded because there were few whites enlisted, and most so-called militiamen were Indians, *lobos* (mestizos with more Indian than European blood), *coyotes* (mulattos with some indigenous and European blood), and from as many *castas* as one could describe.[26]

In New Spain, many of the negative epithets hurled at the provincial militias reflected vituperative *peninsular* arrogance that served only to deepen the divisions between the criollos and the European Spaniards. In 1768, Inspector General Marqués de la Torre reviewed the newly established provincial regiments and expressed alarm at the behavior of the *peninsular* officers and soldiers who had been transferred from Europe to serve as training cadres. Torre found that all of these men, idle in their isolated provincial posts, passed their time causing "discords, anxieties, and dissensions in the towns." The fact that they had only remote expectations of transfers left them depressed and without any motivation, discipline, or military vocation. All of them requested transfers to serve with regular army units even if such moves required reductions in rank and seniority. These were desperate men whom Torre described as "consuming their salaries" without service or pride in their occupation.[27] Angry at their fate in lifetime postings in the backwater towns of New Spain and bored with their day-to-day routines in the military jurisdiction, these officers and soldiers challenged the authority of district *subdelegados*, municipal governments, officers of the Consulado (merchant guild), regional mining authorities, the tobacco monopoly, and other local jurisdictions. Through extravagant claims about the special legal powers of the *fuero militar*, attacks on minor officials, and the defense of litigious and borderline criminal elements within the militias, they labored to expand the military legal jurisdiction. Throughout Spanish America these officers added weight to the negative burden of the oppressive gachupines or *chapetones*. Like many other *peninsular* Spaniards in provincial American society, these officers abused their limited powers and provoked chronic clashes by their arrogance and blockheaded aggressiveness.

Bourbons Straight Up: José Antonio de Areche in New Spain and Peru

The heavy-handed behavior of European Spanish bureaucrats—particularly those of modest parentage—was bad enough at the local or regional levels, but truly obnoxious when viceroys and senior government officials expressed anti-Americano views. One of these who served the cause of Bourbon reform was José Antonio de Areche, a truly irascible and pretentious Spanish reform bureaucrat and loyal supporter of José de Gálvez. Areche served as attorney general of the Audiencia of New Spain and beginning in 1777 as *visitador general* of Peru. In 1774 he wrote his "reflections" on the Kingdom of New Spain that was little more than a diatribe that damned the inhabitants from the criollos of Spanish descent to the *castas* and Indians. He opened his study by describing New Spain as "almost a desert." There were only four or five cities, with weak economies and at great distances apart, that deserved the name. Areche described other places populated by Indians and only a few people of Spanish origin as no more than collections of badly constructed huts that "usurp" the name of town. Surveying the population of Spanish origins, he doubted whether these people had achieved enough in New Spain to make up for their loss to the mother country. He observed whites in the plazas of Mexico City who were hungry and almost naked, clothed only in coarse ponchos.

In Areche's view, these unemployed and lazy Spaniards brought shame to their kind, contempt from the rest of society, and embarrassment to the state. The fact that fertile land lay fallow and uncultivated was a commentary on people who refused to follow honorable and essential occupations in agriculture. This area was left to Indians, who lacked adequate method or talent for farming. Landowners of Spanish background depended upon the Indian *gañan* (day laborer) and sacrificed their estates by renting plots to those who did not look after the land. Hacendados exploited their workers by supplying clothing and other items on credit at usurious rates.[28] Areche attacked the magistrates who made their money through managing the evil *repartimiento* business in their provinces and districts. They solicited rich *aviadores* (those who advanced funds on credit) with whom they shared their businesses and borrowed money that they lent to Indian producers in coin or merchandise for later delivery of manufactures and crops.[29] Any individuals who wanted to enter commerce or open a business soon found themselves the victims of the monopolistic *alcalde mayor*, who made war on their interests and worked to diminish their resources. In addition, Areche was critical of the Church, which drew too many men and women into religious lives and owned too much urban and rural real estate. He noted the example of the town of Atlixco near Puebla, which had been a prosperous agricultural center until the eighteenth century when the expansion of religious houses, removal of many productive men and women, and heavy taxation brought the community almost to its knees.[30]

On the issue of race, Areche emphasized the state of general confusion in Spanish America caused by the miscegenation that mixed and blended the Indians, Afro-Americans (blacks), and Europeans (whites). Genealogical lineages had become so complex that some people defied accurate description and were given categories such as *no le entiendo* (I do not understand you). Large numbers of these people were to be seen in the towns and cities, rootless vagabonds who drifted from place to place driven by misery, persecution, or their own caprice. The Indians who cultivated and worked the haciendas were described as "slothful, inclined to excesses, and of little ability to reason."[31] Areche argued that placing confidence in them or expressing kindness toward them produced a contrary result. Hacienda managers who needed workers simply went to the magistrates, who ordered Indian work gangs dispatched to serve them. These people, according to Areche, were confined at night in a building called a *tlapisquera*, since otherwise they would flee with any pay that had been advanced to them.[32]

In Peru, Areche worked to reduce criollo influence on the Audiencia and continued to attack the abuses of the system of *repartimiento*. The outbreak of the Túpac Amarú Rebellion in November 1780 appeared to confirm Spanish fears that leading criollos must be implicated in the movement. Areche criticized the loyalty and efficiency of Peruvian militiamen and demanded that Spanish regulars be sent to garrison the viceroyalty. He dominated the war effort directed against the insurgents and undermined the authority of Viceroy Agustín de Jáuregui, who as captain general should have exercised command. Areche advised Gálvez to reduce criollo dominance of public offices and to make certain that under the reformed administrative system criollos were not named to important posts as provincial intendants. With the suppression of the remaining Inca revolts in 1783, Areche moved to limit the roles of criollos in the militias. Hated by the criollo elites and the popular classes for reducing criollo power, curbing the powers of officials and the lucrative *repartimiento*, and applying new tax monopolies, Areche was a loyal Spaniard who advanced the Bourbon objective of regaining control over the Americas and of mining the hemisphere for the benefit of Spain.[33]

The Bourbon Reformers and the *Castas*

If criollos had cause to criticize the Bourbon system that throttled their aspirations to hold high office and that exported capital from the New World to serve the needs of metropolitan Spain, the *castas* were much worse off. The racist attitudes and haughty superiority of many Bourbon reformers could not help but alienate these people. From New Spain to La Plata, the *castas*—particularly the *pardos* and *morenos*—were a major population sector in tropical lowland regions where the requirements for military defense were highest. In Venezuela the *castas* who lived under restrictive laws and lacked the opportunities of whites in total numbers were almost a majority.[34] They lived in cities where they were artisans and laborers, worked on haciendas as expert horsemen (*llaneros*, or plainsmen), and manned militia companies with disease-hardened, knowledgable veterans who possessed a natural resistance to yellow fever, malaria, and other tropical diseases. They were implacable fighters, accustomed to violence, who in many theaters of war during the independence era made their mark both for the insurgents and the royalists. In New Spain these people served Father José María Morelos and the many insurgent-guerrilla bands that over time eroded royalist military power. In Venezuela, Bolívar's ultimate successes likely would not have occurred if the *llaneros* who fought for the royalists under the ruthless José Tomás Boves had not changed sides. Although the document by José de Cevallos included in the present volume (Chapter 7) demonstrates that some royalist commanders understood the crucial importance of the *castas*, by this point it was too late to shift entrenched opinion and policy. As the wars dragged on, throughout Spanish America the people of the *castas* recognized that their best opportunities lay with independence rather than with possible reforms within the empire.

In 1783, Colonel Francisco Crespo, a veteran of many senior army commands, corregidor of Mexico City, and a respected member of the intellectual community of the Real Academia de San Carlos, undertook a study on how to improve the army of New Spain. Crespo analyzed the defensive requirements and drafted a lengthy reform program that influenced the military up to and even after 1810. While he was a perceptive observer and thoughtful military planner, Crespo was belligerent and racist in his attitudes toward the *castas*. He reported that they "look with deep abhorrence at the noble Spanish caste, and with aversion and contempt upon the pure Indians."[35] In Crespo's view, they were uncomfortable with the honorable customs of Spaniards and rejected the humility and hard work of the Indians. He lumped all the *castas* together and compared them to the gypsies of Spain: "The true gypsy recognizes no permanent domicile; he lives without modesty or pride; he is indifferent whether he is dressed or naked. His science is deceit and lying, his inclination is to commit robbery; his jobs and occupations are those that will help him find a means to steal." Crespo believed that the *castas*, like the gypsies, were guilty of heinous crimes and maintained their culture by wicked traditions: "lascivious dances, sad songs, and coarse language."[36] Having cataloged the propensity of gypsies to drunkenness, vulgarity, obstinacy, and other evils, Crespo proclaimed: "it seems to me that this is the most accurate portrait of a *lobo, coyote, salta atrás* (a lighter-skinned mulatto), or the unidentifiable *tente en el aire*."[37] To Crespo, the multitude of *castas* infected New Spain like a contagious disease. Found everywhere—in the cities, the mining districts, the thinly populated Provincias Internas, the rugged mountainous regions, and along the isolated coastlines—they were thus much more dangerous than the gypsies, who lived in specific regions of Spain where they could be controlled.

Although the Bourbon regime and later the royalist armies had few qualms about employing *pardo* and other *casta* militiamen to defend coastal regions against foreign enemies and to maintain internal tranquility, other segments of the population hated them. Desperate for recognition, they were more willing than others to serve in the army and to undertake unpopular duties. In New Spain, *pardo* and *moreno* militiamen from Puebla in 1691 guarded the viceregal palace during riots by plebeian mobs that damaged the central downtown business district. Unlike other militiamen, they served at Veracruz and Campeche and helped to suppress riots in the major cities. In 1767 they assisted in rounding up the Jesuits destined for deportation to Europe. However, during daily guard duty in Mexico City or Puebla, the *pardos* complained that the ordinary judicial authorities and the agents of the Acordada "treated them outrageously and reviled them."[38] One Juan García suffered arrest and spent six months in the public jail. Others stated that during their incarceration, they were beaten with as many as twenty-five to fifty lashes. After examining petitions that detailed the loyal service of the *pardos* to the state, Viceroy Croix decided to award them the *fuero militar* when they served on active duty.[39]

Despite the examples of racist harassment, the *pardo* and *moreno* militiamen persevered because their uniforms and the *fuero militar* gave them some standing and exempted them from having to pay the degrading *tributo* (head or capitation tax). In 1792, Viceroy Conde de Revillagigedo, one of the most active supporters of Enlightenment themes connected with science and the arts, urban beautification and improvement, and scientific exploration, disbanded the *pardo* battalions in the capital and in Puebla. The subinspector general of the army, Brigadier Pedro de Gorostiza, reported that henceforth provincial militia forces were to enlist only "clean" *castas*. He insisted that since the 1760s, when Lieutenant General Villalba visited New Spain to introduce the militias, blacks or *morenos* were excluded from military service.[40] Gorostiza neglected to mention his fears of resonance from the black revolution in the French colony of Saint Domingue (Hispaniola). Viceroy Revillagigedo ordered an investigation that turned up information that a priest from Havana, José Rodríguez de Hurtado, had assisted the pesky *pardos* with their petitions and drafted their final document.[41] Despite this pressure, Gorostiza dismissed the *pardos* as "the most vice-ridden people of both major cities" who caused numerous conflicts with authority and abused their military privileges. Discipline was poor among them, their uniforms were in bad condition, and their muskets were unserviceable. In fact, the muster rolls contradicted Gorostiza's diatribes. The great majority of these so-called vice-ridden *pardos* were respectable artisans—carpenters, weavers, tailors, ironworkers, blacksmiths, shoemakers, tradesmen, and general laborers.[42] They were scarcely the sort of useless men described by the senior military commanders.

Needless to say, the viceroy reacted negatively when *pardo* officers and soldiers submitted petitions attacking the program to disband their battalions, remove their *fueros*, and force them to pay *tributo*. In one petition, three *pardo* officers exclaimed: "Free us from the yoke of European officers who always have been our capital enemies. Finally, they have managed to accomplish their goal of dominating, ruining, and debasing us." They concluded that "these soldiers although *pardos* by color are noble at heart and willing to sacrifice their property and their lives for the King."[43] In some respects, this was a prophetic statement, since after 1810 for a time many *pardos* and *morenos* fought for the royalists in the independence struggles of Spanish America. While many whites despised and feared them—particularly after the events of Hispaniola—the *pardos* viewed their participation in the independence wars on both sides as a means to achieve status and recognition.

The Impact of the French Revolution

If the American Revolution failed to arouse many Spanish Americans, in the 1790s the French Revolution raised palpable fears among colonial officials as well as proposals to deport French residents of suspect loyalties. The Crown warned that revolutionary agents were on their way from Paris to enflame the Spanish colonies. In 1792, for example, the Conde de Floridablanca ordered the apprehension of six propaganda emissaries who were said to have sailed from Brest for Spanish America with a cargo of printed incendiary documents.[44] Indeed, the combination of ideological attacks and the impact of the Wars of the Coalitions in the 1790s increased the potential for invasion by either side in the European conflicts. Spain declared war on France in June 1793, turning against its old Family Pact ally when the revolution consumed King Louis XVI. In the American provinces, priests warned their parishioners of possible dangers posed by the Godless French and also reminded them of old threats posed by the heretical English Protestants. The imperial government ordered authorities to watch for inflammatory literature and to detain all suspicious persons. In May 1790 the Crown issued an order prohibiting the entry of blacks from the French colonies in the Caribbean or the importation of slaves who might be sold by their owners into Spanish American jurisdictions. The Crown soon extended these prohibitions to include persons of other *castas* who might imbue the subjects of King Carlos IV with seditious ideas and illegal maxims opposed to proper subordination and vassalage.[45]

In New Spain, Viceroy Conde de Revillagigedo informed the Spanish naval explorer, Alejando Malaspina, that the "contagion" caused by the French in their colonies would likely carry to Spanish possessions. In a personal letter to the Conde de Aranda, Revillagigedo described "the foolish new system of the French" but also commented that "its contamination will spread its fatal plague to others." He sent Malaspina a packet of published papers from Hispaniola and discussed the efforts of the French king and his family to escape, purportedly aided by Monsieur Lafayette, who was at Metz with an army of twenty thousand Germans.[46] The viceroy followed European events closely through foreign journals, as did many others in New Spain and the other Spanish colonies. Even after 1796, with the restoration of the old alliance with France, Spanish authorities continued to compare the French to fatal epidemics. In 1807, when Napoleon invaded Spain and Portugal, Spanish propaganda attacks became even more shrill.

During the years commencing in 1790, there were flurries of notices and orders directed to prevent the importation into Spanish America of foreign pocket watches, snuffboxes, medallions, and coins inscribed with revolutionary slogans. In 1791 the coast of Peru was inundated with items engraved with a woman dressed in white carrying a flag in her hand—the female personification of Liberty—with the words "Libertad Americana."[47] In New Spain, port officials exercised special vigilance against the introduction of pictures, coins, and other items from the United States that glorified the liberty of the Anglo-American colonies. Although Viceroy Revillagigedo stepped up customs inspections of all cases of books and other printed materials, he recognized that his officers could not possibly check every item.[48] Throughout the Spanish American provinces, French residents—often pastry cooks, hairdressers, teachers, architects, and other specialized tradesmen—fell under careful scrutiny. Everywhere, Spanish administrators portrayed the French as lepers who went about the world infecting the healthy. In New Spain there were roundups of suspects, Inquisition investigations, and special searches to discover copies of an incendiary tract, published in Philadelphia, entitled *Desengaño del hombre* (Disillusionment of man). Imperial authorities worried that Louisiana, despite its outward acceptance of Spanish rule, was still very French, dubious in its loyalty, and dangerous because of its proximity to the United States. Although the major threat to New Spain was overland by way of thinly populated Texas and the Provincias Internas, New Orleans ships touched at many South American ports.[49]

The threat from Hispaniola came not only from the French and the former slave patriots but also from royalist black soldiers who had fought on Spain's side. Until mid-1794, Toussaint l'Ouverture served the Spaniards until he switched to support the French republicans. Many other black leaders, including Jean François, a Spanish army general, and his subordinate Jorge Biassou, remained loyal to Madrid. In 1795, when Spain delivered the colony to the French, the captain general of Santo Domingo decided to evacuate General Jean François and all of the black pro-Spanish leaders and to resettle them in Cuba or some other Spanish American destination. This news absolutely terrified the white population of Havana, Campeche, and other cities as far away as Caracas. People believed that such immigrants would spark slave insurrections.

Cuba's Captain General Luis de las Casas summed up the widespread fears, noting that in the case of Jean François and Biassou, yesterday's slaves had become heroes—triumphant in battle, wealthy, and highly honored. Such examples could not help but influence any blacks who lived under the oppressive rule of white minorities. Jean François not only wore the uniform and medals of a Spanish army general, but he also owned a magnificent coach with six white horses and household furniture that was more luxurious than anything ever seen in Cuba (or owned by the captain general).[50] Such a person taking up residence in a society of slaves and oppressed *castas* could only be viewed as a redeemer of people who longed for liberty. Although Las Casas dispatched a fast ship to Hispaniola to prevent the departure of the black soldiers, Biassou and twenty-three of his men arrived in Cuba aboard the Spanish warship *San Lorenzo*. Las Casas gave them the choice of settling in Florida or on the Isla de Pinos off Cuba, and they accepted the former.

When General Jean François showed up at Havana with 780 followers—including many women and children—12 were sent to Cádiz, 115 to Campeche, 144 to Trinidad, 307 to Trujillo, and the remainder to Portobello.[51] Las Casas underscored his argument that Cuba was absolutely out of the question. In the previous month, women of Havana had been terrorized when a usually peaceful black man ran amuck with a machete, wounding a man and injuring ten schoolgirls, one of whom died. Many civilians were certain that this event signaled the commencement of a revolution similar to that of France or of neighboring Hispaniola. The mood of the city was not at all improved when an émigré French naval lieutenant reported a conversation passed on to him by his mulatto servant; a Spanish slave of his acquaintance had asked: "Do you think that we will do the same as the blacks of Guarico (Hispaniola)?"[52] Rumors of a black revolution swept through the city. These reports competed with stories of an imminent insurrection by whites who wanted independence and with gossip that French prisoners of war at Havana planned to break out of their prison. All of this hearsay circulated to feed fears and to terrorize much of the population. The Cabildo (city council) of Havana condemned those who spread false information, and one *regidor* (councilman) lamented that "the cursed French have turned the world upside down."[53]

While there was no revolution in Havana, the state of anxiety underscored the mood of people throughout Spanish America who felt that they were locked into struggles beyond their control. The whites, the *castas*, and the blacks anticipated some frightful catastrophe or secretly hoped that a revolution might improve their situations. The band of 115 black men, women, and children in Jean François's household were sent to the Yucatán and settled three leagues from Río Lagartos. They were awarded tracts of good agricultural soil considered suitable for raising sugarcane, indigo, coffee, and other crops. Captain General Arturo O'Neill designated funds to assist the settlers with the construction of thatched palm huts and the purchase of axes, machetes, shovels, and other tools. In considering the location for the settlement, O'Neill was careful to select a site separate from the Indian and other *casta* populations but close enough so that the blacks could be monitored by militiamen in case they caused trouble.[54]

New Fears of Revolution

War with Britain in 1796 brought with it a new threat of an attack led by the revolutionary Francisco Miranda of Caracas, who was well known in London. If Miranda combined with a British expeditionary force, some Spanish authorities expected an invasion attempt directed against New Spain or some other American province. One intelligence report indicated that the British had assembled an expeditionary army of ten thousand troops in Canada and planned to attack down the Mississippi River and overland into northern New Spain, and by sea against Florida from Halifax in Nova Scotia. In New Spain, Viceroy Marqués de Branciforte could not imagine how Miranda might arouse insurrection in New Spain, but he worried sufficiently about the invasion threat to establish a small cantonment of troops at Jalapa to guard against a surprise amphibious assault against Veracruz. Descriptions of Miranda as a man with unhappy brown eyes and a suspicious, treacherous countenance were sent to all relevant authorities.[55]

After a short truce in 1802 resulting from the Peace of Amiens, beginning in 1803 all of Spanish America faced constant threats of interdicted commerce, naval raids on coastal districts, privateering against merchant shipping, and the possibility of full-scale invasions. The fall of Trinidad to the British in 1797, the successful defense of Puerto Rico, and the spectacular resistance to the British invasions of Buenos Aires and Montevideo in 1806–07 served to convince many criollos that their continued attachment to the Spanish empire was exceptionally costly. Militia mobilizations, cantonments, and defensive exercises assembled men from different parts of the enormous provinces. They discovered that they shared common resentments against distant arbitrary government and against excessive taxation by Bourbon viceroys, intendants, *subdelegados*, and other parasitic officials. The defeat of the combined Franco-Spanish fleet at Trafalgar in 1805 and rumors of British projects to invade Venezuela or New Spain intensified apprehensions of danger.

The Impact of Napoleon's Invasion of Spain

In 1807, Napoleon obtained permission from Carlos IV to march his armies across Spain to occupy Portugal and thus to plug a leak in his Continental System, which was designed to exclude British commerce from Europe. Not mentioned were Napoleon's plans to occupy Spain and to overthrow the House of Bourbon. After some sorry spectacles, Carlos IV and his son Fernando VII marched to Bayonne where they both abdicated the throne in favor of Napoleon's brother Joseph (José I), and they spent the succeeding years until 1814 as enforced guests of France. On May 2, 1808, the population of Madrid rose up against the hated French, formed governing juntas, and launched similar movements all over Spain. Cast adrift, the Spanish American provinces found that they were left to their own devices. Like the metropolitan Spaniards, the criollos in many cities organized juntas that would rule in the absence of the king. In the succeeding events that Jaime Rodríguez has described as a political revolution,[56] the old colonial administrations failed to adapt to sudden change.

In the turbulent years between 1807 and 1810, Spanish Americans had to decide whether to maintain the old regime, seek some sort of autonomy under the vestigial Junta Central or Regency governments in Spain, or grasp outright independence for their provinces. Very few persons elected to support Napoleon's appointment of Joseph to the Spanish throne. Throughout Spanish America in cities such as Caracas and Buenos Aires, criollo interests involved with the municipal governments moved to organize juntas along the lines of those established in the Peninsula. If the Spanish claimed that in the absence of the king, sovereignty returned to the people, then the same was true for Americano subjects of Fernando VII. Naturally, European Spaniards—the gachupines and *chapetones*—viewed such moves, innocent or not, as a prelude to outright separatism.

In New Spain, the debate over whether to recognize a Spanish junta or the Junta Central produced a coup on September 16, 1808, involving elements of the Regimiento Urbano del Comercio de México (Urban Regiment of Commerce of Mexico City). Headed by Gabriel Yermo, gachupín merchants overthrew Viceroy José de Iturrigaray, who had appeared friendly to criollo interests. This highly illegal act, while successful in the short term, served to polarize the opinion of criollos. The coup prevented the criollo-dominated Ayuntamiento of Mexico City from setting up an interim governing junta. However, throughout the wars of independence in New Spain, criollos questioned about their support for the insurgency or asked to list reasons for the struggle often referred back to the dastardly acts of Yermo and a few gachupines who toppled Viceroy Iturrigaray and set New Spain on the road to civil war. In Buenos Aires and Caracas, there were similar conflicts between *peninsular* and criollo whites. Throughout the Americas, politically active groups declared support for the deposed Fernando VII and then either worked toward some form of independence or autonomy, or on the other side demanded submission to any remaining vestigial Spanish regime.

To counter possible French overtures to the Spanish American provinces, the Junta Central recognized the overseas territories as kingdoms rather than colonies and permitted the election of a small number of representatives to the metropolitan government. There were too few Americano representatives, and other difficulties intruded, but Virginia

Guedea and Jaime Rodríguez argue that these steps were significant to many criollos who desired home rule rather than outright independence.[57] On the Continent the sudden collapse of Spanish resistance to the French armies during 1809 forced the Junta Central to flee southward until the only unoccupied Spanish territory was Cádiz, which was defended by the guns of the British Royal Navy. By January 1810 the Junta Central surrendered any pretense of governing Spain and its empire. All that remained was a small Council of Regency supported by the British, who were anxious to keep alive at least the pretense of an independent Spain. As might be expected, given Napoleon's military dominance in Europe, many criollo observers in the Americas believed that Spain would be ruled permanently by France. Even before these events, officials in Chuquisaca (Sucre), the capital of Charcas, La Paz, and Quito formed criollo-supported juntas that sparked violent retribution from royalist authorities dispatching military forces from Buenos Aires, Lima, and Guayaquil.

The fall of Spain to Napoleon's armies was a catalyst in the Americas for events that otherwise could have been postponed for some years. In Spain there was no time for mature reflection about replacing Bourbon autocracy in the American possessions with institutions of home rule. Indeed, for years during and after the revolutions for independence, Spanish honor demanded that the military struggle continue.[58] Spain attempted to reconquer Mexico in 1829, and secret dispatches by spies who believed that the old colonies were ripe for a return to the embrace of the motherland may be found in the Archivo General Militar de Segovia. As late as 1864, Spanish warships attacked Callao, Peru, seized the guano-producing Chincha Islands, and bombarded the Chilean port of Valparaiso. On the Americano side, the collapse of Spain in 1809–10 permitted the renewed emergence of Francisco Miranda and of a new generation of criollo leaders such as Simón Bolívar, Bernardo O'Higgins, José de San Martín, and Bernardino Rivadavia, who envisioned new nations in the Americas. Many other criollos were less certain that independence was the best option and came to the idea later based upon their wartime experiences.

The Decline into Violence

Throughout Spanish America, confusion, chaos, and near anarchy swept away Bourbon reason and good order. Even prior to 1807–1810, in many provinces the governing regimes became preoccupied with the perception of danger and lost touch with the population. In viceregal capitals, officials had no idea of how to separate real dangers from the wild ideas of harmless eccentrics and lunatics. For New Spain, Eric Van Young has examined messianic and millenarian themes as well as the ravings of a "mad Messiah" in Durango who was only one among many eccentric or unbalanced individuals investigated.[59] Rumors, gossip, and backbiting were the food and drink of provincial society. Ubiquitous stories surfaced from time to time about conspiracies to blow up the viceregal palace in Mexico City. Two months following the overthrow of Viceroy Iturrigaray, for example, the governor of Baja California intercepted an anonymous letter from Mexico City to a surgeon, Dr. José Francisco Araujo, who had been exiled to the mission of Loreto and was in trouble once again for seducing the wife of a soldier. The letter stated that Europeans had arrested Viceroy Iturrigaray and had shipped him to Veracruz because the criollos wanted to crown him king. The writer claimed that gachupín perpetrators were so frightened of the criollos that following the coup they had been afraid to leave the safety of their houses. Neither the criollos nor the other classes in the capital had shown the fortitude to resist only two hundred to three hundred European cashiers. The army was no better since the commanders, officers, and soldiers looked on passively while forty merchants who had never handled muskets escorted the viceroy, their captain general, to the prison of San Juan de Ulúa at Veracruz.[60]

Iturrigaray's replacement, Interim Viceroy Pedro de Garibay, an octogenarian field marshal with almost sixty years' military service, scarcely knew what to make of the rumors, denunciations, and libels reported to him. He feared the gachupines who had thrust him into office and had no idea what the *casta* and Indian populations might be thinking. In his proclamations, Garibay told the people to avoid using the terms "criollo" and "gachupín"; indeed, "all members of the same nation must be known by no name other than that of the nation of which they are a part." He ordered everyone to denounce traitors and to turn in seditious papers.[61] A priest reported the cavalry commander of Nueva Santander, Colonel José Florencio Barragan, who said that he blamed Fernando VII for all of the troubles of Spain because of the discord with his father, Carlos IV.[62]

During May 1809 vessels arriving at Veracruz from Puerto Cabello brought news of the French occupation of Andalucia, the dissolution of the Junta Central, the establishment of the Council of Regency, and the uprising in Venezuela. In their proclamation, the people of Caracas saw no hope for Cádiz to resist the French since all of the city's food and water came from occupied territory. In rising up to resist Napoleon, the new authorities in Caracas claimed loyalty to the true ruler of Spain, Fernando VII, and promised to do whatever they could to stop the French and to assist the oppressed Spanish population.[63] In the meantime, a conspiracy organized by a small group of criollos at Valladolid (Morelia) discussed rumors of a gachupín plot to turn over New Spain to Britain or France. The so-called conspirators talked about raising an army of eighteen thousand to twenty thousand men from Valladolid and Guanajuato provinces. There was some mention of independence for New Spain, but no action was taken.[64] However, for many older career Spanish officials and army officers, the world as they knew it had changed so radically that they were not certain how to respond.

Viceroy Garibay busied himself with prosecuting one Captain Manuel de Moral of Tehuacán, who had opened a public corral and cockpit on his property to engage in the scandalous sports of running bulls and staging cockfights on religious holidays. The interim viceroy considered these activities dangerous to both sexes and utterly outrageous at a time when the mother country "groans under the oppression of the common tyrant (Napoleon)."[65] Government officials tore down the corral and closed the cockpit, but the matter was not over. Captain Moral proved that he held a legitimate government permit and demanded full compensation for lost income.

By 1810 the defeat of metropolitan Spain and the outbreak of uprisings in South America left the old regime in New Spain almost powerless to make decisions. In Mexico City, Archbishop Francisco Javier de Lizana replaced Garibay as interim viceroy, but he was no more adept than his predecessor at handling a political crisis that soon took on revolutionary overtones. The Ayuntamiento of Guadalajara warned about the impact of hidden enemies upon "an ignorant and gullible common population that has a propensity to the latest fad and is susceptible to seduction."[66] In motivating this concern the city government produced a letter, said to be from Napoleon, that offered the Indians and *castas* freedom from *tributo*. Some small clay pots turned up at the village of Tonalá outside Guadalajara with the inscription, "Viva Nuestro Rey Buenparte (Bonaparte)."[67]

Countering the pessimistic view, some authorities such as Dionisio Cano y Moctezuma, the Indian governor by election at Tecpam near Acapulco, informed Lizana that he worked hard to maintain loyalty, subordination, and love for the Catholic religion, king, and motherland. His people had maintained their loyalty since the Conquest, and "they have not abandoned these sentiments in the difficult circumstances of the day."[68] When Cano learned about the archbishop-viceroy's campaign to raise funds from respectable groups and religious corporations to purchase arms, he convened his population in a public meeting to express their loyalty and to raise a contribution. Although the failure of the maize harvest prevented them from making a financial donation, they would be extremely useful in resisting invasion with rigor. Since their sentiments were honor, loyalty, and subordination to the legitimate authorities, Cano offered their services in defense of New Spain. They knew how to use slings and volunteered to be instructed in firearms. Cano concluded his offer with an assessment that in hindsight seems alarming: "The principal arms that Napoleon uses for his conquests—seduction, intrigue, and proclamations—will be blunted by the rusticity of the Indians, who neither know nor wish to know anything more than that Fernando VII is their king."[69]

No agitator or agent would be capable of persuading these Indian people to work against their beliefs. They would not enter into discussions or be open to reasoning. In a word, they would be "constant supporters of the just cause that we defend, as they are the least exposed to become the victims of seduction and hallucination."[70] He concluded with a proposal to form an Indian volunteer regiment. Doubtless shuddering at this prospect, Lizana thanked Cano for his ideas and for his loyalty.

As Virginia Guedea illustrates in Chapter 2, others such as Father Miguel Hidalgo were about to launch events that would take people similar to these in quite different directions. Depending upon many factors, the Indians and *castas* ended up on both sides in the forthcoming conflicts. Guedea's study of one insurgent courier, José Nemesio Vázquez, reveals some of the confusion that occurred once the fog of war descended. The Hidalgo Revolt in New Spain was no simple fight for Mexican independence. The questions of race, social rivalries, regionalism, and even religion must be examined. Did Father Miguel Hidalgo and his followers desire independence or some form of autonomy? Was the revolt simply one more unplanned conspiracy that went wrong?[71] The rebels who took up the banner of the Virgin of Guadalupe also loudly proclaimed their loyalty to Ferdinand VII. However, in their attacks directed against "bad government," the insurgents in New Spain, like those elsewhere in Spanish America, identified the evil gachupines as avaricious, greedy, power hungry, vicious, brutal, corrupt, condescending, and haughty. The rancorous quarrels and hatreds between the criollos and the *peninsulares* served to harden the views of mestizos, mulattos, and other *castas*. Following Mexican independence, the continuing bad blood led to expulsion laws directed to rid the new nation of the gachupines who still held high offices.

Often, local *curas* (parish priests) who were criollos themselves identified with the broad range of issues behind the rebellions and exercised leadership that extended from the pulpit to actual command of the rebel bands. Similar to the roles played by small ranchers, muleteers, petty bureaucrats, and some local militiamen, the *curas* served as important "linking agents" who had leadership skills together with some knowledge of the larger political issues espoused by urban rebel leaders. The near-spontaneous popularity of the Hidalgo Revolt in some provinces pointed to connections with earlier eighteenth-century uprisings in New Spain and to the rebellions of Túpac Amarú, the Comuneros, and other movements in South America during the independence wars. In New Spain, most creoles feared the revolutionary messages found in Hidalgo's rebellion and the fact that the mestizo and Indian rebels attacked the property of criollo whites as well as that of gachupines. The great majority of the criollos threw their support to the royalist cause until such time as they could take control over the process. In New Spain, the time did not come until 1821, long after the executions of the great leaders, Fathers Hidalgo and Morelos.

The Nature of the Wars and the Need for Coalitions

There were three great continental theaters of conventional and unconventional warfare during the epoch of Spanish American independence. New Spain became an enormous battleground of insurgency and guerrilla warfare. Although there were thousands of sieges, skirmishes, ambushes, and raids, only a few conventional battles deserve the name. As in South America, officers had to eschew the linear formations learned in their training in the disciplined tactics of Frederick the Great. Cavalry was more important in New Spain's than in Europe's wars since the rebels seldom stood to fight and the country was so large. Military operations were exceedingly difficult because there were few roads suitable for wheeled traffic. From the beginning, the rebels tested the logistical skills of the royalists from remote and rugged regions far from the centers of supply. Infantry guarded convoys, manned city and town garrisons, and took part in siege work against rebel forts.

Except for a few transfers of royalist officers, the war of New Spain had limited connections with the other centers of revolutionary fighting. Beginning on September 16, 1810, Father Miguel Hidalgo unleashed what historians often describe as an inchoate mass of disgruntled, ill-armed people from the Bajío provinces upon an unsuspecting and unprepared royalist army dominated by a criollo officer corps. It appeared at first that Hidalgo's popular uprising might sweep to power before opposition mobilized, but Brigadiers Félix Calleja and José de la Cruz—the leading royalist army commanders—mobilized forces and created a military system that permitted the old colonial army to respond. Calleja's "Political-Military Regulations" (Chapters 3 and 4) introduced a tiered system that helped royalist forces to defeat insurgent armies and to control, if not eliminate, guerrilla warfare. After 1815 the war became an exhausting counterinsurgency struggle that gradually wore down the royalists. When the Riego Rebellion in Spain took place in 1820 and restored the liberal Spanish Constitution of 1812, the people of New Spain refused to pay the heavy burdens of regional and district counterinsurgency forces. When Agustín de Iturbide changed sides to negotiate an alliance with the guerrillas of Vicente Guerrero and then proclaimed the Plan de Iguala, the royalist army literally imploded toward Mexico City and a few other urban bases. The final defeat was sudden, but comparatively bloodless.[72]

The second major theater of war included the modern nations of Venezuela, Colombia, Ecuador, Peru, and Upper Peru (Bolivia). In this vast territory of South America, the successes and failures of Simón Bolívar dominate the period and obscure many other themes that need further study. The independence of New Spain produced no major figure even close to Bolívar in terms of longevity and stature. Even today, Mexicans are ambivalent about Iturbide, who won independence, and favor Father Morelos, who was executed in 1815, as the leading progenitor of the nation.[73] During his lifetime, Bolívar aroused true passion among Venezuelans, Colombians, and others who perceived him as the sublime patriot, nation builder, and political thinker. Among his most dedicated image makers, modern historians such as Vicente Lecuna and Gerhard Masur have devoted their research to his remarkable career. A darker side to Bolívar reported by contemporary observers such as Major George Flinter (Chapter 6) and General H. L. V. Ducoudray Holstein (Chapter 8) was ably countered by his leading supporters, such as General Florencio O'Leary (Chapters 8 and 10). Bolívar's detractors criticized his military skills, his seduction of women in preference to the pursuit of war, and his policy of terror and genocide commencing with the June 1813 proclamation of *guerra a muerte* (war to the death). Thereafter, Bolívar was charged with various bloody acts and unnecessary killings of royalists, European Spaniards, and even his own soldiers.

To deal with these assorted "lies, calumnies and errors," Vicente Lecuna wrote a three-volume work in defense of the Liberator.[74] Lecuna believed that the nature of the war in Venezuela differed from other Spanish American countries owing to geography, the special racial mix, and the character of the people. He criticized the royalists for their atrocities but admitted that on one occasion Bolívar had ordered the execution of over eight hundred Spaniards.[75] Pressed by royalist forces and lacking guards to contain the prisoners, Lecuna argued that the patriots either had to kill or be killed. On the other side, royalist scourge José Tomás Boves turned his wild *llanero* troops on patriot forces. In the heat of battle—particularly where racial hatred, superiority, and inferiority compounded enmities—surrender often provoked cruelties such as rape, torture, and cold-blooded murder.

Although atrocities such as the execution of Spaniards ordered by Bolívar are difficult to defend, the Liberator, more than most other major patriot and royalist military commanders in the other theaters of war, came under the direct scrutiny of many outside observers. The immediate proximity of foreign colonies off the coast of Nueva Granada and Venezuela allowed foreigners such as Major Flinter to obtain access to information and to visit such cities as Caracas and Cartagena. In New Spain or Peru, for example, there were few outside observers to publicize atrocities. Even in La Plata, foreign observers were not generally present during the campaigns against Upper Peru that took place far from the coasts. In New Spain, Hidalgo or his subordinates ordered the execution of several hundred gachupines, and Morelos's men massacred Spanish expeditionary prisoners of the Infantry Regiment of Barcelona in a church near Acapulco.

Agustín de Iturbide in his years of service as a royalist commander executed hundreds of insurgents.

On the royalist side, Félix Calleja and other commanders issued proclamations at Guanajuato, San Miguel, and in other communities threatening decimation of the male population as punishment for refusing to resist the rebels. Calleja ordered entire towns incinerated (except for the churches) for supporting insurgency. In the aftermath of Morelos's breakout from the fortress of Cuautla Amilpas, royalist troopers rode down 816 rebels and left the ground strewn with the bodies.[76] In general, royalist forces terrorized the countryside with *destacamentos volantes* (flying detachments) whom Calleja ordered to "make harsh and repeated justice." Soldiers dragged suspected rebels before firing squads and nailed up their reeking remains at crossroads or hung them from trees. Royalist commanders described executions as "healthful examples," and the insurgents reciprocated with similar atrocities.[77]

Unlike the rebels of New Spain, except for the abortive 1817 Javier Mina expedition, Bolívar obtained the services of many foreign army officers and soldiers who were veterans of the Napoleonic Wars. The haughty Europeans criticized the ill-equipped and unsophisticated patriot forces. Few professional army men appreciated *pardo, moreno*, and other *casta* soldiers who appeared incapable of the disciplined formations required for martial display. Even their commander, Bolívar, attracted their negative criticism and chronic backbiting.[78] Based upon comparisons elsewhere in Spanish America, Bolívar was probably no more sanguinary than his patriot and royalist contemporaries. As we have noted, civil wars involving race, class, possession of resources, and intense hatreds fueled atrocities and unleashed violence, much of which took place beyond the eyes of observers. Moreover, propagandists of different political persuasions often manufactured evidence to blacken the reputations of their adversaries.

For years, victory appeared to remain just beyond Bolívar's grasp. In April 1815, General Pablo Morillo landed in Venezuela with an expeditionary army of 10,500 Spanish troops. Although an accidental fire cost Morillo the *San Pedro de Alcántara*, a ship-of-the-line loaded with arms and equipment for his army, he moved quickly to assume control of Caracas. Already, much of Venezuela had been reconquered by Boves's implacable *llanero* cavalry. The Spanish expeditionaries besieged Cartagena for 106 days commencing on August 22, 1815, and when the patriots capitulated, Colombia gave up rebellion (Chapter 9). In May 1816, Spanish forces reoccupied Bogotá. For the royalists, the situation brightened even more when Quito, Ecuador, surrendered to forces led by Juan Sámano and Toribio Montes after only a few major skirmishes. On the negative side, as elsewhere in counterinsurgency campaigns of Spanish America, disease, atrocious conditions, bad food, the mortifying climate, lack of pay, and desertion rapidly destroyed the expeditionary army (Chapter 12). Few criollos, mistrusted by Spanish officers and soldiers, were willing to fight for the royalist armies, whether local or expeditionary.

As might be expected, conflicts soon emerged between expeditionary soldiers and the royalist *llaneros*. As Stephen Stoan concludes in Chapter 9, Morillo, like Calleja in New Spain, recognized that after years of fighting the majority of the population desired independence. Even if effective, the royalist counterinsurgency programs fostered new resentments and more insurgents. After the Battle of Boyacá, a relatively small engagement in terms of numbers of combatants, Bolívar reoccupied Bogotá on August 9, 1819. From this point onward, the royalists slid into defeat that in some respects paralleled the fate of the armies of New Spain. Exhaustion, illness, desertion, and death eroded morale, and there were no fresh reinforcements from Spain to restore lost esprit de corps. Spain abandoned the remainder of Morillo's counterinsurgency reconquerors and left them with no long-term prospects. Following the restoration of the Spanish Constitution on November 27, 1820, Bolívar met Morillo, who quickly abandoned the scene of impending disaster. Caracas fell to the patriots on May 14, 1821, and the royalists surrendered at the second battle of Carabobo on June 24, leaving only the royalist bastion of Puerto Cabello, which held out for a few months. Bolívar now turned his attention to nation-building and to the stalemate between royalists and rebels in Peru.

The third theater of war embraced the territory of the Southern Cone including La Plata (Argentina), Uruguay, Paraguay, Chile, Upper Peru, and Peru. The two latter provinces were a borderland zone where the forces of San Martín encountered those of Bolívar and Antonio José de Sucre. Buenos Aires won its autonomy more or less uncontested in the name of Fernando VII. From the outset, the Atlantic-oriented *porteño* elites attempted to dominate Montevideo and the interior cities including Córdoba, Mendoza, and San Juan. On the distant periphery, Paraguay and Upper Peru shared few interests with the pro-free trade people of the coast— particularly when Buenos Aires dispatched armies to conquer the outlying provinces of the old viceroyalty of La Plata. Beginning in 1810, Juan José Castelli led an army that penetrated Upper Peru and occupied Potosí. Executions, arbitrary rule, and cruel behavior made the patriot soldiers hated, and their brutality soon provoked an uprising. At Potosí and other towns, the people welcomed the royalists from Peru under General José Manuel de Goyeneche, who in turn sent troops to invade the La Plata cities of Salta and Jujuy. Advancing upon Tucuman, the royalists ran into a force commanded by General Manuel Belgrano, who crushed the invaders and chased them back into Upper Peru. Having occupied Potosí, Belgrano tasted defeat in 1813 at the hands of General Joaquín de la Pezuela. Following yet another invasion from La Plata, Pezuela crushed the Argentines at the battle of Sipe Sipe and forced them into an embarrassing flight from Upper Peru.[79]

In many respects, the behavior of the Argentines in Upper Peru alienated those who otherwise might have supported them. The royalists regained control and held on for years. General San Martín recognized that the best way to deal with the Spaniards was to conquer them in Chile and then strike at their main bastion in Peru by amphibious naval attack. When the royalists regained control in Chile with the assistance of Viceroy José Fernando de Abascal of Peru, some Chileans (including the patriot leader Bernardo O'Higgins) crossed the Andes to join San Martín. In 1816, San Martín's small army of 5,000 troops, which included a contingent of slaves and a handful of European veterans of the Napoleonic Wars, crossed the Andes through six high-altitude passes. Catching the royalists by surprise, the Army of the Andes occupied Santiago following two skirmishes. The royalists retreated southward to repair their fortunes and returned in 1818 to assault Santiago. On April 5, 1818, at the battle of Maipó, San Martín definitively crushed the royalists and now could contemplate an attack against Peru.

It took San Martín and his allies two years to organize a navy and an army capable of assaulting royalist Peru. Admiral Lord Cochrane, a famous but controversial British naval officer, won a series of victories but did not get along with San Martín. Cochrane planned to attack at Callao so that the main force of the royalist army could be engaged quickly and Lima occupied. Instead, San Martín invaded Pisco south of Lima with a force of only 4,500 troops and then negotiated with Viceroy Pezuela, who, as we have seen, made his reputation against La Plata forces in Upper Peru. The proclamation of the Spanish Constitution made matters difficult since Pezuela proposed a cease-fire. After a period of indecision, the royalist army officers in Peru overthrew Pezuela and elevated José de la Serna. He concluded that to save the royalist army he would have to lead it out of Lima and into the mountainous interior.

Although San Martín occupied Lima, he was unable to gain sufficient support to win a decisive victory. With his army losing strength and becoming more corrupt, the local population scheming, and the economy of Peru falling into ruin, San Martín went to Guayaquil to seek assistance from Bolívar. The Guayaquil interview took place on July 26 and 27, 1821, without witnesses, thus opening the way for controversy ever since among historians who favor one side or the other (Chapter 10). San Martín departed Guayaquil and returned to Lima where he gathered his belongings and began a long journey into exile in Europe. While the way was opened for Bolívar and his northern forces to complete the patriot victory in South America, as Timothy Anna explains in Chapter 11, even at this point the royalists did not succumb without a protracted struggle.

The Spanish American wars of independence took many different forms depending upon the region, the composition of the population, the economy, and the sort of leadership that emerged on both sides. We can describe the conflicts as revolutions in that the patriot or rebel side desired independence from Spain or a change in governance from monarchy to either a centralist or federal republican system. Often, people supported the federalist approach to break the dominance of the old viceregal capitals and major regional centers. Until recently, the participation of vocal literate classes espousing the principles of liberalism has tended to obscure events that took place in the regions where the people had specific ideas about the nature of systemic alterations to the political system. As Peter Guardino illustrates for Guerrero in New Spain (Chapter 4), the educated classes that aspired to replace Spanish rule could no longer anticipate the somnolent approval of the rural, village, and town populations. It is clear that in many provinces of the Spanish empire, the *casta* and indigenous communities viewed the revolutions as golden opportunities to alter their situations for the better and to redress old grievances.

To win, the leader of a rebel band on the insurgent side or a royalist commander needed to organize coalitions within his community. Since many leaders were formerly traders, innkeepers, muleteers, priests, minor ranchers, and others with knowledge and ties with the *casta* and indigenous communities, they proposed social and political as well as purely military programs. Although some of these leaders appear more like outright bandits, they were often social bandits of a sort who shared loot and were careful to protect their own core supporters. The term "insurgent-bandit" suits them.[80] In Venezuela, Boves, the leader of the *pardo* and *moreno llaneros*, fitted some of these roles. Despite the fact that he was a European Spaniard originally from Asturias, he knew the people of the *castas* whom he molded into a powerful royalist cavalry.[81] In these roles, Boves acted as an effective "linking agent" who welded together coalitions and sent his implacable troops to attack, rape, and murder their patriot opponents—particularly the haughty criollos. His cavalry of tough *llaneros* rolled over conventional forces and made their opponents think twice before engaging them in battle. Exactly the same was true in Upper Peru, where guerrilla chiefs of the *republiquetas* (little republics) mobilized the indigenous populations and, like the *llaneros*, fought on both sides during the course of the lengthy wars.[82] In New Spain as in Peru, hundreds of these *cabecillas* dominated the decade of war and maintained the cause of rebellion following the defeat and executions of the original chiefs, Fathers Hidalgo (d. 1811) and Morelos (d. 1815). The report by Viceroy Juan Ruíz de Apodaca (Chapter 5) underscores the difficulties of fighting a guerrilla war against hundreds of autonomous bands that simply melted away when their members sought refuge in rugged mountainous districts or blended in with the peaceful civilian agricultural population. In this general aspect, the war of New Spain, the conflict of the *llanos* of Venezuela and Colombia, and the struggle in Upper Peru illustrated many common themes that in the twentieth century were evident in many wars of national liberation in Africa and Asia.

The key to success in the different theaters of war depended upon the ability of the royalist or insurgent commanders to forge coalitions that at least temporarily merged the individual interests of the different factions. For all of his weaknesses, Bolívar was the most successful in welding alliances between the criollos and *pardos*, who were not natural allies. He attracted and held the loyalty of some foreign officers and troops who played significant roles despite their small numbers. Bolívar might have been a shifty character, but he was also a consummate politician able to attract the loyalty of excellent officers such as Sucre, who was also a gifted commander—the victor in the 1824 battles of Junín and Ayacucho (Chapter 11). San Martín was popular with his officers and a good soldier, but his support for representative monarchy "as the best adapted to the South Americans"[83] was not a system that could gain him broad support from the spectrum of groups anticipating greater liberty under republican forms of government. In New Spain, despite the popularity of the message of Miguel Hidalgo and José María Morelos with the peasantry and the *castas*, the criollos suspected them of engineering a social revolution. Until they could control the national agenda, most criollos preferred to support the royalists.

On the royalist side, Félix Calleja of New Spain forged coalitions that included criollos and different *castas*, but he also recognized that his army could win all the battles but the last one and still lose the war in a matter of days. Unlike many royalist senior commanders, Calleja had enjoyed long experience in New Spain since 1789 that gave him profound knowledge of the people and the country. Iturbide, in some respects a brutal and overly ambitious royalist commander, recognized how to fashion the broad coalition needed to win the war. He made a deal with the insurgent chief Vicente Guerrero and gained the help of many insurgent *cabecillas*. Iturbide's real strength was that he knew so many army commanders, bureaucrats, priests, and other leaders whom he could recruit into his amalgam of royalists and insurgents. Totally exhausted by permanent mobilizations that removed men from their families and jobs and by high taxation to support the royalist armies, the people of New Spain made Iturbide a hero and declared an end to the war. In 1820 their reading of the renewed Spanish Constitution convinced them that arbitrary taxes levied to support the military were illegal. Almost spontaneously, they stacked their muskets at the local ayuntamiento and went home. In the meantime, under the Plan de Iguala, Iturbide espoused the motherhood slogans of "Independence, Religion, and Union." He won converts across the spectrum from the most tenacious "old insurgents" to European officers who were the flower of the expeditionary regiments serving in New Spain. In the end, very few Spanish soldiers returned to Spain. In Peru, the viceroys and army chiefs were also successful in prolonging the war by attracting different sectors of the population into the royalist coalition.

Throughout Spanish America, over time the royalist leaders experienced difficulties in their promotion of continuity under Spanish rule compared with the rebels, who lacked any track record and could offer grand visions for improved social position and recognition to those criollos, *pardos*, and *morenos* who wished to ameliorate old grievances. This vision often coincided with the aspirations of local people to control their resources and lands. The concept of provincial political autonomy under the Spanish Constitution offered relatively little to regional and district people who had specific economic and social grievances that required more thorough changes. Nevertheless, Jaime Rodríguez and Peter Guardino have pointed out for New Spain that village people participated actively in politics—first under the Spanish Constitution and later under the Mexican Constitution of 1824.[84] Often, villagers wished to topple dominance by a district town, to escape taxation, and to ward off speculators who purchased tracts of land.

As the wars dragged on, both rebels and royalists turned on the civilian population to steal food, abuse noncombatant men and women, and engage in other criminal activities. Often unpaid, ill fed, and poorly clothed, soldiers became accustomed to collecting their remuneration from travelers, produce sellers on their way to market, and anyone who would pay for protection. In New Spain, for example, by 1820 the royalist army as a whole suffered from exhaustion, lack of adequate pay, and declining numbers. Soldiers stationed in fortified towns stopped patrolling the rural districts and rugged mountainous zones that rapidly became permanent preserves of the insurgents. Gripped by a blockhouse mentality, royalist officers traded with the enemy, made deals, and sought to avoid risking their lives. In the Mexico City garrison, for example, there were daily fights, stabbings, sexual assaults, and murders. Hostility and racial epithets exchanged between the European expeditionary soldiers and those born in New Spain added to the violence.

In May 1820, when soldiers stole live pigs and produce from city markets, civilians who witnessed these thefts protested by throwing stones at anyone wearing a uniform. Battalion registers listed the names and crimes of soldiers caught while attempting to rob homeowners, shops, and their comrades.[85] On May 25, 1820, a patrol caught a civilian and two drummers of the expeditionary infantry regiment of Ordenes Militares with three women in the Mexico City cemetery of the Bethlemite Order. They were detained after the members of the patrol observed them in flagrante delicto. The patrol sent the soldiers to their barracks and the civilian and women to jail. Anonymous denunciants reported wild all-night fiestas and gambling at the Fruta (wineshop) that made the place seem like "a whores' and knaves' market." A late-night raid netted the police some forty individuals including a colonel, some officers and NCOs, and several priests.[86] In another typical incident during 1820 and the restoration of the 1812 Constitution, José de Jesús Rivera was arrested for insolence toward a guard at the sentry post of La Piedad market. He refused to pay a tax for the admission of a load of salt, insisting that the Constitution did not permit any taxes whatsoever. When the commander of the post went to see what the commotion was all about, Rivera slapped him in the face for having supported the opinion of the guard.[87]

Conclusion

The Spanish American wars of independence were remarkable conflicts that opened the age of wars of national liberation. Once we move beyond hagiography glorifying the great leaders such as Bolívar, San Martín, Morelos, and other *padres de la patria*, we find conflicts that foreshadowed the numerous revolutions and wars of the nineteenth and twentieth centuries. When poor peasants took up arms against fairly well-organized royalist forces carrying flintlock muskets and rifles, they soon learned to avoid conventional battlefield tactics and to employ stealth, knowledge of the terrain, and surprise. These insurgents emerged as some of the world's best practitioners of guerrilla warfare. Against these self-taught experts, the royalists introduced Draconian counterinsurgency techniques that would not appear foreign to any number of occupying powers in the twentieth century. They rounded up dispersed rural peoples and relocated them by force in defended villages where they could be observed as well as compelled to stand guard duty and to mount patrols. Anyone found in the countryside was in danger of summary execution as a suspected insurgent in a fire-free zone. They burned crops, killed animals, executed blacksmiths who could make lance points, and even went into forests to chop down trees that bore edible fruit. As counterinsurgents, the royalists confiscated draft animals, imposed confiscatory taxes, and boasted that they would make civilians fear them more than death itself. As is so often the case, many army commanders became wealthy in their posts and accustomed to wielding arbitrary powers. With independence, throughout Spanish America they would not return to their barracks or to mundane, poorly paid military tasks associated with internal order and national defense.

Although the wars took place often without close connections between the theaters of conflict, as will be seen throughout the present study there were many more similarities than differences. Race was a factor of major significance. Some leaders such as Bolívar and Morelos recognized that the abolition of slavery was essential in winning over the *pardos* and *morenos* who in many theaters were outstanding fighters. These leaders sought to harness the developing aspirations of the village and town populations while maintaining links with the criollos, an essential factor in any permanent victory. On the insurgent side, lack of adequate weapons, training, and discipline forced them to guerrilla tactics and often to the use of cavalry over infantry and artillery. The revolutionaries of Venezuela, Colombia, and La Plata managed better than others because they could import arms from the enormous stocks available in the Atlantic economy following the defeat of Napoleon. They employed mercenary officers and soldiers who were looking for work and new adventures unobtainable in peacetime Europe. Strangely, given its geographic location, New Spain was more isolated despite the connections by some rebels with New Orleans and American maritime contrabandists. Cut off from the markets for muskets, most insurgents had to learn the technology of military science—boring cannon out of tree trunks, melting down churchbells, and manufacturing swords and sabers so brittle that they broke in the scabbards before they could be put to use.

Looking across the great continental battle zones, it is difficult to condemn one side or one province, such as Venezuela, for being more bloody than the other. As we have seen, Bolívar's proclamation of war to the death was not unique. The killing of prisoners took place where emotions were at a fever pitch and where the captors feared that they could not afford to mount effective guards. Much more often, prisoners were given the opportunity to change sides and to continue as soldiers for their erstwhile enemies. Some men deserted and rejoined rebel and royalist forces as many as eight or ten times. Especially in the case of the royalist forces, the widespread use of amnesties filled the ranks with former rebels who in many cases had not altered their basic sentiments. Finally, it is important to remember that the wars of independence continued for over a decade. Men and women who grew up as rebels knew no other trade than that of soldier or guerrilla-bandit. As might be suspected, they continued these occupations in the new nations that desperately required peace and order to restore devastated economies. Taken together, these factors underscore the fact that the roots of nineteenth-century instability in Spanish America must be traced to the conflicts that gave birth to the new republics.

Notes

1. Charles E. Chapman, *Colonial Hispanic America: A History* (New York: MacMillan Company, 1933), 213.
2. Ibid.

3. Ibid.

4. Ibid., 214.

5. Jay Kinsbruner, *Independence in Spanish America: Civil Wars, Revolutions, and Underdevelopment* (Albuquerque: University of New Mexico Press, 1994), 9; this book is the revised and enlarged edition of a study first published in 1973. For another updated overview, see Richard Graham's revised 1972 study, *Independence in Latin America: A Comparative Approach* (New York: McGraw-Hill, 1994). There are other major works in English that should be mentioned at this point, starting with John Lynch's revised 1973 study, *The Spanish American Revolutions, 1808–1826: A Unified Account of the Revolutions that Swept over South and Central America in the Early Nineteenth Century*, 2d ed. (New York: Norton, 1986); and R. A. Humphries and John Lynch, eds., *The Origins of the Latin American Revolutions, 1808–1826* (New York: Alfred A. Knopf, 1966). For a recent compilation on the origins of the independence wars see John Lynch, ed., *Latin American Revolutions, 1808–1826: Old and New World Origins* (Norman: University of Oklahoma Press, 1994). For chapters on the different regions as well as overviews see Leslie Bethell, ed., *The Cambridge History of Latin America*, vol. 3 (Cambridge, England: Cambridge University Press, 1987). Finally, for detail and overviews see Barbara A. Tenenbaum, ed., *Encyclopedia of Latin American History and Culture*, 5 vols. (New York: Charles Scribner's Sons, 1996). In Spanish, see François-Xavier Guerra, *Modernidad e independencias: Ensayos sobre las revoluciones hispánicas* (Madrid: Editorial Mapre, 1992); and Jaime E. Rodríguez O., *La independencia de la América española* (México: Fondo de Cultura Económica, 1996).

6. Lynch, *The Spanish American Revolutions*, 1.

7. Jaime E. Rodríguez O., *The Independence of Spanish America* (New York: Cambridge University Press, 1998).

8. Alan Frost, *The Voyage of the Endeavour: Captain Cook and the Discovery of the Pacific* (St. Leonards, New South Wales: Allen and Unwin, 1998), 2–5.

9. See Richard Pares, *War and Trade in the West Indies, 1739–1763* (Oxford: Oxford University Press, 1936); and Richard Harding, *Amphibious Warfare in the Eighteenth Century: The British Expedition to the West Indies, 1740–1742* (London: Royal Historical Society Studies in History 62, 1991).

10. See David Syrett, *The Siege and Capture of Havana, 1762* (London: Naval Records Society, 1970).

11. There is considerable literature published on military reform in the Americas, more in fact than on the armies of the era of independence. See María del Carmen Velázquez, *El estado de guerra en Nueva España, 1760–1808* (México: El Colegio de México, 1950); Lyle N. McAlister, *The "Fuero Militar" in New Spain, 1764–1800* (Gainesville: University Presses of Florida, 1957); Leon G. Campbell, *The Military and Society in Colonial Peru, 1750–1810* (Philadelphia: American Philosophical Society, 1978); Allan J. Kuethe, *Military Reform and Society in New Granada, 1773–1808* (Gainesville: University Presses of Florida, 1978); idem, *Cuba, 1753–1815: Crown, Military, and Society* (Knoxville: University of Tennessee Press, 1986); Christon I. Archer, *The Army in Bourbon Mexico, 1760–1810* (Albuquerque: University of New Mexico Press, 1977); Juan Marchena Fernández, *Oficiales y soldados en el ejército de América* (Seville: Escuela de Estudios Hispanoamericanos, 1983); Julio Albi, *La defensa de las Indias (1764–1799)* (Madrid: Ediciones Cultura Hispánica, 1987); Josefa Vega Juanino, *La institución militar en Michoacán en el último cuarto del siglo XVIII* (Zamora: El Colegio de Michoacán, 1986); Santiago-Gerardo Suárez, *Las milicias: Instituciones militares hispanoamericanos* (Caracas: Biblioteca de la Academia Nacional

de la Historia, 1984); and Juan Marchena Fernández, *Ejército y milicias en el mundo colonial americano* (Madrid: Editorial Mapre, 1992).

12. There is a vast literature on the Bourbon Reforms that is much too comprehensive to review here. As an introduction, students should examine Herbert I. Priestley, *José de Gálvez: Visitor General of New Spain, 1765–1771* (Berkeley: University of California Press, 1916); Anthony McFarlane, *Colombia before Independence: Economy, Society, and Politics under Bourbon Rule* (New York: Cambridge University Press, 1993); John R. Fisher, *Government and Society in Colonial Peru: The Intendant System, 1784–1814* (London: Athlone Press, 1970); David A. Brading, *Miners and Merchants in Bourbon Mexico, 1763–1810* (Cambridge, England: Cambridge University Press, 1971); John Lynch, *Spanish Colonial Administration, 1782–1810* (London: Athlone Press, 1958); Mark A. Burkholder, *Politics of a Colonial Career: José Baquíjano and the Audiencia of Lima* (Albuquerque: University of New Mexico Press, 1980); John E. Kicza, *Colonial Entrepreneurs: Families and Business in Bourbon Mexico City* (Albuquerque: University of New Mexico Press, 1983); Linda Arnold, *Bureaucracy and Bureaucrats in Mexico City, 1742–1835* (Tucson: University of Arizona Press, 1988); Jacques A. Barbier, *Reform and Politics in Bourbon Chile, 1755–1796* (Ottawa: University of Ottawa Press, 1980); Brian R. Hamnett, *Politics and Trade in Southern Mexico, 1750–1821* (Cambridge, England: Cambridge University Press, 1971); Kendall W. Brown, *Bourbons and Brandy: Imperial Reform in Eighteenth-Century Arequipa* (Albuquerque: University of New Mexico Press, 1986); Mark A. Burkholder and D. S. Chandler, *From Impotence to Authority: The Spanish Crown and the American Audiencias, 1687–1808* (Columbia: University of Missouri Press, 1977); Jaime E. Rodríguez O., ed., *Mexico in the Age of Democratic Revolutions, 1750–1850* (Boulder: Lynne Rienner, 1994); and Colin MacLachlan, *Spain's Empire in the New World: The Role of Ideas in Institutional and Social Change* (Berkeley: University of California Press, 1988).

13. For a good discussion see David A. Brading, *The First America: The Spanish Monarchy, Creole Patriots, and the Liberal State, 1492–1867* (Cambridge, England: Cambridge University Press, 1991), 422–46.

14. McFarlane, *Colombia before Independence*, 270–71.

15. Archer, *The Army in Bourbon Mexico*, 94–98.

16. J. Eric S. Thompson, ed., *Thomas Gage's Travels in the New World* (Norman: University of Oklahoma Press, 1958), 215.

17. Instrucción de 1 Agosto de 1764 para gobierno y comandancia general de las armas e Instrucción de las Tropas del Reino, Archivo General de la Nación, Mexico, Sección de Indiferente de Guerra (cited hereinafter as AGN:IG), vol. 224-A. Also see Archer, *The Army in Bourbon Mexico*, 11–12.

18. See Kuethe, *Cuba, 1753–1815*, 24–49; and Bibiano Torres Ramírez, *Alejandro O'Reilly en las Indias* (Seville: Escuela de Estudios Hispanoamericanos, 1969).

19. For New Spain, the original Spanish cadre consisted of 4 field marshals, 6 colonels, 5 lieutenant colonels, 10 majors, 109 lieutenants, 7 ensigns, 15 cadets, 228 sergeants, 401 corporals, 151 common soldiers, drummers, and fifers, a trumpeter, and a kettledrummer. There was also a complete regiment of infantry. See Juan de Villalba to Viceroy Marqués de Cruillas, November 1, 1764, AGN:IG, vol. 304-A.

20. Instrucción de 1 Agosto de 1764, AGN:IG, vol. 224-A.

21. Félix de Ferraz to Viceroy Croix, Reglamento para las milicias de Blancos, Pardos y Morenos, March 18, 1767, AGN:IG, vol. 40-B.

22. Noticias venidas de Londres con fecha de 8 de agosto de 1766, AGN:IG, vol. 224-A.

23. Julián de Arriaga to Viceroy Marqués de Croix, Aranjuez, June 24, 1767, AGN:IG, vol. 224-A; Archer, *The Army in Bourbon Mexico*, 12–13.

24. Alonso Basco y Vargas, Alcalde Mayor of Alvarado, to Viceroy Cruillas, November 13, 1762, AGN:IG, vol. 532-A.

25. Arriaga to Viceroy Antonio María de Bucareli, March 15, 1771, AGN:IG, vol. 224-A.

26. Antonio de Llano y Villarrutía to Viceroy Antonio María de Bucareli, February 1, 1775, AGN:IG, vol. 202-B.

27. Dictamen del Marqués de la Torre, Inspector General de Infantería, en punto de milicias del Reino de Nueva España y otros relativos a su conservación, seguridad y defensa, October 24, 1768, AGN:IG, vol. 36-B.

28. Reflexiones sobre el Reino de Nueva España y algunos otros puntos deducidos del dictamen dado por el Fiscal de Real Hacienda, el Señor Areche en 1774 a el Exmo. Sor. Virrey Frey Don Antonio Bucareli, sobre proposiciones que hizo el Exmo. Sor. Inspector Don Pascual Cisneros, punto a formación de Milicias Provinciales en el Reino, Museo Naval, Madrid, ms. 568.

29. For good descriptions of the system of *repartimiento* see Hamnett, *Politics and Trade in Southern Mexico*; and Brading, *Miners and Merchants in Bourbon Mexico*, 47–50.

30. Reflexiones sobre el Reino de Nueva España, 1774, Museo Naval, Madrid, ms. 568.

31. Ibid.

32. Ibid.

33. Leon G. Campbell, "A Colonial Establishment: Creole Domination of the Audiencia of Lima during the Late Eighteenth Century," *Hispanic American Historical Review* 52:1 (February 1972): 16–17; idem, *The Military and Society in Colonial Peru*, 236–37; Fisher, *Government and Society in Colonial Peru*, 17–21.

34. P. Michael McKinley, *Pre-Revolutionary Caracas: Politics, Economy, and Society, 1777–1811* (Cambridge: Cambridge University Press, 1985), 18–20.

35. Francisco Crespo, "Proyecto formado en el año de 1784 sobre el mejor arreglo y establecimiento del Ejército de Nueva España," Archivo General de las Indias, Seville, Sección de Méjico (cited hereinafter as AGI:Mexico), leg. 2418. Also see Archer, *The Army in Bourbon Mexico*, 224–25.

36. Proyecto de Crespo, AGI: Mexico, leg. 2418.

37. For a general discussion see Magnus Mörner, *Race Mixture in the History of Latin America* (Boston: Little, Brown and Company, 1967), 58–59.

38. For an excellent study of the Acordada in eighteenth-century New Spain see Colin MacLachlan, *Criminal Justice in Eighteenth-Century Mexico* (Berkeley: University of California Press, 1974).

39. Petition of the *pardo* sergeants and corporal of the Batallón de Pardos de Puebla to Viceroy Croix, AGN:IG, vol. 40-B; Bando of Viceroy Marqués de Croix, December 24, 1767, AGN: IG, vol. 40-B; Inspector General Pascual de Cisneros to Viceroy Bucareli, May 31, 1777, AGN:IG, vol. 42-B.

40. Viceroy Marqués de Branciforte to the Marqués Campo de Alange, no. 66, June 30, 1792, Archivo General de Simancas, Guerra Moderna, leg. 6970.

41. Petition of *pardo* officers, April 23, 1792, AGN:IG, vol. 100-A. Rodríguez de Hurtado was tracked down and punished with a term of seclusion. He apologized for his unwitting crime and claimed that this was his first error in fifty-two years in the priesthood.

42. Ibid.

43. Petition of Narziso Zigarra, Yldefonso Silva, and Juan Pastor to Viceroy Branciforte, n.d., 1794, AGN: IG, vol. 197-B.

44. Ignacio López de Ulloa to the Conde de Floridablanca, Turin, February 1, 1792, AGI: Estado, leg. 39.

45. "Para evitar los graves prejuicios que podrián causar las sediciosas . . . de la Asamblea Nacional de Francia," Aranjuez, May 21, 1790, AGI: Indiferente General, leg. 662.

46. Revillagigedo to Alejandro Malaspina, October 31, 1791, Museo Naval, Madrid, vol. 280; Revillagigedo to the Conde de Aranda, Archivo Histórico Nacional, Madrid, leg. 4287.

47. Real Orden, Aranjuez, May 18, 1791, AGI: Indiferente General, leg. 662.

48. "Manifiesta el modo con que ha cumplido la Real Orden de 18 de mayo último sobre precaver pinturas o inscripciones seductosas," Revillagigedo, no. 605, October 29, 1791, AGI: Mexico, leg. 1544; Revillagigedo to the Conde de Lerena, no. 504, August 27, 1791, AGI: Mexico, leg. 1546.

49. Revillagigedo to Campo de Alange, reservada, April 30, 1793, AGI: Mexico, leg. 1435; Viceroy Marqués de Branciforte to the Duque de Alcudia, September 2, December 3, 1794, AGI: Estado, leg. 22.

50. Luis de las Casas to the Conde de Aranda, December 16, 1795, AGI: Sección 11 A, Papeles de Cuba (cited hereinafter as AGI:Cuba), leg. 1489.

51. Ibid.

52. Las Casas to Campo de Alange, no. 1025, November 12, 1794, AGI:Cuba, leg. 1488.

53. Ibid.

54. Arturo O'Neill to the Principe de la Paz, Mérida, October 28, 1796, AGI: Estado, leg. 35.

55. Branciforte to the Principe de la Paz, Orizaba, June 30, 1797, AGI: Estado, leg. 28.

56. Rodríguez, *The Independence of Spanish America*, 51–74.

57. Ibid; Virginia Guedea, "The First Popular Elections in Mexico City, 1812–1813," in Jaime E. Rodríguez O., ed., *The Evolution of the Mexican Political System* (Wilmington, DE: Scholarly Resources, 1993), 46–48.

58. Michael P. Costeloe, *Response to Revolution: Imperial Spain and the Spanish American Revolutions, 1810–1840* (Cambridge, England: Cambridge University Press, 1986), 6–7, 98–100.

59. Eric Van Young, "Millennium on the Northern Marches: The Mad Messiah of Durango and Popular Rebellion in Mexico, 1800–1815," Comparative Study in Society and History 28 (1996): 385–413.

60. Carta escrita de Nueva York por F.G. a un amigo de Veracruz con fecha 10 de Noviembre de 1808, AGN:IG, vol. 77.

61. Proclama del Virrey Garibay, April 20, 1809, AGN:IG, vol. 276-B.

62. Sobre varias expresiones sediciosas proferidas por el Comandante de Caballería del Nueva Santander, Don José Florencia Barragan, AGN:IB, vol. 188-B.

63. Audiencia Gobernativa to the Secretario de Estado y de su Despacho Universal, no. 7, May 31, 1810, AGI: Mexico, leg. 1544.

64. See Archer, *The Army in Bourbon Mexico*, 292–93.

65. Pedro Garibay to Subdelegado y Justicia de Tehuacán Salvador de Benavides, July 12, 1809, AGN:IG, vol. 205-B

66. Ayuntamiento of Guadalajara to Archbishop-Viceroy Francisco Javier de Lizana, Guadalajara, May 11, 1810, AGN: IG, vol. 410-A.

67. Ibid.

68. Plan de defensa de Dionisio Cano y Moctezuma, Real Tecpam de San Juan, April 27, 1810, AGN:IG, vol. 410-A.

69. Ibid.

70. Ibid.

71. See Christon I. Archer, "Bite of the Hydra: The Rebellion of Cura Miguel Hidalgo, 1810–1811," in Jaime E. Rodríguez O., ed., *Patterns of Contention in Mexican History* (Wilmington, DE: Scholarly Resources, 1992), 69–93.

72. See Brian R. Hamnett, *Roots of Insurgency: Mexican Regions, 1750–1824* (Cambridge, England: Cambridge University Press, 1986); Timothy E. Anna, *The Fall of the Royal Government in Mexico City* (Lincoln: University of Nebraska Press, 1978); Peter F. Guardino, *Peasants, Politics, and the Formation of Mexico's National State: Guerrero, 1800–1857* (Stanford: Stanford University Press, 1996); John Tutino, *From Insurrection to Revolution in Mexico: Social Bases of Agrarian Violence, 1750–1940* (Princeton: Princeton University Press, 1986); and Christon I. Archer, " 'La Causa Buena": The Counterinsurgency Army of New Spain and the Ten Years' War," in Jaime E. Rodriguez O., ed., *The Independence of Mexico and the Creation of the New Nation* (Los Angeles: UCLA Latin American Center, 1989), 85–108.

73. William Spence Robertson, *Iturbide of Mexico* (Durham: Duke University Press, 1952); Timothy E. Anna, *The Mexican Empire of Iturbide* (Lincoln: University of Nebraska Press, 1990).

74. Vicente Lecuna, *Catálogo de errores y calumnias en la historia de Bolívar*, 3 vols. (New York: Colonial Press, 1956).

75. Ibid., I:276–77, 313–19; McKinley, *Pre-Revolutionary Caracas*, 171.

76. Hugh M. Hamill, *The Hidalgo Revolt: Prelude to Mexican Independence* (Gainesville: University Presses of Florida, 1966), 181–82; Christon I. Archer, "New Wars and Old: Félix Calleja and the Independence War of Mexico, 1810–1816," in B. J. C. McKercher and A. Hamish Ion, eds., *Military Heretics: The Unorthodox in Policy and Strategy* (Westport, CT: Praeger, 1994), 50–51; Archer, "The Counterinsurgency Army and the Ten Years' War," 92–95

77. Christon I. Archer, "La revolución militar de México: Estrategia, tácticas y logisticas durante la guerra de independencia, 1810–1821," in Josefina Zoraida Vázquez, ed., *Interpretaciones de la independencia de México* (México: Nueva Imagen, 1997), 156–76.

78. See Alfred Hasbrouck, *Foreign Legionaries in the Liberation of Spanish South America* (New York: Columbia University Press, 1928), 371–75.

79. Charles W. Arnade, *The Emergence of the Republic of Bolivia* (Gainesville: University Presses of Florida, 1957), 57–79.

80. On banditry see the classic interpretation by Eric Hobsbawm, *Bandits* (New York: Pantheon Books, 1981). For Latin America see Richard W. Slatta, ed., *Bandidos: The Varieties of Latin American Banditry* (New York: Greenwood Press, 1987), 1–9, 34–47; and Christon I. Archer, "Banditry and Revolution in New Spain, 1790–1821," *Biblioteca Americana* 1:2 (November 1982): 59–90.

81. Stephen K. Stoan, *Pablo Morillo and Venezuela, 1815–1820* (Columbus: Ohio State University Press, 1974), 52–53; Rodríguez, *The Independence of Spanish America*, 121–22.

82. Arnade, *The Emergence of the Republic of Bolivia*, 32–56.

83. John Miller, *Memoirs of General Miller in the Service of the Republic of Peru*, 2 vols. (London: Longman, Rees Orme, Brown, and Green, 1829), 1: 425.

84. Guardino, *Peasants, Politics, and the Formation of Mexico's National State*, 6–8; Rodríguez, *The Independence of Spanish America*, 205–6; and idem, "The Constitution of 1824 and the Formation of the Mexican State," in Jaime E. Rodríquez O., ed., *The Evolution of the Mexican Political System* (Wilmington, DE: Scholarly Resources, 1993), 71–90.

85. Colonel José de Mendivil, *sargento mayor* of the Plaza de México to Viceroy Conde de Venadito (Apodaca), May 6–8, 1820, AGN: Operaciones de Guerra (cited hereinafter as OG), vol 597.

86. Report of Capitán de Comisarios, Antonio Acuña, April 19, 1820, AGN:OG, vol. 597.

87. Mendivil to Venadito, September 19, 1820, AGN:OG, vol. 603.

1

Popular Insurrection and Royalist Reaction: Colombian Regions, 1810–1823

Brian R. Hamnett

Why do people revolt, and do their motivations depend upon social, racial, and economic origins? How can we get at the mentality of insurgents who left very few records other than judicial and military documents prepared by their opponents and oppressors? Brian Hamnett's study illustrates many themes that can be found in all parts of Spanish America. The dissident elites, anxious to recruit popular classes, were at the same time opposed to granting meaningful reforms. Old grievances and regional tensions produced rivalries that led to armed conflicts in the Llanos de Casanare, Pasto, and other peripheral jurisdictions where issues of taxation and contraband commerce resulted in banditry and guerrilla warfare. While the royalists were successful in their use of tax concessions granting privileges in some regions, the army failed to control remote areas such as the Llanos de Casanare. Facing chronic insurgency, the royalists relied on terrorism and sent destacamentos volantes *to punish the rebels. Even with the military victories of 1816 won by Pablo Morillo's expeditionary army, counterinsurgency simply delayed the inevitable. Similar to New Spain, these harsh approaches and arbitrary conduct by Spanish officers often made implacable enemies. The insurgents took permanent control over many of the more rugged outlying areas. The* llaneros *contributed much to Simón Bolívar's victory in 1819 at the Battle of Boyacá. The grievances of the lower classes, particularly of the* pardos libres *(free blacks), carried over from the late colony through the epoch of the independence wars and into the nineteenth-century republican era.*

From Brian R. Hamnett, "Popular Insurrection and Royalist Reaction: Colombian Regions, 1810–1823," in J. R. Fisher, A. J. Kuethe, and A. McFarlane, eds., *Reform and Insurrection in Bourbon New Granada and Peru* (Baton Rouge: Louisiana State University Press, 1990), 291–326. Reprinted by permission of Louisiana State University Press.

Brian Hamnett has researched many aspects of the independence movements in different parts of Spanish America. His Roots of Insurgency: Mexican Regions, 1750–1824 *(1986), is the best modern work on the insurgency in New Spain.*

S ources of conflict within New Granada's provinces during the Wars of Independence have received remarkably little attention. Similarly, the question of popular participation has usually receded before the customary emphasis on the leading creole protagonists and their more developed ideological formation. Overridingly important is the extent to which provincial rebellions after 1810 reflected or extenuated existing social tensions. Anthony McFarlane, in his recent examination of the local roots of popular discontent in eighteenth-century New Granada, argues that protest and rebellion were not motivated by any preconceived ideology and usually had scant repercussions beyond their original areas. Yet, at the same time, they constituted authentic evidence of a popular challenge to the existing powers, often beyond simply fiscal protest. The viceroyalty, moreover, contained an estimated 70,000 slaves and 140,000 free blacks in 1800. The Cauca Valley was the center of a slavocracy that dominated western New Granada well into the nineteenth century. Michael Taussig points to the reappearance of slave rebellions and flights in the late eighteenth century "as a major social factor alongside the growing restlessness of free blacks and a general wave of discontent in the colony as a whole." This regional discontent was especially intense in the valley, where "plots were uncovered for regional revolts, some of which included alliances with Indians, and there is a suggestion that secret black societies or slave cabildos, common enough along the Caribbean coast, even existed in some of the Cauca Valley haciendas."

The most striking protest in late colonial New Granada was the Comunero movement of 1780–1781, which went beyond fiscal grievances. The extent and initial impact of the Comunero revolt derived from the ability of the regional elites in Socorro to draw together, at least for a short time, a broad spectrum of popular support. This multiclass alliance rocked the colonial authorities in Santa Fe.[1] A similar type of alliance, though consisting of different social groups, accounted for the early impact of the Túpac Amarú rebellion in Peru in November, 1780.[2] Neither of these two movements brought about the political emancipation of their participants. Nevertheless, the experience of the 1780s provided important guidelines for the independence movements of the 1810s because it demonstrated the efficacy of cross-class alliances and the potential of popular-class recruitment by the dissident elites.[3] Where the elites did not learn this lesson, as in the case of the Venezuelan planters, who sought to transform Spanish abolutism into a slave owners' oligarchy, the popular reaction was decisive. It led to the collapse of the first and second Venezuelan republics in April, 1812, and August, 1814, respectively.[4]

In New Granada, the political fragmentation following the creole revolution of July 20, 1810, in Santa Fe weakened central government, led to a series of interregional civil wars, and compromised the positions of hitherto predominant social groups. Political disarray may well have provided lower-class groups with a chance to redress long-standing grievances at the local level. Similarly, participation, even for a limited time, in a broader-ranging struggle, whether on the patriot or the royalist side, may have been seen as a means of social improvement for the community or upward mobility for the individual.

Colonial New Granada: A Case of Undergovernment

Allan Kuethe argues for the relatively minor impact of the Bourban reforms in New Granada. In contrast to New Spain and Peru, the structure of royal administration remained largely unchanged; the intendant system was never introduced; mining reform proved to be a failure; and the disciplined militia system affected primarily the coastal zone. Neither military reforms nor a *visita* took place in the 1760s before the reforming impulse in metropolitan government circles slowed down again between 1766 and 1776. When the *visita* of New Granada finally took place in the later 1770s, fiscal reform, that is, in reality, new tax impositions, preceded both consensus building around the principle of administrative rationalization and commercial reforms that could redound to the benefit of the creole elites. In consequence, fiscal innovations provided violent responses and polarized colonial opinion across social groups in opposition to government policy. Kuethe concludes that delay of general reform set the stage for Spain's political catastrophes in the 1810s. Spanish colonial government in New Granada had long demonstrated a striking incapacity to mobilize the territory's fiscal potential and to control revenue from commerce. Failure to halt the contraband trade led to relatively scant revenues from commerce and mining. This in the long run denied the viceregal government the opportunity to finance reform.

Contraband had a long history in New Granada. The Bourbon government had inadvertently compounded the problem by creating a state tobacco monopoly, established in stages between 1766 and 1778. The aim was not primarily to encourage exportation but to raise revenue for the crown at a time of pressing imperial defense requirements. Controversial from the start and a contributory factor to the rebellion of 1781, the monopoly confined growing to only four areas: Girón and Zapatoca in Socorro, Ambalema in the Upper Magdalena zone, Pore and Numchia in the Llanos of Casanare, and the Llano Grande on the eastern side of the

Cauca Valley. In many areas illegal cultivation continued. In the Cauca region, for instance, free black peasants began growing tobacco on the periphery of the Arboleda family's slave hacienda in the last quarter of the eighteenth century. Taussig describes these communities as "a type of internal 'republic' or state within the state, cut off from the rest of society except for the illegal cash and crop transfers of tobacco upon which so much of their autonomy depended." This zone on the Río Palo included a runaway slave *palenque*. In the external trade the principal destination for New Granada's contraband was British Jamaica.[5] Along the Caribbean coast gold and tropical produce were exchanged for manufactures. In this clandestine trade Riohacha occupied pride of place. The Río Atrato provided the outlet for gold from Chocó. The large haciendas of the Magdalena Valley, the principal means of access to the interior, were deeply involved in the contraband trade.

Mompós stood at the center of both legal and illegal commerce. Not even the customs house after 1720 nor the deputation of the Consulado of Cartagena after 1796 could halt the illicit trade through Mompós, which by the 1770s had already become one of New Granada's most important towns. In fact, from that time, the contrabandist and mercantile group consolidated its position in opposition to representatives of the official colonial power.[6] In the late colonial period, the Bourbon commercial reforms helped to stimulate the expansion of New Granada's trade, particularly in tropical produce.[7] This, however, did not signify any change in the direction of trade away from the contraband sector. On the contrary, the Cartagena merchant José Ignacio de Pombo estimated the value of imports through the contraband trade to total as much as 3,000,000 pesos, a figure that contrasted with the value of licit trade at 2,562,812 pesos. The suspension of transatlantic trade from 1796 and the prevalence of contraband increased the rivalry between Cartagena and the interior and, in turn, weakened the Cartagena merchants' predominance in the overseas trade.[8] Fals Borda draws attention to the increasing tension between the Mompós contrabandists and the traditional slave-owning planter elite in the coastal zone concerning the question of control of the routes of trade. This conflict reached a climax when, on August 6, 1810, the merchant majority on the Mompós cabildo proclaimed independence from Spain and formed a merchant-controlled patriotic junta. The effort of this group to establish Mompós as a separate province led to civil war with Cartagena during the following year.[9]

The Wars of Independence exacerbated the problem of contraband, which had been endemic and beyond resolution during the colonial period. At the end of the eighteenth century, New Granada's annual gold production reached 3,060,000 pesos, and a considerable quantity, particularly from the placer deposits of the Chocó which accounted for one-third of this total, went into the contraband trade, rather than the colonial exchequer.[10] Indeed, the food supply to the Chocó communities traveled precisely up the Río Atrato. A characteristic route in the Chocó contraband trade in gold was to Panama, with a further trade also to Guayaquil in the south. The lieutenant governor of Buga, in the center of the Cauca Valley, writing in the midst of the conflicts of the *patria boba* era, appealed for royalist authorities to take measures to stop the Panama and Guayaquil contraband trades with the Chocó.[11] A major problem continued to be the remote location of the gold-producing zones and the repeated failure of the colonial administration to remedy the situation. Recurrent conflict across the lines of commercial transit served to make matters worse during the 1810s. Barbacoas illustrated this dilemma. The small settlement lay on the Río de Telembí, which flowed into the Río de Patía, which in turn discharged into the ports of Iscuandé and Tumaco on the Pacific coast. Rich deposits of gold had made the region important in the previous two hundred years, and teams of Negro slaves of both sexes, comprising some four thousand individuals, worked them. White settlement always remained scant, and everything but maize and bananas had to be imported from Pasto on the backs of Indian carriers along the high mountainous paths. There was no road, only the Indians' trails used since the pre-Columbian era. This remote but significant area was drawn into the conflicts in southern New Granada.[12]

As the Barbacoas case illustrated, gold needed a large labor force. The great families of Popayán, such as the Mosquera and Arboleda, rose to prosperity through their ownership of slave teams and their employment in the gold sector during the eighteenth century. Wealth from the Chocó and the Cauca zones passed into Popayán to sustain its elites. The important Cauca-region towns of Cali, Anserma, Buga, Toro, and Almaguer equally rose upon the gold trade and the slave-labor system. The Wars of Independence, however, tended to disperse the labor force and led in some instances to the decline of operations, as in the case of the Chachafruto mine in the Supía region.[13]

It is surprising that the Spanish colonial authorities managed to maintain their position in the Americas at all, in view of the small amount of policing available to them. The scant military establishment in New Granada was a further case in point. In 1799, the army in New Granada consisted solely of 3,576 regulars and 8,460 disciplined militia.[14] Evidently, so small an army, formed with the object of retaining political control of a widely dispersed territory, would be incapable of holding the entire viceroyalty in times of emergency. Such a situation gave insurgency movements the opportunity to establish themselves in remote areas and then extend their influence outward. Precisely because of this state of affairs, the Llanos of Casanare, the lowlands east of the cordillera of Cundinamarca and Boyacá, became a crucially important strategic zone. In itself it had always been rather tangential to the affairs of the viceroyalty, especially after the decline of its textile industries in the later eighteenth century. The official military presence in the Llanos had always been limited, since the central power remained distant and financially constrained through its incapacity to master the sources of revenue. According to Jane Loy, central government control in Casanare was weaker in 1810 than in 1780. This suggests that, were an insurgency to occur in that perennially troubled zone, the central government would lack the means of containing or extinguishing it. Loy argues that the Llanos in 1800–1810 were still experiencing the repercussions of the expulsion of the Jesuits from the missions and of the rebellion of the Comuneros in the cordillera zone. Furthermore, several Comunero rebels had sought refuge in the Llanos, and in some instances they were to take part in the insurgency of the 1810s.[15] The Llanos were in a state of turmoil well before the creoles made their bid for political supremacy in Santa Fe in July, 1810.

We have already remarked on the contraband trade along the river sysems of the Caribbean lowlands. That region, too, was undergoverned in the late colonial period and like the Llanos, though for different reasons, would prove to be a zone of heavy fighting during the Wars of Independence. During the second half of the eighteenth century, the region between Mompós, Cartagena, and Santa Marta revealed little evidence of effective viceregal authority. The central power had made efforts to remedy this lax administrative control by grouping dispersed settlements into new towns during 1744–1770. A major reason for this policy was the need to safeguard the region between Mompós and the coast from the depredations of the Chimila Indians. Even so, unpacified Indians continued to threaten the routes of transit into the interior, including the Magdalena route itself.[16] The situation in this coastal zone was further complicated by the jurisdictional rivalry between the three cities, which continued throughout the Wars of Independence and into the following decades. Even though Santa Marta lacked the commerical importance of Cartagena, its strategic position between New Granada's revolutionary city-state and royalist-controlled Maracaibo guaranteed that possession of it would be bitterly contested in the 1810s. During the struggle for independence long-standing intraregional tensions resulted in armed conflicts. Similarly, the latent social tensions within these zones also rose to the surface to cause further complications. The conflicts within the city of Cartagena itself in 1810–1815 were a case in point. Hermes Tovar has perceptively commented that the Wars of Independence "represented in those early years of the revolutionary juntas and republics a checkboard of hidden vendettas."[17]

Patria Boba

The social conflicts of Cartagena were real and of long duration. The revolution in Caracas in April, 1810, presented the city's aspiring dissi-

dent merchant and lawyer group with the opportunity to launch a swift
bid for political control to make themselves independent of both metropolitan Spain and viceregal Santa Fe. Cartagena proclaimed itself an independent sovereign state on November 11, 1811. This action was central
to the internal struggle in the city, described by Indalecio Liévano Aguirre
as a social conflict between "el partido de los patricios" and "el partido
revolucionario," which took power on November 11, 1811, with the support of "los estratos populares del puerto." With the fall of the "notables,"
power was transferred to Rodríguez Torices, who became president of the
state of Cartagena. The city's military situation became critical during
the next year with the collapse of the first Venezuelan republic in April,
1812, which enabled the royalists of Santa Marta and Panama to intensify
their naval and land blockade. Already, the royalists of Santa Marta had
fortified positions such as Tenerife and Chiriguana along the Magdalena
River. The Cartagena revolutionaries were obliged to launch a campaign
into this region and burned the towns in 1812.[18]

These royalist positions on the coast enabled Benito Pérez to recon-
stitute the viceroyalty of New Granada in the isthmus of Panama. However, the remoteness of Panama and the military expansion of Cartagena
obliged the royalists briefly to abandon control of Santa Marta and the
Ocaña district early in January, 1813, and repair from the Magdalena line
into the safety of Maracaibo. Local resistance to the Cartagena patriots
forced the revolutionaries out on March 6, 1813, and enabled the incom-
ing viceroy, Francisco de Montalvo, to take up residence in Santa Marta
in June and prepare for the reduction of the patriot positions. He described
the city as prostrate and faced by a naval blockade from Cartagena and an
attempt by land to cut off the food supply from Ciénaga Grande and the
right bank of the Magdalena. This danger was not finally dispelled until
royalist ships from Portobelo reopened the food supply in September and
brought troops and émigré civil servants. Montalvo reunited all Santa
Marta forces into a provincial battalion and began to plan for the refortifi-
cation of the Magdalena line. Royalist naval action late in March, 1814,
reopened Ciénaga Grande and forced the patriots to abandon the province
and withdraw across the Magdalena. By June, 1814, the royalist cause was
better placed than ever in the Caribbean zone—especially with the Quito
royalist victories in southern New Granada in May, which led to the capture of Antonio Nariño, and with the impending collapse of the second
Venezuelan republic.[19]

The social and economic impact of these military conflicts is not easy
to quantify. The tithe revenues of the Santa Marta diocese fell from 25,000
to 9,000 pesos between 1810 and 1815. The loss of the city in 1813 made
matters worse, and the royalist commanders, eager to find someone to
blame, complained that the city council was incompetent and the Ciénaga
Indians indifferent. The patriot campaign in that year led to the burning

of towns along the Magdalena line and the dispersal of their inhabitants. The royalist retreat took the military conflict into the region of Valledupar as the patriots pressed towards Riohacha in 1814. Mompós, a revolutionary center, suffered greatly during the advance of the Spanish expeditionary force into the interior in 1815. General Francisco Tomás Morales, who commanded the Magdalena Valley section, ordered the execution of large numbers of rebel supporters after his entry into the town. Colonel Francisco Warletta persecuted prominent patriot families, obliging them to leave the town and abandon their estates. The population of Mompós before the revolution had been eighteen thousand; by the early 1820s, it had sunk to ten thousand. Santa Marta's population fell from eight thousand to three thousand during the war years. Since the city was a royalist position, the victorious patriots after 1821 drafted many of its leading citizens into the army. Furthermore, the neglected condition of the region enabled Indian tribes from the hinterland to sweep into the city in January, 1823, under the command of a former Spanish governor, Pujol, operating possibly in conjunction with Morales, who retained control of Maracaibo, and occupy it for three weeks with disastrous consequences. Cartagena was besieged three times, including the 116-day siege by General Pablo Morillo's Spanish force, which lasted until the capitulation of the suffering city on December 6, 1815. Morillo entered to find a city of death and horror.[20]

Upon the collapse of the second Venezuelan republic, Bolívar fled to Cartagena and thence to Mompós (October, 1814). Inside the Caribbean city social and political tensions had escalated to the point that the notables, strengthened by the military defeats suffered by the popular regime, conspired to recover power therein. Internal conflict led to the withdrawal of Cartagena troops from the right bank of the Magdalena to facilitate this. On November 24, 1814, a constituent college, dominated by the notables, took control, a political change at the top that provoked intense popular opposition. Liévano Aguirre points to the contrast between "the college, controlled by the notables, and the enraged multitude that broke into the area of its meeting place and surrounded the building from the first day, hurling hostile cries at the Cartagena oligarchy." The notables had installed Dr. José María García de Toledo as governor of the Cartagena state, against whom the popular leader, Gabriel Gutiérrez de Piñeres, himself a member of the upper class, incited the *zambos* of the city. Accordingly, troops needed to fight the Santa Marta royalists had to be redeployed to hold back the popular classes inside the city itself to prevent a civil war between the white upper class and the colored majority. Bolívar, who at the end of 1814 had been caught in the conflict between the congress of the United Provinces based in the provincial town of Socorro and the city of Santa Fe, which he had taken on December 12, now found himself caught up in the Cartagena situation. The military commander in Cartagena, Castillo, fearing Bolivarian control of the city, refused to cooperate with Bolívar's efforts to renew the campaign in Venezuela. By March 1815, Bolívar was determined to march against the city to prepare for a general campaign against Santa Marta. These differences benefited only the royalists, who took Mompós on April 29, 1815. The loss of this rich and important position cut off the coast from the interior. In that month, the Spanish expeditionary force under Morillo arrived on the Venezuelan coast. Morillo reached Santa Marta on July 23 and established the blockade of Cartagena on August 22. Royalist seizure of Tierrabomba cut off the fortress of San Fernando de Bocachica and led to the fall of Cartagena. Montalvo took up residence there and reestablished the Consulado on October 23, 1816, and the city's white militia force; he decided not to restore the battalion of *pardos libres* because of revolutionary recruitment among the colored population.[21]

The insurrection in the Cauca Valley was supported by the patriots of Santa Fe, but not exclusively motivated by their example. It derived its origins from local conditions. In the province of Popayán, for instance, whites constituted less than a quarter of the population.[22] The fears of landed proprietors and slave owners resulted from the fact that the Negro and mulatto population, the chief source of labor, was double the white. Gaspar Mollien, the French traveler, commented that "one hardly encounters anyone but Negroes along the entire cordillera between Cartagena and Pasto." Social tensions in these regions, with their marked racial aspect, certainly did not originate in the Independence period, and similarly, they did not terminate with the creation of the Colombian state in 1821. The social conflicts of the Independence period probably had their roots in eighteenth-century economic conditions, such as the expansion of sugar refining in the Cauca Valley. The livestock haciendas depended largely upon slave labor: in fact, the value of the slave population represented one of the largest assets of these estates. The social and racial tensions of the Cauca Valley before 1810 were the context for the struggles thereafter, particularly since the traditional methods of political control through the Spanish colonial system had broken down at the governmental level. The regional elites, who derived their power from control of land and labor, found themselves caught between royalist counterrevolution and revolt from below. Continued tensions in the valley after independence inhibited economic development. Slavery entered a long, terminal crisis. Loss of slaves, as a result of the fighting during the Wars of Independence, could seriously affect the value of properties.[23]

Similar conflicts affected the gold-producing sector of the Popayán economy. The sisters of the Valencia family of Popayán owned the mine of Yurmangín in the southern coastal zone. The slave-labor force rebelled early in the insurrection, and these proprietors, arguing that the prosperity of the province depended upon slavery, warned that the state itself would suffer if the mines were not worked. The slaves, however, not only persisted in their rebellious conduct, but sought to spread the insurrection. In November, 1813, the sisters appealed to the president of Quito to order troops from Tumaco to put down the slave rebellions.[24]

The town councils of Cali, Buga, Cartago, Anserma, and Toro supported in 1811 the insurrection of Santa Fe against the colonial regime and formed the Confederation of the Cauca Valley. These were, however, risings of the creole elites that had broad geographical repercussions among that social group. Nevertheless, the risings in the Cauca region took from the start a decidedly popular character, though it is difficult to ascertain to what degree popular participation was stimulated by elite leadership or example. According to the royalist military commander in Cartago, José Antonio Yllera, who was involved in the concertina warfare across the region in 1813, "unrest in the valley grows in momentum with every day, and the local populace thinks only of renewing their rebellion" (which had begun in 1811). Such activity obliged him to evacuate the area. Yllera warned that three hundred insurgents with eight pieces of artillery in Anserma were ready to attack royalist positions in the Cauca Valley by way of the mountainous passes of the Quindío and Barragán. These actions culminated in the seizure of Cartago by the revolutionary forces of Santa Fe and Antioquia. Such reports as these suggest collusion between local popular leaders within the valley zone and the creole leaders of the revolutions in the main cities. Yllera pointed to the revolutionary role of the dominant group in the city of Cali. Other sources commented on this as well, particularly with respect to Cali's rivalry with Popayán. Royalist authorities complained that the city of Popayán had been the first to witness bloodshed on account of its opposition to the revolution. "The city had been attacked thereafter by its subordinate cities and suffered all the miseries of war brought upon it by the hostility of Cali, which had been continually rained down upon it." In 1811–1812, "the traitors of Cali" occupied Popayán. The president of the republican government in Popayán was Joaquín Caicedo, member of the celebrated family that originated in Cali. His brother, Manuel José Caicedo, was provisor of the diocese. Their uncle was Bishop José de Cuero y Caicedo of Quito, who in 1809 had written to the leading citizens of Popayán asking them to support the Quito revolution. All of them, and a number of other clerics in Popayán, were singled out by Miguel Tacón, the royalist commander, as determined enemies of Spanish rule.[25]

Revolutionary action in southern New Granada depended to a large extent on the survival of the second revolutionary regime in Quito. However, a further military intervention from royalist Peru extinguished that regime in November, 1812. The Consulado of Lima, bastion of the Peruvian counterrevolution, contributed the sum of 100,000 pesos toward this expeditionary army against Quito. Once the royalists had recovered the city, the president of the audiencia, Toribio Montes, began the counter-offensive into southern New Granada.[26] The royalists reoccupied the city of Popayán on June 30, 1813. However, the matter did not end there. The new governor, Colonel Juan Sámano, a confirmed soldier with no civil tact, made himself and his Peruvian troops immediately unpopular with the Popayán creole elite, who regarded themselves as a highly superior and cultured aristocracy. Indeed, the Popayán elite found itself caught between the dangerous revolutionaries of Santa Fe and the Cauca Valley on the one hand, and the rough, increasingly arbitrary, counterrevolution emanating from Quito and Lima on the other. They were squeezed and did not know which way to turn. Sámano pressured the *ayuntamiento* for thirty thousand pesos for the payment and maintenance of his force. Indeed, such requests for instant cash earned him the hostility of the pro-independence faction of the clergy. Sámano himself mistrusted everyone and suspected all of collusion with the enemy: the Dominican prior was "a well-known insurgent"; the Franciscan Joaquín Fernández de Soto was "one of the principal apostles of insurrection in the province, companion of the late Caicedo and fellow member of the revolutionary junta"; the diocesan provisor, Manuel Mariano Urrutia, was "by nature an intriguer and turbulent rebel." Urrutia took upon himself the task of openly confronting Sámano's authority in Popayán when the latter arrested the parish priest of El Trapiche, Belisario Gómez, whom the royalist governor considered to be "the most ardent protagonist of the revolutionary system since its beginnings." Such conflicts point to the evident tendency of the royalist military to blame the American clergy for the outbreak and sustenance of the insurrection in New Granada, and in Popayán the inviolability of suspected insurgent clerics could not be guaranteed.[27]

Once they had recovered Popayán, the royalists attempted to pacify the Cauca Valley, and they formed detachments for the "expulsion of the bandits" from the area of Las Cañas. Even so, they feared at any time the recrudescence in the still unruly Cauca zone of the "insurrectionary movement . . . of the slaves." Furthermore, the threat of a royalist révanche from the south had encouraged the president of Cundinamarca, Antonio Nariño, to bring his main force to the valley. Since Sámano felt too exposed to challenge him, he abandoned Popayán on January 15, 1814, and withdrew to Pasto, leaving the Casa de Moneda and printing press in revolutionary hands. With Nariño's advance, a considerable number of Sámano's locally recruited forces deserted to the rebels.[28] After the capture of Nariño in Pasto, the royalist Teniente Coronel Aparicio Vidaurrazaga reoccupied Popayán on December 29, 1814, and renewed Sámano's controversial measures. The city apparently presented a dismal picture of impoverishment and disarray.[29] Vidaurrazaga's pressures on ecclesiastical immunity led to the protest of Provisor Urrutia and the parish priest of El Tambo, Dr. Manuel María Rodríguez, a member of one of the senior

families, in the spring of 1815. Vidaurrazaga arrested Rodríguez, in what
was perceived to be a scandalous manner, as an alleged collaborator of
Nariño, whom he himself claimed to have opposed, and hauled him before a civil judge. Montes, when informed of such procedures, ordered
his release to prevent an open breach between the civil and the ecclesiastical powers.[30]

The pressures of war, especially in view of the frequent changes of
control in Popayán, fell heavily upon the city's elite, many of whom were
prominent royalists. Few, however, found themselves in any way sympathetic to the new militarism of the counterrevolutionary army. Many were
caught up in the escalating conflict and could not control their situations.
Dr. José María de Mosquera y Figueroa, *procurador supernumerario* of
the city council in 1810 and commander of the militia, contributed 42,000
pesos in loans, livestock, and food to the royalist cause. Nariño's forces
inflicted heavy damage to his estates. In March, 1811, when the royalist
commander, Governor Miguel Tacón, abandoned the city to the revolutionaries for the first time, he asked Mosquera to remain there to prevent
a sack. He stayed there to welcome the Quito royalist forces in December,
1814, and contributed large sums of his own and from the estate of his
business associate, Francisco José Arboleda, to the royalist cause, even
loaning Negroes from the La Tota mine.[31] The Rodríguez family, which
had so greatly incurred Vidaurrazaga's wrath, was strongly royalist. José
María Rodríguez Gil del Valle, captain of Popayán militia forces, had fled
to Pasto in 1811 to avoid being compromised by the revolutionary occupation of his city. He was the son of the regidor Francisco Antonio
Rodríguez. Dr. José María made donations to the royalist cause in 1814
and played a significant role in the counterrevolution by recruiting loyal
natives of the Patía region and contributing thereby to the capture of the
revolutionary junta president, Caicedo, in Pasto. Vidaurrazaga in 1815,
however, suspected him of insurgent sympathies because he was the brother
of the parish priest of El Tambo, who resisted royalist violations of ecclesiastical immunity.[32]

Between 1810 and 1815, the various social groups involved in the
conflicts of the epoch of the *patria boba* coexisted uneasily, each with
distinct perspectives concerning the nature and purpose of the struggle.
The breach between Antonio Nariño and the Congress of Cundinamarca
exposed the degree to which such tensions led to political disintegration
within the revolutionary camp. The continued royalist positions in Panama
and Santa Marta in the north and Pasto and Quito in the south made this
dissolution alarming. Once the royalist counteroffensive opened in the
south in 1812–1813, the patriots had to devise some sort of political response as well as a military one, and they appealed for popular support to
maintain revolutionary momentum. Nariño attempted to recruit support
among the dissident hacienda slave population of the Western Cordillera

for his campaign against the southern royalists in the autumn of 1813. Nariño's military efforts, however, were repeatedly obstructed by the resistance of the provincial authorities in the rival cities of Antioquia, Tunja, and Socorro to placing their forces under a unified command. Antioquia's military commander refused to compromise the sovereignty of the province. Nariño, imitating the royalist practice begun by Tacón and anticipating the policy to be pursued in Venezuela by Bolívar after his Carúpano decrees of 1816, offered slaves their liberty on condition that they serve in his army. Such actions provoked slave rebellions on estates and in mining zones. The situation in the west reached such a serious state of affairs that the patriot dictator of Antioquia, Juan del Corral, advocated a gradual abolition of slavery. Corral, a native of Mompós and closely related to the creole revolutionaries of that region, had become a hereditary city councilor in Antioquia in 1808 and deputy in the first congress of New Granada in July, 1810. When the Quito royalists recovered Popayán, the Antioquia legislature appointed Corral president-dictator on July 30, 1813, with the full support of the Antioquia Revolutionary Junta's president, José Miguel de Restrepo. Antioquia's response to the royalist advance down the Cauca Valley was the campaign to the south by the specially organized "Batallón Antioqueño" of some five hundred men formed at the cost of 337, 518 pesos. The aim of this force was eventually to cooperate with Nariño's offensive towards Popayán and Pasto. Corral urged the Congress of the Union on December 12, 1813, to adopt a policy of emancipation of slaves to prevent royalist attempts to stir up slaves against patriot landowners. Manumission, however, was legislated to apply only within the province of Antioquia because of the general hostility to such a radical policy in Chocó and Popayán, the other centers of slave-manned gold-prospecting operations. In Antioquia, in any case, manumission applied only to the descendants of those in slavery at the time of promulgation. The slave trade into and out of the province was banned, and a progressive emancipation of all slaves was projected. The royalist counterrevolution of 1816 terminated this policy altogether. The Congress of the Union, then located in Tunja, resisted even recognizing the liberty Nariño had offered to combatant slaves.[33]

Popular participation in the struggles of the 1810s took different forms in different places. In the Pasto region, the popular class consistently fought on the royalist side. From the first instant, Pasto had opposed the revolutionary movement, whether launched from Quito in 1809 or from Bogotá in 1810. In response to this royalist sentiment, Tacón in 1811 unilaterally reduced Indian tribute by one peso to four pesos. Nevertheless, when the Quito royalists recovered the city, Montes restored the full tribute in October, 1814, in spite of Indian protests.[34] Patriot campaigns against the city, as in 1812, were met by mass organization to resist them, regardless of the insurrection of the towns farther down the Cauca Valley. This opposition to the patriots did not in any way signify that either Pasto or its adjacent regions had a history of passivity before the official power. On the contrary, the south and the districts of Quito beyond Tulcán had a long tradition of resistance to the fiscal impositions of a central power. Indeed, the Quito populace itself had set the example by its long resistance during 1765 to tax innovations and to exclusive peninsular dominance. Otavalo and the other regions had rebelled in 1777, and Túquerres in 1800. The Indians of Pasto rose in 1780 to oppose the establishment of the aguardiente monopoly, and they were initially supported in their dissent by the *vecinos*. In Túquerres, in 1800, attempts to reinforce the tribute burden precipitated a protest movement among the Indians. A further revolt occurred in Barbacoas. Such rebellions were not revolutionary movements designed to overthrow the colonial system, but protests against specific impositions and evidence of local resentment at incursions by a remote central power tentatively attempting to poach new resources for itself. In these rebellions, many whites acted in collusion with the popular classes of society, in a common, multiethnic front against fiscal measures.[35]

The resistance of Pasto to the new republican order should be understood within this context of opposition to central-government innovations. The city, caught between the revolutionary forces of the Cauca Valley cities in the north and of Quito in the south, fell early in the insurrection and was sacked. *Pastuso* royalists, however, regrouped in the surrounding hills and waged a guerrilla struggle that finally enabled them to recover control. Nariño's surrender in Pasto in 1814 extinguished the revolutionary threat until the autumn of 1819. The loyalty of Pasto to the royal cause encouraged its leading citizens to petition the crown to elevate the region to a civil and military governorship and designate it as a diocese in its own right. They also requested the foundation of a college so that they could circumvent the expensive necessity of sending their sons to Popayán or Quito for their education. Furthermore, they requested exemption from recent taxes on official sealed paper and on strong drink. The city council requested, in addition, "that the Pasto Indians, our constant companions throughout the military struggle over the past five years in Quito and Santa Fe, should be exempted from tribute payments." The Council of the Indies replied on February 27, 1819, and conceded Pasto certain favors: a ten-year exemption from payment of *alcabalas*, exoneration of one-half the tribute payment for a period to be specified by the viceroy, and the right to found its own college-seminary.[36] Such concessions, though never implemented, may have helped to reinforce Pasto's royalist allegiance.

Regions such as Patía, which contained a number of escaped slave *palenques*, and Barbacoas continued to be royalist in sentiment throughout the 1810s. In Barbacoas, the local Negroes struggled against white proprietors. In effect, they were probably taking advantage of disturbed conditions throughout the south to improve their position and weaken the

links that bound them to the political center. They rose in 1811 against
the patriot regime in Santa Fe. In the summer of 1811, "the inhabitants of
El Tambo and Timbío formed common cause with those of Patía. They
abandoned their homes and . . . invaded the Valley of Patía, pillaging and
robbing the local proprietors and even killing several patriot stragglers
from the armies." Patriot authorities regarded such popular insurrections
as "banditry" when they were directed against themselves; royalist authorities adopted exactly the same response. In the colonial period, the
viceregal government, well aware of the warlike nature of the region's
inhabitants, had left them well alone. Republicans, however, feared for
the safety of their forces on campaign against Pasto, since the Barbacoas
zone lay on their flank. Indeed, militia forces from Barbacoas assisted
Miguel Tacón, royalist governor of Popayán, against the patriots in 1812.
A series of coastal and coastal-hinterland positions from Barbacoas,
Iscuandé, and Buenaventura to Tumaco and Esmeraldas long remained in
royalist hands, in spite of periodic patriot actions there.[37] Despite popular
royalism among the castes, royalist military commanders, most of them
property owners or local elites, had their fears of overzealous participation. Captain José María Rodríguez, of the leading Popayán family, played
an important role in the organization of, in his own words, "the counterrevolution," in the pueblos of El Tambo and Patía. He claimed to have
been obliged to hold back the *patianos* to prevent them from committing
any excesses since their "sole objective was robbery and murder, scarcely
compatible with the defense of the crown."[38]

Insurgent corsair activity along the coasts occasionally resulted in
damage or occupation, and trade between Panama and Guayaquil, especially in textiles, was cut off, though such actions never altered the course
of the war, especially because after 1816 the Spanish expeditionary force
controlled the main areas of settlement in New Granada. Buenos Aires'
corsairs attacked the royalist-held port of Guayaquil on February 8, 1816,
and entered the Puerto de Dagua with three large ships in the hope of
joining forces with the Cauca Valley insurgents and threatening Tumaco.
A second attempt took place between February 17 and 29, and a third in
June.[39] In January, 1819, however, Buenos Aires' corsairs reduced the port
of Tumaco to ruins and threatened Iscuandé, the River Barbacoas, and the
port of Esmeraldas until late in February, 1819, when their main thrusts
were directed to the Bay of Guayaquil and the coast of Panama.[40]

The Llanos of Casanare

The royalist insurgency from Pasto, Barbacoas, Patía, etc., derived its
strength from predominance in remote zones. The Spanish expeditionary
force's failure to pacify the Llanos of Casanare enabled a patriot insurgency to develop there within three years of the fall of Santa Fe to Morillo,

with appalling consequences for the restored royalist regime. Indeed, Viceroy Montalvo himself pointed out that the entire kingdom had been pacified militarily, *with the exception of the Llanos*. By September to October, 1817, the Bogotá regime had concluded that a military expedition into the Llanos was, as Sámano himself put it, "absolutely indispensible."[41]

The Llanos of Casanare became the base area of revolutionary resistance after the military triumph of the counterrevolution in 1815–1816, which led to a harsh political repression throughout the subsequent three years. The defeat of the armed forces of the regional revolutionary powers of Cartagena, Tunja, Santa Fe, and Cali left few possibilities of open resistance. Nevertheless, by 1817 conspiracies and limited insurgencies had become the patriot response to the counterrevolution. A guerrilla movement could take root because the royalist reconquest was not complete. The royalist armies, in spite of their punitive measures throughout the main settled areas, had made the classic error of failing to establish absolute military control over all territory. This failure enabled insurgent bands to recover the initiative on the eastern Llanos, a vast, open region linked geographically to the plains of Venezuela, which were still in a state of open rebellion. Of the territory of the viceroyalty of New Granada, only the Llanos of Casanare remained independent of royalist control in 1816. This remote region was distant from the political center, but nevertheless offered relatively easy access to pockets of insurgency in Boyacá by means of the valleys that led upward into the cordillera. There was, however, no attempt by the New Granada revolutionaries—in any case, a severely decimated group—to set up an insurgent provisional government in the Llanos. The whole region continued to be nominally under the authority of the Venezuelan revolutionary authorities based in Angostura.[42]

Jane Loy's recent studies have highlighted the peculiarities of the Colombian Llanos. Miguel Izard's examination of theVenezuelan Llanos has similarly set the region and its people within a historical context. According to Izard, "the Llanos were always a zone of refuge," though "between the second half of the seventeenth and the first half of the eighteenth centuries they became a zone of great unrest, principally because the white oligarchy of the coast sought to bring the inhabitants and wealth of the Llanos under its control." This unsuccessful attempt "in itself let loose a long-lasting confrontation that would endure until the early twentieth century." Banditry had become endemic, and contraband was notorious. Insurgency in the Llanos had already anticipated the Caracas revolution of April, 1810, by several years, and after Venezuelan independence, conflict throughout the Llanos continued just as before. In Casanare, local *caudillos* operated independently of the supreme Venezuelan *caudillo* of the Llanos, José Antonio Páez. Their activities obliged the New Granadan royalists to maintain troops at the points of upward access into the cordillera and to send patrols down to the nearby lowlands. Morillo's expeditionary force failed to establish a position of control in the Llanos and ultimately withdrew from them because of the threat the *llanero* cavalry posed to communications.[43] The *llaneros*, as is well known, contributed decisively to the Bolivarian victory of 1819 in Boyacá and Cundinamarca. After the Spanish reconquest in 1816, several patriot chieftains fled to Casanare for safety. In that zone, a number of rebel bands were already operating under *caudillos* such as Juan Galea, Ramón Nonato Pérez, and the most celebrated of all, the Dominican friar Colonel Fray Ignacio Mariño. By the end of 1817, these bands controlled the entire Casanare zone and were beginning to threaten the royalist position in the Eastern Cordillera.

Insurgency in the Eastern Cordillera

Continued revolt in the Llanos led to pockets of insurgency in the Eastern Cordillera. These, moreover, could be fueled by insurgent recruitment of disaffected troops from the royalist armies. Guerrilla bands were formed within the territory nominally under the control of the Spanish expeditionary force, particularly in regions with a tradition of opposition to the central power, such as Socorro, Tunja, Vélez, and the Cauca Valley. Leaders of these bands were generally persons of wealth and position within their particular provinces, and only rarely were they of lower-class origin. Colonel Juan José Neira, for instance, who operated in Guachetá, was one of the hacendados of the province of Tunja. He had led a band consisting of estate tenants and persons of station in an attempt to hold back Morillo's advance in 1816.[44]

Harsh royalist repression after the recovery of the viceregal capital rapidly alienated sympathies. Viceroy Montalvo himself put the number of persons executed at more than seven thousand, and these he described as "individuals from the principal families of the viceroyalty." Many had been put before the firing squad after being sentenced by the Consejo de Guerra Permanente (a permanent court martial) at Morillo's instructions. This policy of implacable terror had left the population restless and desperate. The cost of the armed forces operating in New Granada in 1816–1817, moreover, already exceeded three million pesos, a sum levied upon that territory itself. In other words, the financial demands of the counterrevolution and the Spanish army took as drastic a toll as the revolutionary turmoil of the preceding five years. Morillo continued to draw on the funds of the royal treasury, regardless of the viceroy's position as *supremo intendente general* of finance. Montalvo's complaints had been ignored. Well after the actual campaign of "pacification" had ceased, Morillo continued to assume that the expenses of the Spanish expeditionary army and those of the viceregal government were one and the same. Montalvo argued that, if Morillo had not interfered, but had instead left for Venezuela to rectify the situation there, the unrest throughout New Granada would have been considerably less. Morillo imposed large contributions on several provinces: thirty thousand pesos on El Chocó, twenty thousand pesos on Antioquia, and comparable sums on Socorro and Popayán, besides appropriations of horses and cash, and levies of fines in Santa Fe. These sums proceeded straight into the treasury of the expeditionary army.[45]

Furthermore, the reestablishment of the Audiencia of Santa Fe at the end of May, 1817, led to a series of major jurisdictional conflicts between the civilian magistrates and the military commanders that further discredited the counterrevolutionary regime and undermined its claim to legitimacy. The connection between conspiratorial activity in the capital and guerrilla activity in the countryside became apparent at this time. In the autumn of 1817, the Almeydas, landowners from the valley of Cúcuta, formed a band of some three hundred men (with only twenty firearms) in the mountains of Machetá. This band, like others formed more or less contemporaneously, cooperated with the insurgents of the Llanos. According to Osvaldo Díaz, "The ramifications of this guerrilla activity were so broad that scarcely a town of the northern Sabana and the slopes of the cordillera could not boast of some participation." These local insurgencies, moreover, incorporated not only former revolutionary soldiers and royalist defectors, but also many peasants and several priests sympathetic to the patriot cause.[46] This situation may not have been drastic in itself, but put together with the royalist failure to establish control of the Llanos, it became potentially disastrous.

Sámano, at that time *mariscal de campo* and commander of the 3rd Division of the expeditionary army, recognized the danger immediately. On September 12, 1817, Sámano began to press the Santa Fe government for instant subsidies to finance an expedition into the Llanos, a campaign he regarded as "absolutely indispensable." The cash he looked to, however, had been sent already to Maracaibo at Morillo's instructions to counter Bolívar's descent on the Venezuelan coast. Sámano requested fifty thousand pesos, which the Junta Superior de Hacienda Extraordinaria voted on October 19 to extend him as an urgent necessity. In mid-November, Sámano reported the presence of insurgents from the Llanos in Guateque and Machetá and identified the Valle de Tenza in the cordillera slopes as a major zone of recruitment. Rebel bands took Chocontá, and the Almeydas operated from Machetá, a town only two or three days' journey from Santa Fe. These bands could apparently rely on the assistance of the villages of the whole region between Honda and Socorro. These risings marked in part a patriot response to the executions planned in Santa Fe for November 14. The public execution of conspirators aroused not only public revulsion in the capital, but also provoked a further and deeper round of conflicts between military actions and civilian jurisdiction. The viceroy and *oidores*, sitting together as the Real Acuerdo, protested to Sámano, military governor of the city, against the flagrant violation of normal legal procedure, since most of the accused were themselves civilians. Sámano, without consulting the Sala del Crimen of the audiencia, had reestablished Morillo's Consejo de Guerra Permanente to try those suspected of a conspiracy to revive the revolutionary movement in the city. Eight men and one woman were executed at 11:00 A.M. outside the audiencia offices in the Plaza Mayor, without either prior consultation with or even notification of the civil magistrates.[47]

In the countryside, the Spanish response to the local insurgencies was a cruel repression. Sámano described them as *bandolerismo*, but organized a type of counterinsurgency to combat them. This took the form principally of a series of *destacamentos volantes* dispatched to the affected zones. In their repression of the insurgency, the royalist commanders executed not only leaders but also peasant and Indian participants, and reduced villagers' crops to ashes. This was particularly the case in the Valle de Tenza, center of the greatest activity until December, 1817. The towns of Machetá, Tibiritá, Nemocón, and Chocontá lay at the center of the revolt and had been patriot since the first days of the independence movement. Sámano put Lieutenant Colonel Carlos Tolrá, already known for his actions in the counterrevolution in the Popayán region, in command of the mobile detachments, which were increased to six hundred men, predominantly experienced infantrymen riding as cavalrymen and with firearms. The Dragones de Granada, moreover, were made up of the fervently royalist inhabitants of Pasto and Patía. Tolrá's proclamation in Chocontá on November 23 established the death penalty for any local authorities guilty of collaboration with insurgency and for the collective punishment of any town guilty of the same.[48] Sámano was promoted to the office of viceroy.

The ferocity of the royalist military response seems to have shocked the patriot guerrillas, who, nevertheless, still retained the option of tactical withdrawal to the Llanos and later reactivation. Even so, rumors of discontent continued to arise from the zones of insurgent activity in 1817. In the autumn of 1818, for instance, the audiencia investigated a supposed conspiracy in the villages of the Guateque area in the Valle de Tenza, with apparently a woman at the center of it. The royalist campaign against the insurgent bands in the northern zones of Tunja province, however, placed major emphasis thereafter upon the remaining zone of rebel activity, the Llanos. In August, 1818, Bolívar sent a volunteer officer from the Cúcuta Valley, Francisco de Paula Santander, into the Llanos with the specific task of coordinating the rebel bands. The objective was to be a campaign by the main armed force, led by Bolívar himself, from the Llanos into the cordillera of Boyacá, with the aim of establishing military and political control over the entire Sabana of Cundinamarca. This strategy culminated in Bolívar's victory at the Puente de Boyacá in August, 1819, and the royalists' loss of the viceregal capital.[49]

The Rebellion of the Cauca Valley

The impact of Boyacá was profound in the interior. Salvador Jiménez de Enciso y Cobos Padilla, the royalist bishop of Popayán, lamented that "a rising has taken place in the Cauca Valley, led neither by members of the clergy nor by any of the decent classes of society, but by deserters and other evil-doers who had sought refuge in the mountains since the last revolution." This rising consisted of "armed groups of bandits" who preyed "upon the loyal and peaceful citizens." In the judgment of Popayán's royalist commander, Sebastián de la Calzada, "several rebels have dared to regroup and form armed bands with the sole object of robbery, as they had shown in the case of Llano Grande, where they sacked private properties and burned down the Royal Tobacco Office. . . . I am convinced that obscure figures lead these bands, since persons of station (*los nobles*) have taken no part in these criminal actions here in the Cauca Valley." Calzada was in fact speaking of a general insurrection throughout the valley, directed against the royalist position there. The governor of Popayán, Pedro Domínguez, perished, and the royalists were forced to abandon the city yet again and withdraw to Pasto.[50]

The intensity of the Cauca risings in the summer and autumn of 1819 may not have represented simply popular responses to the news of Boyacá, but more long-term factors such as hatred of the excesses of the royalist forces there since the reconquest. The governor of Popayán had already complained to Viceroy Montalvo in October, 1817, of what he described as "the terrorism and confusion brought about by Ruperto Delgado, commander of the First Numancia Battalion, and several of his subaltern commanders in their duties with their garrison forces in the towns of the Cauca Valley." Montalvo, himself critical of the arbitrary conduct of Morillo and Sámano, now heard of the "most serious excesses" committed by the army in the king's name, as well as flagrant usurpation of civil jurisdiction by the military and flouting of the rights of municipal councils in the towns under their charge. Army recruitment measures that excepted neither farmers nor married men had driven many families to seek refuge in the hills, where they encountered the remnants of the rebel bands and often joined their ranks. The governor of Popayán had warned in 1817 of the political consequences of alienating the local population through such disdainful treatment. This alienation was not limited to the lower classes. On the contrary, Delgado's arrest of town councilors in Cartago, Cali, Anserma, and Buga had outraged persons of local reputation. In Buga he had brushed aside civilian authority altogether. The military commanders, moreover, had put the burden of paying the army on the region itself. Troops consumed what livestock was left in the private estates after seven years of warfare; local artisans had been forced to work on military equipment with only an insignificant remuneration; labor gangs had been recruited and put to work on road construction. The results had been simmering discontent.[51]

It has often been wrongly concluded that Bolívar's victory at Boyacá led to rapid extinction of royalist rule in New Granada. Although the Cauca Valley remained a principal area of revolutionary support throughout the 1810s, the south's firm resistance—as much to Bolívar in 1819–1822 as to Nariño in 1810–1814—continued undiminished. The strong royalist position in Pasto enabled Calzada to recover the city of Popayán on January 24, 1820, a serious threat to the political solution Bolivarian forces thought they had accomplished with the fall of Santa Fe. This royalist counter-offensive in the south prepared the way for a campaign of reconquest along the Cauca Valley by March, 1820. Calzada, aware of the support Santander had given to the Cauca patriots, struck into rebel-held territory with three thousand troops to extinguish a "mass insurrection, which had taken the lives not only of Europeans but also of loyal and distinguished Americans in the valley." This campaign threatened to deprive the main patriot army of the possibility of extending the revolution southward into Quito and thence to the royalist stronghold of Peru.[52]

As had been the case with the Llanos of Casanare in 1816–1817, the royalist pacification in 1820 was incomplete, owing to lack of manpower and resources, insurgent strength in the east, and above all, the nature of the terrain. Calzada's campaign left the Chocó region unsubdued. The insurgency disintegrated in the Cauca Valley only to fester and rekindle in El Chocó, particularly in the Vega de Supía with its Negro slave population. The continued insurrection in El Chocó meant not only that communications with one of the principal gold-producing zones remained beyond the reach of royal power, but also that other provinces were able to open new theatres of insurgency. Accordingly, just as the royalists believed they had pacified the Cauca Valley, the province of Antioquia renewed the revolutionary struggle.[53]

In contrast, the Pasto royalists contributed a royalist battalion for the war in Popayán in 1819 and 1820. Calzada had a low opinion of its composition: "they are all peasants, with no military training and no discipline: even worse than their unruliness is the fact that they have only a few rifles that are any use." The *pastusos* responded to the patriot victories of 1819 with a regional solidarity that cut across social groups. When they proposed to form a second battalion, hacienda owners offered their livestock for its sustenance, and an appeal was made for assistance from the twenty-six Indian towns of the city hinterland. This confrontational zeal extended into the year 1821, when Basilio García informed Mariscal de Campo Mechor Aymerich, president of Quito, that "enthusiasm for the royalist cause is general, not only in Pasto and its district, but throughout the province . . . the entire Valley of Patía, furthermore, is ready *en masse* for the enemy, should he appear, and the province of Almaguer is of the same mind." Nevertheless, enthusiasm had to be paid for, and soon enough the fiscal burden of warfare fell upon the *pastusos*. Ramón Zambrano levied a special 1 percent contribution in January, 1822, for the purpose of sustaining local troops. This tax did not exempt even the convents, where it was met with wounded indignation. The bishop of Popayán, in exile once more, commented on the warlike capacities and skilled marksmanship of the *pastusos*, particularly when called to defend their native soil, but warned of their extreme reluctance to fight for anything beyond it. Within their own territory, they were natural guerrilla warriors.[54]

It has been argued that Pasto's continued resistance to the new Colombian republic established in Bogotá placed the region effectively beyond the reach of central authority for much of the early 1820s.[55] Bolívar and his close associate, Antonio José de Sucre, were extremely preoccupied with what they saw as the deteriorating situation in the south. Sucre's Quito campaign, which culminated in his victory on the slopes of Pichincha on May 24, 1822, was designed to resolve the problem definitively; however, it did not. Initially, Bolívar's capitulation provisions for Pasto on June 8 permitted all royalist employees to remain in office in the city, as a means of preserving harmony, until the complete establishment of the new constitutional system of the Republic of Colombia. Accordingly, Ramón Zambrano, colonel of the royalist militia, became republican governor, without, however, a serious commitment to the patriot cause. When the financially hard-pressed Bogotá government sought to levy a tax on Pasto as part of its contribution to a forced assessment, the city rose in rebellion on October 28 with general popular support. Bolívar described Pasto as "bitterly hostile to the republic."[56] The new republican authorities in the Quito zone were alarmed at the prospect of isolation from Santa Fe in the face of a supposed *pastuso* and *patiano* advance on Tulcán and appealed for aid from the city of Quito to combat it. After yet another tenacious resistance, Pasto fell at the end of December.[57]

The new republican state found it as difficult as the former viceregency had to control the extent of national territory. The towns of the Cauca Valley early in 1821 had maintained their revolutionary tradition, but this time in opposition to the republican state in Bogotá. The Cauca rebellion had seriously compromised the precarious patriot position in the south. Bolívar had threatened a punitive example. In the remote coastal zones of the south, republican commanders in 1823 reported local resistance from Esmeraldas to Tumaco and denounced it as the work of "facciosos" and "bárbaros, enemigos acérrimos de Colombia y de la tranquilidad pública."

In Esmeraldas, local resistance seemed to have formed around the Casierras, a group of mountain chieftains. The local republican commander claimed to have Bolívar's authorization to make "an imposing example" of these dissidents by shooting them in whatever number he saw fit, since "the ferocity of their resistance defied any claim to leniency."[58]

Pasto itself remained for decades in sporadic opposition to the central power. The former royalist guerrilla commander, Colonel José María Obando, who had defected to Bolívar in Popayán on February 7, 1822, led the Pasto rebellion of 1839–1841 in opposition to the abolition of the convents. Similarly, the insurrection of May, 1851, formed part of a Catholic reaction to liberal anticlerical measures between 1849 and 1854.[59]

Conclusions

New Granada's long history of governmental weakness in outlying areas allowed insurgency movements to form and later flourish at sporadic intervals during the 1810s and 1820s. Regions such as the Caribbean hinterland, the Llanos of Casanare, Chocó, and the remote zone of the Pacific south were cases in point. It did not matter whether insurrectionary action was directed against royalist or republican regimes; it took similar forms and was responded to in similar ways. The Pasto zone in the far south stood in constant opposition to the revolutionary system throughout the 1810s and early 1820s, and this fierce resistance delayed the establishment of a Bolivarian state in the New Granada region. When popular action supported the royalist cause, as in the case of risings of the Negroes of the southwestern regions of Patía and Barbacoas, royalist commanders feared the social implications of lower-class revolt as much as their republican counterparts. Whenever they could, both royalist and republican authorities sought to bring popular militancy under control and channel it into a subordinate role within their own movements.

This common fear of lower-class autonomous action existed irrespective of the divisions within the elites concerning ideology and political forms. Such fears in themselves demonstrated the existence of spontaneous popular participation in the conflicts at the regional and local levels during the Wars of Independence. Participants and observers of opposing political views similarly commented on the repeated evidence of popular rebellions. Lower-class social groups probably saw in escalating violence and the disintegration of central authority the means to press for the improvement of their condition. In such a way, long-standing local tensions, such as those in the Cauca Valley, became to an extent subsumed within the broader civil struggles. In themselves, however, these local rebellions could not have generated a national movement. Without the superstructure of elite resistance to metropolitan rule, combined with the temporary collapse of peninsular Spain during 1808–1814, it is likely that they would simply have resembled the local rebellions of the colonial era. Since political independence, won between 1819 and 1822, did not involve any necessary commitment to the resolution of lower-class social grievances, the sources of tension that had generated spontaneous popular participation during the 1810s and early 1820s probably continued to simmer below the surface thereafter.

The survival of insurgent bands in the Llanos of Casanare kept the spirit of resistance alive, in spite of the apparently complete military victory of the Spanish expeditionary army in 1816. Savage Spanish reprisals combined with the arbitrary conduct of the military commanders, many of them detested even within the royalist camp, undermined the prestige of the Bourbon cause and threw into doubt the legitimacy of Spanish rule after what had seemed to be a successful campaign of reconquest.

Rivalry between Cali and Popayán led to outright conflict during the Wars of Independence. The Cauca Valley, like the Caribbean coastal zone, was an area of high concentration of Negroid population, where the livestock estates and sugar production were sustained by slave labor. The collapse of central authority after 1810 provided the opportunity for popular rebellion against the slave owners, who traditionally controlled town councils in the region and derived their social position from mastery of land and labor. Attention to the struggles within the elites, between those who wanted to preserve the empire and those who wanted to separate from it, or between the centralists and the regionalists, has tended to obfuscate the intense social conflicts that characterized these areas. In the Pasto zone, social relations were not torn apart by comparable ethnic tensions, mainly, of course, because the economic system there was entirely different from that prevalent in the Cauca Valley. A common opposition emerged to the intervention of outside power, which in this case was perceived to be the revolutionary regime of Santa Fe.

Notes

1. Anthony McFarlane, "Riot and Rebellion in Colonial Spanish America," *Latin American Research Review*, XVII (1982), 212–21; McFarlane, "Civil Disorders and Popular Protests"; Leslie B. Rout, Jr., *The African Experience in Spanish America, 1502 to the Present Day* (Cambridge, 1976), 95, 134, 236–49; Michael Taussig, "The Evolution of Rural Wage Labour in the Cauca Valley of Colombia, 1700–1970," in K. Duncan and I. Rutledge (eds.), *Land and Labour in Latin America* (Cambridge, 1977), 397–434, 408; Phelan, *The People and the King.*

2. See Scarlett O'Phelan Godoy, "Elementos étnicos y de poder en el movimiento tupacamarista, 1780–81," *Nova Americana*, V (1982), 79–101.

3. See J. R. Fisher, "Royalism, Regionalism and Rebellion in Colonial Peru, 1808–1815," *Hispanic American Historical Review,* LIX (1979), 232–57; and Fisher, "La rebelión de Túpac Amaru."

4. Germán Carrera Damas, *Boves: Aspectos socioeconómicos de la guerra de independencia* (Caracas, 1972); Miguel Izard, *El miedo a la revolución: La lucha por la libertad en Venezuela (1777–1830)* (Madrid, 1979).

5. Phelan, *The People and the King,* 18–23; Taussig, "Rural Wage Labour," 407–408.

6. Orlando Fals Borda, *Mompox y Loba: Historia doble de la costa* (Bogotá, 1980), I, 85A, 86A, 87A, 124B.

7. Anthony McFarlane, "El comercio exterior del Virreinato de la Nueva Granada: Conflictos en la política económica de los Borbones, 1783–1789," *Anuario Colombiano de Historia Social y de la Cultura,* VI–VII, (1971–72), 78–81. McFarlane argues that although precious-metal exports reached a value of over two million pesos in 1787, commercial reform had a greater overall impact on agricultural produce than on mining.

8. Fals Borda, *Mompox y Loba,* I, 88B, 102A, 118A–20A; McFarlane, "Comerciantes y monopolio en la Nueva Granada," 64, 67–69.

9. Fals Borda, *Mompox y Loba,* I, 118A, 119A, 122A, 128A, 135A, 136A. Mompós had a reputation for unruliness as the center of construction for the *champanes* that carried trade and passengers from the coast to the interior. Most of the *bogas* who manned these craft, generally Negroes and *zambos*, lived in the town. See Charles Stuart Cochrane, *Journal of a Residence and Travels in Colombia* (London, 1825), I, 104–105. John P. Hamilton, *Travels Through the Interior Provinces of Colombia* (London, 1827), I, 74–75, considered the *bogas* "as drunken and dissipated a set of fellows as any under the sun."

10. Restrepo, *Minas de Colombia,* 76, 185. Popayán, Barbacoas, Iscuandé, and El Raposo produced 670,000 pesos in gold.

11. Juan Sámano (governor of Popayán) to Toribio Montes, Popayán, November 6, 1813, ANHE, PQ, Vol. 483 (1813), doc. 27, fol. 27. The propensity of Guayaquil merchants (in a royalist-held city) for the contraband trade with the insurgents (in control of Quito until November, 1812) occasioned comment. Governor Juan Vasco y Pascual to Montes, Guayaquil, July 16, 1812, ANHE, PQ, Vol. 471 (1812), III, doc. 94, fols. 114–15v.

12. "Expediente sobre la apertura de la montaña de Barbacoas para el libre tránsito de los traficantes," ANHE, PQ, Vol. 564 (1818). VI, exp. 12,308, fols. 101–16; Procurador General Pedro Díaz del Castillo to Juan Ramírez (president of Quito), Barbacoas, February 18, 1818, *ibid.*, fols. 103–107. The object was to open trade to Panama, Cartagena, Popayán, Pasto, and Quito as an alternative to Guayaquil, where the Río Guayas flooded for six months of the year, and to the Magdalena route.

13. Restrepo, *Minas de Colombia,* 65–67, 70–73, 75, 79, 184; Germán Colmenares, *Historia económica y social de Colombia, 1537–1719* (Cali, 1973), 267, 285–87, 298–303.

14. Kuethe, *Military Reform and Society,* 210–11, 217–18.

15. Jane M. Loy, "Forgotten Comuneros: The 1781 Revolt in the Llanos of Casanare," *HAHR,* LXI (1981), 235–57. These features of the history of the Llanos recurred at several intervals, most notably during the *Violencia,* when a "guerrilla campesina" formed a major aspect of the provincial response to the events of April 9, 1948, in Bogotá. The Llanos became one of the first nuclei of resistance: by the end of 1952, at least twenty thousand combatants had fought there and in the following year passed on to the offensive. See Gonzalo Sánchez and Donny Meertens, *Bandoleros, gamonales y campesinos: El caso de la violencia en Colombia* (Bogotá, 1983), 32–33, 38–40.

16. Fals Borda, *Mompox y Loba,* I, 106A–14B.

17. María Dolores González Luna, "La política de población y pacificación indígena en las poblaciones de Santa Marta y Cartagena (Nuevo Reino de Granada), 1750–1800," *Boletín americanista*, XX (1978), 87–118; Cochrane, *Journal*, I, 57–59; Tovar, "Guerras de opinión," 196.

18. Indalecio Liévano Aguirre, *Los grandes conflictos sociales y económicos de nuestra historia* (7th ed.; Bogotá, 1978), II, 864–65, 879–86, 902–903; Eduardo Lemaitre, *Breve historia de Cartagena* (Cartagena, 1958), 91–138; T. Blossom, *Nariño: Hero of Colombian Independence* (Arizona, 1967), 92; Tovar, "Guerras de opinión," 192–93; Hamilton, *Travels,* I, 62.

19. R. Blanco-Fombona (ed.), *Ultimos virreyes de Nueva Granada: Relación de mando del Virrey Francisco Montalvo y noticias del Virrey Sámano sobre la pérdida del reino (1813–1819)* (Madrid, 1918), 10–20, 30–35, 45–48.

20. Tovar, "Guerras de opinión," 197; Juan Jiménez (commander in La Ciénaga) to Viceroy Francisco de Montalvo, Portobelo, June 26, 1813, Governor Manuel Zegueira to Montalvo, Riohacha, September 5, 1814. Ayuntamiento to Montalvo, Santa Marta, January 8, 1814, Gonzalo Aramendi to Montalvo, Riohacha, January 17, 1814, Aramendi to Montalvo, no. 92, Valledupar, June 22, 1814, all in AHNC, Anexo, Guerra y Marina, tomo 117, fols, 919–22v, tomo 120, fols, 209–209v, 283–83v, 605–11; Cochrane, *Journal,* I, 104–105; Hamilton, *Travels,* I, 74–75; Fals Borda, *Mompox y Loba,* I, 139A, 141A; Cochrane, *Journal,* I, 57–59; Hamilton, *Travels,* 15, 20–21; Pablo Morillo, *Mémoires du General Morillo, Comte de Carthagéne, Marquis de la Puerta: Rélatifs aux principaux événements de ses campagnes en Amérique de 1815 à 1821* (Paris, 1826), 60–61.

21. Blanco-Fombona, *Ultimos virreyes,* 57, 63; Liévano Aguirre, *Los grandes conflictos,* II, 879–86, 902–903; Blanco-Fombona, *Ultimos virreyes,* 64, 70–73, 77–89, 93, 100, 122.

22. Hermes Tovar Pinzón, "El estado colonial frente al poder local y regional," *Nova americana,* V (1983), 42–43. Tovar includes Pasto in this southern zone and gives the following proportions: free Negroes and mulattoes, 32,766; Indians, 27,764; whites, 21,066; Negroes, 18,761; total, 100,356 (12.5 percent of the population of the viceroyalty).

23. Gaspar Théodore Mollien, *Viaje por la República de Colombia en 1823* (Bogotá, 1944), 275; Germán Colmenares. *Historia económica y social de Colombia, II Popayán: Una sociedad esclavista, 1680–1800* (Bogotá, 1979), 269–71; Keith Christie, "Antioqueño Colonization in Western Colombia: A Reappraisal," *HAHR,* LVIII (1978), 260–83; José Escorcía, "Haciendas y estructura agraria en al Valle del Cauca, 1810–50," *ACHSC,* X (1982), 119–38.

24. Ignacia Valencia to Montes, Popayán, November 6, 1813, ANHE, PQ, Vol. 483 (1813), XI, doc. 23, fols, 23–23v.

25. José Antonio Yllera to Sámano, Buga, December 8, 1813. Yllera to José Esteban de Dorronsoro (teniente general del asiento), Cartago, December 2, 1813. Yllera to Sámano, Tulúa, December 8, 1813, all in ANHE, PQ, Vol. 484 (1813), XII, no. 55. Fol. 60, no. 7, fols. 7–7v, no. 69, fols. 75–76; J. M. Rodríguez to Montes, Quito, October 2, 1815. ANHE, PQ, Vol. 512 (1815), III, exp. 11,364, fols. 10–16; ANHE, PQ, Vol. 510, exp. 11,332, fol. 181v; Miguel Tacón to Molina (president of Quito), Tumaco, November 23, 1811, ANHE, PQ, Vol. 468 (1811), IV, fols. 264–65v.

26. Luis de Ariza and Gabriel Fernández de Urbina to Montes, Guayaquil, June 4, 1812, ANHE, PQ, Vol. 471 (1812), II, doc. 81, fols. 99–99v.

27. Sámano to cabildo, Popayán, November 4, 1813, Sámano to Montes, Popayán, November 9, 1813, Fray Pedro de Paredes to an anonymous cleric, Popayán, October 21, 1813. Sámano to Montes, Popayán, November 11, 1813,

all in ANHE, PQ, Vol 483 (1813), doc. 24, fols. 24–24v, doc. 44, fols. 45–47v, doc. 47, no. 3, fols. 50–50v, doc. 65, fols. 74–75. B. R. Hamnett, "The Counter-revolution of Morillo and the Insurgent Clerics of New Granada, 1815–1820," *Americas*, XXXII (1976), 597–617, studied this problem in the Bogotá context, with particular reference to Fernando Caicedo y Flores, to whom Pope Leo XII granted canonical recognition as Archbishop of Santa Fe in May 1827.

28. Ildefonso Gil de la Tejada to Montes, Buga, November 22, 1813, Sámano to Montes, Popayán, November 23, 1813, both in ANHE, PQ, Vol. 483 (1813), no. 131, fols. 152–52v, no. 134, fols. 156–57; Montes to Benito Pérez, Quito, April 7, 1814, in Sergio Elías Ortiz (ed.), *Colección de documentos para la historia de Colombia (época de la Independencia)* (Bogotá, 1964), primera serie, 52–53. Montes censured Sámano for this retreat.

29. Montalvo to Montes, Santa Marta, May 10, 1815, ANHE, PQ, Vol. 514 (1814), V, exp. 11,432; J. A. Balcázar Sánchez to Montes, Popayán, January 5, 1815, ANHE, PQ, Vol. 515 (1815), VI, no. 41, fols. 46–46v.

30. Rodríguez to Montes, Tambo, June 5, 1815, Rodríguez to Montes, Popayán, June 21, 1815, Provisor Manuel Mariano Urrutia, Quito, December 1, 1815, all in ANHE, PQ, Vol. 513 (1815), no. 4, exp. 11,410, fols. 136–231v. After removal from Popayán, Vidaurrazaga became subdelegate of Santa and Chancay.

31. Documentos que acreditan las erogaciones, suplementos y donativos que han hecho Dr. J. M. de Mosquera . . . , ANHE, PQ, Vol. 556 (1817), II, exp. 12,088, fols. 160–71v, cuaderno I. See also Oidor Joaquín de Mosquera y Figueroa to the king, Madrid, January 31, 1818, in Ortiz (ed.). *Colección de documentos*, primera serie, 100–107.

32. Rodríguez to Montes, Quito, October 2, 1815, ANHE, PQ, Vol. 512 (1815), III, exp. 11,364, fols. 10–16. Montes upheld Rodríguez's position. Upon the news of the Spanish expeditionary force's advance toward Neiva, Sámano moved north from Pasto in company with Ramón Zambrano, commander of the Pasto Militia Battalion, and reoccupied Popayán on June 30, 1816, after the rebels had failed to destroy the Casa de Moneda. Fernando Zambrano to Montes, Pasto, June 13, 1816, ANHE, PQ, Vol. 532 (1816), IV, no. 80, fols. 93–93v; Manuel de Pombo to Sámano, Popayán, July 2, 1816, ANHE, PQ, Vol. 533 (1816), VII, no. 26, fols. 29–30v.

33. Roberto M. Tisnes Jiménez, *Don Juan del Corral: Libertador de los esclavos* (Cali, 1980), 18, 32, 34, 47, 51, 59, 101–102, 116–17, 157, 165–67, 183, 262–73, 276. Corral died on April 7, 1814 (Liévano Aguirre, *Los grandes conflictos*, II, 805–10).

34. Governor Tomás Miguel Santa Cruz to Montes, Pasto, February 27, 1815, ANHE, PQ, Vol. 516 (1815), VI, no. 142, fol. 163.

35. Javier Lavina, "La sublevación de Túquerres en 1800: una revuelta antifiscal." *Boletín americanista*, XX (1978), 191–92, 195–96. According to this source, the Túquerres rebellion began on May 18 and lasted two days. See especially Moreno Yañez, *Sublevaciones indigenas*, 147–70, and (for the Otavalo rebellion of 1777) 359–79.

36. "Representación del Cabildo de Pasto ante Su Majestad sobre el mérito de la ciudad en las pasadas convulsiones," Sala Capitular del Ayuntamiento Constitucional de Pasto, June 13, 1814, in Ortiz (ed.), *Colección de documentos*, primera serie, 54–64: Consejo de Indias en sala segunda, Madrid, February 27, 1819, *ibid.*, 110–14.

37. J. M. Cabral to Dr. Miguel de Pombo, Popayán, August 4, 1811, in Sergio Elías Ortiz (ed.), *Colección de documentos para la historia de Colombia (época de la Independencia)* (Bogotá, 1966), tercera serie, 206–207; Nicolas de Quiñones

y Cienfuegos (comandante de milicias disciplinadas de la ciudad de Barbacoas) to Gabriel de Torres (subinspector general del reino), Barbacoas, April 6, 1817, in Ortiz (ed.), *Colección de documentos*, primera serie, 93–97.

38. Rodríquez to Montes, Quito, October 2, 1815, ANHE, PQ, Vol. 512 (1815), III. Exp. 11,364, fols, 10–16.

39. José de Maruri (jefe político y militar) to Montes, Tumaco, May 22, 1816, ANHE, PQ,Vol. 531 (1816), V, no. 139, fols, 164–64v; Vasco to Montes, Guayaquil, February 17, 1816, Vasco to Montes, Guayaquil, February 19, 1816, ANHE, PQ, Vol. 528 (1816), II, no. 115, fols. 140–40v, no. 192, fol. 222; Antonio Mingues to Montes, Barbacoas, June 6, 1816, ANHE, PQ, Vol. 532 (1816), VI, doc. 44, fols, 51–52. Iscuandé and Micay were defended by fifty militiamen.

40. *Vecinos* to Ramírez, Barbacoas, January 6, 1819, Andrés de Castro to Ramírez, Esmeraldas, February 24–25 and March 25, 1819, all in ANHE, PQ, Vol. 567 (1819), I, no. 11, fols, 11–11v, nos. 82, 86, 116, fols, 89, 93, 131.

41. Montalvo to Sámano, Cartagena, January 30, 1818, in Blanco-Fombona, *Ultimos virreyes*, 217; Sámano to Oidor Decano Juan Jurado, Santa Fe, September 12, 1817, AHNC, Anexo, Historia, tomo 23, fol. 119.

42. David Bushnell, *The Santander Regime in Gran Colombia* (Delaware, 1954), 10.

43. Miguel Izard, "Ni Cuartreros ni Montoneros, Llaneros," *Boletin americanista*, XXIII (1981), 88, 109, 113–18; Osvaldo Díaz Díaz, *Los Almeydas: Episodios de la resistencia patriótica contra el ejército pacificador de Tierra Firme* (Bogotá, 1962), 187–94; Izard, "Ni Cuartreros," 121–24.

44. Díaz Díaz, *Los Almeydas*, 41–42, 138–41.

45. Blanco-Fombona, *Ultimos virreyes*, 158, 141, 147–48, 152–53, 156.

46. Díaz Díaz, *Los Almeydas*, 57–59, 72–74, 81–82, 88–90, 95, 105, 116, 123–25.

47. Junta Superior, Santa Fe, October 19, 1817, Sámano to Jurado, Santa Fe, September 12, 1817, Sámano to Teniente Coronel Vicente Sánchez de Lima, Santa Fe, October 24, 1817, all in AHNC, Anexo, Historia, tomo 23, fols, 117–19, 124; Díaz Díaz, *Los Almeydas,* 95–105; Real Acuerdo de Justicia, Santa Fe, November 14, 1817, AHNC, Anexo, Historia, tomo 23, fols, 58–58v.

48. Díaz Díaz, *Los Almeydas*, 116, 123–25, 128–29, 133–34, 145, 152–53, 156, 170–71. Tolrá executed possibly some one hundred "infelices indios y campesinos," described by him as "insurgentes."

49. Audiencia of Santa Fe to Sámano, Santa Fe, October 1, 1818, AHNC, Anexo, Historia, tomo 24, fols. 309–10; Díaz Díaz, *Los Almeydas*, 133–34, 165–81.

50. Bishop to Sámano, Popayán, September 8, 1819, in Ortiz (ed.). *Colección de documentos*, primera serie, 132–33; Sebastián de la Calzada to Sámano, Popayán, September 8, 1819, Calzada to Melchor Aymerich (president of Quito), Mercaderes, October 11, 1819, Aymerich to Calzada, Quito, October 23 and October 30, 1819, all in Oritz (ed.), *Colección de documentos*, primera serie, 134–35, 143–44, 148–49, 153–55.

51. Governor José Solís to Montalvo, Popayán, August 5, October 6, and October 20, 1817, AHNC, Anexo, Guerra y Marina, tomo 152, fols, 241–43, 246–48v, 251–52v.

52. Calzada to Aymerich, Popayán, January 24, 1820, Aymerich to Sámano, Quito, February 7, 1820, both in Ortiz (ed.), *Colección de documentos*, primera serie, 206, 207–10.

53. Bishop of Popayán to the crown, Popayán, March 21, 1820, *ibid.*, 211–16.

54. Calzada to Aymerich, Mercaderes, October 11, 1819, Bishop of Popayán, Pasto, May 18, 1820, "Actas celebradas en Pasto por la Junta de Autoridades," Pasto, July 17–21, 1820, *ibid.*, 143–44, 217–18, 221–28; Basilio García to

Aymerich, Pasto, January 1, 1821, García to Aymerich, Campo de Matabojoy, January 29, 1821, both in ANHE, PQ, Vol 584 (1821), I, doc. 2, fols. 4–4v, 121–121v; Abadesa y Monjas del Convento de Conceptas to Juan de la Cruz Mourgeon (captain general, jefe superior y político of the Kingdom of New Granada), Pasto, January 14, 1822, Bishop of Popayán to Mourgeon, Pasto, January 18, 1822, ANHE, PQ and RC, Vol. 596 (1822), I, doc. 418, fols. 160–60v, no. 219, fols. 244–45v.

55. Ospina Vásquez, *Industria y protección*, 127.

56. Bolívar, Cuartel General de Pasto, June 9, 1822, in (Simon Bolívar), *Decretos del Libertador* (Los Teques, 1983), I, 254–55; "Capitulación de Pasto, Cuartel General Liberatador en Pasto," June 8, 1822, in José M. de Mier, *La Gran Colombia* (Bogotá, 1983), V, 1676–79. See ANHE, PQ, Vol. 567 (1819), I, doc. 142, fols. 160–60v, on Zambrano in the Pasto resistance of 1819.

57. Manuel López Pardo to Governor Joaquín Gómez de la Torre, Cumbral, November 3, 1822, ANHE, RC, Vol. 603 (1822), VIII, no. 2, fols, 2–3v; Bolívar, Cuartel General de Pasto, January 13, 1823, in (Bolivar), *Decretos del Libertador,* I, 273–74.

58. Bolívar, Cuartel General de Bogotá, January 7, 1821, in (Bolívar), *Decretos del Libertador*, I, 221–22; Pedro José Villegas to Intendant Vicente Aguirre, Esmeraldas, February 13, 1823 (three letters), ANHE, RC, Vol. 607 (1823), I, no. 178, fols, 202–202v, no. 184, fols. 208–208v, no. 190, fols. 214–14v.

59. ANHE, RC, vol. 596 (1822), I, doc. 229, fol. 254; Tulio Halperín Donghi. *The Aftermath of Revolution in Latin America* (New York, 1973), 9, 11; Orlando Fals Borda, *Subversion and Social Change in Colombia* (New York, 1969), 86. The Obando family were Pasto landowners who fulfilled administrative duties such as the lease of tribute and tithe collection and were connected to the Popayán elite.

II

Insurgency and
Counterinsurgency in New Spain

2

José Nemesio Vázquez: An Insurgent Courier, 1812–1816

Virginia Guedea

Virginia Guedea's essay on José Nemesio Vázquez illustrates the advantages and the necessity of examining the microhistory of the independence wars. Basing her work on one small incident involving a poor worker in rural New Spain who became caught up in the confused world of insurgency and counterinsurgency, Guedea underscores a number of highly significant themes. Clearly, neither the royalists nor the insurgents had the upper hand in the endless series of small guerrilla-style actions that tied down the royalist army and forced the regime to adopt a cumbersome system of heavily escorted convoys. If the royalists could not control the most strategic routes from Mexico City to Puebla and to the port of Veracruz, they could not expect to win the war. At the district level, if they were to survive, the royalist army commanders had to alter the implementation of harsh orders emanating from Mexico City. While Vázquez was captured red-handed in possession of a weapon and a document that tied him to the insurgents, the imposition of an automatic death sentence as demanded by the edicts of the central regime was not forthcoming.

Guedea's study highlights the interface between a militarized system and the realities of administering and maintaining some semblance of a legal structure. The people of the small town of Juchitepec petitioned rigorously against the execution of Vázquez by a firing squad. Ironically, however, their motives were self-protective rather than humanitarian. They feared reprisals by the rebel and insurgent-bandit gangs that inhabited the rugged territory surrounding the town. Guedea's essay points out many of the anarchic themes that affected the lives of the people during the long and confusing wars. In a word, she describes small and dirty wars—really chases and skirmishes—between enemies who seldom comprehended the motivations of the other side. There are no heroes in Guedea's essay,

From Virginia Guedea, "José Nemesio Vázquez: Un correo insurgente," in *De la Historia: Homenaje a Jorge Gurría Lacroix* (México: UNAM, IIH, 1985), 287–95. Reprinted by permission of Virginia Guedea and the Instituto de Investigaciones Históricas.

and no great causes. The concept of independence was foreign to humble men and women such as Vázquez who found themselves compelled to serve either side.

Virginia Guedea is directora *of the Centro de Estudios Históricos of the Universidad Autónoma de México (UNAM). Her outstanding works on the insurgency include* En busca de un gobierno alterno: Los Guadalupes de México *(1992).*

José Nemesio Vázquez was one of many individuals upon whom the insurgents of New Spain relied to undertake the dangerous but necessary task of transporting compromising papers. While his activities as a courier were hardly as important to the insurgency as the actions of some of his more illustrious colleagues, his case is interesting because it demonstrates how profoundly the war of insurgency came to affect the distinct strata of New Spain's society—particularly those who occupied the lowest societal classes.

During the years of the war of insurgency (1810–1821), frequently Mexico City was surrounded by numerous insurgent bands that almost continuously interdicted the flow of foodstuffs and other articles indispensable for subsistence. They also blocked communications—always important and especially in wartime—between the center of viceregal power and the rest of the territory of New Spain. Although these rebel groups attained neither the notoriety nor the fame of other groups, they often distracted the attention of the colonial authorities, and tied down army units that otherwise may have been better employed in other theaters of conflict. A particularly targeted region was the rugged zone situated between the capital and the city of Puebla. A careful study of these bands illustrates many of the special characteristics of insurgency. The region embracing the capital and the city of Puebla was the scene of numerous and quite diverse insurgent activities that not only represented constant threats to the security and provisioning of both cities, but also blockaded the vital transportation and communications corridor between Mexico City and Veracruz. This was an artery of vital importance to New Spain and the metropolis since it was the essential route of communications and the carrier of a very active commerce.

In order to confront the insurgents who obstructed roads, particularly a strategic route of such significance as that connecting the interior with the port of Veracruz, the authorities adopted a system of employing large convoys guarded by strong armed escorts to protect travelers and commercial shipments. This system was not always effective since it took time to plan, to organize, and to dispatch a convoy. Because the departure date had to be published and the passage of the ponderous cavalcade of freight vehicles and animals was slow, the rebels were able to organize their forces and to launch attacks from strategic points along the road. However, the individual insurgent groups that occupied the region between Mexico City and Puebla generally operated independently of one another. While this flexibility permitted the small bands great mobility to attack minor targets, the total lack of coordination often impeded them from achieving successes in larger enterprises requiring the amalgamation of autonomous forces. On more than one occasion, the insurgents failed when they attempted joint operations simply because they lacked the ability to form sufficiently unified forces.

Among the rebel chiefs who operated in this zone between 1812 and 1816, José Vicente Gómez stood out for his military activities and unfortunately for the cruelties with which he treated some prisoners who fell into his power when they traveled the Mexico City-Puebla road. According to the historian Lucas Alamán, this insurgent chief was known by the nickname of *El Capador* (the Castrator), "because he castrated Spanish prisoners who he did not wish to kill saying that he did so to prevent them from propagating their *casta* (racial group)."[1] In his evaluation of Gómez's actions, Carlos María Bustamante wrote with some sarcasm that Gómez's behavior was "to the detriment of humanity and served only to benefit the choirs of theaters and coliseums that will have a nursery of excellent singers. If Calleja seriously considered relieving their miserable fortunes, he would have sent them to a chapel school."[2]

Gómez's horrendous practices led Governor Ortega of Puebla to issue a circular designed to frighten any soldiers who considered desertion from the royalist ranks.[3] Gómez dominated a broad zone surrounding the town of San Martín Texmelucan that he occupied first in February, 1812.[4] The following year he took part in the famous victory won on 14 October, 1813, by Mariano Matamoros at San Agustín del Palmar over Juan Cándamo and José Manuel Martínez, who commanded a tobacco convoy from Orizaba.[5] His influence was felt very close to the capital by way of Milpa Alta where José Mariano Jiménez commanded a small rebel band. Between this town and the district connecting with the town of San Martín Texmelucan, the rebel chief Mateo Colín operated under the orders of Gómez from his headquarters at San Salvador el Verde.

Despite the fact that the rebel chiefs of the different bands of this zone acted on their own in the majority of their operations, they maintained frequent communications with each other to inform themselves of their activities and to request assistance when they undertook major actions. They also served as points of contact with other rebel chiefs of more distant zones, and between these and the supporters of the insurgency in Mexico City, Puebla, and in other important centers.

In order to circulate information that they needed to transmit, the insurgents utilized the services of numerous persons of all social classes and conditions. Some were discovered by the royalists as they undertook their missions and they suffered severe punishments. Nevertheless, many of the insurgent couriers were individuals who believed completely in the justice of their cause and they did not hesitate to risk their lives. Others became couriers simply because they expected to benefit personally from this activity. There were still others—neither partisans of the insurgency nor greedy opportunists—who for diverse reasons found themselves obliged to fulfill a role that they had not sought. Often, they did not even understand the consequences of their actions. This was the case of José Nemesio Vázquez, who was apprehended by royalist forces on 18 April, 1814, at the Hacienda de la Asunción for having in his possession a receipt signed by José Mariano Jiménez that acknowledged the arrival of papers sent by Mateo Colín. The receipt stated, "17 April 1814. The three letters and the dispatch are received. Camp and date and they continue on to their final destination. Signed, Captain José Mariano Jiménez."[6]

According to his statement, taken three days after being taken prisoner, Vázquez was a native of Tetelco, a *labrador* (farmer), of between sixteen and seventeen years of age. When questioned how it was that he had become mixed up with the insurgents, he explained his pathetic situation in simple words. He answered that:

> . . . he had been in the town of Tlalmanalco working in an aguardiente (sugar cane alcohol) distillery belonging to Don José María Cacho. Around midnight, as he walked by Don Andrés Pliego's store on his way to guard Don Cacho's distillery, by surprise he encountered the band of [the insurgent] Cabecilla Mateo Colín. Forced by *cintarazos* (blows with the flat of a sword), Vázquez had to carry a leather container of aguardiente that they had purchased at the store. They made him carry this burden to the top of a hill, where another man took it from him and carried it to the hacienda de Contla on the other side of the mountain. They arrived there at around eleven the next morning, stopping only to throw forage to their horses. Then they left for the town of San Salvador, going to José Aponte's house, where he had his headquarters situated in the *plaza mayor*. For the next three days, Vázquez remained under arrest after which the insurgent Mariano Espinosa took him to the house of the surgeon where he received treatment for a wound that had resulted from the blows he received at Tlalmanalco. Thereafter, he was released and given the responsibility to care for the horses until the day that the convoy passed. . . .[7]

The convoy mentioned by Vázquez in his declaration appears to be one that departed from Mexico City under escort by a force commanded by the royalist commander, Colonel Luis del Aguila. He was the same officer who on 1 November, 1812, attacked the forces of José María Morelos in the Cumbres de Aculcingo, obliging the rebels to flee and to abandon their artillery during the return of the insurgents to Tehuacán from Orizaba. This convoy protected by Colonel Aguila guarded eighty-seven passenger coaches, many other travelers on horseback, and 7,000 mules that freighted five million pesos in silver for the Peninsula and other cargo. Lucas Alamán was an eyewitness to these events as he traveled with the convoy to Veracruz where he embarked for Cádiz. In addition to Alamán, two judges of the Audiencia traveled to Spain, Manuel de la Bodega, who had been named overseas minister by the Regency, and Pedro de la Puente, ex-superintendent of police during the administration of Viceroy Francisco Xavier Venegas. Among other important figures traveling with the convoy, Field Marshal Don Nemesio Salcedo was returning to Spain after having served as Comandante General of the Provincias Internas where he had amassed a large fortune, and Don Jacobo de Villaurrutia, who had been ordered against his will to serve as a judge in the Audiencia of Seville.[8] This appointment resulted from Villaurrutia having been chosen as parish elector in the tumultuous November, 1812, popular elections for the new Constitutional Ayuntamiento held in Mexico City.[9] The day before the convoy departed, Viceroy Calleja ordered Dr. José María Alcalá, senior canon of the Mexico City cathedral, and Licenciado Manuel Cortázar, attorney of the Intendancy of Mexico, to leave for Spain where they were to take up posts as deputies to the Cortés for the province of Guanajuato. They also joined the convoy.[10] Villaurrutia, Alcalá, and Cortázar had provoked the viceroy's annoyance by demonstrating sympathies toward the insurgent cause. In addition, the latter two formed part of the secret society of the Guadalupes that from Mexico City aided the insurgent chiefs and Villaurrutia also was involved with the society although the colonial authorities were unaware of these ties. In Bustamante's opinion, the presence of so many distinguished persons in the convoy resulted from Morelos's capture of Acapulco and plans to assault Valladolid that "made many Spaniards to think seriously about their fate, and some requested passports to Spain and permission to travel with the convoy. They carried with them their riches and anything they possessed of value, whether honestly or dishonestly acquired."[11]

The problems for the convoy commenced on the road to Puebla when, after arriving at Río Frío, various passengers who traveled on horseback became impatient with the laborously slow pace and decided to ride ahead. They paid dearly for their impatience since some died at the hands of the rebels of the region who hung their cadavers from trees along the road. When the insurgents occupied the mountain heights, the convoy was forced to halt at Texmelucan bridge until the escort force drove them away. Finally, after nightfall and in some confusion, the convoy entered the town of San Martín Texmelucan.[12] The vicissitudes suffered by the convoy did not end there. On the road from Jalapa to Veracruz it was attacked again this time at San Juan Pass by the insurgent José Antonio Martínez, who captured part of the cargo and many official papers.[13]

From Vázquez's confession one can assume that the rebel chiefs who obstructed the convoy without winning major successes in its passage from Mexico City to Puebla were men commanded by Vicente Gómez. They coalesced their bands around Río Frío under the command of Mateo

Colín. While these events took place, Vázquez had been left behind, charged with the task of corralling the insurgents's horses at a nearby hacienda so that they would not fall into the hands of the royalist convoy escort force. However, shortly after Colín had departed, Vázquez saw that the rebels:

> fled pursued by the light cavalry of the convoy. With others, the declarant (Vázquez) fled to the hacienda of Santiago Colcingo seeking to reunite with Mateo Colín who had gone in that direction. From there they re-turned to San Salvador. A few days later, having arrived at Venta de Córdoba, they ordered Vázquez to go to the town of Milpa Alta with dispatches for the cabecilla (rebel chief) José Mariano Jiménez who gave him a receipt. Jiménez and his gang of twenty to thirty men who had come up the mountain were well armed, but not very well mounted. The declarant (Vázquez) spent the night in that town and the next day during his return trip, he was apprehended by a patrol of the convoy escort on the lands of La Asunción. He was taken to the cuartel (bar-racks) where he had remained in jail until the time of this statement. At the time of his capture, Vázquez had in his possession a saddled horse, a second without a saddle, a sword, and the receipt for the dispatches that he had carried. . . .[14]

At the beginning of Vázquez's declaration, he stated that after having been surprised by Colín's band, he was obliged to follow the rebels "un-der the force of sword slaps" and that after his arrival at San Salvador el Verde he was held prisoner for three days. However, following these state-ments there was not a word in his testimony suggesting that he was forced to remain with the insurgents or that he resisted the tasks assigned to him. Moreover, according to Vázquez's own statements elsewhere in his decla-ration there was no mention that he intended to flee from the rebels at some moment when he was not well guarded as did other prisoners. It appears that he accepted his fate with resignation either because he feared the reprisals of the insurgents if he abandoned them, or because he be-lieved that he would be rejected by his own people if he returned after having disappeared for some months. Or, he was simply at a loss about what he should do.

Like his capture by the insurgents, Vázquez's apprehension by the royalists was entirely accidental. Since horses were scarce and indispens-able to fight the insurgents, Buenaventura Manzo, the royalist commander of Juchitepec, had sent a detachment under the command of Sergeant Gutiérrez to recover a horse that the insurgents had hidden at the haci-enda de Ayocingo. Returning from this mission, the troops ran into Vázquez.[15] His sword and two horses were distributed among the royalist recruits, and the receipt issued by Jiménez that Vázquez carried for Colín was taken as irrefutable proof of his complicity with the insurgents. The day following Vázquez's capture, Manzo informed the Interim Delegate and Military Commander of the Province, Manuel Torres at Chalco of this event. In his report, Manzo inquired about the kind of punishment that should be inflicted upon the prisoner.[16] Torres replied immediately that in his opinion following the preparation of the appropriate summary charges, Vázquez "has committed a capital crime for which he must be executed in that town by firing squad as an enemy spy and for bearing arms against the King." In his reply, Torres also informed Manzo that upon carrying out these orders, "after executing the sentence" he should provide a detailed report so that the viceroy would be fully informed.[17] The dispositions taken by the provincial military *comandante* were, without a doubt, very harsh, but on invoking them he complied with the instructions issued by superior authorities concerning the treatment of insurgent prisoners. Immediately after learning of Torres's decision, Manzo initiated procedures to bring summary charges, and to carry out the appropriate sentence against Vázquez. On April 21, he appointed a scribe to record the prisoner's declaration. This took place the same day,[18] but without all of the appropriate formalities. However, Manzo did not proceed with the order to execute Vázquez.

While the military authorities took all of these dispositions, the inhabitants of the district of Santiago Domingo Juchitepec became greatly alarmed at the news that a prisoner would be shot. There never had been an execution in the town and they did not wish this to be the first. They sought the assistance of *bachiller* Gregorio Antonio García, deputy curate and ecclesiastical judge of the district, who immediately wrote a letter to Comandante Torres. After informing the commander of his great desire to please his beloved parishioners who always had been submissive, García invoked God to beg that if it was possible Torres should spare Vázquez's life. García implored Torres in the name of the town whose inhabitants promised that "further to the contribution that all residents of this district are making to maintain the royalist urban patriots company of cavalry (*compañía de patriotas urbanos de caballería*), they would obligate themselves to give one hundred pesos cash to help pay the expenses of these troops if they could obtain the grace and favor requested. Thanking García first for the "excessive charity" represented by the people, Torres explained that the concession solicited was not possible because the delinquent's crimes were so serious that it was necessary to invoke the death penalty. However, Vázquez could be transferred to Chalco headquarters so that the execution would not take place in the town. García noted that until that moment both he and the district curate, *Bachiller* José María Sánchez y Lara, always had enjoyed the favor of the military commanders and that the town had not been the site of any executions.[19] Torres's reply, dated April 22, while cordial was negative regarding the petition. He informed García that although he wished to please the town and the deputy curate, he lacked the power to overturn the sentence. He had to enforce orders received from higher authorities and it was necessary to put Vázquez to death.[20]

Torres's reply to García was identical to the one he gave the same day to the residents of Juchitepec who traveled to Chalco to make personal solicitations that if the execution of Vázquez must take place, it should not be done in their town. Despite the denial of their request by the provincial commander, even though the residents of Juchitepec did not challenge Torres's jurisdiction they were not ready to accept defeat. They appealed to Miguel Sánchez y Lara, the curate's brother, to intervene on their behalf with Manzo so that in turn he would appeal to Torres. As can be seen from Sánchez y Lara's statement to Manzo, the insistence of the residents of Juchitepec on pursuing their appeal did not originate from purely humanitarian grounds. They were moved primarily for reasons of their own security since they feared a large insurgent band in the nearby mountains that would attack the town if the authorities carried out the execution of Vázquez. Sánchez y Lara did not doubt the valor of the local royalist troops to confront the enemy, "but we fear that the force against us may be great and the one that we have for our defense is small." If a misfortune occurred in which the division of Juchitepec suffered destruction, the insurgents would attack the populace "as is their custom." With courtesy, Sánchez y Lara implored Manzo to propose that Torres send all of this information about their concerns to the viceroy. After all, Viceroy Calleja who had declared himself "protector and father of all honorable residents" would not make a decision that could harm them.[21]

Manzo did not appear inclined immediately to comply with Torres's orders since, despite placing the prisoner in the chapel after having taken his declaration, he delayed organizing a firing squad to perform the execution. Neither inactive nor lazy, Manzo took advantage of the opportunity presented to him by Sánchez y Lara's memorandum; that same day, he sent the document to Torres accompanied by an official letter of his own. In it he explained that the people of the area had conducted themselves well, and he believed that their request should be granted. Subsequently, little by little they would succeed in losing their fear of insurgents who inhabited their environs. Manzo took pains to stress that, although he had limited forces under his command, the rebels occupying the surrounding mountains did not intimidate him. Instead of executing Vázquez, Manzo believed that it would be more convenient to send him to a presidio or to condemn him to life in the King's armed forces. If his request received a positive response, he would be very grateful "because (Vázquez) is a young man who inspires pity since he is a youth who has not yet reached eighteen years of age."[22]

Despite Manzo's efforts not to show fear instilled by rebels of the nearby territory, it appears that this was the primary motive for his conduct and not any preoccupation for the life of his prisoner. Nor did the fate of this unfortunate man preoccupy the rebels themselves who did not make the slightest effort to rescue him. In spite of the fears expressed by the residents of Juchitepec and the military commander of the town himself, there were no threats to avenge his death in the event that he suffered execution.

Torres's response to Manzo's official letter is not found in Vásquez's dossier. Manzo ordered him transferred to Chalco on 26 April, together with two other prisoners, the file of summary charges, Jiménez's receipt, and García's and Sánchez y Lara's statements on his behalf. Nevertheless, Vázquez's departure did not imply necessarily that the insurgents of the surrounding territory would withdraw. Although the possibility of an insurgent attack diminished somewhat, in the same report in which he informed Torres of Vázquez's departure, Manzo requested the shipment of a case of munitions since he did not have enough should the rebels attack.[23]

When Torres received the prisoner and the papers that accompanied him, he acknowledged their arrival while he reproached Manzo for his delay in communications.[24] The following day, 27 April, the provincial commander prepared a statement delineating responsibility in which he declared that he had received Vázquez, who had "confessed and been convicted" of serving as an insurgent courier. For this crime, the prisoner deserved the death penalty, a punishment that should have been carried out at Juchitepec near where he was apprehended. This had not occurred due to the negligence of Comandante Manzo who had been communicated precise orders. Therefore, Torres decided to inform Viceroy Calleja of the events in the hope that he would resolve the case as he considered appropriate.[25] That same day, Torres submitted an official report to Calleja and enclosed the summary charges formed by Manzo against Vázquez.

To protect himself from any accusations of wrongdoing, Comandante Torres explained to the viceroy in detail everything that had occurred since Vázquez's capture, as well as the correspondence with Manzo regarding the prisoner's fate. He also notified Calleja that Vázquez was now to be found under his care in the Chalco jail, where he would remain until the viceroy determined what must be done with him. Torres concluded by informing Calleja that he considered it necessary that: "Captain Don Buenaventura Manzo be reprimanded so that in the future he does not commit the error of obstructing the orders of his superior officers, as he has done in this instance with notable scandal in that town and province after I had made my just determination."[26] While Torres was correct in accusing the Juchitepec commander of negligence and of confounding his orders, he was not right that the matter resulted in a scandal in the town and province. In preventing the execution of Vázquez, Manzo clearly succeeded in restoring tranquillity among the local residents.

Torres sent his report and the summary charges to Pedro Menoso who forwarded them to Viceroy Calleja. On 6 May, he in turn submitted the matter to Auditor de Guerra Melchor de Foncerrada. The following day, the auditor issued his opinion. Vázquez, by his own admission, was a courier and a spy for the insurgent chiefs Gómez and Colín. However, ". . . by virtue of declarations lacking the formalities prescribed by law, without the signature of the party concerned, the auditor could not go so far as to recommend the death sentence inasmuch as it was not carried out there *in flagranti* [*sic*], and because the man who apprehended him doubted the propriety of such action." This had given the local residents and the deputy curate time to intervene and to offer one hundred pesos for the prisoner's life. He concluded, "Your Excellency has the opportunity to exercise clemency, by pardoning the death sentence of this man, and sending him to an overseas prison for eight years." That was after accepting the hundred pesos offered for expenses of the army and with "the town continuing to maintain the urban cavalry as it has until the present."[27]

The last document which appears in Vázquez's case file is the resolution of Calleja dated 12 May, 1814. The viceroy agreed, of course, with Foncerrada's opinion. He ordered that the hundred pesos be applied to the treasury of the patriot company of Juchitepec to cover their expenses. As for Vázquez, he ordered ". . . that the prisoner be delivered in this capital to the presidio of Santiago so that, at the first opportunity, he may be forwarded to Havana. The corresponding official documentation is to be sent to the military governor and the intendant."[28] This is all we know about the sad fate of José Nemesio Vázquez.

Clearly, his case was not an exceptional one in the annals of insurgency. There were many like him who, without having made a decision to take an active part in the struggle, found themselves forced to act and as a result faced terrible consequences. This occurred because the very nature of the war did not permit the contenders to show mercy to the enemy. José Nemesio Vázquez's experience, and the problems which his imprisonment caused to both his captors and the residents of the zone where these events took place, is interesting not because of its uniqueness but precisely the opposite. Cases such as his allow us to understand the degree to which the war of insurgency affected all of those whose fate it was to experience it.

Notes

1. Lucas Alamán, *Historia de Méjico desde los primeros movimientos que prepararon su independencia en el año de 1808 hasta la época presente* II (México: Imprenta de J. M. Lara, 1850), p. 568.

2. Carlos María de Bustamante, *Cuadro histórico de la revolución mexicana, comenzada por el ciudadano Miguel Hidalgo y Costilla, cura del pueblo de los*

Dolores, en el obispado de Michoacán, 2a edición, III (México: Imprenta de José Mariano Lara, 1843–1846), p. 28.

3. C. M. de Bustamante, *Cuadro histórico,* III, p. 29. Bustamante expanded on the matter to criticize the governor of Puebla for having published a list of the unfortunate victims of castration who would thereafter suffer the contempt of society. In a note, he added that Gómez managed to convert this operation "into a science, such as that of pulling teeth so that many got better and were bright enough although their faces were beardless and their skin became pallid."

4. L. Alamán, *Historia de México,* II, p. 568.

5. L. Alamán, *Historia de México,* III, 537–539; and Carlos María de Bustamante, *Cuadro histórico,* II, p. 368.

6. Recibo expedido por José Mariano Jiménez, 17 de abril de 1814, "Sumaria contra José Nemesio Vázquez, inodado de insurgente y correo de los mismos, aprehendido por las tropas del rey y destacamento de Juchi," Archivo General de la Nación (cited hereinafter as AGN), Infidencias, vol. 83, exp. 1, f. 1.

7. Declaración de José Nemesio Vázquez, Juchitepec, 21 de abril de 1814, "Sumaria contra José Nemesio Vázquez," AGN, Infidencias, vol. 83,1, f. 2 and 2v.

8. Carlos María de Bustamante, *Historia de México* III, p. 30.

9. On the elections see Virginia Guedea, "Las primeras elecciones populares en la ciudad de México, 1812–1813," *Mexican Studies/Estudios Mexicanos* 7:1 (Winter, 1991), 1–28.

10. Lucas Alamán, *Historia de Méjico,* IV, p. 37–38.

11. On these activities see Virginia Guedea, *En busca de un gobierno alterno. Los Guadalupes de México,* (México: Universidad Nacional Autónoma de México, 1992).

12. L. Alamán, *Historia de Méjico,* IV, p. 39, and Carlos María de Bustamante, *Cuadro Histórico,* t. III, p. 30–32.

13. L. Alamán, *Historia de Méjico,* IV, p. 39.

14. Declaración de José Nemesio Vázquez, Juchitepec, 21 de abril de 1814, in "Sumaria contra José Nemesio Vázquez," AGN:Infidencias, vol. 83, exp. 1, f.

15. The great preoccupation of the viceregal regime with providing horses needed for military operations for the royalist army is evident from the many repeated initiatives to obtain them. Some of these efforts were difficult to enforce such as the decree issued by Viceroy Venegas on 1 February, 1812, ordering the requisition of all horses. This decree was published in the *Gazeta de México,* III, n. 184, (15 February, 1812) , p. 174.

16. Buenaventura Manzo to Manuel Torres, Juchitepec, 19 de abril de 1814, in "Sumaria contra José Nemesio Vázquez," AGN: Infidencias, vol. 83, exp. 1, f. 5-5v.

17. Manuel Torres to Buenaventura Manzo, Chalco, 20 de abril de 1814, "Sumaria contra José Nemesio Vázquez," AGN: Infidencias, vol. 83, exp. 1, f. 6-6v.

18. Declaración de José Nemesio Vázquez, Juchipan, 21 de abril de 1814, "Sumaria contra Nemesio Vázquez . . .," AGN, Infidencias, vol. 83, f. 2.

19. Gregorio Antonio García to Manuel Torres, n. 1. and n. d., "Sumaria contra José Nemesio Vázquez," AGN: Infidencias, vol. 83, exp. 1, f. 7-7v.

20. Manuel Torres to Gregorio Antonio García, Chalco, 22 de abril de 1814, "Sumaria contra José Nemesio Vázquez," AGN: Infidencias, vol. 83, exp. 1, f. 7.

21. Miguel Sánchez y Lara to Buenaventura Torres, hacienda de Tlajomulco, 23 de abril de 1814, "Sumaria contra José Nemesio Vázquez," AGN: Infidencias, vol. 83, exp. 1, f.8-8v.

22. Buenaventura Manzo to Manuel Torres, Juchitepec, 23 de abril de 1814, "Sumaria contra José Nemesio Vázquez," AGN: Infidencias, vol. 83, exp. 1, f. 10-10v.

23. Buenaventura Manzo to Manuel Torres, Juchitepec, 26 de abril de 1814, "Sumaria contra José Nemesio Vázquez," AGN: Infidencias, vol. 83, exp. 1, f. 12-12v.

24. Manuel Torres to Buenaventura Manzo, Chalco, 26 de abril de 1814, "Sumaria contra José Nemesio Vázquez," AGN: Infidencias, vol. 83, exp. 1, f. 13.

25. Constancia de Manuel Torres, Chalco, 27 de abril de 1814, "Sumaria contra José Nemesio Vázquez," AGN: Infidencias, vol. 83, exp. 1, f. 3-3v.

26. Manuel Torres to Félix María Calleja, Chalco, 27 de abril de 1814, "Sumaria contra José Nemesio Vázquez," AGN: Infidencias, vol. 83, exp. 1, f. s. n.

27. Parecer de Melchor de Foncerrada, México, 7 de mayo de 1814, "Sumaria contra José Nemesio Vázquez," AGN: Infidencias, vol. 83, exp. 1, f. s. n.

28. Resolución de Félix María Calleja, México, 12 de mayo de 1814, "Sumaria contra José Nemesio Vázquez," AGN, Infidencias, vol. 83, exp. 1, f. s. n.

3

Political-Military Regulations That Must Be Observed, New Spain, 1811

Félix Calleja

Faced by the dangerous popular revolt of Father Miguel Hidalgo that produced many separate centers of insurgency, Brigadier Félix Calleja, commander of the Army of the Center, confronted the debilitating problem of counterinsurgency directed against people who adopted traditional guerrilla warfare techniques. Calleja's response was to force the residents of towns, villages, and haciendas to raise and to fund local defense units. The goal was to militarize New Spain and to permit the regular army the flexibility that it needed to attack the centers of coalesced rebel power. With some modifications, Calleja's program continued until the 1820 restoration of the Spanish constitution. With the popular collapse of this burdensome and expensive system coinciding with the rise of Agustín de Iturbide's rebellion, the royalist army lacked the manpower or the will to hold the country.

To: Viceroy Don Francisco Xavier Venegas
Most Excellent Sir:
Your Excellency,

I am sending you herewith provisional regulations that appear to me as being indispensable for containing the egoism that unfortunately is generally widespread (in New Spain). These regulations will establish the rules necessary for strengthening the establishment of militia companies for towns and haciendas.

Once implemented, these regulations will extinguish the revolution, but there is no shortage of potential inconveniences. The principal one is

Translated and reprinted from Félix Calleja, "Reglamento político militar que deberán observar bajo las penas que señala a los Pueblos, Haciendas, y Ranchos a quienes se comunique por las Autoridades Legítimas y Respectivas . . . , Aguascalientes, 8 de junio 1811," in Archivo General de la Nación, Mexico, Ramo de Operaciones de Guerra, vol. 19, part 2, ff.75–78.

87

that by arming and reorganizing the Kingdom for its own defense, those we arm may turn against us at some point in the future. If so, they will create many new dangers.

In the meantime, if our military detachments are carefully unified, they will obtain the subjection and trust of the towns, and be enabled to pursue the insurgents.

Moreover, they will make the insurgents their natural enemies, as occurred at Leon, Irapuato, Real del Catorce, and other towns. After they have fought the insurgents successfully, and suffered from enemy misdeeds, it will be difficult for them to join forces with the insurgents.

In general, man is guided by education, custom, and convenience, and for these reasons, I believe, we can accomplish our goals in a short time. However, Your Excellency will have the kindness to tell me if we are in a position to adapt and introduce this plan.

May God provide Your Excellency with a long life.
Félix Calleja
Aguascalientes, June 8, 1811

Political-military regulations that must be observed by towns, haciendas, and ranchos, as ordered by the legitimate and respective authorities. Failure to comply with these regulations will result in punishments as established by law. In the meantime, the Most Excellent Viceroy to whom I am reporting will decide to make these regulations public knowledge, if he considers it to be convenient.

The most absurd, impolitic, and barbarous insurrection is reduced to its true state. Composed of mere gangs of thugs (gavillas), these insurgents embrace criminals from justice isolated from intercourse with decent men. These delinquents from each town occupy themselves by taking advantage of the vastness of the countryside to disrupt public order. Due to their atrocious crimes against innocent parties, they cannot be offered amnesty. They rob and interdict all movement of commerce and agriculture on the roads, and they disrupt mining. They threaten everyone and sometimes they coalesce larger forces by recruiting rabble from other gangs.

The towns fear them and for the lack of unity and method, the people permit themselves to witness atrocities. They foresee their ruin, the state of misery that threatens them, and the epidemics that are the natural consequences. And yet, they (the people) cannot resolve themselves to avoid those ills by adopting the only sure direction that lies within their reach. They want the King's troops deployed everywhere. They insist that each town, hacienda, and rancho have a garrison to defend them. Their cowardliness and egoism have caused their major catastrophes. These factors must be excised before they ruin the kingdom. But each individual cannot by himself build a dam to stop disorder, rapine, violence, and assassinations. For that, it is necessary for the government to establish general and simple rules so that all individuals be aware and willing to comply with their assigned roles in the plan of pacification. As general of His Majesty's Armies, and with the powers granted to me by the Viceroy of these kingdoms (New Spain), I have established the following regulations:

1. Army detachments will be stationed at all locations that do not require long marches to achieve the rapid destruction of rebel gangs (gavillas) that due to their numbers terrorize the towns. To avoid the coalescence of these gangs, district administrators (justicias), owners or managers of haciendas will be zealous and active in their obligations to report any assembly of criminal bands to the commanders of army detachments.

2. In each city or headquarters town the respective generals will name a commander for the local defense forces. To avoid rivalries, and costly delays, whenever possible the military appointee will take charge of and incorporate the powers of the Royal jurisdiction within his office so that there will be no more than one leader. Depending upon the exact nature of the topography and the population, the commander will take immediate steps to enlist an urban unit of either cavalry or infantry. Without exceptions, all honorable local residents will serve according to their social class in this corps. If some men refuse to fulfill their duty— something which I hope shall not happen, for the offense they shall be sentenced to exile at a location at least fifty leagues away from their normal place of domicile.

3. These infantry and cavalry corps shall be armed for now with dispersed weapons that may be available in the towns. Having ordered their collection, the commander will have these weapons at his disposal. Wherever there are shortages of arms, lances and machetes manufactured locally shall be issued to the troops.

4. Each one of these units will provide between one-hundred and one-hundred fifty men for active duty. They shall be remunerated according to their origins from a provisional special tax fund. If these tax funds are not available, the commander will order a mandatory general levy upon the population. The amounts to be collected shall be determined and collected by the local cabildo (municipal council). The cabildo shall ensure that these special taxes are applied with strict impartiality, and according to the particular resources of each individual. To enforce the decisions

entailed in this process, the cabildo shall name a commission composed of three trustworthy individuals and a treasurer who will manage the militia funds.

5. With this permanent force, military commanders and royal magistrates will enforce the rules of their police mission with severity and exactness. They will ensure that all pertinent parties are properly notified regarding this matter, and of the circumstances under which punishments will be applied against those who fail to comply with these regulations.

6. On fiesta days the remainder of the urban militia shall receive appropriate training in the use of arms and they shall always be ready to assemble when ordered to do so.

7. A magistrate shall be charged with ensuring that all eligible residents enlist based upon their neighborhood of domicile. He will be responsible for including every man capable of bearing arms in the mobilization. The magistrate will be responsible for providing those assembled with suitable arms and equipment. In the cases where there is a shortage of weapons, those enlisted will be provided with slings and stones. Also, the magistrate will be responsible for directing these men to the local military commander when requested to do so.

8. In each of these urban neighborhoods or rural militia assemblies, a virtuous and patriotic ecclesiastic will be appointed who must be capable of fulfilling the objective of serving as spiritual director and of exhorting and motivating the militiamen.

9. In each hacienda of the respective districts, the landowners will organize a company of 150 men according to the terms stated above for the towns, under the command of a captain with the support of subalterns of the appropriate ranks. In those haciendas of lesser importance, a company of thirty men under the command of an ensign will be deployed, and for smaller ranchos, a squadron commanded by a sergeant.

10. The district army commanders will keep muster lists of all units in their jurisdiction, and all military and civil authorities will be responsible to maintain surveillance over the roads of their districts. They will arrest any persons who appear suspicious. The district commander must be informed of everything that takes place and any matter that is worthy of his notice. If any of these operations result in information about the coalescence of bandit gangs (gavillas), the district army commander will take the appropriate steps needed to assemble all or part of the local forces of the haciendas needed to disperse and to punish those delinquents.

11. When necessity dictates, the neighborhood militia units of the headquarters towns under their respective magistrates will join

forces with those units assembled by the district commander. Even when neighborhood forces do not participate in combat operations, they will remain assembled and well-informed of their respective duties. During these emergencies, individuals who fail to report to their units without justified cause will be considered and dealt with as insurgents without any exceptions.

12. Any person who is not a member of the regional military forces, regardless of class or status, will be absolutely prohibited from bearing any kind of arms. In order to identify those enlisted in the royalist companies, at all times each individual militiaman will carry a signed identity certificate issued by his captain and countersigned by the district commander that confirms his military affiliation.

13. Individuals who are detained for carrying identification that lacks the signature of their appropriate company commander and the endorsement of the district commander, will have their documents confiscated. Those guilty of a first infraction will be punished with a fine of six pesos. These fines will be deposited in the urban provincial militia treasuries of the district to help finance the war effort. Those guilty of a second offense will be punished with a fine of twelve pesos, and third time offenders will be sentenced to exile fifty leagues from their usual places of residence.

14. Muleteers, and other individuals who usually require iron tools for conducting their individual occupations, shall be allowed only to possess an ax, and a short knife without a point that is suitable to cut through ropes and straps, etc.

By these regulations, good patriots will be identified and recognized, without the many errors that until now have prevented the punishment of evil traitors. Furthermore, haciendas will be safe, and their inhabitants will be able to dedicate themselves to their crops, and to avoid misery and sickness. The towns will have militia units of the haciendas at their vanguard to assist collective defense, they will not be surprised by unexpected insurgent activities, and it will be impossible for even a single man to transit the region without being discovered.

Once implemented and generalized, this simple plan will extinguish the last vestiges of insurrection within a very few days. It will restore peace to the breast of families and purge the country of those who have caused so much pain. The implementation of the plan does not involve any extraordinary difficulties, nor does it require sacrifices that many towns have not made already voluntarily.

However, if contrary to my expectations there is some tenacious egoist who intends to frustrate this program, I shall order all commanders and judicial authorities to report to me immediately all those regardless of class or status who fail or refuse to comply with these regulations.

In accordance with the seriousness of this type of offense, the guilty shall be punished with exile fifty leagues from their normal place of domicile. No lesser punishment can be imposed upon any man who is indifferent to the evils that suffocate the country that provides him with his daily sustenance. The town or hacienda that under unacceptable or suspicious pretexts fails to fulfill its obligations shall suffer the levy of a heavy military tax, payable to the Royal Treasury, plus any other punishment that individuals may deserve as a result of their misguided conduct.

Félix Calleja
Aguascalientes, June 8, 1811

4

The War of Independence in Guerrero, New Spain, 1808–1821

Peter F. Guardino

In his study of the region that became Mexico's Guerrero state, Peter Guardino tests many general themes and ideas about politics, insurgency, and counterinsurgency in New Spain. Both peasants and local elites in Guerrero shared interests and approaches on politics, justice, and legitimacy so that they could work out a common program. They hated the gachupín merchants and bureaucrats whom they described as monopolists, usurers, and afrancesados *(supporters of the French and of Napoleon). Since this region was insurgent territory throughout the independence wars, leaders such as José María Morelos and Vicente Guerrero were able to construct a system to replace the Spanish regime based in distant Mexico City. They abolished the tribute tax paid by Indians, mulattos, and other* castas, *declaring that all inhabitants were to be known as Americanos.*

In a region settled in large part by mulattos who had suffered the worst deal from the Spanish regime—they paid tribute as well as the alcabala *(sales tax) from which the Indians were exempt, and they suffered the stigma of slave origins—these people became committed insurgents. Although there were few slaves, the abolition of slavery helped to elevate the mulattos to a position of greater respectability. They served Father Morelos and became highly effective guerrilla fighters who, over time, eroded the ability of the royalist army to regain permanent reconquest. Guardino views the period as one of constant fighting and profound change in which the Spanish colonial regime lost its legitimacy. The appointment of Agustín de Iturbide to command the region in 1820 was a desperate step by an exhausted royalist military command. When Iturbide dealt with Guerrero to produce the Plan de Iguala and a new coalition that proclaimed independence, this region and its peoples hastened the total defeat of the royalist regime.*

 Peter Guardino is associate professor of history at Indiana University, Bloomington. He is currently researching the changes in popular political culture in Oaxaca from the pre-Bourbon reform era to La Reforma.

> We should take precautions so that the usurper does not catch us unready and unarmed. . . . The *patria* is based upon patriotism; only this support is firm, and patriotism consists in the virtue of each, and in the union of all . . . the present generation will decide the fate of future generations.
> —The Cathedral Chapter of Michoacán, Valladolid
> April 5, 1810

> Except for the European Spanish, all other inhabitants will not be called Indians, mulattos, or other castes, but instead all Americans. No one will pay tribute, nor will there be slavery in the future. . . . There will be no community treasuries and the Indians will receive the rent from their lands as their own.
> —José María Morelos, Aguacatillo
> November 17, 1810

> It is necessary that Your Graces, who are the most loyal to your Nation, defenders of the Sacred Religion and most loving of your *Patria* . . . gather all your fathers and sons and come with me, leaving as many people as are necessary to protect the village.
> —José Eduardo de las Cabadas, San Marcos
> January 17, 1811

The area that later became the state of Guerrero was a major arena of social and political conflict during Mexico's 1808–21 independence war. Beginning in 1808, the social and political landscape changed fundamentally. Before 1808 the primary forum for social and political disagreements was the colonial court system; after 1808 it became rebellion and the threat of rebellion. Before 1808 political action and peasant resistance were atomized in lawsuits and riots that rarely extended beyond a single village; after 1808 political actions in which peasants from more than one village cooperated became common. Moreover, many of these rebellions were joined or even led by people from other social classes. Through the nineteenth century and beyond, these movements have been the primary means through which groups of peasants have influenced the shape of the Mexican state and its relations with Mexican society. Thus the year 1808 is a watershed in the history of the Mexican state and the Mexican peasantry.

Post-1808 social movements were characterized by the involvement of more than one village and by the formation of alliances between groups of villages and "outsiders."[1] These phenomena required not only some congruence in material interests, however short-term, but also some ideology or programmatic content capable of uniting diverse parties who had never before acted in concert. These two elements are essential to the forms of political conflict and alliance that have prevailed in Mexico since 1808. Neither existed in central Mexico before 1808: both were common thereafter. In this way too, 1808 represents a turning point.

The keys to understanding these changes are found in the movement for independence, its program, and popular consciousness. Not surprisingly, the insurgency in different regions of New Spain has drawn a great deal of interest from scholars. In Guerrero, New Spain's political crisis of 1808–10 provoked violent and unexpected responses that, although rooted in diverse social tensions, were focused by the political leadership that led the insurgent alliance in the area. The program and discourse that articulated the movement effectively appealed to distinct social groups while constructing a vision of a new Mexican society that was to address the concerns of all and harmonize their interests. This vision changed significantly during the fluid political conflicts that characterized Mexico and Spain in the second decade of the nineteenth century. The rebels effectively governed the Guerrero area for several years, and their organization provides more insight into insurgent goals and how the insurgent state in practice differed from the colonial order it sought to replace. Although the movement suffered severe setbacks in the middle of the decade, it survived through guerrilla warfare and won a place in the 1821 alliance that led to Mexican independence.

Popular Violence and Mexican Independence

In recent years, several scholars have analyzed popular participation in the movement for independence in New Spain. Most depict a sharp division between the elite's political motivations for rebellion and the social motivations that they attribute to New Spain's peasantry. These scholars postulate parallel and disarticulated movements at different levels; indeed, at first blush the activities and motivations of elites and peasants seem to have little in common apart from their timing. These scholars thus devote little attention to the programmatic statements of what they consider to be the elite movement, and they explain the lack of such statements attributable to the parallel popular movements by stressing the expression of popular discontents and grievances through unfocused acts of violence and occasional traces of millenarianism.[2]

This study will take the opposite tack by examining the concrete motivations of both local elites and the rural poor and showing how the program elaborated by the movement's leaders articulated both sets of concerns. Certainly there were tensions within the movement, and not all peasant concerns were consciously championed by elite leaders. I will argue, however, that peasants and local elites shared concrete interests as well as basic notions of politics, justice, and legitimacy from which a common program could be fashioned. The positions of elite and peasant rebels varied greatly over time and across regions; nonetheless, the idea that local elites joined the movement because they agreed with its program and peasants did so only to revenge past wrongs and restore a traditional equilibrium does not adequately describe events in Guerrero.

Interpretations of the movement for independence have cited two sets of factors that are not necessarily mutually exclusive. The first consists of the negative effects of the various Bourbon reforms on both peasants and elites, which include increased economic demands and attacks on the power and autonomy of various corporate groups in New Spain, among them peasant villages. Economic demands increased with changes aimed at more effective tax collection, the drive to secure "voluntary" donations and loans for the Crown, and the famous Consolidación de Vales Reales. Politically, the reforms reduced the autonomy of peasant groups in some areas of New Spain as well as the access to offices previously enjoyed by elite Creoles. The reforms also reduced clerical privileges, particularly in legal matters; William Taylor and Serge Gruzinski have detected a general drive to secularize peasants and reduce the role of the clergy in peasant life, desacralizing politics.[3]

The second cause often cited is agrarian change driven by economic development and population growth. This factor has been convincingly demonstrated for such important areas as the Bajío, Morelos, and the Guadalajara region, where Mexico's dominant class invested heavily in haciendas. They constructed irrigation works and granaries that allowed them to reap enormous profits in years of harvest failure and to hold their grain production off the market until prices rose late in the annual agricultural cycle even in good years. In the Bajío hacienda tenants were driven to more marginal, unirrigated lands, whereas in the Guadalajara region Indian villagers were forced out of the market as grain producers and back into it as workers. In Morelos competition over resources increased with rural population growth and the opportunity presented by the growing demand for agricultural products in Mexico City. Morelos provided some support for the insurgents, and the Bajío and Guadalajara regions contributed large contingents to the Hidalgo revolt.[4]

In Guerrero several features of the Bourbon reforms contributed to the rebellion. José María Morelos and other rural priests resented Bourbon attempts to limit church autonomy. Bourbon moves to tap cofradía resources and cajas de comunidad, increase tribute collection, and secure funds through voluntary loans and donations also contributed to the revolt. Nevertheless, the Bourbon reforms were implemented throughout Spanish America over a 50-year period, and although many contributed to increasing tensions it is difficult to sustain an argument citing them as a direct cause of the 1810 explosion.

There is no evidence to suggest that Guerrero experienced the severe agrarian changes that took place in the Bajío, Morelos, and Guadalajara regions in the late eighteenth and early nineteenth centuries. Population pressure was a factor in some parts of Guerrero but its effect was uneven: it contributed to tensions in the Tierra Caliente, where repúblicas sought to evict ranchero tenants and bring their lands into production for their own expanding populations, but it does not seem to have been important on the Costa Grande or in the Tlapa region, the other two areas of insurgent strength in Guerrero.

The response of village Indians to the independence movement has been of particular interest to historians. This type of peasantry has dominated the historical literature on rural Mexico since the 1930s. The assumption that villagers were traditional in orientation leads Brian Hamnett to suggest that they were in general indifferent to the 1810 movement, which he believes sought to abolish corporate privileges. John Tutino hypothesizes that in crucial areas of the central plateau villages were part of a stable symbiotic order in which they combined the use of their own resources with employment opportunities on nearby estates. Villages in these areas thus did not support the independence movement. William Taylor and Eric Van Young have noted that at least some communities in Jalisco supported the insurgents. Van Young suggests that although communities became increasingly split in the late colonial period tensions within them may have been displaced toward outsiders, leading to unified community action in moments of stress. In contrast, Rodolfo Pastor notes that communities in the Mixteca did not react unanimously. There wealthier Indians were insurgent but poorer ones and more traditional nobles were either apathetic or openly royalist.[5]

Some historians have suggested that communities participated in the movement in order to regain community lands lost to outsiders or to gain new lands.[6] Others are skeptical of this interpretation, noting the dubious origins of the only programmatic statement found to date referring to the redistribution of land.[7] Van Young has argued that the desire of communities to regain lost lands or expand their holdings was deflected through intervening variables; his hypothesis would still rank land hunger as a major motivation of the participants while accounting for the fact that no programmatic statements about land have come to light.[8] Christon Archer suggests that a great deal of unofficial agrarian reform took place during the fighting, as peasants and rancheros farmed hacienda lands in the absence of their owners.[9]

But the debate over the "agrarian nature" of peasant participation, with its implicit assumption that land must be the primary issue in peasant political action, may be misdirected. In this regard, the quintessential model is based on the events of Zapatista Morelos in 1910–20. This chapter will show how other issues could also drive peasant collective action. This shift in emphasis should not be surprising, as Taylor has noted that land was not an issue in the majority of the village riots he studied for the colonial period.[10] In Guerrero, the areas where peasant support for the movement was strongest and most tenacious were not places in which haciendas had expanded at the expense of communities or even controlled a significant amount of land. The salience of issues other than land is important because many problems that concerned peasants also concerned at least some nonvillagers. Even when they did not share peasant concerns, local elites often acquiesced to changes desired by villagers.

The Outbreak of the Insurgency in Guerrero

In 1808 French troops crossed the frontier into Spain and both Fernando VII and Carlos IV resigned their rights to the Spanish throne, precipitating an uprising against the French in Spain. In New Spain these events resulted in a crisis of legitimacy. Whose authority should be recognized? Neither the new French government of Spain nor those who organized resistance to it had a clear claim. In Mexico City urban Creoles attempted to persuade the viceroy to set up a junta to rule the viceroyalty in the name of the captive king until the situation was resolved.[11]

A group of peninsular merchants led by Gabriel de Yermo deposed the viceroy and imprisoned many of the Creole leaders involved in the autonomy attempt. Yermo's coup was conservative, designed to maintain the status quo, yet it was a direct antecedent to the Hidalgo revolt and did more than anything else to hasten the coming social explosion. In the highly charged atmosphere of 1808 the coup only exacerbated the confusion and tensions, shattering the constitutional continuity already shaken by events in Spain. In particular it replaced the reigning representative of the king in Mexico. To paraphrase Luís Villoro, the government of New Spain left the sphere of what "was" and entered that of what was "made": government had become the result of concrete and quite unsacred human will.[12] This event allowed future conspirators to view their efforts as plans to restore constitutional order.[13]

The events in Mexico City and Spain had ramifications throughout the viceroyalty. The terms of the debate were grafted onto many older disputes.[14] In Guerrero, various repúblicas de indios met to send expressions of loyalty to the king. Anti-French sentiment grew: in Tixtla that August local officials embargoed the goods of a Frenchman without superior orders. But the French were not the only targets of unauthorized actions. In Acapulco, a minor colonial official named Mariano Tabares organized an unsuccessful conspiracy that foreshadowed events to come. The conspiracy, which involved mulatto garrison soldiers and sharecroppers in the nearby district, sought "to crown a new king in America since there no longer was any in Spain and to kill the *europeos* because they were tyrants."[15] Tabares fled after he suspected that the plot had been discovered.

Responses to this crisis varied greatly, even within single villages.[16] Although a few areas can be identified as having insurgent or royalist tendencies, the inhabitants of most places oscillated from one side to the other throughout the 1810–20 period in response to opportunities, risks, and the actions of both insurgent and royalist governments.[17] This maneuvering was facilitated by the policies of both royalist and insurgent armies, which continually offered pardons to villages and individuals who wished to switch sides. There are even cases of revolts against the insurgent government when it attempted to impose unpopular measures.[18]

The prevalence of coercion further complicates attempts to explain the positions of various social groups on the basis of their interests and ideologies. Coercion was a factor in every rebellion in Guerrero throughout the early nineteenth century. Both the organizers of movements and authorities seeking to repress them used coercion to enforce loyalty. The literature on social movements often assumes the kind of unanimity that their organizers dream of but rarely encounter.

The first area of Guerrero to be affected by the independence movement was the Costa Grande. José María Morelos, a parish priest from Michoacán, arrived in the area in early November 1810 with only twenty men but by late November had recruited 3,000. This number may seem small in the light of the huge numbers Hidalgo recruited in the Bajío in the same period, but the coast was sparsely populated. By November 19 Acapulco's merchants and garrison were the only nearby groups still opposing the movement; under siege by Morelos, the city was the westernmost point of royalist control in the area. The response of the residents of the Costa Grande to Morelos was overwhelming.[19]

On October 18, 1810, the subdelegado of Tecpan, the largest population center on the Costa Grande, reported to the viceroy that he had seen no signs of disloyalty but considered his position weak because of the extreme poverty of the area's mulatto residents. The subdelegado noted that he had already exempted mulattos and Indians from the tribute because both groups resented its payment. When he reported again on November 8 the situation had changed drastically, for by then he had word of a priest from Michoacán advancing through the area, recruiting from the same villages that only a few days earlier had presented themselves voluntarily to the subdelegado to defend the king. The few Indians who answered the subdelegado's call to arms quickly deserted, leaving him with only the militia company of mulattos, who accompanied him on the first few miles of his retreat to Acapulco but soon asked for permission to leave him and return to their families. They, too, joined the insurgents.[20]

Actually, the wavering of the mulatto militia of Tecpan was rare on the Costa Grande: the other militia units in the area went over to Morelos even more quickly. These units consisted of mulatto sharecroppers who grew cotton commercially, and some officials and landowners also joined, although notably no coastal merchants became insurgents. The wealthier insurgents became leaders, often organizing their own sharecroppers. Several Indian villages also supported the movement.[21]

Although individuals and groups vacillated somewhat during the course of the war, there seems to have been a consistent base of support for the insurgents on the Costa Grande throughout the decade.[22] Even in November 1810 the area was a hotbed of anti-*gachupín* resentment. No group in Guerrero directed more hate at the European Spanish than the mulatto sharecroppers and Indian villagers who grew cotton on the Costa Grande.[23]

After securing the coast Morelos delayed several months before pushing on into the Montaña and other more northern areas. In the meantime the royalist authorities of the Montaña area began to organize for defense. Their most immediate concern was pressure from the northwest, where many villages in the Tierra Caliente and the Taxco region had risen. The nucleus of insurgent activity in the Tierra Caliente and Taxco regions began to spread south and east to the extent that royalist authorities in Chilapa and Tixtla did not feel that they could send reinforcements to Acapulco to help with the defense of that strategic position.[24]

These royalists were less concerned about insurgency closer to home. In the first few months of the war the entire elite of the Montaña remained loyal to the Mexico City government, led by the subdelegado Joaquín de Guevara (also a local landowner), the priest Manuel Mallol, and the powerful merchant and landowning Leyva family. The group also began organizing the Indians of the surrounding villages to aid in counterinsurgency efforts to the immediate north.[25] However, already there were some disturbing signs of what was to come. In early November the village Indians of Chilapa imprisoned ten europeos who had fled the insurgency in nearby Tepecoacuilco, mistaking them for insurgents. This incident suggests that the villagers were somewhat biased as to who they thought their enemies really were. Also, the authorities suspected the loyalty of the villages of Atenango del Río, Xochipala, and others who showed signs that they were "very uppity."[26]

The authorities' biggest worry, however, was the fragility of the local elite's own consensus. Accusations and counteraccusations began to dominate their correspondence. When Chilpancingo and Zumpango del Río were attacked by the insurgents in December not only the Indians but some of the Creoles and mestizos welcomed them. They later apologized when royalist forces forced a retreat. Furthermore, officials suspected the loyalty of the key elite family of the Chilpancingo area, the Bravos, because they dragged their feet when asked for money and men for the defense effort. Troops were sent to arrest the Bravos but the family fled into the *monte*.[27] This well-connected family eventually went over to Morelos.

The royalist effort to maintain control of the Montaña collapsed in the summer of 1811. In early May the Bravo family left hiding to join the insurgency, and later that month Morelos's forces took the strategic town of Tixtla. Until August an uneasy balance of power persisted in the area: the insurgents held Tixtla but the royalists continued to control Chilapa, less than 25 kilometers away. The stalemate ended in mid-August when the insurgents crushed a royalist force sent to recapture Tixtla, and royalist authority subsequently collapsed in the entire area from Chilpancingo east to Huajuapan in present-day Oaxaca.[28]

Although Morelos clearly received some support in the Chilpancingo area, particularly from the village of Xochipala and the Bravo family, the situation in the Tixtla-Chilapa area was not as clearcut. No spontaneous rising took place there, even when the insurgents approached. This ambivalence is particularly interesting because Chilapa was the area of Guerrero with the most frequent and acrimonious land disputes between villages and haciendas or ranchos. Even the village of Atenango del Río, which royalist authorities had suspected previously of insurgent sympathies, did not present itself to the insurgents after they had established military control of the area.[29] Farther east in Tlapa, where villages controlled virtually all of the land, the situation was different; there a relatively small force of insurgents quickly recruited large numbers of villagers and insurgent control was quickly organized with few outside forces.[30]

This pattern continued throughout the 1811–20 period. For instance, in 1812 when Morelos took the bulk of his troops to Cuautla a very small royalist force was able to spark a counterrevolution in the Chilapa area. Then and later, support for the insurgents seems to have been lukewarm and fragmented if not lacking entirely.[31] In contrast, in the Tlapa area at the lowest moments of insurgent military strength very small insurgent forces were able to catalyze large guerilla movements.[32] This pattern implies that land conflict was not the primary motor driving social movements in Guerrero.

Farther north in the area of Tepecoacuilco, Iguala, and Taxco the story was different. A conspiracy that began in 1810 before the Hidalgo revolt linked many arrieros with the Indian gobernadores of Tepecoacuilco, Iguala, Huitzuco, and other towns. The situation was exacerbated by food scarcities and high prices near Taxco. In late 1810 the insurrection was centered in these same places and quickly spread to other villages near Taxco, often under the leadership of elected Indian officials, many of whom soon began ignoring orders sent by the subdelegado of Taxco. They were supported by forces from the Tierra Caliente. Taxco was essentially under guerrilla siege until it was finally captured by the insurgents on December 25, 1811. It was retaken by the royalists in May 1812 but the surrounding villages continued a guerrilla war against the royalists.[33] In this region the insurgency split villages: several villages joined the insurgency through "internal revolutions" in which one peasant faction deposed and exiled another, usually alleging that the exiled group was closely identified with colonial authorities and merchants. Those exiled were sometimes referred to as *agachupinado*.[34]

In the Tierra Caliente, where Indian villages owned most of the land, the insurrection began immediately without outside military support. The composition of the local insurgency was relatively complex: it was led by parish priests, landowners, and village governments, but other landowners and priests opposed it. Furthermore, the allegiances of local elites do not explain those of the rest of the local populace. For example, the owner of the Hacienda del Cubo was royalist, but many of its residents were insurgents, and the royalist pastor of Teloloapan had to be rescued from his parishioners.[35] Generally people in the Tierra Caliente seem to have been inclined to support the insurgents and continued to do so despite repeated royalist counterinsurgency campaigns from 1811 to 1820. Royalist commanders attributed this tendency to the willingness of the inhabitants to question colonial authority even before 1810.[36] Like colonial disputes, peasant support for the insurgency stemmed from tensions over such village resources as rental lands, cofradías, and cajas de comunidad.

The one area of Guerrero whose loyalty to the royalists rivaled that of the Tierra Caliente to the insurgents was the Costa Chica. This fact is puzzling, as the Costa Chica was socially and economically similar to the Costa Grande, which ignited so quickly and thoroughly upon the arrival of Morelos. Until 1813 the Costa Chica royalists held out against the insurgents who controlled the rest of Guerrero without aid from the viceregal government. They provisioned the garrison of Acapulco by sea, allowing the port to withstand the insurgent siege until the Costa Chica was subjugated by Morelos's main army in 1813. Even then the royalist forces on the Costa Chica did not surrender but instead dispersed and fought as guerrillas until the decline of Morelos's fortunes allowed them to reconquer the area. Even when the Plan of Iguala united insurgents and royalists in 1821, the residents of the Costa Chica were reluctant to accept the compromise.[37]

The Costa Chica's population of mulatto sharecroppers lived dispersed along the banks of the rivers used to irrigate their cotton crops. Their fierce loyalty to the royalists can be explained by four factors that stand out in contrast to their counterparts on the Costa Grande. First, they had been organized in militia companies since the late seventeenth century, a factor that seems to have figured prominently in their construction of their identity. Second, as militiamen they had continually and successfully sought exemption from tribute payments and thus had escaped much of the impact of increasing state demands in the Bourbon period.[38] Third, the role of European Spanish merchants in financing cotton production and thus controlling cotton trade seems to have been much smaller there, perhaps because of the success enjoyed by the Indians of the Tlapa area to the north, who employed cofradía capital in the trade.[39] The fourth factor is less abstract: Francisco Paris, who commanded royalist forces in the area and who had been subdelegado since the early 1790s, had continually supported the efforts of the militiamen to obtain exemption from tribute, and although he may have either participated in or allowed some repartimiento or habilitación in the area, he seems to have kept such activity at a level below that found on the Costa Grande, at least judging from the lack of documented complaints. Paris seems to have been one subdelegado who avoided actions that would lead to his characterization as "bad government," and his approach won him immense loyalty from the impoverished mulatto troops he commanded.[40]

Leadership

Brian Hamnett and Christon Archer have noted the importance of networks of insurgent leaders during the War of Independence.[41] Understanding which nonpeasants supported the insurgency and why they did so is necessary to any explanation of this movement. Leaving aside village officials and wealthy villagers, three overlapping groups of nonpeasants provided most of the officers of the insurgent army and its civil administration.

The first and probably largest group of leaders were arrieros, or muleteers. Arrieros were important in the first insurgent conspiracy in the region and remained prominent throughout the insurgency.[42] The most prominent arrieros (and former arrieros) were Morelos himself, who had worked as a muleteer before becoming a priest and even afterward engaged in small-scale trading, and Vicente Guerrero, who came from a family of muleteers centered in Tixtla. Others include Valerio Trujano and Juan del Carmen.[43] In this and other areas of New Spain whole villages and towns specialized in this activity and sometimes participated collectively in the revolt.[44]

Muleteers were a diverse group both ethnically and socially. They included European Spaniards, Creoles, mestizos, mulattos, and Indians;

some owned their own mules, from as few as two to as many as hundreds, and others worked for the owners, either controlling a whole train or working in lesser capacities. Muleteers who traded on their own account were the independent entrepreneurs who held together New Spain's economy.[45] They were very useful to the insurrection because of their knowledge of the physical, economic and social geography of large areas and a wide variety of contacts with whom they had developed trust through business arrangements. Some had learned Indian languages through their trading activities.[46] In addition, arrieros were traditionally one of the most important conduits through which news and rumors flowed in rural areas, a factor that gave them an additional edge in recruitment.

Muleteers' support for the insurrection seems to have been rooted in their resentment of the commercial domination of well-financed peninsular merchants centered in Mexico City, though this motivation is difficult to document directly. These merchants had often obtained the cooperation of local royal officials to limit competition. The connection between anti-gachupín sentiment and economic practices will be examined in detail below; for now it should be noted that the same exclusionary practices that kept prices paid to rural producers low also affected muleteers. Colonial officials often harassed muleteers who tried to compete with protected interests.[47]

Many insurgent leaders were parish priests. The most prominent in Guerrero was José María Morelos, but numerous others also served with the insurgent forces or aided in their civil administration.[48] Much of the discourse used to justify and motivate the movement was religious in tone and substance. Two features of clerical participation must be considered. First, why did members of this group rebel? Second, how effective was their participation on either side, especially in recruiting their own parishioners?

Two basic theses have been advanced to explain the participation of priests in the movement. The first is the great disparities in income among the clergy, whose social stratification mirrored the class structure of colonial society. The most well-remunerated and important posts were those of bishoprics and their attendant cathedral chapters; lower on the scale were a few particularly wealthy chaplaincies, and then others that allowed priests to enjoy the relative comfort and security of major cities. Below these were urban parishes and relatively wealthy rural parishes near major cities and markets. The least desirable positions were in isolated, poverty-striken, and often unhealthy, rural areas. The placement of priests was controlled by the bishoprics, cathedral chapters, and ecclesiastical courts—posts held by men of the colonial dominant class.[49]

The life of José María Morelos illustrates the lack of opportunity that could frustrate a poor parish priest. Son of a moderately prosperous mestizo artisan and his Creole wife, he entered the priesthood at a relatively late age after working for some years as an arriero and rancho administrator. Morelos was denied a chaplaincy after a lengthy lawsuit during and after which he worked in two different impoverished parishes in the Michoacán hot country. In the first his mother, whom he supported, became ill and died. The colonial church certainly had not done well by Morelos.[50]

A second motive for clerical unrest in the late colonial period was the drive to reduce the privileges of the clergy as part of the general Bourbon assault on corporations and their rights. Among the measures that most irritated the lower clergy were limitations on clerical immunity, the extension of royal authority over such sources of income as chaplaincies, and the Consolidación de Vales Reales.[51] At his trial, Morelos himself listed Spanish attacks on priests and ecclesiastical wealth as among his motives for revolt.[52]

How effective were priests as recruiters for political causes in 1810–20? Their influence was obviously great, although not as overwhelming as the literature sometimes suggests.[53] Parishioners did not invariably follow the lead of their pastors. Often captured insurgents cited the pernicious influence of their pastors as a defense at their trials, but royal officials did not always accept this defense.[54] Priests who preached for one side or another against the wishes of their parishioners were imprisoned and otherwise persecuted.[55] Perhaps the most important way that priests aided the insurgency was in giving it a vital and effective ideological content.

One of the relatively unusual features of the insurgency in Guerrero was the support it received from two important landowning families. The Bravos owned the large and fertile hacienda of Chichihualco near Chilpancingo. To the insurgency they contributed five brothers, Leonardo, Miguel, Máximo, Victor, and Casimoro, as well as Leonardo's son Nicolás. The Bravos seem to have wavered for several months in 1810–11, refusing to cooperate in organizing royalist forces in their area but also not joining Morelos. Only after this attitude led the royalists to seek their arrest did they join the insurgency. Their reasons are still not clear. In an 1828 description of his political life, Nicolás Bravo admitted that he had everything to lose by revolting but did not specify why he did. One suspects that the decision was taken as a family. Later, after Leonardo was captured, Nicolás and his uncles offered to surrender and also help pacify the area if Leonardo's life was spared. The deal fell through, however, and after Leonardo was killed the family remained important in the insurgency until late in the second decade of the century.[56]

The Galeanas were the other important landowning family that joined the insurgency. Their motivation seems clearer: they were a numerous family that possessed several cotton-producing haciendas on the Costa Grande, and several were also local militia officers.[57] They contributed several leaders to the movement, the most important of whom was

Hermengildo. Like the Bravos, the Galeanas were by no means one of the families that made up Mexico's ruling class; their holdings were the largest on the Costa Grande but were dwarfed in value by those of Mexico's first families. The family's culture and educational levels were similar to those of their peasant tenants.[58] The Galeanas' sharecropping of cotton land left them in the same disadvantageous position in the cotton market as their tenants,[59] and it is thus not surprising that just before the revolt Hermengildo Galeana was involved in an acrimonious dispute with two coastal europeos, apparently merchants.[60]

The Galeana and Bravo families led not only their own tenants but also other peasants during the insurgency. Their class position as local landowners did not preclude this mingling with their subordinates; rather, both families seem to have maintained relatively paternalist attitudes toward their tenants and other nearby peasants.[61] Neither family thought that the insurgency posed a threat to their position as landholders. This lack of fear suggests that these families did not consider land hunger the most important issue motivating peasant insurgents.

Ideology and Program of the Movement

The ideology of the insurgency articulated the cross-class alliance evident in the movement, providing a program that seemed to represent the aspirations of such diverse groups as Indian peasants, mulatto sharecroppers, provincial muleteers, hacendados, and priests. The various elements of this program were closely related to the political culture prevalent before 1810. Generally peasants and the provincial elite that led them focused on European-born Spaniards as the root of New Spain's problems. However, the insurgents also expressed more direct demands, and these aspirations changed as events progressed and old formulas were adapted to maintain their relevance.

The social and political explosion that rocked New Spain in 1810–11 was unforeseen and unprecedented, though the fact that New Spain's poor were capable of expressing their discontent by defying authorities was not surprising. Resistance, both through the courts and in village riots, was a common element of New Spain's political life. The shocking features of the early years of the insurgency were two: first, large numbers of poor people over a wide area cooperated in the resistance; second, the poor were joined and in fact led by substantial numbers of wealthier and more respectable folk. Certainly the latter's cooperation with the poor did not necessarily indicate that they shared the same practical and material goals and grievances. Perhaps they were simply successful manipulators of the desperate and vengeful rabble—temporarily, at least. Even in that case, their success requires explanation.

Historians who believe that the peasants who formed the mass of the rebels and the priests, muleteers, and even landowners who led the insurgents had very different goals may very well be correct. However, these different aims were not expressed in radically different ways. Late colonial Mexico did not experience the kind of "remarkable dissociation between the polite and the plebeian culture" that E. P. Thompson detected in England at the same time.[62] New Spain's poor and elite shared a common political culture to a striking degree. They were unified, in fact, by the same basic beliefs that were the only ones shared by the poor across village boundaries, namely, that the king was the ultimate guardian of justice and the Catholic Church the only guarantee of eternal salvation. Within these limits there was enormous room for disagreement, and neither parish priests nor the king's appointees were safe from sometimes violent opposition. However, even that opposition, whether in the courts or the village plaza, stressed loyalty to the king and the church.

In 1810 the shared nature of this political culture was extremely important because it allowed alliances and cooperation across class lines. The influence of the Enlightenment, Bourbon reforms, and even the French Revolution were seeping into the cracks of this edifice, and a breakup was only a few years away. However, those with doubts certainly did not make them public or attempt to recruit mass support by voicing them. Moreover, when New Spain's hegemonic political culture fragmented it did not fracture along class lines, and thus cross-class alliances remained possible.

Eric Van Young has recently remarked on the seeming incongruity of peasants claiming that their loyalty to Fernando VII required that they kill European Spaniards or drive them from New Spain. Revolution against the established order was carried out in the name of the very embodiment of that order.[63] However, this apparent contradiction is quite understandable because one of the most important ideas in the political culture of New Spain's peasantry was that the king's subjects sometimes had to speak and act in his name against the "bad government." The common village riot studied by William Taylor relies on this basic notion that the will of the king's representatives is not always that of the king.[64] The slogan "Long live the King, death to the Bad Government" was not coined on September 15, 1810.

Furthermore, this feature of peasant political attitudes dovetailed with ideas adopted by a significant portion of New Spain's Creoles in 1808. They argued that God did not confer sovereignty on the king directly. Instead sovereignty first passed through "el Pueblo." This idea had been enunciated by pre-absolutist theologians like Francisco Suarez whose influence was never really eliminated from theological texts during the eighteenth century. The Creoles argued that in the absence of the king the

"Pueblo" of New Spain, represented by such bodies as town councils, was required to exercise sovereignty to prevent chaos.[65] In an important step they included Indian village governments among those bodies on which sovereignty fell by inviting the Indian governor of the barrio of San Juan to their 1808 deliberations.[66] First Hidalgo and then Morelos drew on this body of thought to justify their actions.[67] The Indian peasant tradition in which the village (pueblo) sometimes was required to act in the name of the king was married to the political tradition in which royal sovereignty was conferred through the people (Pueblo) and sometimes devolved to them.

Thus, invoking the name of the king while recruiting for the insurgency was not a "yawning contradiction," as Van Young would have it.[68] Originally, Hidalgo and Morelos, like the Creole municipal council of Mexico City in 1808, sought not independence but status as a coequal kingdom, that is, they desired autonomy from Spain under the king. They differed from the Creole autonomists of 1808 in that, after the European Spaniards resorted to force, any who sought to oppose them must also use the same means.[69]

The strength of the association between the figure of the king and popular notions of justice was such in 1808–10 that the "royalist" hue of insurgent discourse was inevitable. However, the evidence suggests that it need not have fixed on the defense of Fernando VII. In the 1808 Acapulco conspiracy mentioned earlier, the conspirators, led by Mariano Tabares, sought to crown a new king in Mexico because there was no longer a king in Spain.[70] Nevertheless, Fernando VII soon became the undisputed symbol of popular hopes, and even Tabares began to support his return. Fernando dominated the symbolic field of battle, his captivity and obvious claim to the throne making him the perfect wild card because in his absence practically any agenda could be attributed to him. Also, by pinning their appeal on the existing king the insurgents avoided the thorny question of choosing a new one. No doubt Hidalgo's decision to support the legitimacy of Fernando VII was also influenced by events in Spain, where the resistance to the French was legitimated in this way.

If the insurgent movement retained a royalist hue, it also did not break with the past in the religious tone of its rhetoric. As Enrique Florescano and David Brading have noted, religion was *the* "unifying element of the ethnic, economic, cultural and political diversity which was New Spain."[71] Religion was the linchpin of the ideological system that organized everyday life and political relations, and it is impossible to imagine any movement mobilizing large numbers of people with a purely secular ideology.

The religious tone of the insurgency actually had two distinct components. The first originated in Old Testament stories of the oppressions and rebellions of the Hebrews, which were held up as examples of just rebellion that God rewarded with success. Documents in which Morelos, other priests, and nonclerical insurgents made this kind of reference are almost unlimited in number. These references remained common in political proclamations in Guerrero even after the death of Morelos. Most also contained references to the impiety of the Spanish, an element examined in greater detail below.[72] It should be noted that these ideas were not exclusive to New Spain: in the Andes, Túpac Amarú also frequently used such images "comparing, for instance, the situation in Peru with the oppression of the Hebrews in Israel."[73]

The second component is more well known. The Virgin of Guadalupe was the most pervasive symbol of the movement, used on flags and uniforms and in proclamations and passwords.[74] This symbol has been the subject of countless works; perhaps the most important for our purposes is the recent work of William Taylor, who rejects the notion that Guadalupe was already an object of devotion for large masses of Indian villagers before 1810 but instead suggests that the symbol became nationally important only after independence. He does note, however, that the symbol of Guadalupe, unlike others, was recognized in various regions and among distinct social groups well before the insurgency and that it exerted a more general appeal than that of other patron saints, even if it signified different ideas to different groups.[75]

Guadalupe, however, did not necessarily represent the overthrow of the established order. In fact, she was used quite frequently in royalist propaganda and religious observances.[76] As Taylor demonstrates, Guadalupe was a two-sided symbol: on the one hand, she offered a new beginning, "inviting her believers to escape the restraints of the established order"; on the other hand, she served as a mediator who fostered the "acceptance and legitimation of Spanish authority."[77] This insight suggests a parallel with ideas about the Spanish king: the king was a symbol of the ultimate legitimacy of the colonial order, yet it was in his name that peasants and others attacked aspects of that order.

A crucial element in the discourse of the insurgency was enmity toward European-born Spaniards. When the insurgency exploded on the coast in late 1810 this anti-Spanish prejudice was its major banner.[78] Anti-Spanish sentiment was obviously related to political attitudes about the legitimacy of the king and the illegitimacy of the government of New Spain as well as the religious facets just discussed. Notably, the words used to describe the European Spanish in the first years of the insurgency were "europeo" and "gachupín." More formal documents occasionally included the term "español europeo," never simply "español"; these usages consciously excluded Creoles from being identified as enemies of the movement.

The ire displayed against gachupines in Guerrero was intense. Actions against them resulted both from the official insurgent policy elaborated by Morelos and his lieutenants and from popular hatred. For instance, when twelve Spaniards were beheaded in Tecpan in early 1811, the executions were ordered by a Creole leader, but, according to a witness, "even the women demonstrated great pleasure."[79] Official policy and popular ire coincided to a remarkable degree. Both stemmed from conscious and unconscious ideas about the role the European-born Spanish played in local and viceregal society. The prevalence of anti-Spanish feelings among certain kinds of peasants makes it difficult to attribute these feelings exclusively to Creole resentment of Spanish predominance in filling civil and ecclesiastical posts. At the same time, the appearance of such sentiment in late 1810 and early 1811 implies that it could not have been solely or primarily a reaction to the ferocity of the counterinsurgency tactics employed by peninsular troops who arrived after 1812. Also, despite royalist misconceptions, this anger was not directed against all white people.[80]

The basic axis of anti-gachupín sentiment was, paradoxically, anti-French. The connections are surprisingly clear. Most viceregal officials in 1810–11 had been appointed under the influence of the royal favorite Manuel Godoy, seen as the man who betrayed Spain to Napoleon. Furthermore, many of Godoy's allies had remained in José Napoleon Bonaparte's government in Spain, rather than joining the groups resisting France. Also, the Europeans' 1808 coup in Mexico City nipped in the bud a movement against recognizing the Bonaparte government in Spain. Although the new government of the viceroyalty also refused to recognize Bonaparte, its anti-Napoleonic credentials seemed weak. More important, in the twenty years since the beginning of the French Revolution the Spanish Crown had propagandized extensively against the French, arguing that the French were atheist and impious as well as the declared enemies of the Crown. This flood of material appeared in two waves. The first surged in the early 1790s after the execution of the French king. After Spain became an ally of revolutionary France, anti-French propaganda subsided until the events of 1808 released a new flood. Much of the literature in the new wave was nationalist in tone, using such words as *patria* and *nación*. In one of the ironies of history, during most of the war insurgents applied to the royalists such terms as *esclavos* and *tiranos*, which had been introduced into the political discourse of New Spain to stiffen the resolve of the king's subjects and extract funds for use against Napoleon.[81]

Considered in the above context, the idea that the gachupines and their government in Mexico City were secret allies of Napoleon and traitors to the king was not at all absurd or naïve. Nor was this a strange peasant millenarian belief: it was a cornerstone of the discourse elaborated by the leaders of the insurgency.[82] Its importance continued even after the viceregal government recognized the Spanish Cortes and outweighed, in Morelos's mind at least, loyalty to the Crown. At his trial Morelos insisted that he thought Fernando VII would never return to Spain and that even if he did, Morelos would not have obeyed him if he returned "*napoleónico.*"[83] The anti-French hysteria encouraged by official propaganda before the revolt was transformed into anti-gachupín sentiment very quickly. Even the measures taken were the same: in August 1808 local officials in Tixtla embargoed the goods of a Frenchman; by 1811 the wealth being confiscated belonged to the European Spanish.[84] The insurgents in fact identified very closely with the resistance to the French on the Peninsula and assumed that these good or loyal Spaniards would recognize the insurgency or at least fulfill many of its goals.[85]

Two other aspects of the idea that gachupines were afrancesado are important. First, as noted above, much of the anti-French discourse in New Spain before 1808 stressed French atheism, heresy, and impiety. Insurgent propaganda also emphasized these characteristics when portraying the gachupines. The image of the Spanish heretic jibed with the notion that the insurgency was a holy war in defense of religion and clerical privilege, a justification used with frequency.[86] The idea that the europeos were heretics and the king had ordered their death had also surfaced in the earlier Tupac Amaru rebellion in the Andes.[87] Furthermore, at least occasionally the gachupines were identified as Jewish,[88] an association interesting because of two possible connotations. The first was the notion of the alien trying to blend into society contained in the history of the Spanish preoccupation with the *conversos*, Spanish Catholics who converted from Judaism under royal pressure. The second is the symbol of the greedy and usurious Jew prevalent in European anti-Semitism.[89] This image of greed resonated with the other connotations of the word "gachupín."

European Spanish merchants, often working with European Spanish officials, were able to corner the market as buyers and sellers of certain commodities in late colonial Guerrero. They did this by advancing goods against the production of cotton, textiles, and maize. The vast majority of the merchants and local colonial officials involved in these practices were born in Spain, and these business tactics were important in determining attitudes toward the gachupines. This was particularly true on the coast, where mulatto sharecroppers produced cotton for markets in the interior of New Spain. Their welfare varied widely from year to year not so much because of agricultural problems as because of variations in the cotton market driven by the vicissitudes of the Napoleonic Wars.[90] When Great Britain was at war with Spain, British control of the sea prevented European textiles from reaching the colony and textiles produced there sold well, raising the price of cotton. When peace prevailed European textiles depressed the market for goods woven in New Spain and the sharecroppers saw their income decrease substantially. This fall in welfare took the concrete form of a Spanish merchant protected and aided by Spanish officials giving sharecroppers less for the fruits of their labor. This phenomenon also affected some Indian peasants who spun cotton, but its impact was less profound because they were not exclusively dependent on the textile trade. Spanish merchants had become the personification of market forces in Guerrero, especially on the coast. Thus it is not surprising that merchants were singled out for harsh treatment.[91] In Guerrero the Spanish were persecuted first and most thoroughly on the Costa Grande, where Spanish merchants most thoroughly controlled trade.

Criticizing the greed of Spanish merchants was a strand of the popular ideology of the insurgency, but it also formed part of the official discourse of the movement. In documents produced by insurgent leaders the European merchants were "monopolists" and only wanted to "fatten their purses, extracting the blood of the poor like leeches with their usurious monopolies and frauds."[92] Official insurgent policy called for imprisoning the European Spaniards and confiscating their goods in the name of the Nation. Imprisoned Spaniards were harassed by their jailers. Eventually the insurgents killed many Spaniards either to prevent their escape when royalist forces neared or in reprisal for the executions of insurgent prisoners.[93]

Although the goals of both leadership and masses of the movement coincided in the repression of the European Spanish, there was room for disagreement over exactly who could be defined as a gachupín. Confining popular ire to the Europeans and maintaining unity among the various castes and classes that composed his coalition constantly preoccupied Morelos. In the summer of 1811, for instance, two of Morelos's officers tried to take control of the movement on the coast, redefining the category "gachupín" to include all whites. Morelos quickly repressed their conspiracy. Interestingly enough, one of the two was Mariano Tabares, leader of the 1808 Acapulco conspiracy.[94] Nevertheless, Morelos seems to have been generally successful in preventing the arbitrary imprisonment or execution of Creoles who did not actively oppose the insurgency.

Anti-gachupín sentiment was tied to business practices characterized as usury and monopoly. Monopoly was criticized as an infringement of free trade, an argument used in the courts and in administrative dispositions from at least the mid-eighteenth century. The idea that usury was a sin was a tenet of Catholicism discussed, along with disapproval of defrauding the poor of their daily sustenance, in books Morelos read as a seminarian and a parish priest. The insurgents criticized Spaniards for both monopoly and usury and, not surprisingly, converted these beliefs into practical measures.[95] For instance, the confiscation of gachupín wealth made the debts owed to them property of the Nation. These debts were in turn forgiven, effectively relieving many peasants and other individuals of debts incurred for at least one year of agricultural or handicraft production. Village Indians were given official sanction to trade with whomever they preferred, another symbolic and practical blow to the repartimiento system. In some areas the insurgents explicitly abolished the repartimiento to secure the support of villagers; in others merchants' flight from the insurgents caused its de facto abolition. Later, after insurgent administration was more established, officials took further measures against "monopolists," including provision for each village's election of "a public attorney, to prevent all monopoly."[96]

The insurgent leaders also sought peasant support through more direct appeals. Conflicts over the control of village lands rented to outsiders were important in some parts of Guerrero, particularly the Tierra Caliente. An early decree of Morelos returned such lands to the villages and prohibited outsiders from renting them in the future. Aware that the colonial administration had borrowed large sums from village cajas de comunidad and cofradías in the name of the Crown without repayment, the insurgents were careful to offer interest when asking for loans, along with assurances that the loans would be repaid soon. More important, the management of such village resources underwent a de facto change: during the war, villages stopped depositing the money earned by cofradías and other communal institutions in government treasuries and submitting their accounts for approval. Later, some insurgent leaders tried to regain control over this potential source of revenue but the earlier system was not successfully reestablished.[97]

The insurgents abolished the tribute, which was particularly resented by the mulattos of the Costa Grande, and publicized the abolition to secure the loyalty of Indian villagers. The royalists likewise considered tribute an important issue for Indians, and an early response to the Hidalgo rebellion was a viceregal order ending tribute payments in New Spain. The Spanish Constitution of 1812 again abolished tribute, but Fernando VII reinstated it in 1815. Later the insurgents legislated a graduated head tax that taxed the poor, including Indians and mulattos, at about half the rate previously charged for tribute, but this tax may not have been actually implemented. After the insurgents abolished tribute, Indians became liable for the alcabala, but this excise tax was lowered from 8 to 4 percent.[98]

One of Morelos's first acts on arrival in coastal Guerrero in 1810 was to decree that "with the exception of the Europeans, all other inhabitants will not be called Indians, mulattos, or other castes, but instead all generally *americanos*" (his emphasis).[99] This measure was an obvious attempt to construct an alliance of all groups against the European Spanish. Moreover, Morelos was trying to recruit the mulatto sharecroppers of the coast, who resented the payment of tribute associated with their caste identification. Mulattos were the only group in New Spain that gained absolutely nothing from the caste system: they did not receive the guaranteed access to resources and legal protection enjoyed by Indians, yet they were expected to pay tribute as well as the alcabala, which Indians were not required to pay. Mulattos were thus most likely to favor the abolition of the caste system and applaud the related idea that all men should enjoy equal rights and obligations. The insurgents also abolished slavery. There were few slaves in New Spain but the abolition of slavery removed a further stigma from mulattos, the only group in the region that could be enslaved under colonial law.[100]

There is no evidence that peasant villages in Guerrero attempted to recover land from neighboring haciendas during the insurgency; nor were such attempts condoned by the insurgent leadership.[101] To my knowledge, there exists only one documented case in which the insurgent leadership was asked to resolve a land dispute between a village and a hacienda. Although this case did not take place in Guerrero, it illustrates the attitude of the leadership. In 1812 he village of Tlastitaca in Xanteleico tried to recover lands and water it had lost to two haciendas forty years before. Morelos wrote to the villagers that because "the actual circumstances of the War do not permit us to verify lands or waters, you should stay in the same state you are in, and petition when we are in Mexico, when we will take care of you in Justice."[102] Notably, although several haciendas were confiscated from Spaniards, these were not distributed among peasants or others but instead were cultivated to provide revenue for the movement.[103]

The ideology of the insurgency evolved substantially over time. The "legitimist" orientation of 1810–11 had become by 1813–14 a drive for an independent Mexico governed by a republican constitution. The transition was rapid but not without roots in colonial political culture: in the eighteenth century the Enlightenment and the reinvigorated Bourbon monarchy had begun to change the political culture of New Spain. Competition with other European powers had led the Bourbons to enthusiastically embrace the new intellectual trends sweeping Europe while simultaneously striving to control innovations that might limit royal power. The monarchy proved to be the most active and important promoter of the Enlightenment and a new official orthodoxy soon coexisted uneasily with its Hapsburg predecessors.

These changes affected New Spain's political culture in three ways. First, the Crown itself weakened some of the corporate bodies and estates that formed the Old Regime by reducing their privileges and autonomy.[104] Second, the new ideas introduced a new role for the monarch as a promoter of public well-being rather than a relatively simple upholder of natural law.[105] Third, the monarchy's enthusiasm for economic development led it to support new forums for the exchange and production of information, including newspapers and organizations where educated individuals could meet to discuss the issues of the day. According to François Furet, similar developments in France led directly to the growth of what he calls a "new political sociability" in which individuals met outside their previous roles in traditional corporations to develop and express consensual opinions.[106]

However, the impact of these changes should not be exaggerated. In New Spain the strength of the new political sociability or public sphere was limited by the relatively small size of the social strata that was able to participate. The new Bourbon Enlightenment ethic did not replace its predecessors but instead joined them in a system that allowed multiple and contradictory discourses to coexist. Thus, although Hidalgo and Morelos had some previous familiarity with Enlightenment political thought, they did not rely on this repertoire in 1810. Hidalgo was not even accused of owning or using such forbidden works when he was tried by the Inquisition after his capture.[107]

As was mentioned earlier, in its first years the insurgent leadership generally justified its actions in the name of the king. The leaders defined their movement in opposition to the Napoleonic invaders of Spain and the gachupín government of New Spain that was planning to betray the king and turn New Spain over to Napoleon. The leadership justified its right to govern New Spain in the King's name using an amalgam of pre-absolutist political doctrine under which God conferred sovereignty on the king through the "people" and common notions of the right of the aggrieved to oppose "bad government" while continuing to recognize the authority of the king. The insurgents identified with the peninsular resistance to Napoleon and expected the juntas and later the Cortes to recognize them as the true patriots of New Spain.

This legitimist orientation was gradually transformed between 1810 and 1814. Two elements acted in succession to drive this transformation: the first was the increasing sense that Fernando VII himself had betrayed Spain, becoming "Napoleonic"; the second was the refusal of the Spanish Cortes to recognize the insurgency and the independence of New Spain under the sovereign. Obviously neither the king nor the Spanish patriots could be relied on, and "America" would have to go it alone. By the 1814 writing of the Constitution of Apatzingán the insurgents had embraced the basic tenets of liberal nationalism and popular sovereignty so conspicuous in their absence from the Grito de Dolores.[108]

By 1814 insurgent views of the constitution of the polity were substantially different from those prevalent in 1810. The Kingdom became the Nation, the subject became the citizen. A new repertoire had been embraced, most elements of which had been introduced under the direction of the Cown itself in the late eighteenth century. Other elements became prominent in royal appeals for funds to support the Crown in the years immediately prior to the insurgency. These appeals, usually addressed through parish priests and local officials, often stressed patriotic themes, using words like nación and patria, and emphasized how vital the contributions of all subjects were to the defense of the king and his kingdom.[109] The influence of the rapidly evolving situation in Spain on the insurgent leadership was crucial; the Cortes's own transition from legitimation on the basis of pre-absolutist doctrine to liberalism and constitutionalism pulled the leadership of the insurgency in the same direction. Newspapers brought Spanish news and political discussions to the insurgents.[110]

The efforts first of Bourbon monarchs and then of the liberal Cortes to forge a Spanish nation provided the repertoire the insurgents drew on in forging their own. Both the liberal Cortes and the insurgent leadership justified their entrance onto the historical stage by invoking seventeenth-century theologians but then rapidly embraced new idols. Nevertheless, what occurred in both Mexico and Spain was less a sudden change in hegemonic political ideas than a melding of "modern Enlightenment principles with the Spanish political and legal tradition."[111] It was thus not unthinkable for the insurgents to accept a constitutional monarchy in 1821. The actual functioning both of the insurgent Constitution of Apatzingán and the Spanish Constitution of 1812 in New Spain clearly demonstrates the syncretic nature of political culture in the early nineteenth century.

The Insurgent State

Until 1815 the insurgents controlled most of what is now the state of Guerrero. There they set up an organized, functioning government; in this way Guerrero's experience with the insurgency differed from the relatively short-lived reign of the Hidalgo movement in the Bajío and the Guadalajara region as well as the effective military control insurgent guerrillas enjoyed at various times in other areas of the viceroyalty. Moreover, the insurgent government produced large numbers of documents, some of which were confiscated by royalist forces and survive in the Archivo General de la Nación in Mexico City, affording a more complete view of insurgent government organization than that offered by propaganda and constitutions. Although the demands of the war itself obviously modified insurgent practice, these documents provide key information on the state and society the insurgents sought to construct. In Guerrero the rebels were consciously *constructing*, and not just destroying, as is shown by the extensive use of such phrases as "our new system" and "our national system."[112]

Village-based organization was the one constant of the insurgent state during the war. Though organizational structures over the villages varied from complex administrative and fiscal bureaucracies appointed and overseen by congresses to more minimalist military command systems, the insurgents relied on the village as the basic cell of their government for many of the same reasons the colonial state did, and kept in place many of the colonial regulations governing village elections. First, collecting resources to support higher government and the army would have been impossible without making individuals acquainted with local society responsible for quotas. Also, village governments enjoyed a legitimacy that more innovative arrangements would have lacked.[113] Unlike Hidalgo, Morelos organized a relatively traditional army, but he also provided for a militia system based on the villages that became ever more important as the insurgents were increasingly forced to adopt guerrilla tactics.

In other ways the insurgent system did not imitate its predecessor. The 1814 Constitution of Apatzingán called for the indirect election of both a congress and a three-person executive but did not discuss the election of officials of lower rank. Although the constitution in theory called for universal male suffrage, there was considerable variation in the actual elections for this and other congresses.[114] In practice, Indians and other local residents elected local officials and replaced functionaries who they felt had abused their offices,[115] thus facilitating the practical desire of insurgent leaders to ensure maximum support for their movement through the consensual choice of officials.

Much insurgent correspondence suggests that first Morelos and later the Congress took over many of the functions carried out in the colonial period by the viceroy and the Audiencia. Disputes that were not resolved at the local level were sent further up the chain of authority. This procedure was not spelled out in early rebel decrees and may have begun simply because it was the most logical thing for aggrieved parties to do. However, later both Morelos and Congress explicitly upheld the right to appeal decisions taken by insurgent officials.[116] The disputes documented varied considerably, including, for instance, several disputes between villages over resources, factional disputes within villages, and disagreements between priests and their parishioners over parochial fees or the control of cofradías.[117] Some cases were carried over from the late colonial period, and arguments were generally similar to those used in colonial days, but claimants' loyalty or disloyalty to the movement became a further issue. Groups sometimes complained of the excesses of insurgent military commanders in collecting rations and money for the war.[118]

Both on paper and in practice, the rudimentary state constructed by the insurgents resembled the viceregal government it sought to replace, but with important differences. The insurgents' need for the active support of the populace in the areas they controlled, combined with the loss of legitimacy that the Crown had suffered before 1808, eventually forced the insurgents to adopt a representative form of government justified by the sovereignty of "the people." Besides the practical power conceded by the insurgent government, localities were also organized for defense, and if power truly grows out of the barrel of a gun, it was shared widely. At times the insurgent drive for an armed populace went to ridiculous extremes: when Viceroy Felix Calleja published a counterinsurgency plan that restricted the carrying of arms in New Spain, Morelos countered with a "Contra Plan de Calleja" that *required* all males over the age of twelve to carry arms.[119]

The Guerrilla War

Between 1810 and 1814 the insurgents sought to destroy the government of New Spain by forming large armies, steadily conquering the viceroyalty, and setting up civil administrations in the territories they came to control. In areas left without large troop formations the insurgents relied on guerrilla militias to frustrate royalist counteroffensives. This strategy almost worked, but the royalist army continually prevailed in large-scale battles because of its advantage in training and armament. The failure of the insurgent approach became definitive when Morelos's last large army was defeated near Valladolid in December 1813. From that moment, Morelos concentrated on defending previously gained territory, reinforcing the guerrilla system, and protecting the Congress that headed his civilian government.[120] Morelos was performing this last task when he was captured in November 1815.

Once the strategy based on large armies had failed, the ground rules of the contest changed. From 1814 to 1820 the insurgents' ability to organize local support for their cause vied with the royalists' efforts to pacify areas. As Christon Archer points out, the war was not over. From 1814 to 1820 bands of insurgents exercised effective political control over large areas of New Spain, disrupting commerce, preventing the collection of revenue, and winning many relatively small military actions. Although arguably the insurgents no longer had much hope of a military and political victory, they were not losing, especially in the area covered by this study, where Vicente Guerrero and other leaders were able to consistently revitalize their support despite unfavorable military odds.[121]

The insurgents' strength in the South ebbed and flowed. In 1814 the royalists advanced on three regions that had been under insurgent control since 1811 and in all three met fierce guerrilla resistance. In the Tierra Caliente and Tlapa this resistance was organized around village governments whereas on the Costa Grande it was led by the hacendado Hermengildo Galeana until his death that June.[122] The defeat of Morelos's armies outside the South had little impact on local support for the movement: from 1814 to 1817, the insurgents under Vicente Guerrero controlled the Tlapa area and guerrillas held out in large numbers both on the Costa Grande and in the Tierra Caliente. After his military defeat in Tlapa, Guerrero simply shifted his efforts to the other two areas and rapidly regained strength.

Insurgent strength in Tlapa was concentrated in the villages. There were no haciendas in Tlapa, and the villages controlled almost all of the land. Guerrero received broad support, and only eight to ten families of the market town of Tlapa itself consistently aided the royalists. In October 1815 the local royalist commander Juan Mota recommended abandoning the whole area. In November 1815 his superior, José Gabriel de

Armijo, reported that over 100 villages in the area were actively aiding the insurgents. However, by May 1817 the royalists' ability to bring large detachments to bear on rebel strong points and carry out severe repression had taken its toll. After losing several pitched battles Vicente Guerrero left Tlapa.[123]

On the Costa Grande west of Acapulco, the mulatto sharecroppers had joined Morelos in large numbers early in the movement and the insurgents governed there until royalist detachments began to operate in the area in 1814. Royalist counterinsurgency measures initially seemed to be effective and quickly led to the death of Hermengildo Galeana in 1814. But the inhabitants of the coast continued to resist because, according to royalist commanders, they wished to continue "the independent and abandoned life that the flags of the insurrection provided them."[124] Continuing under Isidro Montes de Oca and Juan Alvarez against superior royalist forces, the insurgency there reached a low point in mid-1817, then rebounded quickly, so that by April 1819 even the royalists admitted that the rebels could concentrate groups of 400 to 500 men for attacks. Insurgent forces diminished again later that year, then began to recover strength in 1820.[125]

Guerrillas also resisted the royalists in the Tierra Caliente. Royalist commanders repeatedly complained of the peasants' willingness to provide the rebels with information and food while refusing to give intelligence to the counterinsurgency forces.[126] However, the preponderance of resources enjoyed by the government again took its toll and by June 1818 many rebels had accepted royalist pardons.[127] Soon thereafter Vicente Guerrero resumed ambushing patrols, and by the autumn of 1818 insurgents had overrun the area. Guerrero began issuing his own pardons to individuals who had accepted those of the government. This revival raged unchecked until the royalists inflicted some military reverses on Guerrero's troops in late 1819, but in 1820 the insurgents began yet another resurgence.[128]

Royalist Tactics

José Gabriel de Armijo, commander of the royalist military in the South during the guerrilla war, fully understood that the real issue was control of the population.[129] The guerrillas sought to bring their forces in concentrated numbers against small detachments of royalist troops and to avoid larger ones, only actually fighting when victory was certain. They relied heavily on the rural population to conceal their movements and provide information and food. The royalists responded with tactics designed to cut off the insurgents from the rural population in various ways.[130]

The royalists relied heavily on the timeworn strategy of making a few individuals responsible for the conduct of larger groups.[131] Royalist troops executed the governors of Indian villages that provided food to the rebels or failed to report insurgent troop movements. This method was of such obvious utility to royalist commanders that at least one settlement that did not have a village government before the war was given one.[132] Royalists also copied the colonial practice of making villages collectively responsible for the actions of their members by threatening that villages that aided the insurgents would be *diezmados* (tithed). Every tenth villager, apparently selected randomly, was killed.[133]

The royalists also organized village defense forces called "patriot companies." This tactic was another way of making villages collectively responsible for their attitudes toward the insurgency. Previously, villages could justify giving rebel bands whatever they wanted by claiming that armed insurgents had coerced them. Once the village's men had been organized into groups and given arms, no matter how useless, they were faced with a choice between resisting the insurgents and being shot for cowardice upon the arrival of royalist regulars.[134] This policy varied in effectiveness. At its best it provided the royalists with enthusiastic and knowledgeable local auxiliaries; at its worst the inhabitants pressed into service simply deserted at the earliest opportunity.[135]

Royalist officers often issued pardons to former insurgents. This practice became so ubiquitous that the numbers of rural people who accepted pardons came into use as an indicator of the effectiveness of royalist policies and officers, and long lists of pardoned individuals were sent to Mexico City.[136] However, like the body counts military officers have used to demonstrate their prowess in other times and places, pardon lists were often misleading. Individuals and villages that accepted pardons often were just waiting for more favorable conditions before resuming the struggle. As noted above, the insurgents sometimes offered their own pardons to those who had accepted royalist offers.[137]

Royalist officers worked to concentrate the rural population in the centers of villages, where it was easier to control and isolate from the guerrillas. This policy was difficult because pueblos were not the nucleated settlements prescribed by colonial law and often agricultural lands were far-flung and inaccessible. The montes, or areas beyond the boundaries of village and hacienda settlements, had always been areas outside of the practical and symbolic supervision of colonial officials. Whole villages literally deserted from colonial society when royalist troops arrived. Convincing such a village to return and accept royal authority was considered an important accomplishment.[138] Other royalist measures required that people taking up residence in a village report to the royal judge; in areas that were particularly isolated and supportive of the rebels this policy was enforced to the extent of moving whole villages and destroying all crops.[139]

After the army had reestablished military control over a particular area, or had claimed to do so, the next challenge was to reestablish colonial administration. This task proved difficult, as the insurgents had often destroyed archives, making the collection of alcabalas and tribute almost impossible. Furthermore, the destruction and insecurity of the war diminished economic activity to the point where the taxes and lawsuits that officials relied on for their salaries were not sufficient. The hostility of the residents was sometimes aroused by attempts to collect back taxes for the years they lived under insurgent government. These problems were compounded by the extra burden placed on the population by militia service and extra levies to supply royalist garrisons.[140]

The problems of defeating tenacious guerrilla resistance and then reestablishing civil authority were simply insurmountable in Guerrero. As Armijo understood, every time he was forced to reduce troop strength in an area the insurgency reappeared. It was clear to him that he was facing a mobile and resilient enemy that had the sympathies of the bulk of the population.[141] The colonial government would never regain the legitimacy that had allowed it to rule New Spain with minimal force for hundreds of years.

The Plan of Iguala and Mexican Independence

One of the most durable misconceptions in Mexican history is that of "conservative independence." According to this formula, the insurgents were defeated and both the Plan of Iguala and Mexico's subsequent independence stemmed from a conservative reaction to the reinstatement of the liberal Constitution of 1812 in Spain: Mexico's dominant class chose independence to preserve the traditional power structure of the viceroyalty from pressures for reform originating in Spain.[142] This interpretation is based on a series of assertions, the first being that the insurgents had been virtually eliminated from the political scene by 1820,[143] the second that the settlement reached in 1821 abrogated the Constitution of 1812 recently reimplemented in New Spain,[144] and the third that the insurgents were forced by their own weakness to accept independence "under principles very different from their own."[145] The "conservative independence" thesis was first advanced by Lucás Alamán in the mid-nineteenth century and has remained attractive to twentieth-century historians.[146] These historians have correctly identified the Plan of Iguala as an important moment in the political life of the new nation but have erred in most of their specific reasons for doing so and have consequently undermined their overall interpretation. This section will examine each of their three assertions in the light of the evidence available.

New Spain had not been pacified as of 1820. Furthermore, it could never have returned to the degree of consensus that had maintained the colonial system with very little recourse to force before 1808. The crisis that had touched off the war was unresolved, and this crisis, combined with the effects of the war itself, had irrevocably damaged the legitimacy of the colonial system. In the words of Jaime Rodríguez, by 1820 "New Spaniards obeyed the government principally because it possessed the monopoly of force."[147] For instance, royalist commanders in Guerrero understood that even where insurgent support was relatively weak any reduction in royalist troop strength could lead to an outbreak of violence.[148] Moreover, from the point of view of New Spain's dominant class the situation was exceedingly fragile because the provincial Creole military officers who actually exercised the monopoly of force did not differ greatly in social origins and political attitudes from those whom the colonial dominant class had thwarted in 1808.[149]

The idea that the insurgents had been defeated by 1820 was an optimistic assessment that not even royalist commanders believed. The rebels were again recovering strength in Guerrero and could not be eliminated without a massive commitment of troops that rebel activity elsewhere in New Spain would not permit. Furthermore, as has been noted, insurgents who had accepted pardons often returned to the struggle when circumstances became more favorable. Although Brian Hamnett's estimate that in the autumn of 1820 the rebels could muster only about 900 men in the South is a reasonable one, it hardly indicates that the war was over.[150] Modern counterinsurgency doctrine, in an age in which technology allows regular forces to move hundreds of miles per day and restricts guerrillas to the same 20 or 30 they could make in 1820, suggests that even a stalemate against 900 guerrillas would require about 9,000 troops. The royalist army, which could move no faster than the guerrillas themselves, never was able to commit more than 4,000 men to the South after 1814. In other words, despite royalist propaganda, there was no end in sight in 1820. Royalist commanders knew this and insisted that they needed more troops to have a chance of defeating the insurgents.[151]

The problems of Mexico's dominant class were compounded when Spanish liberals forced Fernando VII to republish the Constitution of 1812.[152] It seems doubtful that the dominant class feared reform from Spain. In the preceding 50 years, the Mexican dominant class had succeeded in blunting or turning to its advantage most Bourbon reform efforts.[153] In 1820, however, the liberal constitution, with its implied radical reordering of Mexican society, already had several potential political bases in Mexico. These included the insurgents, the royalist military officers mentioned above, and a diverse array of provincial Creole and mestizo rancheros, hacendados, merchants, minor officials, muleteers, and Indian townspeople. Some had overtly or covertly supported the insurgency at various moments and others had not, but many found the Spanish constitution attractive.

The viceregal government's impotence against the insurgency put the insurgents and the royalist military in touch immediately. Royalist commanders approached the insurgents throughout the viceroyalty to suggest that the revived Constitution of 1812 offered the insurgents everything they sought. Both José Gabriel de Armijo and Carlos Moya wrote Vicente Guerrero to convince him that the constitution's representative system of government and abolition of caste distinctions would end the domination of New Spain by the European Spanish. Other rebels received similar offers. The royalists supplemented these private overtures with proclamations aimed at rank-and-file insurgents.[154] Pamphlets published in Mexico City under the new press freedom also stressed this theme. Other pamphlets, aimed at royalists, emphasized the need to negotiate with the insurgents.[155]

The newly operative constitution had other supporters in Guerrero. One of its most revolutionary provisions allowed locations with more than 1,000 inhabitants to become municipalities, electing officials with political autonomy to counterbalance officials appointed from above. Many such municipalities were erected in New Spain in 1820 and 1821.[156] Between July 1820 and January 1821 no less than 71 municipalities were set up in Guerrero, including many organized around Indian villages.[157] Both municipalities and the constitution's abolition of caste distinctions and tribute were popular. Furthermore, as Christon Archer points out, the first acts of many municipalities ended extraordinary war taxes and disbanded the militias that towns were required to support.[158] Meanwhile, Mexico City pamphleteers tried to sell New Spain's poor on the benefits of the constitution; distrusting the colonial dominant class, these writers suggested that a new revolution might be needed to preserve the new freedoms.[159]

José Gabriel de Armijo resigned as commander of royalist forces in the South in November 1820, claiming that his poor health prevented him from effectively dealing with the latest insurgent offensive. Agustín de Iturbide replaced him. Iturbide had a relatively simple plan: he sought to quickly defeat the rebels and then unilaterally declare Mexico's independence from Spain, offering the Bourbon family a chance to continue their dynasty in the New World. This "Brazilian solution" to the problem faced by Mexico's dominant class would secure continued political legitimacy *and* guarantee proprietorship of the Mexican state. The problem with this plan was that the insurgents refused to fade away[160] but instead continued their recent successes, defeating Iturbide's forces repeatedly and convincing him that he could not end the war quickly.[161] Iturbide was forced to enter into negotiations with Guerrero.

The insurgents had not accepted pardons under the Spanish constitution for three reasons. First, accepting pardons would have constituted an admission that their cause was illegitimate. Second, the insurgents were not confident that future political events in Spain would not at some date undo what the Spanish liberals had accomplished. Third, the constitution denied the rights of citizenship to mulattos.[162] All these issues were discussed when Iturbide and Guerrero began negotiating via written correspondence in December 1820. Iturbide first suggested that Guerrero accept a pardon, in exchange for which Iturbide would allow Guerrero to continue in command of his troops and the Mexican representatives to the new Spanish Cortes would propose that the constitution be amended to provide citizenship for mulattos. Iturbide further suggested that Fernando VII or another member of the Bourbon family might be persuaded to transfer his throne to Mexico. Iturbide ended this letter by remarking that he was not worried by the battles he had just lost because the government would send as many troops as he needed to defeat the insurgents.[163] Guerrero responded that if the Spanish liberals did not accept the Mexican deputies' proposals in 1812 at the height of the war with France they were not likely to when they faced no such threat. He reiterated his rejection of racial limitations on citizenship but offered to put his forces under Iturbide's command if Iturbide accepted the principle of independence.[164] Thus Guerrero's position was laid out: independence under the Spanish constitution with the condition that citizenship be extended to all men. Iturbide accepted this model and it became the basis for the Plan of Iguala. Notably, Guerrero had proposed essentially the same compromise to another royalist officer in August 1820, soon after the constitution was promulgated in New Spain.[165]

The Plan of Iguala did not bring a "conservative independence" in reaction to the liberal Spanish constitution; it specifically left that constitution in effect in New Spain, but it varied from the constitution in preserving the clerical legal privileges and extending to all suffrage and eligibility for public office.[166] The settlement also offered the insurgents other important concessions: it reaffirmed the legitimacy of their cause and their ability to participate in the politics of the new Mexico, and it effectively ceded to them control of the areas in which they were strongest. The man who succeeded Iturbide as military commandant of the South was none other than Vicente Guerrero.

Between March and September 1821 resistance to Iturbide and Guerrero collapsed. Guerrero's adherence quickly assured that of other insurgents. Relatively little fighting took place as both leaders concentrated on convincing the officers of the former royalist army to embrace their proposal.[167] José Gabriel de Armijo was sent back to the South to contain the rapidly spreading movement but soon despaired, informing his superior that the entire region was lost because the troops and militias there would not oppose the new alliance. Former insurgents who had previously accepted pardons also joined the movement. The collapse was swift and sudden, but it left many issues unresolved.[168]

The study of the social movement that mobilized large numbers of rural Mexicans between 1810 and 1821 has been impeded by its characterization as an "independence" movement. The idea that it resulted in independence with relatively few social changes has obscured the initial motivations of both poor and relatively wealthy participants. The insurgency and its program must be viewed in the context of the political culture of colonial New Spain. The initial justifications of both peasants and nonpeasants were conservative and legitimist in nature, and although the program later became more republican it continued to reconcile this "progressivism" with its preoccupation with ancient rights. Significantly, both peasants and the rural priests, landowners, and muleteers who led the movement subscribed to this relatively cohesive set of ideas, sharing enough common assumptions about politics, legitimacy, and justice to fashion a discourse based on reconciling their interests in conscious contradiction to the group they considered their common enemy, the European Spanish who made up the colonial dominant class centered in Mexico City. Socially the movement in Guerrero sought to end the abuses of state power endemic to the colonial system by making local officials accountable to the populace.

The timing of the insurgency in New Spain is critical to understanding its nature. Guerrero did not experience the agrarian changes that primed the Bajío and the Guadalajara region for revolt. The Bourbon reforms placed more fiscal pressure on various social groups in rural Guerrero and reduced the autonomy of peasant villages, but these changes do not seem sufficient to explain the cataclysmic collapse of order that took place. Moreover, the insurgency was not triggered by the breakdown of the state's repressive capacity, a factor so crucial to Theda Skocpol's theory of revolutions. New Spain's government had never relied heavily on force to preserve order.[169] The proximate cause of the explosion was instead the colonial government's loss of legitimacy due to the confused events in Spain and the attendant split in New Spain's upper classes. The trigger was more a legitimacy vacuum than a power vacuum, and it was this legitimacy vacuum that allowed the articulation of the cross-class alliances that turned New Spain into a battlefield. Nothing inherent in Mexico's class structure made the explosion inevitable. As Steven Topik suggested recently, Mexican independence might have been more like Brazil's truly conservative independence if the Spanish royal family had joined their Portuguese peers in fleeing to the New World.[170]

The poor rural people who fought and bore the brunt of the war were not motivated by the agrarian demands so often attributed to Mexican peasants. A review of the areas that supported the insurgents most constantly and thoroughly clearly suggests that Indian peasants were more likely to participate in areas where village communities dominated both demographically and in resource ownership. In these areas villages controlled almost all the land and other resources. As a consequence non-Indians who wished to prosper economically had to do so by manipulating resources that the peasants claimed as their own, including village lands rented to outsiders as well as cattle and money held by cofradías and cajas de comunidad. Mulatto peasants who sharecropped on coastal lands also were stalwart insurgents, but significantly they did not revolt against the owners of the land but instead targeted the merchants who connected them to the wider economy.

The independence war clearly defied the dichotomies between national and local, elite and poor, and modern and traditional that permeate much social scientific research on rural resistance and state formation. The 1808 political crisis was viceregal or "national" in scope but it provided the opportunity for diverse groups to express local grievances. The crisis first split Mexico's elite but that division encouraged impoverished people to press claims outside the courts. Both elites and the poor first justified their actions through calls for a restoration of traditional justice, but the backward-looking movement forced major changes in Mexican politics. Nationalism in Guerrero, as elsewhere, may have been a "modern" ideology but its force originated in a vision of the past. Moreover, the political vision of the rebels changed dramatically during the decade of fighting, as shown by the leadership's embrace of republican representative government. Although evidence of changing popular attitudes is more difficult to find it is noteworthy that by 1821 Guerrero stressed the need to extend citizenship rights to his mulatto followers.

The New Spain that became Mexico in 1821 was profoundly different from that which existed in 1808, particularly in rural areas. Politics in the countryside changed forever with the collapse of the legitimacy that had channeled most conflict into the colonial courts. From then on village peasants most commonly sought social and political goals through alliances with other villages and nonpeasants. The insurgent coalition was the first of these movements, and it suggests several necessary aspects of such phenomena: the need for a common set of enemies; the need for congruent if not common goals, at least locally; and finally the need for a program capable of uniting it and articulating the desires of its members in a way understandable to all. Such a program only became possible in 1808, but the collapse of colonial assumptions about politics, justice, and legitimacy made such programs easier to fashion in subsequent years. Movements of many peasant villages in alliance with other actors became the most important tools with which Mexico's peasantry exerted pressure on the shape of the state in the nineteenth and early twentieth centuries.

Notes

1. This is defined here to include practically anyone not an Indian peasant. Included are rural priests, *rancheros*, muleteers, small merchants, *hacendados*, military leaders, and a wide variety of other rural people.

2. Christon Archer, "Banditry and Revolution in New Spain, 1790–1821," *Bibliotheca Americana* 1 (1982), pp. 61, 68, 71; Brian Hamnett, "The Economic and Social Dimension of the Revolution of Independence in Mexico, 1800–1824," *Ibero-Amerikanisches Archiv* 6 (1980), pp. 13–14; Brian Hamnett, *Roots of Insurgency: Mexican Regions, 1750–1824* (New York: Cambridge University Press, 1986), pp. 74–75; John Tutino, *From Insurrection to Revolution in Mexico: Social Bases of Agrarian Violence, 1750–1940* (Princeton: Princeton University Press, 1986), pp. 42–46; Eric Van Young, "The Age of Paradox: Mexican Agriculture at the End of the Colonial Period, 1750–1810," in Nils Jacobsen and Hans Jurgen Puhle, eds. *The Economies of Mexico and Peru during the Late Colonial Period* (Berlin: Bibliotheca Ibero-Americana, 1986), p. 64; Eric Van Young, "Islands in the Storm: Quiet Cities and Violent Countrysides in the Mexican Independence Era," *Past and Present* 118 (1988), pp. 131, 135; Eric Van Young, "Moving Towards Revolt: Agrarian Origins of the Hidalgo Rebellion in the Guadalajara Region," in Friedrich Katz, ed. *Riot, Rebellion and Revolt: Rural Social Conflict in Mexico* (Princeton: Princeton University Press, 1988), pp. 181, 185; Eric Van Young, "Quetzalcóatl, King Ferdinand, and Ignacio Allende Go to the Seashore; or Messianism and Mystical Kingship in Mexico, 1800–1821," in Jaime E. Rodríguez O., ed. *The Independence of Mexico and the Origins of the New Nation* (Los Angeles: University of California at Los Angeles Latin American Center, 1989), especially 11. See Archer's review of the literature, "¡Viva Nuestra Señora de Guadalupe! Recent Interpretations of Mexico's Independence Period," *Mexican Studies/Estudios Mexicanos,* 7 (1991):143–165.

3. William Taylor, "Banditry and Insurrection: Rural Unrest in Central Jalisco, 1790–1816," in Katz, ed. *Riot, Rebellion and Revolt*, pp. 234, 236; For economic demands see Friedrich Katz, "Introduction: Rural Revolts in Mexico," Katz, ed. *Riot, Rebellion and Revolt*, pp. 7–8; Scarlett O'Phelan Godoy, *Un siglo de rebeliones anti-coloniales: Peru y Bolivia, 1700–1783* (Cusco: Centro de las Casas, 1988), pp. 175–222, 273–287; John Lynch, *The Spanish-American Revolutions, 1808–1826* (New York: Norton and Co., 1973), pp. 11–12; Carlos Marichal, "Las guerras imperiales y los préstamos novohispanos, 1781–1804," *Historia Mexicana* 39 (1990):881–907; Josefa Vega, "Los primeros préstamos de la Guerra de Independencia, 1809–1812." *Historia Mexicana* 39 (1990):909–931. Nancy Farriss argues for a loss of peasant political autonomy and access to *cofradías* and *cajas de comunidad* in the Yucatan. See Farriss, *Maya Society under Colonial Rule: The Collective Enterprise of Survival* (Princeton: Princeton University Press, 1984), pp. 355–366. Marcello Carmagnani minimizes the impact of the Bourbon reforms on peasantry of Oaxaca. See Carmagnani, *El regreso de los dioses: La reconstitución de la identidad étnica en Oaxaca, siglos xvii y xviii* (Mexico: Fondo de Cultura Económica, 1988), p. 234. The effect of the Bourbon reforms on the prospects for Creoles was first suggested as a cause of the revolt by Alamán. See John Lynch, *The Spanish-American Revolutions, 1808–1826* (New York: Norton and Co., 1973), pp. 17–19. For the effect of the reforms on clerical privilege and possibly peasant religion see Nancy Farriss, *Crown and Clergy in Colonial Mexico, 1579–1821* (London: Athlone Press, 1968); David Brading, "Tridentine Catholicism and Enlightened Despotism in Bourbon Mexico," *Journal of Latin*

American Studies 15 (1983), pp. 7–13; William Taylor, "Between Global Process and Local Knowledge: An Inquiry into Early Latin American Social History, 1500–1900" in Oliver Zunz, ed. *Reliving the Past: The Worlds of Social History* (Chapel Hill: University of North Carolina Press, 1985), pp. 151–162; Taylor, "Banditry and Insurrection," pp. 234–235; Serge Gruzinski, "La 'segunda aculteracíon': el estado ilustrado y la religiosidad indígena de la Nueva España (1775–1800)," *Estudios de Historia Novohispana* 8 (1985):175–201.

4. Tutino, *From Insurrection*, pp. 41–126; Eric Wolf, "The Mexican Bajio in the Eighteenth Century." in *Synoptic Studies of Mexican Culture* (New Orleans: Tulane University, 1957), pp. 177–199; Enrique Florescano, *Orígen y desarrollo de los problemas agrarios de México* (Mexico: Era, 1976), p. 87; Eric Van Young, *Hacienda and Market in Eighteenth Century Mexico: The Rural Economy of the Guadalajara Region, 1675–1820* (Berkeley: University of California Press, 1981), pp. 224, 269; Van Young, "Moving Towards Revolt," pp. 189–195; Taylor, "Banditry"; Cheryl English Martin, "Haciendas and Villages in Late Colonial Morelos," *Hispanic American Historical Review* 62 (1982):407–427; Cheryl English Martin, *Rural Society in Colonial Morelos* (Albuquerque: University of New Mexico Press, 1985), pp. 99–113. The review of the literature on both the Bourbon reforms and agrarian changes presented above owes much to Michael Ducey, "Peasant Participation in Mexico's Independence: Some Thoughts on the Recent Literature" (Seminar Paper, University of Chicago, March 20, 1986).

5. Brian Hamnett, *Revolución y contrarevolución en México y el Peru (Liberalismo, realeza y separatismo 1800–1824)* (Mexico: Fondo de Cultura Económica, 1978), pp. 96–397; Hamnett, "The Economic and Social Dimension," p. 11; Tutino, *From Insurrection*, p. 140–145; Van Young, "Moving Towards Revolt," pp. 197–199; Taylor, "Banditry"; Rodolfo Pastor, *Campesinos y reformas: La Mixteca, 1700–1856* (Mexico: El Colegio de México, 1987), p. 498.

6. For a relatively recent case see Moises Santos Carrera and Jesus Alvarez Hernández, *Historia de la cuestión agraria mexicana, Estado de Guerrero: Épocas prehispanica y colonial* (Chilpancingo: Universidad Autónoma de Guerrero, 1988), pp. 168, 173.

7. For the document see Juan Hernández y Dávalos, *Colección de documentos para la historia de la Guerra de Independencia de México de 1808–1821* (Mexico: n.p., 1882), Vol. 1, pp. 879–880. For the debate surrounding it see Alfonso Teja Zambre, "Morelos, hombre de guerra y hombre de paz," *Historia Mexicana* 8 (1959), pp. 499–505; Wilbert Timmons, "José María Morelos—Agrarian Reformer?" *Hispanic American Historical Review* 45 (1965), pp. 183–195. See also Miguel Mejía Fernandez, *Política agraria en México en el siglo XIX* (Mexico: Siglo XXI, 1979), pp. 50–57.

8. Van Young, "Moving Towards Revolt," pp. 183–4, 197–199; Van Young, "Islands," p. 155; Van Young, "The Age," p. 83.

9. Archer, "¡Viva Nuestra Señora de Guadalupe!," p. 149.

10. William Taylor, *Drinking, Homicide and Rebellion in Colonial Mexican Villages* (Stanford: Stanford University Press, 1979), pp. 134–138.

11. Jaime Rodríguez, "From Royal Subject to Republican Citizen: The Role of the Autonomists in the Independence of Mexico," in Jaime E. Rodríguez O., ed. *The Independence of Mexico and the Origins of the New Nation* (Los Angeles: University of California at Los Angeles Latin American Center, 1989), p. 38.

12. Luís Villoro, *El proceso ideológico de la Revolución de Independencia* (Mexico: Universidad Nacional Autónoma de México, 1967), pp. 54–55.

13. Jacques Lafaye, *Quetzalcóatl and Guadalupe: The Formation of Mexican National Consciousness 1531–1813* (Chicago: University of Chicago Press, 1976), p. 118; Rodríguez, "From Royal Subject," p. 29.

14. For examples see Martin, *Rural Society,* pp. 190–192 and Reinhard Liehr, *Ayuntamiento y oligarquía en Puebla, 1787–1810* (Mexico: Secretaría de Educación Pública, 1976), Vol. 2, p. 143.

15. Archivo General de la Nación (Hereafter AGN), Historia, Vol. 46, exp. 32, fols. 476–477, exp. 33, fols. 488–500; AGN, Historia, Vol. 50, exp. 21, fols. 363–365; AGN, Historia, Vol. 432, exp. 3, fols. 41–81.

16. See Taylor, "Banditry," p. 219 for comparison with another region.

17. Archer, "Banditry," p. 80. For examples in Guerrero see AGN, Operaciones de Guerra, Vol. 76, fols. 140–142; AGN, Operaciones de Guerra, Vol. 79, fols. 122v, 156–157, 274–278v, 294–295; AGN, Operaciones de Guerra, Vol. 82, fols. 311–311v; AGN, Operaciones de Guerra, Vol. 86, fol. 212; AGN, Operaciones de Guerra, Vol. 201, fol. 192; AGN, Operaciones de Guerra, Vol. 466; AGN, Operaciones de Guerra, Vol. 976, exp. 37, fols. 124–125; Luís Castillo Ledon, *Morelos: Documentos inéditos y poco conocidos* (Mexico: Secretaría de Educación Pública, 1927), Vol. 3, p. 96.

18. AGN, Operaciones de Guerra, Vol. 201, fols. 179–180; AGN, Operaciones de Guerra, Vol. 466. For detailed accounts of the shifting allegiances of individuals see AGN, Operaciones de Guerra, Vol. 89, fols. 109–110v and AGN, Infidencias, Vol. 48, exp. 2, fol. 53.

19. Ignacio Altamirano, *Morelos en Zacatula* (Mexico: Imprenta de Vicente Agueros, 1910), p. 112; Rafael Aguirre Colorado, Ruben García and Pelagio A. Rodríguez, *Campañas de Morelos sobre Acapulco 1810–13* (Mexico: Comisión de Historia Militar, 1933), pp. 12–14; AGN, Infidencias, Vol. 5, exp. 2, fols. 59–61; Carlos Herrejón Peredo, ed. *Morelos: Documentos inéditos de vida revolucionaria* (Zamora: El Colegio de Michoacán, 1987), p. 100; Hernández y Dávalos, Vol. 5, p. 29.

20. AGN, Operaciones de Guerra, Vol. 829, exp. 4, fols. 54–57; exp. 5, fols. 60–61; Herrejón Peredo, *Morelos: Documentos,* pp. 91–95.

21. Aguirre Colorado, García, and Rodríguez, p. 102; Ignacio Altamirano, *Morelos en Tixtla* (Mexico: Imprenta de Vicente Agueros, 1910), pp. 203, 206; Ignacio Altamirano, *Morelos en el Veladero* (Mexico: Imprenta de Vicente Agueros, 1910), pp. 6–77; AGN, Historia, Vol. 104, exp. 33, fol. 143; AGN, Historia, Vol. 409, fols. 239–258v; AGN, Operaciones de Guerra, Vol. 9, fols. 96, 178v; Fernando Díaz y Díaz, *Caudillos y caciques: Antonio López de Santa Anna y Juan Alvarez* (Mexico: El Colegio de México, 1972), p. 100; Francisco Gomezjara, *Bonapartismo y lucha campesina en la Costa Grande de Guerrero* (Mexico: Ediciones Posada, 1979), p. 61; Hernández y Dávalos, Vol. 4, pp. 284–286.

22. AGN, Operaciones de Guerra, Vol. 71, exp. 32, fols. 229–229v; AGN, Operaciones de Guerra, Vol. 72, exp. 4, fol. 14v; Hernández y Dávalos, Vol. 5, p. 26.

23. For some early examples see AGN, Infidencias, Vol. 5, exp. 2, fol. 63; AGN, Infidencias, Vol. 55, exp. 24, fols. 227–227v.

24. Ubaldo Vargas Martínez, *Hermengildo Galeana* (Mexico: Secretaría de Educación Pública, 1964), p. 23; Aguirre Colorado, García and Rodríguez, p. 73; AGN, Infidencias, Vol. 131, exp. 3, fols. 12–13; exp. 34, fols. 185–186v; Hernández y Dávalos, Vol. 2, pp. 245–246; AGN, Operaciones de Guerra, Vol. 829, exp. 7, fols. 63–65; AGN, Intendencias, Vol. 73.

25. Altamirano, *Morelos en Tixtla,* p. 186; Altamirano, *Morelos en el Veladero,* pp. 171, 173; Aguirre Colorado, García and Rodríguez, pp. 32, 51; AGN, Inquisición, Vol. 1452, fols. 309–310v; Miguel Ortega, ed. *Colección de documentos y apuntes para la historia del Edo. de Guerrero* (Mexico: n.p., 1948), Vol. 17, pp. 75, 120.

26. AGN, Operaciones de Guerra, Vol. 829, exp. 7, fols. 63–65; Biblioteca Nacional (Hereafter BN), Fondo Alvarez, carpeta 1, documento 102; AGN,

Operaciones de Guerra, Vol. 829, exp. 32, fol. 155; AGN, Operaciones de Guerra, Vol. 917, exp. 4, fols. 13–14. This is a loose translation of *muy sobre sí.*

27. Aguirre Colorado, García and Rodríguez, pp. 81–82; AGN, Operaciones de Guerra, Vol. 976, exp. 1, fol. 7; BN, Fondo Alvarez, Carpeta 1, documentos 22, 100, 105; Carpeta 2, documentos 112, 114.

28. René Aviles, *Vicente Guerrero, el insurgente ciudadano* (Mexico: Sociedad Amigos del Libro Mexicano, 1957), pp. 13–14; Castillo Ledon, 3:91, 92; AGN, Operaciones de Guerra, Vol. 976, exp. 2, fol. 20; AGN, Infidencias, Vol. 24, exp. 9, fols. 228–230; AGN, Historia, Vol. 103, exp. 8, fol. 29, exp. 9, fols. 37–38, exp. 26, fols. 104–105, 110, exp. 27, fol. 109; AGN, Historia, Vol. 105, exp. 30, fols. 107, 109, exp. 41, fols. 146–147, exp. 70, fol. 251.

29. AGN, Historia, Vol. 105, exp. 21, fols. 84–85.

30. AGN, Archivo Histórico de Hacienda, Vol. 1982, exp. 4; Herrejón Peredo, *Morelos: Documentos,* pp. 156, 163–164; AGN, Operaciones de Guerra, Vol. 976, exp. 5, fol. 30v, exp. 15, fol. 70v.

31. AGN, Operaciones de Guerra, Vol. 70, exp. 15, fols. 46–46v; AGN, Operaciones de Guerra, Vol. 976, exp. 19, fols. 83–88, exp. 25, fols. 102–103.

32. AGN, Operaciones de Guerra, Vol. 70, exp. 22, fols. 68–71v, exp. 23, fols. 76–77; AGN, Operaciones de Guerra, Vol. 976, exp. 29, fols. 11–114.

33. Archer, "Banditry," p. 68; Luís Guevara Ramírez, *Síntesis histórica del Estado de Guerrero* (Mexico: Gráfica Cerventina, 1959), p. 40; Herminio Chavez Guerrero, *Vicente Guerrero: el consumador, biografía* (Mexico: Cultura y Ciencia Política, 1971), p. 26; Moises Ochoa Campos, *Breve historia del Estado de Guerrero* (Mexico: Porrúa, 1968), pp. 92–93; BN, Fondo Alvarez, Carpeta 2, documento 115; Aguirre Colorado, García and Rodríguez, p. 73; AGN, Operaciones de Guerra, Vol. 829, exp. 30, fol. 153; AGN, Operaciones de Guerra, Vol. 935, exp. 260, fol. 506; AGN, Historia, Vol. 103, exp. 25, fols. 100–101; AGN, Historia, Vol. 104, exp. 4, fols. 6–8, exp. 5, fols. 9–11; AGN, Infidencias, Vol. 131, exp. 3, fols. 12–13, 116–117, exp. 34, fols. 185–186v, exp. 47, fol. 246v; Herrejón Peredo, *Morelos: Documentos,* p. 187; Vargas Martínez, p. 39; AGN, Criminal, Vol. 174, exp. 12, fols. 403–407v.

34. This was also true in two villages to the south, Zumpango del Río and Chilpancingo. AGN, Operaciones de Guerra, Vol. 919, fols. 6, 48–54, 94, 103–106v, 116–116v, 160–161.

35. AGN, Infidencias, Vol. 131, exp. 19, fol. 80; AGN, Infidencias, Vol. 143, exp. 48; AGN, Criminal, Vol. 5, exp. 4, fols. 35–36; AGN, Infidencias, Vol. 143, exps. 101, 32; AGN, Operaciones de Guerra, Vol. 15, exp. 3, fols. 40–51; Hernández y Dávalos, Vol. 5, pp. 884–885; AGN, Operaciones de Guerra, Vol. 471.

36. Hernández y Dávalos, Vol. 5, pp. 878–879, 884–885, 887; AGN, Operaciones de Guerra, Vol. 15, exp. 3, fols. 40–51; AGN, Infidencias, Vol. 24, exp. 9, fol. 224; AGN, Infidencias, Vol. 131, exp. 19, fols. 82–83; AGN, Infidencias, Vol. 131, fols. 116–117; AGN, Infidencias, Vol. 143, exps. 32, 46, 49, 101. The reference to previous disobedience is from AGN, Operaciones de Guerra, Vol. 470.

37. AGN, Operaciones de Guerra, Vol. 70, exp. 39, fols. 49–50; AGN, Operaciones de Guerra, Vol. 976, exp. 1, fols. 1–6, exp. 2, fol. 15v, exp. 5, fol. 37v, exp. 37, fols. 124–125, exp. 38, fols. 126–129, exp. 42, fols. 140–144; AGN, Historia, Vol. 105, exp. 5, fols. 6–11, exp. 61, fols. 228–230; Hernández y Dávalos, Vol. 5, pp. 252–6; Javier Ocampo, *Las ideas de un día: El pueblo mexicano ante la consumación de su independencia* (Mexico: El Colegio de México, 1969), p. 52.

38. AGN, Tributos, Vol. 34, exp. 1, fols. 1–12, exp. 7, fols. 160–167.

39. AGN, Tributos, Vol. 54, exp. 14, fols. 194–199.

40. Unlike other *subdelegados* elsewhere, Paris rarely shows up in an unfavorable light in the documents about the area. For an example of a dispute which he arbitrated see AGN, Civil, Vol. 454, exp. 1, fol. 33v. Interestingly enough, in contrast to most assessments royal officals made of the loyalty of their jurisdictions, Paris placed far more confidence in his relatively poor mulattos than in the local *vecinos de razón.* See AGN, Historia, Vol. 105, exp. 5, fols. 6–11.

41. Archer, "Banditry," pp. 71–73; Hamnett, *Roots,* pp. 125–149.

42. Chavez Guerrero, *Vicente Guerrero,* p. 26; Ochoa Campos, *Breve historia,* pp. 92–93.

43. For Morelos see Wilbert Timmons, *Morelos: sacerdote, soldado, estadista* (Mexico: Fondo de Cultura Económica, 1983), pp. 14–24 and Carlos Herrejón Peredo, ed. *Morelos: Vida preinsurgente y lecturas* (Zamora: El Colegio de Michoacán, 1984), pp. 28–29, 38. For Guerrero see Aviles, pp. 9–10; Chavez Guerrero, *Vicente Guerrero,* 23–24, 30; Mario Salcedo Guerrero, "Vicente Guerrero's Struggle for Mexican Independence, 1810–1821" (Ph.D. Dissertation, University of California at Santa Barbara, 1977), pp. 8–9. For Carmen and Trujano see Enrique Cordero y T., *Historia comprendida del Estado de Puebla* (Puebla: Bohemia Poblana, 1965), p. 462; Moises Ochoa Campos, *Valerio Trujano.* (n.p: colección Letras Guerrerenses, 1972), pp. 6–9; Moises Ochoa Campos, *Juan del Carmen: El brazo derecho de Vicente Guerrero* (n.p: n.p., 1972), p. 9.

44. Archer, "Banditry," p. 66; Hamnett, *Roots,* p. 25.

45. Salcedo Guerrero, "Vicente Guerrero's Struggle," pp. 6, 12; Gerardo Sánchez, "Mulas, hatajos y arrieros en el Michoacán del siglo XIX," *Relaciones* 5 (1984), pp. 41–42, 45; Claude Morin, *Michoacán en la Nueva España del siglo xviii* (Mexico: Fondo de Cultura Económica, 1979), p. 160; AGN, Padrones, Vol. 18 and AGN, Padrones, Vol. 16, fols. 107–221.

46. Archer, "Banditry," p. 66; Stanley Green, *The Mexican Republic: The First Decade 1823–1832* (Pittsburgh: Pittsburgh University Press, 1987), pp. 163–164; Ernesto Lemoine, "Vicente Guerrero, úlima opción de la insurgencia," in *Memoria de la mesa redonda sobre Vicente Guerrero* (Mexico: Instituto Mora, 1982), p. 9; Ochoa Campos, *Valerio Trujano,* p. 6; Pastor, *Campesinos,* p. 321; William Sprague, *Vicente Guerrero, Mexican Liberator, A Study in Patriotism* (Chicago: Donnelley and Sons, 1939), pp. 1–2.

47. Gomezjara, pp. 61–62; Morin, p. 177; Rodolfo Pastor, "El repartimiento de mercancias y los alcaldes mayores novohispanos: un sistema de explotación, de sus origenes a la crisis de 1810," in Woodrow Borah, ed. *El gobierno provincial en la Nueva España, 1570–1781* (Mexico: Universidad Nacional Autónoma de México, 1985), pp. 215–216. In discussing muleteer support for the Tupac Amaru movement in Peru Scarlett O'Phelan points to the burden of increased *alcabala* payments and restrictive regulations to ensure its payment. See O'Phelan, pp. 273–287.

48. For a few examples see Altamirano, *Morelos en el Veladero,* pp. 176–177, and Cordero y T., p. 449.

49. David Brading, "El clero mexicano y el movimiento insurgente de 1810," *Relaciones* 2 (1981), pp. 13–19; Farriss, *Crown,* pp. 18, 119.

50. Timmons, *Morelos,* pp. 12, 23–4, 31–33; Herrejón Peredo, *Morelos: Vida,* p. 151. Villoro, 122 offers an interesting view on how the split between the high and low clergy may have affected future Church-state relations in Mexico.

51. Farriss, *Crown,* pp. 95, 99, 238–245; Taylor, "Between Global Process," pp. 151–152; Taylor, "Banditry," pp. 236, 245.

52. Carlos Herrejón Peredo, ed. *Los procesos de Morelos* (Zamora: El Colegio de Michoacán, 1985), pp. 395–396.

53. Farriss, *Crown,* p. 199.

54. See, for instance, AGN, Operaciones de Guerra, Vol. 15, exp. 4, fols. 55v–70v.

55. AGN, Operaciones de Guerra, Vol. 9, fols. 199–200; AGN, Operaciones de Guerra, Vol. 15, exp. 3, fols. 40–51; AGN, Infidencias, Vol. 54, exp. 3, fols. 122v–132v.

56. AGN, Operaciones de Guerra, Vol. 194, exp. 21, fol. 36; Nicolás Bravo, *Manifiesto* (Mexico: Imprenta de Galvan, 1828), pp. 5–6; BN, Fondo Alvarez, Carpeta 1 documento 105; Carpeta 2 documentos 112, 114.

57. AGN, Criminal, Vol. 173, exp. 11, fol. 246; AGN, Criminal, Vol. 583, exp. 1, fol. 32; AGN, Tierras, Vol. 2827, exp. 10, fols. 15v–16; AGN, Tierras, Vol. 2828, exp. 3, fol. 4: Chavez Guerrero, *Vicente Guerrero,* p. 30; Ochoa Campos, *Valerio Trujano,* p. 8: Edgar Pavía Guzman, *Provincias guerrerenses en la Costa de la Mar del Sur* (Chilpancingo: n.p., 1985), p. 31.

58. Hermengildo could not read or write and married a mestiza. Timmons, *Morelos,* pp. 54–55; Vargas Martínez, pp. 10, 13–4; Humberto Ochoa Campos, *El brazo derecho (Tata Gildo)* (Mexico: Cuadernos de Lectura Popular, 1967), p. 18.

59. See AGN, Ex-indiferente de Alcabalas, Acapulco, caja 4, exp. 8, caja 16, exp. 7, caja 19, exp. 7, caja 21, exp. 2; AGN, Real Hacienda, Administración General de Alcabalas, caja 25; Morin, pp. 172–174, 177. The evidence seems to confirm the hypothesis presented by Brian Hamnett. Hamnett, *Roots,* pp. 145–146.

60. H. Ochoa Campos, pp. 21–22.

61. H. Ochoa Campos, pp. 16–20; Gomezjara, p. 61.

62. E. P. Thompson, *Customs in Common: Studies in Traditional Popular Culture,* (New York: The New Press, 1993), p. 53.

63. Van Young, "Quetzalcóatl," pp. 110–111.

64. On the centrality of the king to legitimacy see Van Young, "Quetzalcóatl," pp. 113–114; Fernando García Argañarás, "Historical Structures, Social Forces, and Mexican Independence," *Latin American Perspectives* 13 (1986), p. 31; and José Luís Mirafuentes Galvan, "Legitimidad política y subversión en el noreste de México. Los intentos del indio José Carlos Ruvalcaba de cornoarse José Carlos V, rey de los naturales de la Nueva Vizcaya (Sonora-Sinaloa, 1771)," *Históricas* 26 (1989):3–22. For village rebellions in general see Taylor, *Drinking,* pp. 113–151.

65. François Guerra, *México: del Antiguo Régimen a la Revolución* (Mexico: Fondo de Cultura Económica, 1988), Vol. 1, p. 44; Rodríguez, "From Royal Subject," p. 26; Carlos O. Stoetzer, *The Scholastic Roots of the Spanish American Revolution* (New York: Fordham University Press, 1979), pp. 192–194. For Suarez see Bernice Hamilton, *Political Thought in Sixteenth Century Spain: A Study of the Political Ideas of Vitoria, Suarez and Molina* (Oxford: Oxford University Press, 1963), pp. 37, 41; Colin MacLachlan, *Spain's Empire in the New World* (Berkeley: University of California Press, 1988), pp. 10–12.

66. Luís Chavez Orozco, *Las instituciones democráticas de los indígenas mexicanos en la época colonial* (Mexico: Insitituto Indigenista Interamericano, 1943), p. 35; Rodríguez, "From Royal Subject," p. 8; Ernesto Lemoine, *Morelos: su vida revolucionaria a través de sus escritos y otros testimonios de la época* (Mexico: Universidad Nacional Autónoma de México, 1965), p. 191.

67. Carlos Herrejón Peredo, "Hidalgo: La justificación de la insurgencia," *Cuadernos Americanos* 42 (1983), pp. 162–180; Carlos Herrejón Peredo, *Hidalgo: Razones de la insurgencia y biografía documental* (Mexico: Secretaría de Educación Pública, 1986), pp. 34–36; Lemoine, *Morelos: Su vida,* p. 264.

68. The quote is from Van Young, "Quetzalcóatl," p. 121.

69. Rodríguez, "From Royal Subject," p. 30; MacLachlan, p. 132; Jaime Rodríguez, "La independencia de la América Española: Una reinterpretación," *Historia Mexicana* 42 (1993), p. 590.

70. AGN, Historia, 432, exp. 3 fol. 41.

71. The quote is from Enrique Florescano, *Memoria mexicana* (Mexico: Joaquín Mortiz, 1987), p. 187. David Brading makes an almost identical statement in Brading, *Los orígenes del nacionalismo mexicano* (Mexico: Era, 1988), p. 15.

72. Lemoine, *Morelos: Su vida* , pp. 185–186; Herrejón Peredo, *Morelos: Vida*, pp. 49, 74; Timmons, *Morelos*, p. 63; AGN, Operaciones de Guerra, Vol. 83, fols. 295–296; AGN, Operaciones de Guerra, Vol. 467; AGN, Infidencias, Vol. 133, fols. 86–87; Santos Carrera and Alvarez Hernández, *Historia*, p. 185.

73. Alberto Flores Galindo, "In Search of an Inca," in Steve Stern, ed. *Resistance, Rebellion and Consciousness in the Andean Peasant World: 18th to 20th Centuries* (Madison: University of Wisconsin Press, 1987), p. 200.

74. Florescano, *Memoria*, p. 291; AGN, Infidencias, Vol. 24, exp. 3, fol. 120v; AGN, Infidencias, Vol. 131, exp. 1, fols. 5–6; William Taylor, "The Virgin of Guadalupe in New Spain: An Inquiry into the Social History of Marian Devotion," *American Ethnologist* 14 (1987), p. 24. Felipe Castro Gutiérrez notes that the failed rebels of the Mariano scare in Nayarit in 1801 also planned to portray the Virgin of Guadalupe on a banner. See Castro Gutiérrez, "La rebelión del indio Mariano (Nayarit 1801)," (Unpublished manuscript,. n.d. Instituto de Investigaciones Históricas, Universidad Autónoma Nacional de México, Mexico City), p. 5.

75. Taylor, "The Virgin," esp. pp. 19, 23–4. See also Lafaye, pp. 280–1; Florescano, *Memoria*, p. 294; Brading, *Los orígenes*, pp. 15–16, 42; Brading, "Tridentine Catholicism," pp. 1–3.

76. Taylor, "The Virgin," p. 23; AGN, Operaciones de Guerra, Vol. 829, exp. 7, fols. 63–65.

77. Taylor, "The Virgin," pp. 20–21.

78. AGN, Infidencias, Vol. 131, exp. 11, fols. 59v–60; AGN, Infidencias, Vol. 55, exp. 24, fols. 227–227v.

79. AGN, Infidencias, Vol. 131, exp. 11, fol. 58. Even literate correspondents of Morelos displayed considerable enthusiasm for the idea of "Cutting off European heads." AGN, Operaciones de Guerra, Vol. 15, exp. 4, fol. 55v.

80. For opposing views see Hamnett, *Roots*, p. 13 and Jaime Rodríguez, "Introduction," in Jaime E. Rodríguez O., ed., *The Independence of Mexico and the Origins of the New Nation* (Los Angeles: University of California at Los Angeles Latin American Center, 1989), p. 7. For royalist fears see AGN, Infidencias, Vol. 131, exp. 29, fols. 167–169.

81. For Godoy as a Francophile see Hugh Hamill, *The Hidalgo Revolt: Prelude to Mexican Independence* (Gainesville: University of Florida Press, 1966), p. 2. For the first wave of official anti-French propaganda see Herr, pp. 304–312, 335. For the second wave see Hamill, pp. 14–15; Dorothy Tanck de Estrada, *La educación ilustrada (1786–1836): Educación primaria en la Ciudad de México* (Mexico: El Colegio de México, 1977), p. 227; and Herrejón Peredo, *Morelos: Vida*, pp. 231–232. For its echo in insurgent discourse see Santos Carrera and Alvarez Hernández, *Historia*, p. 199; AGN, Operaciones de Guerra, Vol. 77, fol. 296; and AGN, Operaciones de Guerra, Vol. 933, exp. 27, fol. 33.

82. For an opposing view see Van Young, "Quetzalcóatl," pp. 120–121. Note that even the idea that Fernando VII was in New Spain leading the resistance was sometimes used among Morelos' forces. Lemoine, *Morelos: Su vida*, p. 169. For some of the myriad expressions of the idea that the Europeans were planning to turn New Spain over to Napoleon see AGN, Infidencias, Vol. 60, exp. 4, fols.

181,184 ; AGN, Operaciones de Guerra, Vol. 15, exp. 4, fol. 61; AGN, Operaciones de Guerra, Vol. 917, exp. 5, fols. 15–16; AGN, Operaciones de Guerra, Vol. 939, fols. 210, 685; Rodríguez, "From Royal Subject," pp. 23–24, 31; Villoro, p. 102; Lemoine, *Morelos: Su vida*, p. 191; Archer, "Banditry," p. 60.

83. Herrejón Peredo, *Los procesos*, p. 189.

84. AGN, Historia, Vol. 50, exp. 21, fols. 363–365.

85. Villoro, p. 136; AGN, Infidencias, Vol. 60, exp. 4, fol. 181v.

86. Villoro, pp. 74–75; Lemoine, *Morelos: Su vida*, p. 192; Herrejón Peredo, *Los procesos*, 3 pp. 95–396.

87. Jan Szeminski, "Why Kill the Spaniard? New Perspectives on Andean Insurrectionary Ideology in the 18th Century," in Steve Stern, ed. *Resistance, Rebellion and Consciousness in the Andean Peasant World, 18th to 20th Centuries* (Madison: University of Wisconsin Press, 1987), pp. 168, 171–174.

88. Villoro, pp. 74–75.

89. See Norman Cohn, *The Pursuit of the Millenium: Revolutionary Millenarians and Mystical Anarchists of the Middle Ages* (New York: Oxford University Press, 1976), pp. 79–80 on this point.

90. For the determinants of price see Guy Thomson, "Protectionism and Industrialization in Mexico, 1821–1854: The Case of Puebla," in Christopher Abel and Colin Lewis, eds. *Latin America, Economic Imperialism and the State: The Political Economy of the External Connection from Independence to the Present* (London: Athlone Press, 1985), pp. 129–130.

91. This has been noted elsewhere in New Spain, also. See Hamnett, *Roots*, pp. 26–27, 32–33; Lafaye, p. 118; Taylor, "Banditry," p. 217.

92. AGN, Infidencias, Vol. 144, exp. 29, fol. 31; and AGN, Operaciones de Guerra, Vol. 939, fol. 684.

93. AGN, Infidencias, Vol. 55, exp. 24, fols. 227–227v; AGN, Infidencias, Vol. 133, fol. 3; AGN, Operaciones de Guerra, Vol. 917, fol. 28; AGN, Operaciones de Guerra, Vol. 919, fol. 3; AGN, Operaciones de Guerra, Vol. 919, exp. 23, fol. 32; AGN, Operaciones de Guerra, Vol. 939; AGN, Operaciones de Guerra, Vol. 72, exp. 23, fols. 157–158.

94. Aguirre Colorado, García and Rodríguez, pp. 15, 86; Carlos María de Bustamante, *Cuadro histórico de la revolución mexicana de 1810* (Mexico: Instituto Nacional de Estudios Históricos de la Revolución Mexicana, 1985), Vol. 2, pp. 20–22; Herrejón Peredo, *Morelos: Documentos*, pp. 120–122, 151. On the identification of the enemy in eighteenth century Andean revolts see Karen Spalding, "¿Quienes son los indios?" in Karen Spalding, ed. *De indio a campesino* (Lima: Instituto de Estudios Peruanas, 1974), p. 191; Szeminski.

95. Herrejón Peredo, *Morelos: Vida*, pp. 58–60; MacLachlan, p. 91; AGN, Infidencias, Vol. 144, exp. 29, fol. 31; AGN, Operaciones de Guerra, Vol. 939, fols. 684–685v.

96. Lemoine, *Morelos: Su vida*, pp. 162, 265–266; AGN, Infidencias, Vol. 144, fols. 4, 60; AGN, Operaciones de Guerra, Vol. 919, exp. 24, fols. 33–34; Hamnett, *Roots*, p. 149; Rodolfo Pastor, "Estructura y vida social en la Mixteca Alta del siglo XVIII," in María de los Angeles Romero Frizzi, ed. *Lecturas históricas de Oaxaca: Epoca Colonial* (Mexico: Instituto Nacional de Antropología e Historia, 1986), pp. 427–428.

97. Lemoine, *Morelos: Su vida*, pp. 175–176, 164–165, 265; Santos Carrera and Alvarez Hernández, *Historia*, pp. 178–179; AGN, Operaciones de Guerra, Vol. 924, exp. 53, fol. 80.

98. Lemoine, *Morelos: Su vida*, pp. 264–265; AGN, Operaciones de Guerra, Vol. 914, exp. 22, fols. 29–30; AGN Operaciones de Guerra Vol. 829, exp. 5, fol. 61; AGN, Historia, Vol. 105, exp. 21, fol. 84; Archivo Parroquial de Chilapa,

(microfilm MXE-3-432 roll 1, located in the AGN); AGN, Tributos, Vol. 62, exp. 2, fol. 117; Lemoine, *Morelos: Su vida*, pp. 566–572; Castillo Ledon, 1:143; Timmons, *Morelos*, p. 108. The taxes collected by the insurgents varied considerably over time and area. See AGN, Infidencias, Vol. 133, fol. 2.

99. Lemoine, *Morelos: Su vida*, pp. 162, 264; AGN, Infidencias, Vol. 144, exp. 5.

100. Hernández y Dávalos, Vol. 5, p. 108; Lemoine, *Morelos: Su vida*, pp. 162, 265, 384–385; Timmons, *Morelos*, p. 105.

101. AGN, Operaciones de Guerra, Vol. 935, exp. 242, fols. 476–476v.

102. AGN, Operaciones de Guerra, Vol. 919, exp. 74, fols. 129–129v. In another case Morelos' intervention was asked for but his decision is not in surviving documents.

103. Hernández y Dávalos, Vol. 3, p. 450; Herrejón Peredo, *Los procesos*, p. 261; AGN, Infidencias, Vol. 914, exp. 18, fol. 22; AGN, Operaciones de Guerra, Vol. 917, exp. 13, fol. 37; AGN, Operaciones de Guerra, Vol. 917, exp. 164, fol. 285; AGN, Operaciones de Guerra, Vol. 918, exp. 40, fols. 54–55; AGN, Operaciones de Guerra, Vol. 918, exp. 47, fols. 64–65.

104. This is an old argument about eighteenth century enlightened monarchies. See Alexis de Tocqueville, *The Old Regime and the French Revolution* (New York: Doubleday Anchor Books, 1955), p. 68; Lyle McAlister, "Social Structure and Social Change in New Spain," *Hispanic American Historical Review* 43 (1963), p. 369; and Richard Morse, "The Heritage of Latin America," in Louis Hartz, ed. *The Founding of New Societies* (New York: Harcourt, 1964), p. 142.

105. MacLachlan, pp. 76, 85–86, 101, 128.

106. The argument for France is from Keith Baker, "Enlightenment and Revolution in France: Old Problems, Renewed Approaches," *Journal of Modern History* 53 (1981), p. 284; and François Furet, *Interpreting the French Revolution* (New York: Cambridge University Press, 1981), pp. 15, 173–174, 179–180, 185. Evidence for Spain and its New World that seems to indicate similar developments can be seen in Richard Herr, *The Eighteenth Century Revolution in Spain* (Princeton: Princeton University Press, 1958), pp. 73, 154–163, 183–200, 262–263, 282, 349, 355–357; MacLachlan, pp. 81–82; and Hamill, pp. 6–8, 69, 72, 82.

107. For Hidalgo see Herrejón Peredo, *Hidalgo: Razones*, pp. 35–36. Morelos, however, was so accused. See Herrejón Peredo, *Los proceso*, pp. 293–383, especially pp. 334–335.

108. Ernesto Lemoine traces this transition ably in *Morelos y la Revolución de 1810* (Mexico: Gobierno del Estado de Michoacán, 1984), pp. 259–310. Lemoine believes that the insurgents' invocations of Fernando VII were disingenuous. However, this does not detract from the importance of the transformation of the manner in which they legitimated their actions with their followers. See Lemoine, *Morelos y la Revolución*, pp. 260–265; and Ernesto Lemoine, "Morelos y la generación de la independencia," in María del Refugio González, ed. *La formación del estado mexicano* (Mexico: Porrúa, 1984), pp. 33–37.

109. For donations in Guerrero see AGN, Archivo Histórico de Hacienda, Vol. 396, exp. 3; AGN, Ex-indiferente de Alcabalas, Tlapa caja 4, exp. 12; exp. 13. For an example of an appeal read by Morelos see Herrejón Peredo, *Morelos: Vida*, pp. 231–232.

110. Herrejón Peredo, *Morelos: Vida*, pp. 52–56. For an interesting interpretation of the Spanish transition see Guerra, Vol. 1, 189–190.

111. Villoro, pp. 99–109, quote from 108. See also Herr, p. 347.

112. AGN, Operaciones de Guerra, Vol. 74, exp. 44, fol. 137; AGN, Operaciones de Guerra, Vol. 917, exp. 150, fols. 261–262; AGN, Operaciones de Guerra, Vol.

919, fols. 31–34v, 55; AGN, Operaciones de Guerra, Vol. 935, exp. 242, fols. 476–476v. For a comparison to Peru in the same period see Peter Guardino, "Las guerrillas y la independencia peruana: Un ensayo de interpretación," *Pasado y presente* 2 (1989), p. 112.

113. AGN, Infidencias, Vol. 133, fols. 108–108v, 119, 127, 210; AGN, Operaciones de Guerra, Vol. 74, exp. 121, fol. 386; AGN, Operaciones de Guerra, Vol. 917, exp. 152, fols. 265–265v; AGN, Operaciones de Guerra, Vol. 918, exp. 25, fols. 38–38v; AGN, Operaciones de Guerra, Vol. 933, exp. 107, fols. 137–141; Ortega, *Colección*, 17:160; Lemoine, *Morelos: Su vida*, pp. 412–417. Villages resisted attempts by insurgent officials to depose or impose their officials as fiercely as they had the efforts of colonial officials. AGN, Operaciones de Guerra, Vol. 91, exp. 68, fols. 119–120v.

114. The constitution is found in Bustamante, *Cuadro*, Vol. 3, 157–189. For instance, electors for the 1813 Congress of Chilpancingo were chosen by the "pastors, military commanders, republics, and principal residents" in Tecpan while in Cutzmala they were chosen by "owners and renters of *haciendas* or *ranchos*, military chiefs, and other upright persons" AGN, Infidencias, Vol. 144, exp. 14, fol. 16; AGN, Operaciones de Guerra, Vol. 943, exp. 74, fol. 84. See also Virginia Guedea, "Las elecciones entre los insurgentes," in Virginia Guedea and Jaime Rodríguez, eds. *Five Centuries of Mexican History/Cinco Siglos de Historia de México*, Vol. I (Mexico: Instituto Mora-University of California at Irvine, 1992), pp. 309–310.

115. AGN, Operaciones de Guerra, Vol. 917, exp. 142, fols. 248–249; AGN, Operaciones de Guerra, Vol. 917, exp. 158, fols. 276–277; AGN, Operaciones de Guerra, Vol. 918, exp. 48, fols. 66–67; AGN, Operaciones de Guerra, Vol. 918, exp. 45, fols. 61–62; AGN Operaciones de Guerra, Vol. 919, exp. 68, fols. 119–120v.

116. Herrejón Peredo, *Morelos: Documentos*, p. 174; Lemoine, *Morelos: Su vida*, pp. 531–532; AGN, Infidencias, Vol. 144, exp. 21, fol. 23.

117. AGN, Operaciones de Guerra, Vol. 914, exp. 19, fols. 23–23v; AGN, Operaciones de Guerra, Vol. 943, exp. 75, fol. 87; AGN, Operaciones de Guerra, Vol. 943, exp. 132, fol. 190; AGN, Operaciones de Guerra, Vol. 943, exp. 141, fol. 203. For disputes within villages see AGN, Operaciones de Guerra, Vol. 914, exp. 12, fols. 13–13v; AGN, Operaciones de Guerra, Vol. 919, fols. 6, 48–54, 68–84v, 94, 103–106v, 116–116v, 160–161, 164. For disputes between priests and peasants see AGN, Infidencias, Vol. 133, fol. 163; AGN, Operaciones de Guerra, Vol. 919, fols. 23–25, 56–67v, 85–88v, 92.

118. AGN, Operaciones de Guerra, Vol. 918, exp. 48, fols. 66–67; AGN, Operaciones de Guerra, Vol. 919, exp. 8, fols. 9–10; Lemoine, *Morelos: Su vida*, pp. 328–329, 403–405.

119. AGN, Infidencias, Vol. 144, exp. 16, fol. 18; Lemoine, *Morelos: Su vida*, pp. 331–335.

120. Hamnett, *Roots*, pp. 150–177; Salcedo Guerrero, "Vicente Guerrero's Struggle," p. 35.

121. Christon Archer, "La Causa Buena: The Counterinsurgency Army of New Spain and the Ten Years War," in Jaime E. Rodríguez, ed. *The Independence of Mexico and the Origins of the New Nation* (Los Angeles: University of California at Los Angeles Latin American Center, 1989), pp. 102–105; Archer, "¡Viva Nuestra Señora de Guadalupe!," p. 147. See also Salcedo Guerrero, "Vicente Guerrero's Struggle," p. 80; Lemoine, "Vicente Guerrero," pp. 9–10.

122. Timmons, *Morelos*, p. 133.

123. The recommendation to abandon the area is found in AGN, Operaciones de Guerra, Vol. 74, exp. 127, fols. 410v–411v. Armijo's report is in AGN, Opera-

ciones de Guerra, Vol. 74, exp. 156, fols. 529v–533v. Salcedo Guerrero, "Vicente Guerrero's Struggle," pp. 29–81; and Sprague, pp. 23–26 provide military histories of the guerrilla struggle. For various assessments of the support given to the insurgents see AGN, Operaciones de Guerra, Vol. 73, fols. 37v, 103; AGN, Operaciones de Guerra, Vol. 70, exp. 22, fols. 68–71v; exp. 23, fols. 76–77; AGN, Operaciones de Guerra, Vol. 74, exp. 126, fol. 401v; exp. 127, fols. 410v–411v; exp. 164, fols. 568–569; exp. 156, fols. 529–533v; AGN, Operaciones de Guerra, Vol. 305, exp. 31, fols. 65–65v; Luís Ramírez Fentanes, *Vicente Guerrero, Presidente de México* (Mexico: Comisión de Historia Militar, 1958), pp. 78–79.

124. AGN, Operaciones de Guerra, Vol. 73, fol. 204. For other comments on the *costeños* obstinate opposition to the royal government see AGN, Operaciones de Guerra, Vol. 72, fols. 216–228; AGN, Operaciones de Guerra, Vol. 73, fols. 242–242v; AGN, Operaciones de Guerra, Vol. 75, fols. 20–23.

125. The April 1819 estimate is from AGN, Operaciones de Guerra, Vol. 86, fols. 347–350. For the coastal war see AGN, Operaciones de Guerra, Vol. 466; AGN, Operaciones de Guerra, Vol. 73, fols. 6–7; AGN, Operaciones de Guerra, Vol. 77, fols. 106v, 276–277; AGN, Infidencias, Vol. 144, exp. 89, fol. 205; exp. 92, fol. 212; AGN, Operaciones de Guerra, Vol. 78, fols. 62–62v; AGN, Operaciones de Guerra, Vol. 86, fols. 84–84v, 370–371; AGN, Operaciones de Guerra, Vol. 939, fols. 271, 275–276, 574v; AGN, Operaciones de Guerra, Vol. 924, exp. 12, fol. 14; Aviles, p. 36; Chavez Guerrero, *Vicente Guerrero*, p. 83.

126. AGN, Operaciones de Guerra, Vol. 466; AGN, Operaciones de Guerra, Vol. 73, fols. 195–197; AGN, Operaciones de Guerra, Vol. 467; AGN, Operaciones de Guerra, Vol. 468, fols. 107, 172; AGN, Operaciones de Guerra, Vol. 75, exp. 119, fol. 373; AGN, Operaciones de Guerra, Vol. 74, fols. 1–3, 189v, 479; AGN, Operaciones de Guerra, Vol. 469, fols. 2v, 12v; AGN, Operaciones de Guerra, Vol. 470; AGN, Operaciones de Guerra, Vol. 915, fols. 205–206; AGN, Operaciones de Guerra, Vol. 81, fols. 438–444.

127. AGN, Operaciones de Guerra, Vol. 81, fols. 448–449; AGN, Operaciones de Guerra, Vol. 80, fols. 56–57.

128. Ramírez Fentanes, *Vicente Guerrero*, p. 123; Salcedo Guerrero, "Vicente Guerrero's Struggle," pp. 119, 137–140; Aviles, pp. 37–38; AGN, Operaciones de Guerra, Vol. 80, fols. 298–307, 313v, 317v; AGN, Operaciones de Guerra, Vol. 82, fols. 74, 276–294; AGN, Operaciones de Guerra, Vol. 83, fols. 166v, 194–195; AGN, Operaciones de Guerra, Vol. 83, fol. 280.

129. See for instance, his June 2, 1815 report to the Viceroy in AGN, Operaciones de Guerra, Vol. 74, fols. 562–562v.

130. For the general outlines of royalist stategy and tactics see Brian Hamnett, "Royalist Counter-Insurgency and the Continuity of Rebellion, Guanajuato and Michoacán 1813–1820," *Hispanic American Historical Review* 62 (1982), pp. 1–26; and Archer, "La Causa Buena."

131. AGN, Operaciones de Guerra, Vol. 73, fols. 42v, 103, 213–213v, 335; AGN, Operaciones de Guerra, Vol. 74, fol. 189v.

132. AGN, Operaciones de Guerra, Vol. 74, fols. 568–569v.

133. AGN, Operaciones de Guerra, Vol. 73, fol. 317.

134. AGN, Historia, Vol. 103, exp. 46, fols. 184–186; AGN, Operaciones de Guerra, Vol. 71 exp. 17, fols. 85–86; exp. 22, fol. 102; AGN, Operaciones de Guerra, Vol. 78, fol. 227v.

135. For examples see Ramírez Fentanes, *Vicente Guerrero*, pp. 58, 95, 100; AGN, Operaciones de Guerra, Vol. 86, fols. 84–84v.

136. AGN, Operaciones de Guerra, Vol. 80, fols. 56–57; AGN, Operaciones de Guerra, Vol. 81, fols. 438–444; AGN, Operaciones de Guerra, Vol. 82, fols. 276–294. See also Archer, "¡Viva Nuestra Señora de Guadalupe!," pp. 158–159.

137. AGN, Operaciones de Guerra, Vol. 82, fols. 311–311v. See also Archer, "¡Viva Nuestra Señora de Guadalupe!," p. 165. For an insurgent counter-offer see Salcedo Guerrero, "Vicente Guerrero's Struggle," p. 119.

138. AGN, Operaciones de Guerra, Vol. 71, exp. 11, fols. 51–51v; exp. 32, fols. 229–229v; AGN, Operaciones de Guerra, Vol. 81, fols. 448–449; AGN, Operaciones de Guerra, Vol. 82, fols. 361–362; AGN, Operaciones de Guerra, Vol. 467. Christon Archer notes this phenomenon but suggests that it represented a type of land reform. My suspicion is that the fiscal and political dimensions were more important. See Archer, "The Young Antonio López de Santa Anna: Veracruz Counterinsurgent and Incipient Caudillo," in William H. Beezeley and Judith Ewell, eds. *The Human Condition in Latin America: The Nineteenth Century* (Wilmington, DE: Scholarly Resources, 1989), p. 6; Archer, "¡Viva Nuestra Señora de Guadalupe!," p. 149.

139. Archivo Parroquial de Chilapa (microfilm MXE-3-432, roll 1, located in AGN); AGN, Operaciones de Guerra, Vol. 77, fol. 92v.

140. AGN, Archivo Histórico de Hacienda, Vol. 219, exp. 10; Vol. 266, exp. 22; Vol. 266, exp. 33; Vol. 441, exp. 1; Vol. 441, exp. 15; Vol. 441, exp. 19; AGN, Civil, Vol. 559, fol. 372; AGN, Ex-indiferente de Alcabalas, Tetela, caja 4, exp. 6; AGN, Indios, Vol. 77, exp. 14, fol. 288; AGN, Intendencias, Vol. 60.

141. AGN, Operaciones de Guerra, Vol. 71, exp. 39, fols. 250–250v; AGN, Operaciones de Guerra, Vol. 81, fol. 136; AGN, Operaciones de Guerra, Vol. 83, fols. 194–195.

142. For some works that support this interpretation see Brading, *Los orígenes*, p. 83; Farriss, *Crown*, pp. 246–251; Carlos San Juan Victoria, "Las utopias oligarquicas conocen sus limites (1821–1834)," in María del Refugio González, ed. *La formación del estado mexicano* (Mexico: Porrúa, 1984), p. 93; and the others cited below.

143. Brading, *Los orígenes*, p. 97; Romeo Flores Caballero, *Counterrevolution: The Role of the Spaniards in the Independence of Mexico, 1804–1838* (Lincoln, Nebraska: University of Nebraska Press, 1974), p. 57.

144. Villoro, p. 191.

145. Flores Caballero, p. 58.

146. Lucás Alamán, *Historia de Méjico* (Mexico: Editorial Jus, 1942), Vol. 4, pp. 666–68, Vol. 5, pp. 331–33.

147. Rodríguez, "From Royal Subject," p. 39. See also Archer, "Banditry," p. 59; Pastor, "Estructura," p. 429. For an interesting comparison with contemporary England see E. P. Thompson, *The Making of the English Working Class* (New York: Vintage, 1966), pp. 605, 625, 682.

148. AGN, Operaciones de Guerra, Vol. 71, exp. 39, fols. 250–250v.

149. Guadalupe Jiménez Codinach, "Introducción al Libro Uno," in *Planes en la Nación Mexicana: Libro Uno 1808–1830* (Mexico: Cámara de Diputados, 1987), p. 44; Frank Samponaro, "The Political Role of the Army in Mexico, 1821–1848" (Ph.D. Dissertation, State University of New York at Stonybrook, 1974), pp. 11–12.

150. Hamnett, *Revolución*, p. 307.

151. AGN, Operaciones de Guerra, Vol. 777. This oft-repeated counter-insurgency ratio shows up in Robin Higham, *Air Power* (London: MacDonald, 1972), p. 219 among other places.

152. Hamnett, *Revolución*, p. 297; Ernesto Lemoine, "1821: ¿Consumación o contradicción de 1810?" *Secuencia* 1 (1985), p. 29.

153. Rodríguez, "La independencia," p. 581.

154. AGN, Operaciones de Guerra, Vol. 83, fols. 270, 277–278; AGN, Operaciones de Guerra, Vol. 777; AGN, Operaciones de Guerra, Vol. 941, fols. 81–82.

155. *Los insurgentes rendidos a la Constitución* (Mexico: Imprenta de Valdes, 1820); *Proclama de un americano a los insurgentes y demás habitantes de Nueva España* (Mexico: Alejandro Valdes, 1820); Carlos María de Bustamante, *Memoria presentada al Exmo. Ayuntamiento Constitucional de México* (Mexico: Imprenta Constitucional, 1820), pp. 3–13; AGN, Operaciones de Guerra, Vol. 83, fol. 289; AGN, Operaciones de Guerra, Vol. 941, fols. 81–82.

156. François Chevalier, "La emancipación y el municipio rural libre en México: De los comuneros al liberalismo," *Cuadernos Americanos* 43 (1983), p. 157. Apparently when the same constitution was in force in 1812–14 very few were set up outside important urban areas, possibly due to the more tenuous military position of the viceregal government then. Roger Cunniff, "Mexican Municipal Electoral Reform, 1810–1822," in Nettie Lee Benson, ed. *Mexico and the Spanish Cortes, 1810–1822* (Austin: University of Texas Press, 1966), pp. 70–80.

157. AGN, Ayuntamientos, Vol. 120, exp. 2; Archivo de la Cámara de Diputados del Estado de México (hereafter ACDEM), Expedientes, 1821, libro 4, exp. 7, fols. 1–2; AGN, Gobernación, caja 13, exp. 1; Archivo Parroquial de Chilapa, (microfilm MXE-3-432, roll 1, located in the AGN).

158. Archer, "La Causa Buena," pp. 106–108.

159. *El indio constitucional a todos los Americanos, segundo papel* (Mexico: n.p., 1820), pp. 6–8; *El indio y la india del pueblo de Actopan* (Mexico: José María Betancourt, 1820).

160. Chavez Guerrero, *Vicente Guerrero*, p. 87; Hamnett, *Revolución*, pp. 308–310.

161. Chavez Guerrero, *Vicente Guerrero*, pp. 103–104; Sprague, pp. 41–42; Salcedo Guerrero, "Vicente Guerrero's Struggle," pp. 164–167.

162. Vicente Guerrero to Iturbide, January 20, 1821, in *Cartas de los señores generales*, pp. 3–6. This was Article 22 of the Constitution, found in Antonio Padilla Serra, ed. *Constituciones y leyes fundamentales de España (1808–1947)* (Granada: Universidad de Granada, 1954), p. 12. See also *Instrucción que para facilitar las elecciones parroquiales y de partido . . .* (Mexico: n.p., 1820), article 4 on citizenship.

163. Iturbide to Guerrero, January 10, 1821 in *Cartas de los señores generales D. Agustín de Iturbide y D. Vicente Guerrero* (Mexico: Imprenta Imperial, 1821), pp. 1–3.

164. Guerrero to Iturbide, January 20, 1821 in *Cartas de los señores generales*, pp. 3–6.

165. Lemoine, "Vicente Guerrero," p. 13. For more on the negotiations see Jiménez Codinach, pp. 46–48; and Sprague, p. 41.

166. The Plan de Iguala can be found in Bustamante, *Cuadro*, Vol. 5, pp. 115–118. See also Jiménez Codinach, pp. 46–47; *Advertencia importante sobre las próximas elecciones de los Ayuntamientos* (Mexico: Alejandro Valdes, 1821), p. 1.

167. AGN, Civil, Vol. 69, exp. 5, fols. 45–52; AGN, Operaciones de Guerra, Vol. 70, exp. 61, fols. 251–252; AGN, Operaciones de Guerra, Vol. 89, fol. 485; Vito Alessio Robles, ed. *La correspondencia de Agustín de Iturbide después de la proclamación del Plan de Iturbide* (Mexico: n.p., 1945), p. 13; Sprague, p. 47.

168. AGN, Operaciones de Guerra, Vol. 70, exp. 63, fols. 261–262; AGN, Operaciones de Guerra, Vol. 89, fols. 467–469; Archer, "La Causa Buena," pp. 107–108.

169. See Theda Skocpol, "France, Russia, and China: A Structural Analysis of Social Revolution," *Comparative Studies in Society and History* 18 (1976), pp. 178, 181, 209. Karen Spalding notes that the Spanish colonial system did not rely on the state's military capacity to maintain order. See Spalding, "Introducción," in

Karen Spalding, ed. *De indio a campesino* (Lima: Instituto de Estudios Peruanas, 1974), p. 21.

170. Steven Topik, "Mexican Independence in Comparative Perspective," in Jaime E. Rodríguez O., ed. *The Independence of Mexico and the Origins of the New Nation* (Los Angeles: University of California at Los Angeles Latin American Center, 1989), p. 333. See also Rodríguez, "La independencia," p. 581.

5

An Update for the Minister of War on the Military Occurrences of the Kingdom of New Spain During the Month of March 1818

Viceroy Juan Ruíz de Apodaca

The following military dispatch by Viceroy Apodaca serves as a kind of snapshot that stops time in March 1818 to illustrate many themes in the Spanish American independence wars. The geographic and social complexities of a vast American nation tested the abilities of any military commander and his subordinates. In each of the theaters of war, both the rebels or patriots and the royalists developed strategies and tactics to confront developing military needs. In New Spain, despite his optimistic prognostications designed to impress his superiors in Madrid, Apodaca probably recognized that his forces were nowhere close to eliminating the root causes of insurgency. In 1816, as the newly appointed viceroy and captain general of New Spain arrived to take up his post, he had witnessed firsthand the effectiveness of insurgent forces that stalked his own well-defended convoy from Veracruz much of the way to Mexico City. His constant references to the successes of pacification programs and to the numbers of amnestied rebels were as illusory as body counts in modern conflicts. These same fighters shifted back and forth, depending upon conditions, from insurgent-bandit to royalist employing the use of many amnesties and of the anonymity possible in a society ripped apart by turbulence.

Many men and women became accustomed to war and to the opportunities for brigandage opened by the absence of order. Moreover, by 1820 the amnestied rebels often came to form a significant proportion, if not

Translated and reprinted from Viceroy Juan Ruíz de Apodaca, "El Virrey de Nueva España Don Juan Ruíz de Apodaca: Continua dando cuenta de las ocurrencias militares de aquel Reino en el presente mes al Excelentísimo Ministro de la Guerra, México, 31 de marzo de 1818," in Archivo General de la Nación, Mexico, Sección de Historia, vol. 152, ff.222–32.

outright majority, of the soldiers enlisted in some units of the royalist forces. Apodaca's optimism reflected his own ambitions to rise in the Spanish bureaucracy and until 1821 his refusal to dwell upon any hint of defeatism. However, on certain occasions he recognized that the royalist campaign could wilt and the heavy taxes forced upon the population to support the war might not be acceptable on a permanent basis. Of special interest, Apodaca saw the dangers posed by the United States and other foreigners to the unsettled northern regions of New Spain. The references to the Gazeta de México *illustrate the use of battlefield combat reports as a means to influence public opinion as well as to showcase the exploits of royalist army commanders.*

D espite the reinforcement of troop units and other assistance to destroy rebel malefactors and to advance the state of pacification, Veracruz Province remains in a precarious state beset by hostilities by the bands under Vergara[1] and Guadalupe Victoria.[2] Our most recent misfortune was a rebel surprise attack on the 12 March mail convoy that resulted in thirty-two casualties from the detachment of seventy grenadiers assigned to the escort force. The Veracruz rebels have frustrated my efforts to suppress the rebellion and to reestablish tranquility and order in Veracruz Province, a goal I have accomplished already in the vast majority of the kingdom. I will defer no measure nor set aside any means available within my discretion to obtain the laudable end of pacification. To achieve this end, I have relieved Brigadier Don Diego García Conde[3] from the military command of Veracruz Province. To replace him, I have conferred command of Veracruz under the same orders upon Brigadier Don Ciriaco de Llano[4] who also will retain his post as Comandante General of the Province of Puebla. Llano has fulfilled his duties as military governor effectively, for the benefit of His Majesty and the Province. The governance of Puebla Province will be assigned to the care of the deputy governor and provincial administrative officer who will take prompt action on all matters that require immediate resolution. As a result of these new duties, Llano must reside in Jalapa so that he can oversee all military operations and if the circumstances require, he will exercise personal command of his forces.

I have been obliged to take these measures by the prospects for success offered by Brigadier Llano who in his previous posts has exhibited energy, dedication and knowledge. Moreover, the Province of Puebla is in a good state as I have reported to Your Excellency in my previous dispatches. This Province will provide support in the form of troops and other resources that are necessary for waging war effectively in Veracruz. Brigadier Llano's joint military command of both Puebla and Veracruz provinces will facilitate opportunities and advantages that would not be possible if the military command of those provinces remains divided.

I have assigned the interim governance of the City of Veracruz and the provincial intendancy to Artillery Colonel Don Ignacio Cincunegui, who commands the artillery forces and whose zeal and great efficiency offer enormous advantages for the successful implementation of military operations, and the administration of the delicate commission to govern the principal port and customs house of the kingdom. Colonel Cincunegui replaces Colonel Don Francisco Hevia[5] in that post, who repeatedly has requested to be relieved. He will return to command the Infantry Regiment of Castilla and military governance of the towns of Códoba and Orizaba that he held with great utility to the service and advanced the pacification of that region. Brigadier Don Joaquín Castillo y Bustamante[6] will return to Jalapa as its military commander and to cover for Don Ciriaco de Llano during his absences from the town on combat operations.

After arriving in Jalapa during the past week, Llano fulfilled my orders to organize two strong detachments that at the appropriate time will coordinate attacks on the bands of the traitors of Victoria and Vergara at Arenal de Monteverde, where they have usurped control. They shall be pursued relentlessly, and will not be permitted to get out of our reach before they are crushed. In this regard, I have notified Llano of the particular *modus operandi* of these rebels, their special characteristics, and movements. Regarding the policies and issues concerning the pacification of Veracruz Province, I have warned Colonel Llano to be very strict in the implementation of his orders. One of these is to reinforce the army units protecting the *camino militar* (military road).[7] I ordered three additional detachments garrisoned at the Paso de Ovejas, Callejones de Guanicaluco, and the third just outside the City of Veracruz at Molino de Santa Fe. With frequent patrols between one point and another, the army will ensure the uninterrupted movement of mail and commerce. Also, these deployments will prevent a repetition of the loss of these three places that occurred because the defenders did not follow the letter of my precautions on military operations in the province. Unacceptable excuses were made by army officers who argued the impossibility of these military assignments and made other similar complaints.

On 26 March, bands of the two rebel chiefs attacked the town of San Antonio Huatusco in the district of Orizaba where they were repelled by our forces, although not before the regrettable deaths of a royalist officer and twenty-seven soldiers. Relying on information gathered from the battlefield report, I believe that these losses were the result of a lack of precautionary measures and vigilance by the commander at Huatusco. For this reason, I have decided to remove him immediately from his command.

As I have already told Your Excellency, the coastal areas of Veracruz remain properly defended and in a good state of defense. I have also taken necessary precautions to ensure that these garrisons remain on high alert so as to avoid any surprises or attacks by pirates and foreigners. On the windward coast (*barlovento*), hundreds of individuals belonging to the rebel side have continued to present themselves for royal amnesties. I have no news that there are any *gavillas* (gangs) still operating in all of the coastal region between Boquilla de Piedras[8] and Tampico.

In the Sierra Baja districts of Zacatlán and La Huasteca that border on the Province of Veracruz, military operations have continued successfully against the rebel gang leaders Simón Díaz, Serafin Olarte, and their followers. In the past month, 1,225 men with their women and children have presented themselves for the royal amnesty. Among them were one-hundred and fifty-eight children seven years of age and younger who have not been baptized. There were thirty-three men who held officer ranks in the insurgent forces, including nine foreigners and Negroes from Santo Domingo—all pirates and corsairs who disembarked at Boquilla de Piedras before royalist forces captured that town. I have ordered those individuals embarked at Veracruz for transport to Spain, where they can seek amnesties and return to their own countries, thereby freeing New Spain of these seditious persons of poor morals who cause major disturbances and damage. The efforts of the royalist officers and troops serving in the expeditions into the Huasteca region have been invaluable. The climate there is the worst in the world, and the dense forests where the rebel forces conceal themselves are practically impenetrable. The absence of healthy conditions and proliferation of poisonous reptiles have caused the commander of the region, Colonel Manuel de la Concha,[9] and some of his officers and troops to fall victim to dangerous diseases. For their invaluable services to God and the King, these men are worthy of recompense as I shall explain at greater length for the benefit of your generous disposition, when we have completed the pacification of the Sierra Baja.

The remainder of the military region of Apan,[10] which encompasses the Huasteca and the Sierra de Zacatlán, as well as several other districts, including Tulancingo, Pachuca, Texcoco, Otumba, and other jurisdictions, remain in a peaceful state as I have expressed to Your Excellency previously. Throughout the region, fields are being cultivated and commercial traffic and industry are restored under the protection and vigilance provided by local detachments and military posts manned by loyal royalists. These forces serve at their own expense or as paid troops supported by special militia taxes administered by the respective ayuntamientos and municipal juntas that have been approved previously by this government. These activities are monitored continuously, according to the Ordenanza General of this army issued 20 June, 1817, as I reported to Your Excellency.

The provinces of Puebla and Oaxaca also remain in a peaceful and stable state. During this month there have been no new developments that are worthy of Your Excellency's attention. The jurisdictions pertaining to Toluca with its military districts of Tenancingo, Tecualoya, Calimaya, Santiago Tianguistengo, Ocuila, Ixtapa, Cuatepec de las Arinas, Metepec,

Almoloya, and other districts under this command remain peaceful and tranquil. These also include Ixtlahuaca, Maravatio, and Acámbaro, that are located along the left side of the road that connects Mexico City to Valladolid (Morelia), and in Temascaltepec, Sultepec, and Zitácuaro situated to the west, one finds a state of peace and tranquility under the same military regulations as are implemented in the district of Apan. Merchants, artisans, traffickers, and laborers enjoy complete security in their daily tasks to work their fields and to engage in industry and commerce. For this reason, the recent maize harvest in the Toluca region has been very abundant.

The military detachment operating in the Valley of Temascaltepec has made several extremely useful and successful penetrations into Tierracaliente (the tropical regions) to the south of this jurisdiction. They routed the forces of the old insurgent, Colonel Pedro Campos.[11] As a result of this development, Campos and two other rebel colonels named Lorenzo and Luis Ortiz, with their followers, presented themselves to appeal for royal amnesties. Now attached to royalist forces, these same men are pursuing and harassing their erstwhile allies. Also there has been a high proportion of towns, haciendas, and hamlets of the region where the people have turned in their arms and offered to form militia companies and picket guards to support *la causa buena* (the good or royalist cause). This region shows that it is well along in the process of pacification and I expect that this will be consolidated under the advice and warnings that I offer incessantly to the commander of the royalist forces, Lieutenant Colonel Don Miguel Torres.[12] I have requested him to give me nominal lists of all those who have presented themselves for militia duty so that they can be provided with the appropriate amnesty certificates. I appointed Lieutenant Colonel Torres, who *accidentalmente* [by happenstance] commands the battalion of the Infantry Regiment of Santo Domingo, to govern this very rugged district. This entire region has been rebel territory since the beginning of the war in 1810, and the advances made by the troops of Torres's battalion have been worthy of great appreciation. As with the troops of the Huasteca region, these soldiers have extracted families and even entire towns from the forest, and they have encountered many children who have not been baptized. The effective performance of those troops has been such that they are in direct contact with military units belonging to the Sección del Norte of the Acapulco Division.

After having concluded the siege and capture of the enemy fortress at Jaujilla, as I reported in my extraordinary dispatch dated 17 March of this year, I ordered the Comandante General of the Province of Valladolid, Don Matías Martín y Aguirre,[13] to remain at Jaujilla with a strong detachment in order to prevent any new attempt by the rebel troops to reoccupy that highly advantageous site. Following my appropriate advice, he divided the troops under this command into three sections, sending one to the town of San Juan Huétamo to operate in close coordination with troops of the Acapulco Division. Their mission is to destroy the *gavillas* that operate in those regions, to reorganize the towns and haciendas of the tropical lowlands, and as I have ordered to establish good order by recruiting new companies of royalist militias (*realistas*) to sustain the defensive line along the banks of the Mezcala River.

Pursuing its own military objectives, the second section marched to the Valleys of Ario and Pururarán, forming a rear guard for Huétamo and providing defensive support for the first section. This tactical deployment has created a defensive chain of military posts that extends from Valladolid (Morelia) to the City of Pátzquaro, and onward to the shores of the Pacific Ocean. In between there are great sugar mills, cattle ranches, and haciendas that produce valuable commodities that since the outbreak of the rebellion until the present have been in rebel hands. In the future, under the renewed control of their legitimate owners, the resources of the province will be directed to support the royalist troops.

The third section under the command of Colonel Martín y Aguirre, marched to Puruándiro, in the northern part of the province to pursue the apostate cleric Miguel Torres.[14] They defeated these enemy bands in several skirmishes, killing eighty-one rebels from whom the royalist soldiers recovered forty muskets, and some machetes, lances, horses, and other items. In one of those clashes, Cadet Don Manuel de Arana of the Provincial Dragoon Regiment of Potosí distinguished himself in combat leading only six soldiers when he forced the surrender of eighteen rebels armed with muskets. For his actions, in the name of the King I have conferred upon him the rank of ensign. I inform Your Excellency so that you can obtain the official approval of His Majesty.

In a raid by the garrison from the town of Acámbaro, a dependency of the military command of Valladolid, conducted by forces commanded by Sublieutenant Don Rafael Silva of the Infantry Regiment of New Spain, against the rebel band led by the so-called Brigadier José María Velasco, the royalist troops killed nineteen rebels and captured twelve prisoners including the insurgent chief Francisco Rubi. They also captured twelve muskets, forty saddled horses, and some lances, machetes, and other items. Your Excellency can read about the details of this action from the *Gazeta de México*, no. 1238, which I have attached to this report. For his successful operations, I promoted Sublieutenant Silva to the rank of lieutenant. I am informing Your Excellency of my actions in this regard so that His Majesty will grant his approval.

The royalist military division of Acapulco district crushed the rebels in an action at the hills of Aguacate and Cusamala. They killed thirty rebels, captured twenty, and wounded many others. The troops captured eight muskets, three pistols, fifteen machetes, and one hundred saddled horses, twenty mules, and sundry other equipment. Also, as a result of this successful operation, the troops imprisoned the rebel chief and apostate cleric, Matías Zavala.[15] After the arrest of rebel leader Nicolás Bravo,[16] about which I informed Your Excellency, Zavala titled himself Comandante General of the district. He has been transferred to the town of Cuernavaca, where charges are being prepared against him to determine the proper application of justice.

Immediately, Colonel Don José Gabriel de Armijo, Comandante General of the *División del Rumbo de Acapulco* (the Division of Acapulco Direction), occupied Cusamala when a rebel unit attempted to surprise the rebel chief, Pablo Campos, before he presented himself to be amnestied, as has been described in the *Gazeta*, no. 1237. During the defense of that town, First Sergeant Don José Manuel Jalabán, of *Escuadrón Provincial de Dragones del Sur* (the Provincial Dragoon Squadron of the South) distinguished himself in combat. In the name of the King, I promoted him to ensign pending royal approval. I include a complete report of the actions taken by this individual and of the other two soldiers whom I recommended previously in this dispatch. The troops operating in this region continue following my orders to pursue the *gavillas* that are still operating there. Before the commencement of the rainy season, I expect that tranquility and good order will be reestablished, as well as the required level of stability that will approach complete pacification.

As I have already informed Your Excellency in my previous reports, the territory between Mexico City and Querétaro, which includes the jurisdictions of Tula, Ixmiquilpan, Zimapán, Huichipán, and San Juan del Río remains in a good state. The towns and haciendas are garrisoned by companies and picket forces of *fieles realistas* (loyal royalist militias) that serve at their own expense or with their costs supported by their own expense or by *contribuciones militares* (special local militia support taxes).[17] They escort convoys and royal mail deliveries coming and going from the Provincias Internas. As a direct result, there have been no calamities during the time that I have held this command. Notwithstanding the work of these militias, regular troops continue to patrol the roads and to protect agriculture and commerce.

The troops of the Querétaro division continue their raids against the rebels based in Xalpa and they escort the convoys from San Luis Potosí and from San Luis de la Paz. To guarantee the safe passage of our convoys and the mail, at present they are occupied with the construction of fortifications at San Luis de la Paz and at the Hacienda of Puerto de Nieto.

Brigadier Don Domingo de Luaces,[18] Colonel of the expeditionary Infantry Regiment of Zaragoza, who has been serving as military and political Governor of Querétaro, informed me recently that his poor health will not allow him to continue in that post. I did not agree to his first request, arguing that all of us must make sacrifices under the present circumstances. Upon receiving his second request, however, I conceded

Luaces a two-month leave of absence from his post so that he can come to Mexico City to recover his health and I appointed the commander of the Dragoon Regiment of Sierragorda, Colonel Don Francisco Guizanoteguí, to serve as interim governor of Querétaro.

To achieve the destruction of the rebel bands operating in Sierragorda, situated to the north of Querétaro, I have ordered the mobilization of 400 *realistas* (royalist militiamen) from the Ríoverde detachment, 100 from the district of Tula, and another 100 from Cadereyta under the command of Lieutenant Colonel Don Manuel de la Llata, commander of the latter district. In a clash with these rebels, amnestied (former insurgent and now royalist) Captain Don Epitacio Sánchez and his troops killed twenty-six men, wounded many more, and captured seven prisoners. The royalist troops recovered twelve carbines, six machetes, sixteen lances, and other equipment as reported in the *Gazeta*, no. 1242. Lieutenant Colonel Llata has my orders to work in accord with Lieutenant Colonel Don Cristóbal Villaseñor, who commands the line between Querétaro and San Luis Potosí. I will not relax my iron fist from these cursed rebels until either they are annihilated totally or pacified after they receive royal amnesties. At that point I will establish *compañías de realistas* (royalist militia companies) in the towns and on haciendas that will pay to sustain these forces and to banish rebellion forever from that mountainous region.

In the province of Guanajuato, the troops continue an active pursuit of the rebels and on the 18th of this month Colonel Don Anastacio Busta-mante,[19] *comandante de la Sección del Sur* (commander of the division of the south of Guanajuato province), dispersed the *gavillas* led by the Apostate Miguel Torres, causing them the loss of dead, wounded and prisoners. In addition, as has been reported in the *Gazeta*, no. 1263, some weapons and horses were recovered. This information has been verified by the commander of the Salvatierra detachment, Lieutenant Colonel Don Antonio Larragoiti, who led his forces against rebel concentrations in his district as reported in the *Gazeta*, nos. 1238 and 1239.

The interim Comandante General of Guanajuato, Colonel Don Antonio Linares,[20] escorted a convoy for Celaya that carried ninety-three silver bars belonging to private interests and the crown. Of these, eleven bars that belonged to the King had to be exchanged at Guanajuato to pay the garrison troops. In fulfillment of my orders to relieve the needs of the mining industry, 400 *cargas* of salt and magistral required urgently for silver refining arrived safely at the mines. To facilitate economic recovery, communications have been reopened between Guanajuato and the provinces of Guadalajara and Zacatecas through the town of San Pedro Piedragorda and the hacienda of Cantera where I stationed military detachments. The goal of these dispositions is to facilitate the recovery of commerce and to provide the Guanajuato mining industry with supplies and materials needed to reestablish the mining and refining industries.

Also, I have decided to dispatch a weekly convoy from Querétaro carrying state and private cargo shipments for Guadalajara, Zacatecas, and the Provincias Internas de Occidente. They will travel the route through Guanajuato with protection provided by the Cantera detachment that will help them to reach their destinations. The same routing will be followed by couriers of those provinces as I ordered in November, 1816, avoiding a detour of more than 80 leagues through San Luis Potosí. For public knowledge of these changes, I ordered the publication of this information in the *Gazeta*, no. 1242, to inform merchants and shippers about the considerable advantages and the great savings in the cost of freightage. These steps will speed up and increase the flow of commerce and enhance private and royal treasury business. In general, these changes will improve commerce and communications between the capital and the Provincias Internas.

The garrison of Villa de León that pertains to the district of Guanajuato has made some very effective raids against the rebels. Recently, as was reported in the *Gazeta* on the 14th of the present month, this royalist force encountered an insurgent cavalry unit belonging to the Apostate Torres at the Hacienda of Cueramaro. The ensuing action resulted in a number of enemy dead before the remainder dispersed under the pressure of our courageous forces.

The fortification of the Hacienda de Cantera and of the town of Pénjamo, situated at the foot of Cerro de San Gregorio, has been concluded in accordance with my dispositions to prevent the enemy from returning to that advantageous position. I informed Your Excellency in my dispatch no. 41, that a section of the troops from the garrison of Guadalajara will be sent to occupy these locations and to defend the town of Puruándiro that is located on the border between Valladolid and Guanajuato provinces.[21] These dispositions are designed to remove the cursed rebel bands that mutually assist each other from both provinces, steal from the resources of the region, and gain advantages by diverting commerce.

I notified Your Excellency of my plans in dispatches no. 28 and 39 dated last August 31 and January 20 about the capture by the division commanded by Field Marshal Don Pascaul de Liñán[22] of the rebel forts of Comanja and San Gregorio in the Province of Guanajuato. In those reports, as well as in previous correspondence, I informed Your Excellency about the fatigues, travails and deprivations suffered by our troops during the almost five months of sieges directed against those enemy fortifications. In order to assault those positions, there were great obstacles that our troops had to overcome caused by the inaccessibility of the rugged terrain and the strong defensive works constructed by enemy engineering and artillery officers who disembarked in New Spain with the traitor Javier Mina.[23] The obstinate and dogged resistance presented by the enemy caused us the loss of many distinguished officers and soldiers who perished, and even more who were injured and crippled. They gave their best in all the operations that took place, giving proof of the courage and valor exhibited by the troops of the King against the audacity and tenacious resistance demonstrated by our nefarious enemies. Your Excellency can read about their exploits yourself in copies of the *Gazeta*, nos. 1192, 1222, 1224, and 1230, that include the battlefield reports of General Liñán.

In view of such valuable services and with Liñán's corroboration following his arrival here with verbal information to support the original reports, I have awarded promotions that I have outlined in an attached report no. 2 in the name of Our Lord, the King, to the officers, cadets, and sergeants, who distinguished themselves in combat. Although I have acted within the powers granted to me by the King, I beg Your Excellency to assist me obtain a favorable approval of this petition to the Sovereign on behalf of vassals who with their blood sealed their the love and determination to sustain the laws of the throne.

In addition, I include a report no. 3 an attachment that lists the names of the officers whom I consider worthy of the award of the Cross of Caballeros and Comendadores of the Royal American Order of Isabel the Catholic, for their distinguished conduct during the sieges and assaults on those forts. I have sent this information to the *Asamblea Provincial del Reino* (Provincial Assembly of the Kingdom) to make the statutory publication as is mandated by law. Regarding General Liñán, I recommended in my report no. 39 that His Majesty consider the grace of conferring upon him the Great Cross of the above mentioned Royal Order.

Additionally, I have ordered the preparation of reports by seniority on more than 400 officers, cadets, and sergeants belonging to military units that participated in the sieges. Although these men are not eligible for regular advancements by rank or seniority, I will issue promotions of one grade to those individuals of each rank who are most senior in their units. Including the pickets of different army units assembled for the sieges, this totals about 400 men. To the most senior of the above mentioned ranks who have not been promoted through regular seniority or otherwise rewarded, in the name of His Majesty, I acted to raise them one rank immediately pending royal approval. As the opportunity arises, I shall send the appropriate reports to Your Excellency regarding the names of those who have benefited from this award, so that His Majesty will be properly notified with the end of obtaining his sovereign approval.

Finally, I conferred badges of distinction to those officers and enlisted men who took part in the victories at Comanja and San Gregorio. They shall wear these badges made of sky-blue cloth emblazoned with a motto commemorating the capture of the enemy forts on their upper left arms. And to make these military siege operations better known, I am sending a sealed tube for Your Excellency with a map and two views of the hill of San Gregorio that will help to inform His Majesty. The director of the post has been charged with providing adequate security so that this package will arrive safely in your hands as did the materials illustrating the operations at Comanja that I sent with my dispatches last September 30th.

The Guadalajara division, subdivided into a number of sections and detachments has continued its raids and useful surprises against the rebels of Guanajuato and Valladolid provinces. These units defeated several *gavillas*, costing the enemy dead, injured, captured, and the loss of horses and arms. Your Excellency can see the battle reports in the *Gazeta* for the present month.

The provinces of Zacatecas and San Luis Potosí continue in a good state of pacification, as I have explained already to Your Excellency in my previous reports. During this past month there have been no further developments to report, other than the fact that the last convoy from the north delivered 686 silver bars belonging to private owners, 507 *cargas* of merchandise, and 35,000 sheep[24] to supply the needs of this capital city. Since Pedro el Negro was brought to justice and the rebel chiefs Vargas and González petitioned for amnesties, it is clear that we have entered a period of greater security.

The Provincias Internas de Oriente y Occidente (East and West) have not experienced any new developments that deserve the attention of the King, but I have received diverse communications from our plenipotentiary minister in the United States, Don Luis de Onís, on projects planned by the Anglo-Americans to take possession of countries belonging to the Spanish Crown. I enclose an attached copy for Your Excellency that includes three Acts issued in the United States during the years 1811 and 1812, that according to the above-mentioned Minister were kept from public knowledge until recently when they were published in newspapers. Those sources stated the intentions of the United States to occupy the territories to the east of the Río Perdido, to the south of the state of Georgia, and the territory of the Mississippi, under the specious pretext that they do not wish these regions to be occupied by some foreign nation. They assumed arbitrarily that His Majesty is in no condition to defend these areas and to keep them for Spain. On this aspect, they are very wrong concerning the provinces that the King has placed under my charge, and I can assure Your Excellency that these fractious elements will pay dearly if they enter New Spain. They will not be able to keep a single inch of our territory under their command.

I have explained to Your Excellency in all of my previous reports, since I found myself in this command, about the evil intentions of the Anglo-Americans and the perfidious conduct that they have demonstrated towards us in fomenting and assisting the rebels of this kingdom in making war against their legitimate sovereign (particularly when the Anglo-Americans were not denied free communications with our coasts which I removed upon my arrival in Veracruz). They have sent several emissaries back and forth and have made plans to overthrow this government and to establish independence. In United States ports, they armed and supplied pirates who caused and are causing so much damage to our commerce. In these same ports, the authorities declare Spanish vessels captured as legal prizes and sell them publicly. Last year, they equipped the traitor Mina with everything that he needed to cause so much damage to the pacification of these provinces, bringing with him on his vessel some Anglo-American officers, soldiers, and mariners. In sum, there is no shortage of evils and prejudicial acts that nation has not caused to this country since the beginning of the rebellion. I have no doubts that the revolt would have ended entirely by now if the insurgents did not keep alive the hope that they would be assisted by the United States. Since the beginning, they have counted upon that nation as their principal benefactor.

After I disembarked in Veracruz, I issued my orders to expel the rebels from Boquilla de Piedras, which was the principal point of communications with the United States where ships from New Orleans and other ports arrived every day. It was through this conduit that they introduced aid and emissaries came and went with such open disregard for royal authority that the same ships continued their voyages to Veracruz. Often, they carried rebel agents aboard who were able to meet and to conspire with other rebels hidden within the population of the city of Veracruz. One of these plots was for a coordinated attack involving a land assault by the bands of Guadalupe Victoria with the pirates and Anglo-Americans invading from the sea.

After Boquilla de Piedras was occupied by royalist troops, the rebels used Nautla, Misantla, and many other places that had to be watched and guarded with great vigilance. As a result of this effort, all communications between those cursed rebels and the United States have ceased which also has terminated clandestine commerce and the introduction of military assistance. These efforts have obstructed and made much more difficult the destructive work of the rebel bands that occupied the Huasteca region and operated in the districts near Papantla. Misantla, Tampico, and other places. Many thousands of inhabitants who followed the enemy party now recognize the paternal dominion of His Majesty.

The Anglo-Americans cannot view the advanced state of our pacification efforts in this kingdom with indifference and the fact that we have wrested from their hands the prize that already they considered secure. They watched with great pain the destruction of the perfidious Mina and his followers, most of whom were citizens of that country, and the backers of that adventurer suffered considerable financial losses. According to papers captured from Mina, one man called Shmit of New Orleans, expressed great expectations about provoking a general rebellion in this Kingdom capable of upsetting my government. Possibly they could have succeeded had it not been through Divine protection, and by the measures that under such protection I took to neutralize their rebel projects and to consummate their extermination, as we did thanks to the grace of God.

Seeing their contraband operations that had allowed them to introduce assistance designed to foment rebellion thwarted, and having lost the hope of establishing their pretended independence in this kingdom, the Anglo-Americans have published their Acts that previously had been kept secret in an effort to reanimate rebel spirits, and to endeavor by this means to give some new impetus to the insurrection that they are greatly pained to see heading toward total annihilation and ruin. In the first of those Acts, issued on January 19, 1812, when the first chiefs of the rebellion took over the Provincias Internas de Oriente and dispatched their emissaries to the United States, it was declared that *Local Authority* would be held by the rebels who occupied the provinces and that the legitimate government and commanders of the troops of the King would not participate in the plots.

In the copy of the document from the Plenipotentiary Minister, he included a letter in which he informed me of the departure from the United States of 156 French officers including Napoleon's former generals Clausel and Lefebvre-Desnouettes, with the objective of establishing a post at Tombigbee. They carried with them plows and other farm implements needed to cultivate the soil. Minister Onís says that he has given a passport and a letter of introduction to me to one General Lallemand, who also served Napoleon, so that he could come to this capital to discuss the settlement of an establishment in the Province of Texas for himself and for those adventurers. Onís stated in his letter that he used this pretext to distract these people from their principal idea of organizing an invasion. This measure seemed to me not only unproductive, since I am not authorized to concede such an establishment which is contrary to the Laws of Indies and the orders from His Majesty, but it is exceedingly prejudicial. Among other serious threats, the project proposes to settle a species of subjects in the countries of the King who extraordinarily would attract to themselves the attention of the people included in the rebellion. In addition, they would attract other people to embrace the causes that were the pretext for the revolt.

Guided by these principles, I have cautioned the governor of Veracruz and the Commander of Tampico that if General Lallemand arrives there, they should confiscate his letters and passport, and inform him courteously that our laws and royal orders issued by His Majesty the King do not permit any foreigner to establish himself in this kingdom, and that he must return to the place from whence he came. The governors should facilitate this with hospitality, but without permitting Lallemand or any other member of his party to disembark. I sent the same warnings to the Comandantes Generales of the Provincias Internas of the Oriente and Occidente, and to the Governor of Texas in case the above-mentioned general should attempt to go there despite the warnings made by Minister Onís. In my letter of response to his letter, I outlined my dispositions, adding my fears that the project of General Lallemand may very well be a distraction so that he can first impose himself upon those countries and afterward work with the knowledge he obtains on his invasion projects.

Minister Onís says at the end of his letter that the success or failure of these developments, (which I assume are those projects being promoted by the Anglo-Americans to take control of Spanish territories), depend on my actions. His assertions in this matter appear to me very strange given the strict orders that I received from His Majesty not to give motives for complaints by the United States, and that I should only take precautionary measures, as I have already done and notified Your Excellency. In truth, I would be the first to celebrate the destruction of the Anglo-American plans by depending solely upon my own response. I would act as I did against the traitor Mina, against his ships and against those who disembarked with him. The Minister frequently confuses the Floridas and Amalia Island subject to the Captaincy General of the Island of Cuba (the only jurisdiction that can aid them, and not me due to lack of naval forces) with the provinces subject to this Viceroyalty. He believes that I will remove the pirates and Anglo-Americans from that island as he expresses in his letters that I include with my responses in this dispatch.

No less extraordinary are his suggestions that I send troops to the Tombigbee River[25] at its confluence with the Black Warrior River[26] to impede the progress of the French adventurers in that place on the east side of the Mississippi River at 32 degrees 30 minutes North latitude, and 11 degrees west of London[27] according to the map that I have which was published in Philadelphia in 1816 by John Melish. This is hundreds of leagues beyond the most remote frontiers of this kingdom. In addition to having to make an immense march through dreadful deserts and unknown countries, any force from New Spain would have to cross large stretches of the territory of the United States.

I conclude this matter by assuring Your Excellency that I have taken and will continue to take all the necessary measures that are in my powers to prevent any damage to the precious domains that Our Lord the King has placed under my care. In their defense, I will shed the last drop of my blood and that of the valiant troops under my command.

During this month, following the pious intentions of His Majesty, I have declared royal amnesties for 1,223 individuals who have embraced the royal pardon within the legal time limit, and others to whom I extended the period of the amnesty offer. Among those pardoned is Licenciado Don Andrés Quintana,[28] who was a member of the revolutionary junta of this Kingdom, but with the condition that he depart for the Iberian Peninsula with his wife, Doña Leona Vicario,[29] who followed him always in his deviations and has played a large part in the rebellion. Another individual receiving pardon is Don Mariano Tercero, a member of the ridiculous Junta of Jaujilla that will attempt to establish itself in the places organized by troops of the King.

All these details, although my account of the military, economic, and political operations concerning them is very succinct, will contribute to the knowledge of Your Excellency. In case you need information you will need to take into consideration the climates, distances, and the inconveniences that all of these factors produce upon energetic responses. At the same time, in such distinct places and across the extensive breadth of the rebellion, I will keep doing what is necessary to arrive at the desired and happy end, which is the total pacification of these Dominions. I will exercise as much vigilance, efficiency, knowledge, and tenacity as are needed to attain this goal as well as that of the meritorious commanders, officers, and troops who are assisting me. One day, I will be able to say to our beloved Sovereign and Lord that we have concluded the war of the rebellion of New Spain. May God grant us this satisfaction that I hope will occur shortly. In the interim, I desire to inform Your Excellency of this knowledge for His Majesty that I am honored to communicate.

May God guide Your Excellency,
Mexico City, March 31, 1818.
Juan Ruíz de Apodaca
To: Minister of War Marqués de Campo Sagrado, Madrid

Notes

1. Unlike some other insurgent leaders, little is known about Vergara's career in Veracruz province. In 1817, he accepted a royal amnesty at Arenal and for a time became a militia captain in the royalist forces. When Javier Mina arrived in New Spain, Vergara rejoined the rebellion. In 1818, he died in an internecine fight between rebel bands.

2. Guadalupe Victoria (b. 29 September 1785–d. 21 March 1843) or José Miguel Ramón Adaucto Fernández y Félix as he was known before he changed his name, joined the rebellion in the province of Veracruz during 1812 under José María Morelos. He was a tenacious guerrilla chieftain who spurned all amnesty programs and withstood the counterinsurgency campaigns of Spain's best field officers of the period. He survived the attacks of General Pascual de Liñán and of the Captain Antonio López de Santa Anna who was determined to establish his reputation by terminating Victoria's career. Following independence, Victoria was the first constitutionally elected president of the Mexican republic (1824–1829).

3. A veteran dragoon officer of the Spanish army who began his career in the blockade of Gibraltar during the War of American Independence, García Conde spent many years in sedentary colonial military service in New Spain prior to 1810 and the outbreak of the Hidalgo Revolt. Indeed, he was still a career lieutenant colonel in 1809 and had been directing road construction projects for the army. With a wife and six children to support, he was anxious to move away from the limited possibilities of promotion in a country in which there were only two regular dragoon regiments and into a more lucrative posting in the civil

administration. When the war broke out, García Conde was appointed colonel of the Provincial Dragoon Regiment of Puebla and shortly thereafter Comandante de las Armas of Michoacán province. With his career soaring, he headed for Michoacán, but was captured by the rebels. While he survived a period of captivity and viewed the chaos in the army of Hidalgo firsthand, like many other older career officers, García Conde was not successful in developing flexible counterinsurgency roles that were demanded of a new generation of royalist combat officers.

4. Like some other commanders, Ciriaco de Llano arrived in New Spain as a naval officer. Since there was a desperate need for army commanders, Viceroy Francisco Xavier de Venegas—likely his uncle—transferred Llano to the army. By 1813, he was colonel of the regular Fixed Infantry Regiment of Mexico and Gobernador Militar y Político of the province of Puebla. Llano was an excellent field officer and administrator who held a succession of posts until 1821 when he capitulated to Agustín de Iturbide at Puebla after a brief struggle. Unlike many senior officers who stayed in Mexico, Llano returned to Spain by way of Cuba, recommending the dispatch of a new expeditionary army from Spain to reconquer Mexico.

5. Colonel Francisco Hevia arrived at Veracruz in 1812 commanding a battalion of the Infantry Regiment of Castile that was dispatched with the first expeditionary units from the Spanish army sent to crush rebellion in New Spain. Although the infusion of new blood was an essential factor to support the royalist cause, Hevia's unit was besieged at Veracruz by rebel forces that used the climate to their advantage. Beset by *vomito negro* (yellow fever), Hevia's battalion lost over 300 soldiers before the remnants broke through the enemy cordon and reached the healthy climate of upland Jalapa. Hevia became an implacable enemy of the rebels and unlike most royalist officers who surrendered, in May, 1821, he perished in combat at Córdoba during Iturbide's rebellion.

6. Another of the colonial career officers, Castillo y Bustamante worked hard prior to 1810 to achieve success in the provincial militias. He served in the cantonments during invasion scares before 1810 and became colonel of the Provincial Infantry Regiment of Tres Villas based at Jalapa. In 1809, Castillo y Bustamante became a caballero in the Order of Santiago and in 1810 just before the Hidalgo Revolt, he was named to join the senior staff of the army of Castilla la Vieja in Spain based at Santander. The war prevented his departure from New Spain, but also enhanced his career. He became an active Callejista (supporter of Félix Calleja), a brigadier general, and governor of Tlaxcala. As governor of Jalapa during the war, he became wealthy during his campaigns against Guadalupe Victoria and other rebel chiefs. In 1820 with the restoration of the liberal Spanish Constitution of 1812, Castillo y Bustamante was charged at Jalapa with destroying public liberty.

7. One of the major weaknesses of the royalists was that they could not control the insurgents of Veracruz who blockaded the roads, interdicted commerce, and collected their own taxes on any shipments from or to the interior of the country. Since flexible counterinsurgency did not work effectively against guerrilla-bandit gangs that disappeared or coalesced according to available opportunities, the royalists constructed a series of blockhouses and gradually built a system of semaphore towers and other signal devices to protect the narrow road corridor used by the convoys. However, even this expensive system failed for lengthy periods in which rebel bands cut off all communications between Mexico City and Spain. Massive expeditions reopened the road temporarily, but the insurgents returned as soon as the royalist forces withdrew or became exhausted by constant combat.

8. One of the great problems for the insurgents of New Spain concerned the supply of adequate weapons and munitions. While there was no adequate supplier capable or willing to arm the rebel forces, weapons were introduced from United States ports—particularly New Orleans—to small harbors along the Mexican Gulf coast. The royalists recognized the importance of closing these ports such as Nautla and Boquilla de Piedras in Veracruz province which in 1816 fell to the royalists. The role of the counterinsurgency forces was to keep the insurgents off the coast and to cut them off from foreign suppliers. Barring this approach, they had to prevent rebel bands in the coastal region from penetrating the interior.

9. Beginning his military career in 1811 as commander of a light infantry company at Valladolid (Morelia), Concha emerged as one of the more effective royalist counterinsurgency campaigners. His program in the Apan region and elsewhere involved a forced militarization of the population that was required to support locally raised and district funded forces. Concha fought tenaciously until the chaos of 1821 when he was assassinated by an armed band.

10. The Apan region was of great strategic importance throughout the war and a testing ground used by both sides to develop strategies and tactics to advance insurgency or counterinsurgency. See Virginia Guedea, *La insurgencia en el Departamento del Norte: Los Llanos de Apan y la Sierra de Puebla, 1810–1816* (México: UNAM/Instituto Mora, 1996).

11. Pedro Campos first emerged in 1811 when he was part of a failed conspiracy to kidnap Viceroy Venegas and to hand him over to the rebel leader Ignacio López Rayón at Zitácuaro. He continued to fight the royalists as a guerrilla band leader.

12. Although he was an acting lieutenant colonel, Torres's actual rank was major of the regular Infantry Regiment of Santo Domingo. This unit was difficult to manage since its troops were often criminals and deserters from other units who deserted again when provisions ran short or they came to know the people of a given district. Torres suffered poor health caused by his advancing age, the mortifying climate, and the terrible conditions that he and his men endured during their campaigns in rugged terrain.

13. A very active career combat officer and commander of the Provincial Regiment of Fieles de Potosí, in 1820 with the restoration of the Spanish Constitution, Martín y Aguirre was elected to the Spanish Cortes for the province of San Luis Potosí. After years of active duty, he became a proponent of the mulatto and mestizo soldiers who served in the royalist forces.

14. Brother of the much more famous rebel commander, Padre José Antonio Torres, Miguel Torres led guerrilla bands in the Sierra de Guanajuato.

15. Padre Zavala joined the insurgency early in support of Morelos and led rebel troops until 1817 when he was captured in a skirmish at Cerro de Aguacate. He was exiled to the Spanish presidio of Ceuta in North Africa.

16. This of course was the famous Nicolás Bravo (1786–1854), who joined Morelos in 1812 and designed the fortifications for the siege of Cuautla Amilpas. Following the Independence war he was a major player in the centralist politics and life of the new nation—an unsuccessful presidential candidate in 1824, a rebel exiled to Ecuador, interim president of Mexico in 1839 and 1843, and vice-president of the nation in 1846.

17. These militia support taxes were a crucial element in the royalist counterinsurgency program in New Spain. It was essential as Félix Calleja (see his Reglamento in this volume) understood that the people must be compelled to pay for and to man the defense of their home districts so that army units would be free to concentrate upon the dangerous *focos* (centers) of insurgent power. After years of

paying graduated income taxes and other imposts to support militias and to build and maintain town fortifications, the populace of all classes became exhausted. With the restoration of the Spanish Constitution, local officials were quick to realize that these local military taxes were illegal. As they disbanded their militias, the royalist army lost its ability to hold territory. Given this situation, Agustín de Iturbide was able to stage what was in fact a glorious victory march across New Spain absorbing rather than defeating most of the remaining royalist forces.

18. Luaces arrived in New Spain in 1816 from Spain as chief of the second battalion of the Infantry of Zaragoza commanded by Field Marshal Pascual de Liñán. Before long, he tired of the drudgery and lack of glory of an endless guerrilla war that he recognized probably could not be won. He criticized Viceroy Apodaca, claimed illnesses that no one believed, and requested permission to retire. By 1818, he complained to Liñán that while his regiment had a distinguished history of 157 years' existence, never had it suffered such abandonment and miseries of every sort. In 1821, Luaces joined with Iturbide under the Plan de Iguala and by 1822 he was dispatched with orders to defeat the remaining Spanish garrison at San Juan de Ulúa, the guardian fortress of Veracruz.

19. Bustamante was yet another officer who launched a major military and political career during the Independence war. He was Vice-President of Mexico (1830–1832), and President (1837–1841). After beginning his career as a student of religion and medicine, Bustamante followed Calleja and later participated in the campaigns against Mina. He joined Iturbide and was a major figure in the early republic. See Brian R. Hamnett, "Anastacio Bustamante y la guerra de Independencia," *Historia Mexicana* 24:4 (1979), 515–545.

20. Linares began his career as a militia captain in the Provincial Dragoon Regiment of Querétaro. He served under Brigadier José de la Cruz in Nueva Galicia, distinguished himself in the campaigns against Mina in 1817, and in 1818 he became Comandante General of Guanajuato. He was slow to join Iturbide, but did not wish to engage in internecine bloodshed as New Spain collapsed. He joined the independence movement and played an active role in the affairs of the city of Celaya after independence.

21. Rebel forces often took advantage of the weaknesses of the border regions between royalist military districts and provinces. Often, royalist commanders did not coordinate their operations and the insurgent bands could move back and forth between jurisdictions with relative impunity. Brian Hamnett examined this major problem thoroughly in "Royalist Counterinsurgency and the Continuity of Rebellion: Guanajuato and Michoacán, 1813–1820," *HAHR* 63:1 (February 1982), 19–48; and in *Roots of Insurgency: Mexican Regions, 1750–1824* (Cambridge: Cambridge University Press, 1986).

22. Pascual de Liñán (1775–1855) arrived in New Spain with the last major overseas reinforcements of almost 2,000 Spanish expeditionary troops. Although this force was to have gone to Panama and on to Peru, fears that the insurgents of New Spain might permanently blockade communications between the interior and the coast forced the Madrid authorities to arrange these reassignments. Indeed, General Pablo Morillo was to have dispatched 4,000 troops from Venezuela to support this operation. While these troops did not arrive in New Spain, Liñán was successful in driving back the Veracruz rebels and he commanded the operations against Mina. Viceroy Apodaca used Liñán in numerous difficult situations until 1821 when he failed against Iturbide. In New Spain at different times he was Comandante General of the Army of the North, Comandante General of the provinces of Querétaro and Guanajuato, and Sub-Inspector General of the Army of New Spain. Until 1822, when he was expelled from the country, Liñán stayed in Mexico to look after the remaining Spanish peninsular troops who desired

repatriation to Spain. He continued his military career and proposed the reconquest of New Spain.

23. Javier Mina (1789–1817) fought in Spain against the French invasion during which he suffered capture and later he sympathized with the cause of Spanish American independence. An enigmatic figure, Mina organized an expedition in the United States in 1817 that landed with the intention of reanimating the insurrection in New Spain. While some amnestied former rebels returned to insurgency, the royalists were successful in isolating and attacking Mina's forces. Finally on 27 October 1817, at Rancho El Venadito, Mina was captured. He died before a royalist firing squad on 11 November 1817. When Viceroy Apodaca was elevated to the noble rank as a count, in recognition of the royalist victory he selected the name Conde de Venadito.

24. On some occasions, even larger numbers of sheep and cattle were driven from San Luis Potosí, Celaya, Querétaro, and other ranching centers to meet the inexhaustible demands for meat in the capital. Given the guerrilla and bandit elements of the war years, it is easy to see why the royalist commanders had no alternative other than to keep these transport corridors open and safe from raiders. One of the great threats posed by the insurgents was that they might be able to starve the metropolis of Mexico City.

25. This river is in the state of Alabama.

26. In Apodaca's document, this river appears under the incorrect name Blake Warnion.

27. The latitude is fairly accurate, but the meridian of longitude mentioned was not measured from London or Greenwich, England.

28. This was the famous Andrés Quintana Roo (1787–1851), who joined the rebels in 1812 and used his pen in support of the cause of independence. He assisted Ignacio López Rayón and then the Plan de Iguala of Iturbide. He became a federalist deputy after independence and was sent by Santa Anna to negotiate an end to separatism in Yucatán.

29. Leona Vicario (1789–1842) was one of the great insurgent heroines of the independence era. Born to a wealthy family, she supplied clothing, arms, and munitions to the rebels. She married Quintana Roo, lived on the run pursued by royalist forces, and rejected many offers of amnesty. In 1817, she was captured and Quintana Roo turned himself in to seek a royal pardon. The couple was to have been exiled to Spain, but they remained in New Spain until the restoration of the Constitution in 1820 when they were liberated from incarceration.

III

Caudillismo, War, and
Insurgency in South America

6

The Commencement of the Revolution in Venezuela

Major George Flinter

Love him or hate him, Simón Bolívar was the most important figure in the independence of Spanish America. The Liberator's longevity, ideas, military role, and influence upon Venezuela, Colombia, Ecuador, Peru, and Bolivia (named after him) make him a unique force who towers over the most famous of his contemporaries in Spanish America. Bolívar was an extremely complex and vulnerable figure who shared many of the weaknesses as well as the strengths of other patriot and royalist leaders. In Venezuela, similar in some respects to some regions of New Spain, he recognized the racial divisions between the whites and pardos; *racial questions were of particular importance in Venezuela, where the mulatto and* pardo *populations opposed dominance by the white elites. To achieve military success, Bolívar needed to deal with many insubordinate caudillos such as José Antonio Páez, who led guerrilla forces and kept the independence cause alive during the difficult years of Spanish counterrevolution led by General Pablo Morillo.*

George Flinter supported the Spanish royalist cause, and, as his observations confirm, he was no friend of Bolívar or the Venezuelan patriot forces. In 1812, Flinter, who knew the Spanish language, was posted with his British regiment on the island of Curaçao. There, he met with Spanish refugees from Caracas and absorbed their views about the nature of the revolt in Venezuela. In 1815, Flinter visited Venezuela and with Spanish permission traveled in areas controlled by the royalists. In 1816, like so many veterans of the Napoleonic Wars, he found himself unemployed when the British army disbanded his regiment. He went to Caracas as a translator and import-export business agent. A partisan royalist supporter,

From George Flinter, *A History of the Revolution of Caracas Comprising an Impartial Narrative of the Atrocities Committed by the Contending Parties Illustrating the Real State of the Contest both in a Commercial and Political Point of View: Together with a Description of the Llaneros, Or People of the Plains of South America* (London: T. and J. Allman, 1819), 12–56.

Flinter wrote: "I had not only an opportunity of observing every part of the country, and the disposition of its inhabitants, but also the conduct of the Spanish government, towards the natives; and I do not hesitate a moment in declaring, that it was always humane and conciliatory, whilst, on the contrary, the insurgent leaders have continually endeavored to outvie each other in acts of barbarity" (p. x). His descriptions of the geography and climate of the Puerto Cabello region underscore the difficulties of making war in the Americas. Like any good propagandist, Flinter purported to be shocked by the "falsehoods propagated by the agents of the insurgent government" that painted the Spaniards as "guilty of atrocities the most abhorrent to humanity."

Although we must exercise care with Flinter's admitted biases in favor of the royalists, what he has to say on military topics and in general is interesting and informative. He liked the revolutionary precursor, Francisco de Miranda, who had resided in London and worked for the British government. Despite his own views, Flinter described the chaos in Caracas at the outbreak of the independence revolution that was similar to many other parts of Spanish America. The European Spaniards demanded loyalty while the criollos believed that they could take control of their nation. In Venezuela as in many other Spanish American regions, the mulattos, pardos, *mestizos, and other* castas *had a different view of the future that did not include simply changing white masters. Flinter recorded the opinions of royalist refugees, most of whom were whites, who opposed major changes that would raise the* castas' *position and status in Venezuelan society.*

When it came to responsibility for the horrendous atrocities that marked the Venezuelan conflict—perhaps in part because they were publicized so widely—Flinter damned patriots such as Bolívar and Antonio Nicolás ("El Diablo") Briceño and made Spaniards such as General Domingo de Monteverde appear to abhor any summary executions. In fact, both sides committed atrocities, which resulted in Bolívar's famous June 15, 1813, Proclamation of Guerra a Muerte *(war to the death). Any Spaniard who refused to pledge his active loyalty to the patriot side was to be punished by death before a firing squad (Chapter 11). While death threats were common in all of the Spanish American independence wars, Bolívar's Proclamation received broad circulation, and some notable atrocities were used by opponents to darken his reputation.*

The history of all civil wars, shows, that when once the sword is drawn from its scabbard, and the minds of men are exasperated by mutual insults and injuries, there are no measures, however desperate, that a colony will not have recourse to, sooner than again acknowledge submission to the parent country: such was the case with the United Provinces (the Netherlands), which withstood, for upwards of thirty years, the whole power of Spain, when at her zenith, and at last succeeded in emancipating themselves.

The cantons of Switzerland opposed, successfully, the power of the house of Austria; and at a still more recent period, North America, established her independence, notwithstanding all the efforts of Great Britain.

These and many other examples show, that to oppose a people unanimous in asserting their liberty, is a mere parade of power; it serves only to protract the war, to make the inveteracy between them more rooted; it may retard, but cannot prevent them obtaining the desired object.

The people of South America acted on a very different principle: they demanded concessions from Spain, and they withheld their assistance at a moment when their mother country was engaged in one of the most glorious struggles that the page of history records; when, with the exception of Cádiz, the whole of the peninsula was occupied by the legions of Bonaparte; and this most ungrateful offspring, most ungenerously took advantage of the moment, when the sun of its parent's glory was on the verge of setting for ever, when her limbs were fettered by the chains of despotism, to strike the fatal blow and consummate her fall. Great as may be our enthusiasm in the cause of liberty, yet purchased at the price of honor and gratitude it loses much of its splendor.

The conduct of the cortes of Spain was certainly intemperate, in declaring the ports of Caracas under blockade, at a moment when it had not power to enforce its edicts; it produced that effect, when all the reasoning of the world, perhaps, would have been exerted in vain; it alienated the minds of the people of Caracas from the common cause, but they were immerged in superstition and ignorance, and although, they wished to be free, yet they feared to encounter the danger, and they dreaded a separation from the mother country.

The European Spaniards, residing in Caracas, were treated in the most illiberal manner, they were publicly insulted in the streets, and the most opprobrious language was heaped upon them. In this state of anxious uncertainty, when the minds of all classes were worked up to the highest pitch of exasperation, arrived at Caracas, the unfortunate general Miranda, that patriot and friend to mankind. His reception on his arrival in his native country, was not of the most flatterring description, and would have damped the hopes of most men; but Miranda possessed a spirit which rose superior to every obstacle, and as his views were directed solely to the good of his country, all minor considerations of personal interest, vanished before the greatness of the thought.

General Miranda had many enemies among the superior classes in Caracas; they were apprehensive of being eclipsed by the lustre of his shining talents, which would no doubt raise him to the first employments; and as he was naturally an enemy to tyranny and disorder, they dreaded his censure. They were too proud to yield obedience to him as a superior; and as they could not stand his competitor for fame, they were determined on thwarting his views, and henceforward they declared themselves his most inveterate enemies.

The day previous to his arrival in Caracas, a circumstance occurred, which is worthy of remark, merely because it shews to what a height of malevolence the enemies of Miranda carried their inveteracy. His effigy was dressed up in a most magnificent manner, and carried through the streets by the mob (who were excited to this degrading insult by some of his enemies), and it was afterwards conducted to the market place, and burned, amidst the acclamations of an idle multitude.

General Miranda made his entry into Caracas, without being attended by a single person, and none of the inhabitants went out to meet him, as is the custom, when any individual of distinction arrives: he was surrounded by a number of boys, who running before him, announced his arrival, by crying out, "Here comes Miranda, who was burned!"

Notwithstanding every discouraging circumstance, and all the united efforts of his adversaries to make him appear ridiculous to the public, yet his abilities soon made his importance known, for he was shortly after elevated to the rank of lieutenant-general of the armies of Venezuela. He endeavoured, by every means in his power, by force of argument and persuasion, to induce the people of Caracas to declare themselves independent of the mother country; he pointed out to them the necessity of taking such a step, if they had any regard to their own welfare, and did not wish to entail a shameful slavery on their posterity; but the great mass of the people still preserved an attachment to the mother country: the force of long established custom and national prejudices operated strongly on their minds; they wavered in their resolutions, and dreaded to resort to measures so decisive; but the antimonarchical leaders, finding that the majority of the white population were extremely averse to an open rupture, had recourse to a plan, which secured their present purpose, but has since proved the means of subverting their own government, and of bringing destruction on their country: they succeeded in getting the people of color to join their party, by holding out to them promises of equality.

A congress was convened in May, 1811, and on the 5th of July, of the same year, it declared Venezuela to be independent of the mother country; but alas! How different were the hopes, how various the interests, of those who had seemingly combined to bring about an event of such importance. The Creoles looked upon it as an era, from which to record the day which would render them citizens of a grand and rising empire; they looked forward to personal aggrandizement and riches. The free people of color, who formed by far the greatest proportion of the community, hailed it as the glorious day, that placed them on an equality with the whites; when they would no longer be considered inferior to their employers; they had a deep sense of the importance of their own number and strength, and they were anxious to profit by this opportunity of laying prostrate every distinction of rank and of color; they carefully availed themselves of every circumstance to evince their equality, by their insolence, and by taking the most signal vengeance on the Creoles. The slaves triumphed at the prospect of emancipation. The Indian alone remained a passive uninterested spectator; enjoying the repose of torpid tranquillity, either swinging to and fro' in his hammock, or ranging the woods in quest of the chase—he felt no sensation burst upon his mind, from the convulsed agitation that surrounded him.

The circumstances of civil discord and party divisions, having arisen among the different provinces under the direction of the government of Caracas, the inveterate animosity which subsisted between the different classes of inhabitants, their extreme ignorance, and the strong prejudices which they had imbibed from their earliest infancy, together with the scanty population that was dispersed over their wide extended territories, and the total absence of the arts and sciences, rendered it almost impossible for them to become independent for many generations; besides these insurmountable difficulties, there were no men of talent in the country, who would unite their abilities with a true patriotic spirit, to reconcile these jarring interests, or to direct the helm of state, at such a critical juncture.

When we reflect, that the first revolution which took place in this country was brought about without a drop of human blood being shed, without even the shadow of opposition, we would be led most naturally to impute it to the concurrence of all parties, in absolving themselves from their allegiance to the crown of Spain; but far different were the motives that actuated them on that momentous occasion. The opinion was general at that time—that the deposition of the constituted authorites was merely to prevent the country from being delivered up to the French, and to secure it more firmly for their captive king.

The rooted antipathy which had always subsisted between the different grades of colour, did not subside, but, on the contrary, it received a new accession of force, from the freedom of speech not being restricted within due bounds of propriety. The Negroes and Mulattoes had the privilege of greeting any person, be his rank or situation in life what it might, with the familiar appellation of citizen. No public balls, or dinners, were given to which they were not invited with marks of particular preference; and to such a height did this levelling distinction arrive, that in a country like Caracas, where it was, previous to the revolution, considered as a mark of infamy to have any connexion, or even acquaintance, with people of color, they used to take out the ladies, to dance at the public balls. On one occasion some ladies, indignant at an insult of this nature, refused to dance, when an immense multitude of people of color gathered round the doors of the assembly room, threatening to put every white person to death, if they should again refuse their sable companions for partners; they even carried their insolence so far, as to demand in marriage the daughters of any person of distinction whom they fancied; and the parents dare not give them an absolute denial, but on some pretence would delay the ceremony, till they could get some favorable opportunity of sending their daughters to some distant part.

Nothing could present a more unpromising appearance, than the situation of Caracas at this moment; the inhabitants of the provinces of Maracaybo, Guayana, and Coro, remained steady in their attachment to the royal cause; they refused to acknowledge the authority of the new government of Caracas, and they were preparing to repel the army sent from Caracas, to reduce them to submission by force. The troops which placed themselves under the royal standard, were composed almost entirely of natives, (for perhaps in the whole province, a force of one thousand regular troops of Old Spain, could not have been collected) who were inured to the climate, and acquainted with every defile; and they were consequently enabled to make the most of every local advantage. Long marches, under the scorching rays of a tropical sun, to them by habit were rendered easy, but would prove the destruction of an European army. This was the gloomy aspect which Caracas presented at a very early period of her political regeneration; torn by intestine divisions, and menaced on all sides, by enemies who aimed at her destruction, whilst the profligate and debauched life of her rulers, portended her speedy dissolution.

All the attempts of the armies of Caracas to reduce the people of Coro and Guayana to submission, were ineffectual; they were repulsed in every attack, her armies were guided by impotence, as were her councils presided over by prejudice and impolicy.

Miranda no longer enjoyed the confidence of the inhabitants; his enemies were too powerfully leagued against him, and they easily found means of undermining his reputation, in a country where there was too much ignorance to discover the deception—or to appreciate his invaluable talents. With all the discernment of a philosopher, and the policy of a wise legislator, Miranda, who well understood the dangers which would arise from great and sudden innovation, insinuated, that there was no necessity of overturning every old institution of the former government, and customs long established; and that it would be much more beneficial to the country, to follow a plan of progressive reformation: for this sage advice, he was pointed out as a suspicious person, and it was even hinted that he was an emissary of the Spanish government.

A conspiracy of the most formidable nature was now discovered in Caracas, which had for its object, the re-establishment of the Spanish government. Ten of the conspirators were taken and put to death, and the heads of these unfortunate men were placed on poles round the city. Thus did the independent government commence, by sullying the dawn of their emancipation, and perpetrating the very acts which they had imputed to the Spaniards. The conspirators who escaped, took refuge in the city of Valencia, which they placed in a state of defence.

Valencia is situated on a large plain at the further extremity of the vallies of Aragua; it is forty leagues distant from Caracas, and nine from the port and fortress of Puerto Cabello, from which it is divided by a chain of the Andes: it contained a population of about eight thousand persons. General Miranda marched against this place, stormed and took the town; but, on attacking the barracks defended by the people of color, he met with such a warm reception as to oblige him to retire with considerable loss. The Spaniards now renewed their exertions, and poured a destructive fire on the assailants, from the houses and monasteries. The patriot forces retreated, but, on the following August, receiving reinforcements, they again attacked the town, which they succeeded in capturing. Miranda next proposed to send an army against Coro, but showers of invective were heaped on him from all sides, and his advice was disregarded.

The congress of Venezuela next proceeded to form a constitution, on the model of that adopted by the United States of North America: the only article which it contained worthy of remark, was, that the abolition of the slave trade was decreed.

An army was also sent across the Oronoco, to attack Guayana; whilst another was detached to protect the frontier towns from invasion, on the side of Coro. But an event now took place which suspended every hostile movement, and destroyed, in one short moment, the fondest expectations of the republicans.

Between the hours of four and five o'clock, P.M. March 26, 1812, the province of Venezuela was visited by a most tremendous earthquake, which, in one moment, buried upwards of thirty thousand persons beneath the ruins of their houses. For nearly two minutes the earth was convulsed with the most frightful agitation; presenting the appearance of a troubled sea. The tremendous crash, occasioned by the fall of so many edifices, reverberated through the adjacent mountains like peals of thunder; the dust and powder which they raised, wafted by the wind, for a moment obscured the horizon, and enveloped the whole in the darkness of night. Some of those who escaped destruction, ran to and fro', half frantic, calling on heaven for mercy, whilst others, petrified with terror and amazement, stood motionless, and the heart rending cries of distress, uttered by those who were buried alive in the ruins, or had their limbs fractured, added to this scene of horror; but what rendered it still more dismal, was the mournful howlings of the dogs and other animals, who rent the air with their cries. Mothers called in vain on the names of their children, and children of their parents; but alas! many were to meet each other no more, who that morning parted, unconscious that in a few fleeting hours, they should be in eternity.

This awful event happened to fall on Holy Thursday, a day, which, in catholic countries, is kept by the most solemn commemoration of the sufferings of our Saviour, and at the very moment, when the churches were crowded with people. Fifteen churches came to the ground, as did also the barracks, which buried, under its ruins, a great many soldiers, together with their arms and ammunition. The whole north-east part of the city of Caracas was destroyed, as were also the cities of La Guayra, Barquisemieto, Merida, and San Felipe. To show what an effect fear and superstition have on the mind of man, I will relate the following circumstance.

The government, to prevent the contagion which would be the consequence, if so many dead bodies were left unburied in such a warm climate, ordered them to be collected together, and carried to the foot of the mountain, outside the town, and burned. It was night, and all the inhabitants had taken refuge in the squares and market place, to be out of the reach of the houses, which were tumbling down in every direction; when the blaze and smoke occasioned by the burning of the dead bodies, was perceived, dismay was pourtrayed in every countenance, voices were heard crying in all directions, "A volcano has burst out in the mountain!" Many persons, from fright, dropped down dead, and tranquillity was not again restored, till the orders of the government were publicly announced. A dreadful calm succeeded, and now that the apprehension of immediate danger was past, every one was alive to the horrors of their situation: fathers who that morning saw a blooming offspring play around them, were left solitary beings, without the soothing cares of filial duty, to smooth the complicated miseries of their declining years, and children were left orphans, without a friend or protector: in vain did they look towards the place, where the stately mansion of their forefathers had stood for ages; it was now a mass of shapeless ruins. Every one had to deplore the loss of some relative, and many were that day left without a single relation to join them in their lamentations.

Amidst this scene of destruction, the Negroes were to be seen entering the houses that were still standing, but whose inmates had deserted them, carrying off every thing they could lay hands on; and it has been related to me, by many persons of the strictest veracity, who were on the spot at the time, that these barbarians even stripped the dead of their ornaments, and that those who were buried up to the necks in the ruins, and implored their assistance, had the earrings dragged out of their ears, and were then left to the chance of somebody passing by, to extricate them.

The effect which the earthquake had on this superstitious people is truly astonishing; they looked upon it as a signal mark of the divine vengeance for their rebellion, and the priests, who in general were addicted to the royal cause, employed themselves, most assiduously, in taking advantage of their present turn, to inculcate maxims unfavorable to the independent cause; even some of the most zealous partisans of liberty wavered, and few indeed were those, who were not tinctured with this religious awe. This gave a fatal blow to the independence of Caracas, the people of which were not enlightened enough to conceive it to have been the natural consequence of their local situation, a similar event having occurred about an hundred years before. Nothing was to be seen, for many months, but people doing penance for their sins: some gravely walking through the public streets with immense wooden crosses, and dressed in sack cloth; others to make atonement for their past bad conduct, married the women with whom they had cohabited for many years previous; and even instances have occurred of men of property espousing their slaves, with whom they had illicit intercourse. In fact, every thing was forgotten but a regard to the salvation of their souls. It would have been a much more proper time to collect volunteers for a crusade, than to attempt such a chimerical enterprise, as to make Venezuela independent.

The royalists of Coro, under the command of general [Domingo de] Monteverde, taking advantage of this favorable change in the minds of the patriots, and of the general opinion in favor of the king, detached a body of troops, to occupy the immense plains, which form part of the provinces of Caracas and Barinas, and from whence the city of Caracas, and all the other towns, situated in the mountainous parts of this province, are supplied with cattle, whilst he advanced in person towards Caracas. The badness of the roads, and the immense distance of country which he had to traverse, were trifling obstacles to an army led on by religious enthusiasm, and encouraged by the people of every town, throwing open their gates, on their appearance, and affording them every assistance to facilitate their progress; whilst entire bodies of the independent troops deserted and joined their standard; this victorious army therefore soon arrived in the vallies of Aragua, where general Miranda had concentrated his forces to oppose it; and the defile of La Cabrera, leading between a lofty mountain and the lake of Valencia, and which was considered to be impregnable, he had rendered still stronger, by constructing gunboats on the lake, which completely enfiladed the narrow road, and made it almost impossible for an army to advance, without being destroyed. Trees were also felled, which falling across the road, and entangling their branches, presented another very formidable obstacle. However the royalists, having guides conversant with the intricacies of the country, avoided this pass, by crossing the mountain, in a place hitherto deemed impassable, and threatened to cut off general Miranda's retreat; to avoid which, after some skirmishing, the general fell back on the town of Vittoria, sixteen leagues distant from Caracas; abandoning to the enemy, a magazine of ammunition and provisions, which had cost the republic half a million of dollars. From this disaster, and the continual desertion of his troops to the enemy; the enmity of his colleagues, to which he knew he would be sacrificed; the defeat of the army sent against Guayana; the treacherous surrender of the strong fortress of Puerto Cabello, to the Spaniards; and the very general feeling of the country in favor of Ferdinand VII, induced him to propose terms of capitulation, which were accepted by the royalist general.

General Miranda being one of the prime movers of the revolution, was apprehensive of his personal safety being endangered, as much from the malice and revengeful disposition of the patriot party, as from the decided hostility of the Spanish government to his political opinions, and his exertions in revolutionising her colonies: therefore the evening previous to the capitulation being ratified, he proceeded secretly to the port of La Guayra, for the purpose of embarking in a vessel, which was to have sailed the same night; however, through the duplicity of the commandant of that place, who had always professed himself to be his friend, Miranda was arrested as he was stepping into a boat to go on board, and delivered up to the Spanish general, who immediately sent him as a prisoner to Spain, where he has since died in captivity. Among the many misrepresentations which have been laid before the British public, in order to affix the stigma of cruelty on the Spanish name, the statements which have appeared in various works and journals, respecting the fate of this unfortunate man, are equally false and absurd. It has been asserted that when he was delivered up to the Spanish general, he treacherously caused him to be beheaded. It is a well known fact, that general Monteverde has always been characterised for the extreme humanity of his disposition, and that Miranda died a short time ago, in the island of Leon, near Cádiz, of a natural death, being far advanced in years.

Many persons, without reflecting on the peculiar circumstances under which the unfortunate Miranda was situated, have laid the failure of the project of the emancipation of Caracas to his timidity and misconduct; whatever may have been his failings, he possesed many great and noble qualities, and shining talents; but what could these avail, situated as he was? He was assailed by circumstances which no mortal could have foreseen; he acted on the whole as a friend to humanity, and although his patriotic views did not meet with that success which he was rather too sanguine in anticipating, yet his efforts were not, on that account, to be considered less glorious; his plans were great, although prematurely carried into execution: the germ of freedom had not yet expanded into maturity, in South America. His philanthropic views in refusing, in face of the strongest opposition, to persecute the Spanish settlers, throws a splendor around him, which envy can never darken, and he may confound his enemies in the words of Philip, king of Spain, when news was brought to him, that the invincible armada was destroyed; "Why," says the monarch, "I sent my ships to contend with men, and not against the elements and the will of providence."

The Spanish commander finding himself in possession of Caracas, although actuated by sentiments of the most humane feelings, allowed himself to be led away by some persons of vindictive minds, who, to be avenged for the indignities they suffered during the continuance of the patriot government, raised false alarms of conspiracies, and the general resorted to the impolitic step of arresting and throwing into prison, many persons engaged in the late rebellion; but notwithstanding these imprisonments were not aggravated by cruel treatment, or a single execution, yet it gave general umbrage to the Creoles, who considered it to be a gross violation of the capitulation, which he had solemnly ratified in the name of his sovereign, to bury every past act of rebellion in oblivion, and that no one should suffer for their former opinions.

The province of Cumana, not having suffered much by the late earthquake, raised the standard of revolt, under the direction of a young man named [Santiago] Mariño, who took possession of the Indian town of Maturin, which he fortified; he defeated a Spanish force which was sent against him by the governors of Barcelona and Cumana; and he also defeated, in April, 1813, General Monteverde, who marched from Caracas to attack him. Whilst the city of Caracas remained in a defenceless state for want of troops, the patriots had invaded Venezuela, in the direction of New Granada.

A native of Caracas, named Simón Bolívar, of a good family, and possessed of considerable landed property, had, on the country being delivered up to the Spaniards in 1812, emigrated, with many others, to the island of Curaçao, from whence he proceeded to Carthagena, and from thence to New Granada, and obtained from the congress of that place, a division of six hundred men; with these he crossed the Andes, and invaded the province of Venezuela; he at the same time, dispatched an officer named [Antonio Nicolás ("El Diablo")] Briceño, to invade the province of Barinas, which this officer executed, committing the most horrid cruelties on the unfortunate Spaniards, who happened to fall into his hands. He caused their heads to be severed from their bodies, and put into bags, and having wrote a letter with their blood, he dispatched them with all the pomp of military triumph, to the congress of New Granada. This monster, was, however, soon after defeated, and taken prisoner by the Spaniards, and, together with sixteen of his officers, were shot, in expiation of their crimes; a death by far too honorable for men who had forfeited every claim to this distinction, which should be alone granted to the brave soldier. The patriot general, Bolívar, who was on his march, the moment he received news of this event, denounced the "Guerra a muerte" [war to the death] against all Spaniards, and natives of the Canary Islands. Thus did he, who arrogated to himself, the pompous appellation of the liberator of his country, the avowed defender of its liberties, and the avenger of its wrongs, fix a most indelible stain on the arms of liberty, a stain which all the waters of the Oronoco can never wash away: it stabbed the independence, the happiness, nay, the very existence of Caracas, in its most vital parts; its dearest interests were sacrificed to a vile spirit of revenge and party pride. Thus did the sanguinary Bolívar, in the true character of a Nero, callous to the voice of humanity, with the most brutal impolicy, decree the destruction of unoffending men, many of whom, perhaps, were at that moment, landing on the coast of Colombia, hailing it as an asylum from French oppression, unconscious of the fate which was suspended over their devoted heads; yet Bolívar was so dead to every sense of reflection, to the appeal of justice, the suggestions of policy, and the feelings of humanity, as to comprise in one order of indiscriminate destruction, every individual who might casually have received their being in Spain: he signed the death warrant of the fathers of those who were the props and hopes of the republic. Almost all the Spaniards settled in South America, were intermarried in the most respectable Creole families; they generally went to the country poor, and by indefatigable labor, industry, and frugality, in a few years acquired a sufficiency to render themselves independent, whilst on the contrary the Creoles, too proud to attach themselves to any laborious occupation, languished in comparative misery and indolence.

By this intemperate and unprincipled mode of proceeding, Bolívar sowed the germ of eternal discord, for he surely could not suppose there existed under the canopy of heaven, a wretch so abandoned, so execrable, as to behold, with indifference, the murder of the authors of his existence. All men of sense, all men of generous and noble feelings, all men of principle, sighed over the impending misfortunes of their country, and augured ill of a war carried on under the banners of despotism and parricide: what less than miscarriage and destruction could be expected where the most atrocious offences were perpetrated under the plausible pretence of retaliation, under the high sounding name of raising the standard of liberty on the mausoleums of the ancient incas, of rescuing their country from the yoke of Spanish tyranny, and of avenging the blood of the Indians who had fallen in its defence three hundred years before; Bolívar and his associates committed the most wanton and unmanly assassinations, whilst the most violent and insatiable avarice polluted every avenue, and the most cool and premeditated oppression marked every act of their government. From this moment we behold nothing on this vast theatre, but a succession of the most horrid events. Happy had it been for the inhabitants of Caracas, had their leaders followed the sage advice of the unfortunate Miranda, of stretching their arms, now free from shackles, across the deep, and generously offering their country as the asylum of the oppressed friends of liberty, in the other hemisphere: myriads of Spaniards would have fled for refuge to their soil, to avoid the horrors of French invasions.

By this mode of proceeding they would have conciliated the goodwill of all mankind; and from the genial balm of union, the arts and sciences would have been diffused over the immense uncultivated regions of the Western world.

The whole line of march of the patriot general Bolívar was marked by the murder of all the Spaniards, who resided in the towns, through which he passed. In the town of St. Mateo, situated in the vallies of Aragua, an old Spaniard, who was upwards of eighty years of age, went tottering, and surrounded by his children and grandchildren, to implore the clemency of the conqueror, but he answered by ordering the unfortunate supplicant to be shot on the spot, at the threshold of the general's door.

Near Valencia the patriot general encountered an inferior Spanish force, under the command of general Monteverde, which he put to the rout, and obliged him to take refuge in the fortress of Puerto Cabello. On the news of this defeat having reached Caracas, and the rapid advance of the patriots, about six thousand Spaniards, dreading the vindictive fury of Bolívar, embarked, with their money and most valuable effects, in seventy small vessels, and sailed to the island of Curaçao, where they were most humanely received by the British governor.

General Bolívar made his triumphal entry into the city of Caracas, on the 4th of August, 1813, amidst the rejoicings of the multitude; but he was held in detestation by every good man. The balconies of all the houses, in the streets through which he passed, were hung with silk, and the streets were strewed with flowers, his hat and uniform were covered with garlands, and bands of music played before him. At night the city was illuminated; the display of fire-works and a grand ball completed the rejoicing.

The first proceeding of the patriot leader was to lay siege to Puerto Cabello, both by sea and land; but the garrison and inhabitants of this place, under the direction of the intrepid general Monteverde, made a most spirited and vigorous resistance, and every attempt which the patriots made to take it by assault was repulsed.

Puerto Cabello is the place of greatest strength, and the most regularly fortified of any other town in Venezuela. It is distant thirty leagues by sea, and fifty over land from Caracas, and is situated at the extremity of the vallies of Aragua, from which it is divided by a chain of the Andes; at the foot of these mountains, on the sea shore, the town and fortifications are erected. It is by far the best harbour of any to be found in South America, being very capacious and secure; vessels of any burthen coming close to the shore. It is the deposit of all the eastern part of Venezuela. The town is surrounded by the sea, on the north, south and east; but to west, on the land side, a canal has been cut for about a hundred and fifty yards, which communicates with the sea, and is very wide and deep, and very much infested with alligators: the whole is defended by a strong line of batteries.

On a small island to the east, on the opposite side of the harbour, which is not more than two hundred yards across, stands the castle, which is very strong; it is bomb proof, and when provided with provisions, and garrisoned with a thousand men, is considered to be impregnable. From under the batteries of this place, it was that the *Hermione*, a British frigate (the crew of which had mutinied, and barbarously murdered their officers), was cut out by our gallant seamen.

This fortress is dependent entirely on the rains for a supply of fresh water, which is preserved in large cisterns; the river which supplies the town being a mile distant from the batteries, and the water of the wells, which they have in the town, being nearly the same as that of the sea. The heat at this place is excessive, augmented by the situation of the town, which is overhung by such high mountains, that they prevent it from enjoying the land breeze, and the trees on the mountain stand so thick, as to intercept the rays of the sun, and keep the ground in a continual state of dampness; this, together with the swamps and mangrove trees, which flank the town to the north, are the causes of the putrid exhalations which continually hang in dense vapours, over the town, and come down in torrents of rain, making this place so very unhealthy, that it is termed the grave of the Spaniards; the yellow fever raging in it throughout the year, with unabated violence; to the malignity of which the temperate and the dissipated alike fall victims.

In May, 1817, I was at Puerto Cabello, and had a dreadful attack of fever; there were at the same time four hundred persons lying under the same disorder; and, contrary to the opinion of many, Peruvian bark proved the most effectual remedy, few recovering who did not make use of it.

The road leading from Puerto Cabello, to Valencia, and the vallies of Aragua, running over the mountains, it would be difficult to describe; in some places the declivity is so great that the mules can scarcely keep their feet; in others it is nearly perpendicular, and is cut zigzag, like a winding staircase, otherwise the mules could not clamber up it. In some places the road is so narrow, that the mules have scarcely room to set their feet, whilst, on either side, precipices, of immeasurable depth, threaten destruction to the traveller, whilst the hollow shouts of the muleteers, and the tinkling of the bells, suspended from the mules' necks, to give warning of their approach, resound through the mountains. On the top of an elevated mountain, one is surprised to see other mountains towering above them, and covered with trees to the very top. The traveller is under continual apprehension, for the mule walks on the very brink of the precipice, but it is much more prudent to let the animal have its own way, as they advance with the greatest caution; for when they come to a steep part of the road they make a halt, and placing their fore-feet together, and bending their necks and bodies, carefully survey every part of the road for a moment, and then slide down; nor is it necessary for the rider to do any thing more than keep his seat, letting the reins of the bridle loose, for these animals are so very sure footed that they seldom or never fall. Besides all these difficulties, which are inseparable from the nature of the country, there are others which proceed from the supine spirit of the people. The mules that happen to drop down under their burthens, along the road, are left there, till they become in a state of putrefaction, not only obstructing the passage, but rendering the surrounding atmosphere infectious from their stench: they remain until the all consuming hand of time incorporates their bones with the dust. Thousands of skeletons of mules are to be found along the road, for when once they fall down, through fatigue, they cannot be again got on their legs, and they are there left till they expire.

7

Aspects of the Civil State of the *Castas* of Venezuela That Shall Be the Object of Improvement to Prevent Potential Ills and Unrest, 1815

Although the royalists might appear to be the consistent defenders of reactionism, many thoughtful Spanish army commanders and adminis- trators recognized that miscegenation was a force that no expeditionary army of Europeans could overcome. Like his colleagues in other Spanish American provinces, José de Cevallos, interim captain general of Caracas, understood that depending upon many different causative factors the war fragmented the population into royalist and patriot factions. Rather than a struggle between Europeans and Americans, what often emerged was a civil war that cut across the racially mixed populace. With the return to power of King Fernando VII in 1814 and the overthrow of the 1812 Con- stitution, in the present document Cevallos expressed ideas that were no longer acceptable to the regime. The imperial government responded with Pablo Morillo's expeditionary army, which won a brief counterrevolu- tionary respite before the European soldiers lost their zeal and either deserted or perished from combat, disease, and exhaustion.

A career soldier with considerable experience in Venezuela, Cevallos knew that without the assistance of the local and regional populations the royalists could not permanently control enormous continental territories. When Morillo and his officers arrived, Cevallos lost power and was

Translated and reprinted from José de Cevallos, "El Capitán General Interino de Caracas. Representa sobre lo necesario y conveniente que será mejorar por los medios que indica, ú otros, el Estado Civil de las Castas de estos territorios que apunta, y como premio del merito y la virtud," in Archivo General de las Indias, Seville, Spain. For a printed facsimile see James F. King, "A Royalist View of the Colored Castes in the Venezuelan War of Independence," *Hispanic American Historical Review* 33, no. 4 (November 1953): 530–37.

179

granted permission to return to Spain. The effective mestizo and mulatto
llanero fighters who had supported the royalist cause under José Tomás
Boves turned to the patriot commander, José Antonio Páez. Simón Bolívar
accepted the need to grant recognition to the castas *fighters who provided*
the hardy disease-resistant soldiers required to win independence.

Letter No. 42. Confidential

To the Secretario de Estado y del Despacho Universal de Indias
Most Excellent Sir:

The introduction of Negroes in the Americas gave rise to the emergence
of a class of people known in vulgar terms as Castas. Ever since their
arrival, legislation of the government has been designed to define the limits
of their civil status, and to provide necessary rules needed to maintain
vigilance over their conduct and to prevent the possibility of hostile acts
on their part that may affect negatively the security and public order of
provinces where their numbers have increased considerably. At present,
as a result of their expanding numbers over the past two and a half centuries, and due to circumstances that have arisen since 1810, I consider
these people to be one of the problems that require the greatest attention
from the Ministry and its policies. This fact requires me to present Your
Excellency with different approaches from those applied until now. In all
of the countries [within the Spanish Empire] that allowed slavery, the laws
always took care to diminish the stain of this civil state, facilitating the
means of obtaining freedom for slaves and the rights of free men. The
stain of slavery was not to have passed from persons who had been slaves
and various means were taken to erase the stigma. But far from achieving
success, in the New World the indelible mark of the black color endured
many generations to produce a third class of people between free and
slave that to a certain point are considered foreign, so that they do not
enjoy the full civil assets of the freeborn, as do the descendants of the
same freemen in other countries.

Laws, customs, and prejudices deeply rooted in time and more difficult to conquer, caused these castes to be rejected by the secular and regular
clergy, and from exercising occupations in civil government and private
industry. They are refused entry to honorary posts and some religious
congregations and confraternities. They are prohibited from socializing
with peoples of the white race, and they are prevented from approaching
them without exhibiting utmost respect and devotion. Their women are
forced to dress in distinctive clothing, and they are prohibited from using
certain adornments as regulated by laws. Before the formation of the Provincial Militia units for Blacks and Mulattos (Pardos and Morenos), their

young men were prohibited from providing military service that is expected from other men.

Our legislators have not considered it appropriate to correct these injustices, nor to identify the paths needed to correct the situation. Referring to the Royal Order of November 30, 1771, in volume 3 of his collection, Severo Aguirre speaks about the prohibition against admitting Blacks and Mulattos to military service in Spain. In his opinion, honorable residents who are members of these groups are by now remote from their origin and they have good reputations among the people of their towns. The magistrates can screen with care anyone who might cause trouble among families or engage in slander. Although this Royal Decree was made public in Spain, I do not know if it was published in the Indies. In all cases about racial equality—and these are very frequent—the superior courts follow the spirit of the 1771 Royal Order. This is done for the reason given or for many other reasons of great public interest. Without any law, the practice has developed that an individual who with or without a contradictory judgment manages to break the barriers and to enter in some position or special occupation reserved to those classified as whites, this may be taken as a primitive act of whitening for a family. Although the process may be artificial, the state gains through the growth of the superior class. In the Spanish Constitution of 1812, the framers adopted the same principle, excluding only those individuals from the rights of citizenship who originated in Africa. This means of entry facilitates that after some generations, they can erase the memory of their origins. But because this process is so slow and arbitrary, society has not gained from the diminution of this numerous people.

During the interregnum caused by the absence of Our Lord the King (captive in France), a decree of January 1812 was enacted favoring the Castas. That decree of the Cortes has provided for the social empowerment of all those individuals who aside from possessing the standing and resources, can be admitted to university degrees, to be students of seminaries, to enter religious communities, and to receive holy orders. However, they must still fulfill all the requirements identified in the codes of laws of the Kingdom, and of the individual constitutions of the different corporations that they are attempting to enter. For that reason, I consider the Decree of 1812 to be one of the most effective and appropriate measures implemented during that era as it stimulates virtue and opens a wide field to the hopes of so many thousands of families. Without this access, they will form a social class no less dangerous than the Helots of Ancient Greece.

Article 22 of the now abolished Constitution declared that the door to virtue and merit to become citizens was open for anyone, including those with African roots, who had provided valuable service to the nation. It also offered the opportunity of full citizenship to those with extraordinary talents, behavior, and public conduct. The only condition was that potential citizens had to be born of legitimate marriages, of intelligent and literate parents, and of a freeborn mother domiciled in the Spanish dominions. Furthermore, those individuals also had to prove that they were employed in some legitimate trade, profession, business, or industry, and that they had the capital necessary. Following the spirit of our ancient legislation, the matter as explained by Juan de Solorzano in Chapter 30, Book 2, of his *Política indiana* (Madrid, 1648), only those suffering from birth defects, or the personal addictions and vices common to the people of the Castas, and suckled with their mothers' milk, will not be permitted to enjoy any of the privileges of full citizenship.

"The immense number of people of African origins established in the overseas countries, their different conditions, the state of civilization and culture in which the greater proportion of them find themselves, require (according to the preliminary discourse of the cited Constitution), great care and diligence so as to avoid aggravating their present situation while avoiding any compromise of the interests and security of those vast provinces." These factors oblige us to concede everything referred to here, and even more today with respect to Venezuela. There, the whites were two tenths of the total population, but now they are even fewer since young men have been consumed in the present barbarous engagements of both conflicting parties and during the late war. Consequently, all of the advantages of physical force lie with the remaining mass of individuals who must be natural enemies of the society that excludes them from political equality. This is especially the case after they have seen a revolution here that flattered their aspirations, and another in all of the empire that opened the road for them to attain the major part of all of their prerogatives.

The numerous European garrisons destined to these provinces, and the progress made by the expeditionary army that will continue to Nueva Granada province, will free us for some time from the imminent danger of seeing played out here the tragic scene suffered by the French of Santo Domingo. We found ourselves in that state six months ago as I reported to Your Excellency from Coro on this past December 31st. Attaining the permanence and stability of the social edifice are works of primary importance that we will not win in a day, especially when we must first destroy the enemy. For the misfortune of these provinces, we have not yet taken such necessary steps that may produce results for the generality of the inhabitants. The life of an army of 4,000 men is finite and even shorter where the climate and poor food work against them. Their number diminishes daily, and even without these factors their force is weakened by being scattered over great distances and by difficult transit. They are obliged to deploy their forces in order to occupy the vast extension of the province. In the meantime, the feared class (the Pardos and Morenos) reproduce and grow in size. In addition to their well known physical advantages, today they have discipline and ferocity that they have acquired during the recently ended cruel war in which they made up almost all of the total force on both sides. Ultimately, it is a truth that is too clear that a society cannot endure long when nine tenths of the people—far from having an interest in conserving it—desire to destroy it.

In order to gain the support of this class, making them take interest in the existence of the society that today they view with odium, or at least with disaffection, one does not have to wait for the last desperate moments when granting them concessions will have the look of being forced by dangers. For this reason, and as I have had and have current affairs to deal with, I am taking the liberty of declaring to Your Excellency that now is the opportune moment without any delays to take into consideration such an important matter. Although I am not so bold as to propose what dispositions must be introduced, I can say that my insufficiency is such that I recognize only the need of these people, and the state of depreciation in which they live. Their numbers and other circumstances as noted do not permit them to suffer with tranquillity as in past times when ignorance reigned in these countries. The well known occurrences of the past few years have awakened them.

I must bring to the attention of Your Excellency that after the publication of the previously mentioned Decree of January 29th, shortly after the arrival of Domingo de Monteverde, the Castas reacted very favorably to the national cause, and especially of course the better off families that will be able to enjoy these concessions. It is most important to win these people who set the tone and have principal influence over the class in general. It seems convenient and even essential for us to confirm this same Decree that having the merits and new approval of His Majesty, will conciliate the will of this people toward his Royal person, and erase the idea of grievances caused by memories of injustices against them by the previous system.

Also, those who have distinguished themselves in the military service under arms deserve particular attention. They abandoned their interests, families and hearths into the hands of the revolution. Since they could not stain themselves with it, they went to loyal towns to seek the help of the legitimate authorities. It is well known that Venezuela has returned to the dominion of the King through the endeavors of its own inhabitants, and that the armies that carry the Royal banner are composed almost totally of Pardos and people of the other Castas. Among them are many who have stood out for their dauntless valor, and constant adhesion to the good cause (*la causa buena*). No treasury would have enough money to repay these worthy men (*benemeritos*). Nor would honors that flatter the elite class serve these people very well. They know very well that medals and badges will not elevate them to the upper class and that in the civil ordinances they are considered inferior to the same whites they have defeated in defense of the cause of their sovereign. On the other hand, it is indispensable to reward them and that they may be made to remain content. If they believe themselves to be aggravated after now knowing what they can accomplish, they will convert their class that is the principal instrument that has served us into a force they will use against us.

My continual meditation on this point which is the most thorny and delicate of Venezuela has occupied my thoughts since I was head of armies where the pardo of darkest complexion was accustomed to commanding whites, treating them at least as equals. They have made me conclude that for these men there is no other way to extract them legally from their inferior class by means of a privilege similar to the terms of the above-mentioned Article 22. No other recompense will fulfill their desires completely and at the same time solve other political questions. Giving them that which one fears they want to grab will satisfy them and cure the evil in their own race. With restrictions to control the situation that are necessary to attain this grace, we will avoid the undesirable aspects of their multiplication and the deformity that they would cause in the civil state. Moreover, with His Majesty having conceded the inestimable blessing of liberty to slaves who served in the royal armies, that is as much as they could expect to better their condition. The free Castas will complain if their reward is not proportionate to the perpetual and transmittable advantages of descent that others acquired. Thus, it seems to me that to avoid the results of comparison, if His Majesty should adopt my ideas or better ones that Your Excellency can propose, this will lead to the prompt publication of the law. This law will authorize the Superior Chief with his council to issue provisional declarations that can satisfy the expectations of the aspirants while Royal approval is awaited. Due to the delays and the difficulties in attaining this result, any other procedure would make the award of this grace useless and would depreciate it as illusory.

I shall be honored if Your Excellency brings this matter to the royal knowledge of His Majesty. Although the reflections contained in this paper may appear illusory to the zeal that animates me for the Royal Service and to achieve security and tranquillity in these provinces, it will be advantageous to examine the following points:

1) The need to improve the general civil state of the Castas that form nine tenths of the population of the province since they know already that they can experience their betterment.

2) That the accepted and highly applauded published order of January 29, 1812, be confirmed.

3) Finally, to reward those individuals of the Castas who have served in the war with loyalty and constancy, or manifested these sentiments

without interruption, the most opportune means is to grant them the privileges of whiteness similar to the description of the citizen as defined in the Constitution.

May God guide Your Excellency.
Caracas, July 22, 1815.
José de Cevallos

8

Two Opposing Views of Simón Bolívar

General Daniel Florencio O'Leary
General H. L. V. Ducoudray Holstein

As indicated in previous chapters, Simón Bolívar was a controversial figure during his career. Historians today continue the debate about the nature of his talents, merits, military acumen, and character. Unlike New Spain, where there were relatively few literate foreigners present to witness the war years (at least until the arrival of the Mina expedition discussed by Viceroy Apodaca in Chapter 5), many English, Scottish, Irish, French, and other European officers whose military careers ended abruptly with the defeat of Napoleonic France turned their attention as soldiers of fortune or mercenaries to the Americas for employment in the only profession they knew. Postwar unemployment, famines, contraband opportunities for traders who sold discarded war materials, and love for adventure motivated these veteran soldiers and officers. Lord Cochrane, for example, a former Royal Navy officer, sailed to command the Chilean navy. Some men such as Major Flinter (Chapter 6) served on the Spanish royalist side, but many others took up the patriot cause to help Spanish Americans gain their independence. Effective propaganda that played upon traditional Black Legend views of Spaniards painted the royalist armies as criminal barbarians guilty of genocide in maintaining their old empire. Once in Venezuela and Colombia, many soldiers who imagined themselves as saviors of liberty soon learned that they would have to endure not only hardships and tropical diseases such as yellow fever but also grinding

From *Bolívar and the War of Independence: Memorias del General Daniel Florencio O'Leary: Narración*, translated and edited by Robert F. McNerney, Jr. (Austin: University of Texas Press, 1970), 139–42. © 1970 by the University of Texas Press. Reprinted by permission of the University of Texas Press; and H. L. V. Ducoudray Holstein, *Memoirs of Simón Bolívar, President Liberator of the Republic of Colombia and of His Principal Generals; A Secret History of the Revolution, and the Events which Preceded It, From 1807 to the Present Time*, 2 vols. (London: Henry Colburn and Richard Bentley, 1830), 2:231–70.

poverty when the patriot governments did not or could not pay them. Many foreign soldiers perished, some fled, and a number such as O'Leary and General William Miller adopted their Spanish American nations. Miller was another veteran of the Napoleonic Wars who first served General José de San Martín in the Army of the Andes, fought at the battles of Junín and Ayacucho, and later rose to grand marshal of Peru.

Born in Cork, Ireland, O'Leary became chief aide-de-camp to Bolívar, a post that accorded him unparalleled access to the Liberator during good times and bad. He wrote his memoirs and collected an archive of correspondence and other materials on the war years that his descendants published much later in thirty-two volumes entitled, Memorias del General O'Leary. He was a constant supporter of Bolívar, who promoted him to brigadier general and favored him in many ways.

Ducoudray Holstein's background prior to his service with Bolívar is more difficult to unravel. Born in Germany, he served with the French army in Spain, but his self-designation as general was not bestowed on him by a European army. Ducoudray, a music teacher anxious to find a better career, attached himself to Bolívar in Haiti. Joining Bolívar's 1815 expedition to invade Cartagena, he commanded the forts of Boca Chica and soon became mired in the factious struggles and backbiting among ambitious officers who surrounded the Liberator. Bolívar's great historian and defender, Vicente Lecuna, made a great effort to point out the calumnies, errors, and falsehoods in Ducoudray's memoirs. Lecuna was particularly upset with Ducoudray's depiction of Bolívar "alternatively as a hero or a coward, of great ability or as perfectly inept, absurd contradictions inappropriate of human nature."* Readers can compare the two accounts and form their own conclusions as to the veracity of Ducoudray's portrait of the Liberator. While Ducoudray's critique reflects his own bitterness, some of his observations are worthy of thought. His dislike of the Spaniards and comment that they were so inept that Bolívar looked good by comparison is interesting. In Venezuela and Colombia, of course, Bolívar's reputation as the founder of nations and Liberator places him in a category of heroes beyond the criticism of historians.

General O'Leary's View

Bolívar had a high, rather narrow forehead that was seamed with wrinkles from his early years—a sign of the thinker. His eyebrows were heavy and well shaped, his eyes black, bright, and piercing. On his long, perfectly shaped nose there was a small wen that annoyed him greatly until it disappeared in 1820, leaving an almost imperceptible scar. His cheekbones were prominent, his cheeks sunken from the time that I met him in 1818; his mouth was ugly, his lips rather thick; the distance between his nose and mouth was notable. His teeth were white, uniform,

*Vicente Lecuna, Catálogo de Errores y Calumnias en la Historia de Bolívar, 3 vols. (New York: Colonial Press, 1957), 2:7.

and beautiful, and he took the greatest care of them. His ears were large but well placed. His hair was black, curly, and of fine texture; he wore it long between 1818 and 1821, when it began to turn grey, after which he wore it short. He had side-whiskers and a mustache, both rather blond, and he shaved them off for the first time in Potosí in 1825. He was five feet six inches tall. His chest was narrow, his figure slender, his legs particularly thin. His skin was swarthy and rather course. His hands and feet were small and well shaped—a woman might have envied them. His expression, when he was in good humor, was pleasant, but it became terrible when he was aroused. The change was unbelievable.

Bolívar always had a good appetite, but no one could equal him in the capacity to endure hunger. Though a real connoisseur of good cooking, he found pleasure in eating the simple and primitive dishes of the *llaneros* and the Indians. He was very temperate. His favorite wines were Graves and champagne, but not even at the times when he was drinking most did I ever see him take more than four glasses of the former or two of the latter. At table he himself filled the glasses of guests seated beside him.

He took a great deal of exercise, and I have never known anyone who could endure fatigue so well. After a day's march, enough to exhaust the most robust man, I have seen him work five or six hours, or dance as long with the enthusiasm that he had for this diversion. He slept five or six hours out of the twenty-four. Whether in a hammock, on a cot, on a cowhide, or wrapped in his cloak on the ground out in the open, he slept as well as he would have on soft feathers. If he had not been a light sleeper, quick to awaken, he never would have escaped with his life at El Rincón de los Toros. Not even the *llaneros* excelled him in keenness of vision and fineness of ear. He was an expert in the handling of arms and a most skillful and daring horseman, though rather awkward-looking on horseback. Extremely fond of horses, he personally supervised their care and would visit the stables several times a day, whether on a campaign or in a city. He dressed with great care and kept himself very clean, taking a bath every day, and as many as three daily in regions where the heat was intense. He preferred country to city life. He detested drunkards and gamblers and, even more, gossips and liars. He was so loyal and gentlemanly that he would not allow others to be discussed unfavorably in his presence. To him friendship was a sacred word. Trustful to an extreme, if he discovered deceit or betrayal, he never forgave the one who had abused his confidence.

His generosity was really extraordinary. Not only would he give away whatever he had, but he would also run into debt to help others. Prodigal with what was his own, he was almost miserly with public funds. At times he may have inclined his ear to praise, but flattery angered him.

He spoke much and well; he had the rare gift of conversation and liked to tell anecdotes about his past life. His style was rhetorical and

correct; his speeches and writings are full of daring and original meta-
phors. His proclamations are models of military eloquence. Elegance of
style, clearness, and terseness are evident in his dispatches. He did not
forget even the most trivial details in the orders that he communicated to
his lieutenants: everything was calculated and foreseen by him. He had
the gift of persuasion and was able to inspire confidence in others. To
these qualities are largely due the astounding triumphs achieved by him
despite conditions so difficult that a man without his natural endowments
and mettle would have become discouraged. A creative genius par excel-
lence, he obtained resources when none seemed available. Always great,
he was greatest in adversity. "Bolívar was more to be feared after defeat
than after victory," his enemies used to say. Reverses made him rise above
himself.

In the dispatch of civil affairs, which he never neglected, even when
on campaigns, he was as skillful and prompt as in all other phases of his
life. Swinging himself in a hammock, or walking up and down, usually
with long steps—for his restless nature precluded repose—with his arms
crossed or with his left hand grasping the collar of his coat and the fore-
finger of his right hand on his upper lip, he would listen to his secretary
reading official correspondence and the innumerable petitions and personal letters addressed to him. As the secretary read, he would dictate his
decisions regarding the petitions, and, as a rule, these decisions were irrev-
ocable. Then he would start dictating—to as many as three amanuenses at
a time—official dispatches and letters, for he never left a letter unan-
swered, no matter how humble the person who wrote to him might be.
Though he might be interrupted during dictation, I never heard him make
a mistake or get confused on resuming the interrupted sentence. When he
did not know the correspondent or the petitioner, he would ask a couple
of questions, but this happened very seldom because, gifted as he was
with a prodigious memory, he knew not only every officer in the army but
also all the officeholders and persons of note in the country. A great judge
of men and of human affections, he realized instantly for what sort of
work each man might serve, and very rarely did he turn out to be mistaken.

He read much, despite the scant time for reading that his busy life
allowed him. He wrote little in his own hand—only to members of his
family or some intimate friends—but he almost always added a line or
two in his own handwriting when he signed what he had dictated. He spoke
and wrote French correctly, and Italian quite well; as for English, he knew
only a little, barely enough to understand what he was reading. He was
thoroughly versed in the Greek and Latin classics, which he had studied,
and he always read them with pleasure in good French translations.

Attacks directed against him in the press made the deepest impression on him, and calumny irritated him. Though a public figure for more

than twenty years, he was never able, because of his sensitive nature, to overcome this susceptibility, rare indeed among men in high position. He had great regard for the sublime mission of the press as a guardian of public morals and as a curb on passions, and he attributed the greatness and the moral standards of the English people to the skillful use made in England of this civilizing agency.

General Ducoudray Holstein's View

General Bolívar, in his exterior, in his physiognomy, in his whole deportment, has nothing which would be noticed as characteristic or imposing. His manners, his conversation, his behaviour in society, have nothing extraordinary in them, nothing which would attract the attention of any one who did not know him; on the contrary, his exterior is against him. He is five feet four inches in height, his visage is long, his cheeks hollow, his complexion a livid brown; his eyes are of middle size, and sunk deep in his head, which is covered thinly with hair; and his whole body is thin and meagre. He has the appearance of a man sixty-five years old. In walking, his arms are in perpetual motion. He cannot walk long, but soon becomes fatigued. Wherever he goes his stay is short, seldom more than half an hour, and as soon as he returns his hammock is fixed, in which he sits or lies, and swings upon it after the manner of his countrymen. Large mustachios and whiskers cover a part of his face, and he is very particular in ordering each of his officers to wear them, saying that they give a martial air. This gives him a dark and wild aspect, particularly when he is in a passion. His eyes then become animated, and he gesticulates and speaks like a madman, threatens to shoot those with whom he is angry, steps quickly across his chamber, or flings himself upon his hammock; then jumps out of it, orders people out of his presence, and frequently arrests them. When he wishes to persuade, or bring any one to his purpose, he employs the most seducing promises, taking a man by the arm, and walking and speaking with him as with his most intimate friend. As soon as his purpose is attained, he becomes cool, haughty, and often sarcastic; but he never ridicules a man of high character, or a brave man, except in his absence. This practise of abusing people in their absence, is characteristic of the Caraguins generally. The following is extracted from Colonel [Gustavus] Hippisley's "Narrative of the Expedition to the Rivers Orinoco and Apure, in South America," London, 1819, p. 382.

"I had a full opportunity of surveying the general (Bolívar) while he was conversing with Captain Beire. From what I had heard of him, I was led to expect in appearance a very different man from the one I saw before me. General Bolívar is a mean looking person, seemingly, though but thirty-eight, about fifty years of age. He is about five feet six inches in height, thin sallow complexion, lengthened visage, marked with every symptom of anxiety, care, and I could almost add, despondency. He seemed also to have undergone great fatigue. His dark, and according to report, brilliant eyes, were now dull and heavy, although I could give them credit for possessing more fire and animation, when his frame was less harassed. Black hair, loosely tied behind with a piece of riband, large mustachios, black handkerchief round his neck, blue trowsers, boots and spurs, completed his costume. In my eyes he might have passed for any thing but what he was. Across the chamber was suspended one of the Spanish hammocks, on which he occasionally sat, lolled, and swung, whilst conversing, and seldom remained in the same posture for two minutes together." &c.

General Bolívar occupies himself very little in studying the military art. He understands no theory, and seldom asks a question, or holds any conversation relative to it. Nor does he speak of the civil administration, unless it happens to fall within the concerns of the moment. I often endeavoured to bring him into serious conversation on these subjects, but he would always interrupt me; "yes, yes, *mon cher ami,* I know this, it is very good; but *apropos*"—and immediately turned the conversation upon some different subject.

His reading, which is very little, consists of light history and tales. He has no library, or collection of books, befitting his rank and the place he has occupied for the last fifteen years. He is passionately fond of the sex, and has always two or three ladies, of whom one is the favourite mistress, who follows him wherever he goes.

Dancing is an amusement of which he is also passionately fond. Whenever he stays two or three days in a place, he gives a ball or two, at which he dances in his boots and spurs, and makes love to those ladies who happen to please him for the moment. Next to this amusement he likes his hammock, where he sits or lolls, conversing or amusing himself with his favourite mistress, or other favourites. During this time, he is inaccessible to all others. The aide-de-camp on duty says to those who have important business to transact with him:—"His Excellency is deeply engaged at present, and can see no one." When he is out of humour, he swears like a common bully, and orders people out of his presence in the rudest and most vulgar manner. From his habits of life, or rather from his love of pleasure, it happens that many matters of business are heaped together, and left to his secretary. . . . When he suddenly recollects some business, he calls his secretary, and directs him to write the letter or the decree. This brings more to mind, and it often happens that in one day he hurries off the work of fifteen or twenty. In this manner it often happens that decrees, made on the same day, are in direct opposition to each other.

General Bolívar has adopted the habits and customs of the European Spaniards. He takes his *siesta* (noon nap) regularly, and eats his meals in the manner of the Spaniards. He goes to *tertulias* (coteries), gives *refrescos*, and always dances the first minuet with the lady highest in rank in the company. This old Spanish custom is strictly observed throughout Colombia.

Inasmuch as General Bolívar is the sport of circumstances, it is difficult to trace his character. Bolívar, in success, differs, not circumstantially alone, from Bolívar in adversity; he is quite another man. When successful, he is vain, haughty, ill-natured, violent; at the same time the slightest circumstances will so excite his jealousy of his authority, that he arrests and sometimes condemns to capital punishment those whom he suspects. Yet he, in a great measure, conceals these faults, under the politeness of a man educated in the so-called *beau monde*. They appear in his fits of passion; but not, however, unless he is sure of having the strength on his side; the bayonets at his command. When he finds himself in adversity and destitute of aid from without, as he often did from 1813 to 1818, he is perfectly free from passion and violence of temper. He then becomes mild, patient, docile, and even submissive. Those who have seen him in the changes of his fortune will agree that I have not overcharged the picture.

The predominant traits in the character of General Bolívar, are ambition, vanity, thirst for absolute undivided power, and profound dissimulation. He is more cunning, and understands mankind better than the mass of his countrymen; he adroitly turns every circumstance to his own advantage, and spares nothing to gain those he thinks will be of present use to him. He is officious in rendering them little services; he flatters them, makes them brilliant promises; finds whatever they suggest very useful and important, and is ready to follow their advice. A third person suggests something to him, or he meets with some unexpected success—instantly he resumes his true character, and becomes vain, haughty, cross, and violent; forgets all services and all obligations, speaks with contempt of those he had just courted, and if they are powerless, abandons them, but always manifests a disposition to spare those whom he knows able to resist him.

At Aux Cayes, General Bolívar and I lived very much and very intimately together. Our conversation turned one day upon General [Santiago] Mariño and he said, laughing to me, "Oh, I despise Mariño. He is a brute and not able to command four men." Mariño at that instant came in. Bolívar met him at the door and embraced him warmly, as a dear friend; and we remained together an hour or more.

Bolívar represented General [Juan Bautista] Arismendi to me as a man without education, and yet as a very intriguing and dangerous man. He was evidently afraid of Arismendi. He remembered that when he himself, and Mariño, came as fugitives to Juan Griego, in 1814, Arismendi had prevented his remaining there, and even threatened violence if he attempted to do so. Bolívar had not forgotten this when we came to

Margarita after the sea-fight in May, 1816, and would probably then have been afraid to venture himself on shore, but that [Admiral Luis] Brión, who, on account of his wound, had been put ashore had made such representations to Arismendi as had reconciled him to Bolívar, and induced him to come on board our vessel. As soon as Arismendi came on board, Bolívar immediately took him down into the cabin and conversed with him for a good while. He regained him by giving him a formal promise to convene a new congress, and lay aside his title of supreme chief, which was very offensive to the republican Arismendi. The latter, relying on his word, engaged again to recognise him as commander-in-chief. The day after Arismendi's formal recognition of Bolívar as commander-in-chief, he took again the title of *supreme chief.* And when I told him that Arismendi would be offended, he said, "Never mind, never mind, I care not much for Arismendi; I have gained him over, and he will do as I wish; and besides, he sees no further than the end of his nose." But when, in 1819, at Angostura, Arismendi had compelled [Francisco Antonio] Zea to leave the post of vice-president, and had taken it himself, Bolívar became so alarmed for his own supremacy, that he left his command to General [José Antonio] Páez, marched about two hundred and fifty miles with his bodyguard against Arismendi, and reinstated Zea, with whom he could indeed do as he pleased. But he could and did only send him back to his former command, at Margarita.

Whilst General Bolívar stood in need of the military skill of General [Manuel] Piar, he flattered him highly; but when he came to fear his influence, he sacrificed him. He would not at that time have put Piar to death, if he had not been so advised and supported by others; not that he was unwilling to have Piar put out of the way, but that he would not have *dared* to condemn him.

In 1826, General Páez openly raised the standard of rebellion against the lawful authorities; and he was not only not punished, but suffered to remain in command as before. His impunity, like that of Arismendi, was owing to the strength of his party.

General Bolívar's disposition with regard to money is the reverse of miserly, and he is generally believed to be very generous. His disposition in this respect cannot be better described than by saying, that if he had a hundred thousand pounds to-day, he might very probably not have a cent to-morrow. He very seldom gives money to those that are in want, or to those who from delicacy refrain from asking for it, but he bestows profusely on his flatterers.

He has been compared to Napoleon Bonaparte. Bolívar in his proclamations imitates, or endeavours to imitate, the style of Napoleon. He began with a small body-guard, and afterwards greatly increased it, like Napoleon. He is ambitious, absolute, and jealous of his command, like the other. On public occasions he is simply dressed, while all around him is splendid, like Napoleon, and he moves quickly from place to place like him. With respect to military and administrative talents, there is no resemblance between them.

Bolívar, when dictator of Venezuela, ordered the execution of 1,253 Spaniards and Isleños, prisoners of war, and others, who were put to death in February, 1814. This was done in cold blood, and no entreaties could save them. I have mentioned an instance of his want of feeling, which I witnessed at the port of Juan Griego in May, 1814, and another in the naval combat just before. This first was attended by an additional circumstance of cruelty; that the prisoners were compelled to dig their own graves! Admiral Brión was on shore, on account of his wound, but as soon as he heard of this execution, he sent positive orders, that no more prisoners should be taken on shore, even if Bolívar himself ordered it; and by this means about 120 lives were saved.

The following fact was related to me by a respectable eye-witness, whom I would name, but for the danger of exposing him to the vengeance of the dictator-liberator. The relator, at the time he stated the fact to me, I presume, had no thought of my writing the history of Bolívar.

During a small skirmish which General Bolívar had with a Spanish detachment, not far from Araure, in 1814, one of his officers came full speed and reported to him, that a detached company was attacked on a bushy hill, a mile from his head-quarters, and that they were in great want of cartridges. Twelve soldiers, who heard the report, immediately offered themselves to carry the cartridges. Bolívar ordered the chief of his staff, Thomas Montilla, to send with each of these soldiers a box of cartridges. But, as there was no road at all, they were obliged to seek a passage through a very thick forest, full of briars and thorns, in order to ascend the hill. After having laboured to force their way until they found there was no probability of penetrating farther, they were compelled to return to head-quarters. They explained to the dictator the impossibility of going further, and showed him their clothes, torn in pieces, and their bodies covered with blood and wounds. Bolívar, in a furious passion, called them cowards, rascals, traitors, &c. and ordered the three first who arrived to be shot. His major-general, or chief of the staff, Thomas Montilla, who is a great favourite, his commandant of the artillery, Joseph Collot, and various other of the surrounding officers of the staff, entreated him to revoke his order. The men fell upon their knees, and with pathetic lamentations, entreated him to spare their lives, as they were innocent, and fathers of large families. All was in vain. As they came into his presence, two or three together, he renewed his order; and the whole twelve were bound and shot. On various occasions has Bolívar manifested the same disposition as I have shown.

Colonel Hippisley, in his work already cited, says, p. 464, "Bolívar would ape the great man. He aspires to be a second Bonaparte, in South

America, without possessing a single talent for the duties of the field or the cabinet. He would be King of New Granada and Venezuela, without genius to command, consequence to secure, or abilities to support, the elevated station to which his ambition most assuredly aspires. In victory, in transient prosperity, he is a tyrant, and displays the feelings and little-ness of an upstart. He gives way to sudden gusts of resentment, and be-comes in a moment, a madman, and (pardon the expression) a blackguard; throws himself into his hammock, which is constantly slung for his use, and utters curses and imprecations upon all around him, of the most dis-gusting and diabolical nature. In defeat, in danger, in retreat, he is per-plexed, harassed and contemptible, even to himself, weighed down by disasters, which he has neither skill or strength of mind to encounter, lighten, or remove. In this state he appeared to me at the retreat to and from San Fernando, when he looked the image of misery and despair.

"He has (p. 462) neither talents nor abilities for a general, and espe-cially for a commander-in-chief. The numerous mistakes he has made throughout the whole of his campaigns, for the last eight years, have nearly desolated the provinces and annihilated the population. The repeated sur-prises he has experienced from the enemy, (already seven,) prove my as-sertion, and bear me out in declaring that any one of them would have disgraced a corporal's guard.

"Tactics, movements, and manoeuvres, are as unknown to him as to the lowest of his troops. All idea of regularity, system, or the common routine of an army, or even a regiment, he is totally unacquainted with. Hence arise all the disasters he meets, the defeats he suffers, and his con-stant obligations to retreat whenever opposed to the foe. The victory which he gains to-day, however dearly purchased, (of which his list of killed and missing, if he calls for or keeps such details, must evidently convince him) is lost tomorrow, by some failure or palpable neglect on his part."

Thus it is that Páez was heard to tell Bolívar, after the action at Villa de Cura, that he would move off his own troops, and act no more with him in command; adding, "I never lost a battle wherein I acted by myself, or in a separate command, and I have always been defeated when acting in concert with you, and under your orders." The native and black troops (freed slaves) can and do dash on, in their native country. Yet, under the name of courage, they will rush, without order, regularity, or discretion, upon the enemy, resolved at that moment to conquer or die; and if, in this onset, they are beaten or repulsed, and find themselves "able to go about" and to retreat, "the devil take the hindmost" appears to be the general cry; for they all continue to run until they reach a place of safety; and it is allowed by the royalist troops themselves, that the patriotic army, with Bolívar at their head, was never beaten in this respect." "The final slaugh-ter of the prisoners, after the battle or during the retreat, is completely acquiesced in by Bolívar, who has himself condescended to witness this scene of butchery," &c.

These passages are sufficient to confirm what I have said in the course of these memoirs, of General Bolívar and his troops. I could cite various other writers, to the same purpose.

It is true that his flatterers and courtiers have endeavored to compare General Bolívar with Napoleon; but none of them have suggested to him the idea of aspiring to deserve being compared with Washington.

All who have compared him with the latter were either strangers, or persons who have seen Bolívar perhaps a few hours, or not at all.

Bolívar's conduct as dictator, in Venezuela, in 1813–14, as supreme chief, in 1816–17–18; his project of a monarchical constitution, in which he proposed the creation of a senate for life, with the titles of dukes, marquises, counts, barons, &c., in 1819; the constitution of Bolivia, the secret history of his *protectorate* in Peru; his behaviour in Venezuela; his famous proclamation directed to the grand convention of Ocaña; and his self-nomination as supreme chief or dictator of Colombia, are proofs of his ambition, his hypocrisy, and his secret determination to become an absolute monarch.

A great man would have directed the efforts of the ambitious and ignorant chieftains of Colombia to one point, the driving their common enemies from the country, in the first place, and then establishing a free government. Bolívar's object has invariably been his own personal aggrandizement, to the exclusion of every good and noble purpose. He is certainly a rare example of great ambition, unaided by talent or virtue. Yet, such are the inhabitants of Colombia, that they are ruled by this man.

In his recently published organic decree, dated August 27th, 1828, in title 1, he says:

"Art. 1st. The attributes of the supreme chief embrace the maintenance of the peace in the interior, and the defence from without; the command of the forces by land and sea; the negotiations in war and peace, and treaties; and the nomination of all officers: the right to issue decrees and the necessary rules *(reglamentos)*, of whatever nature they may be; to modify, to reform the established laws; the execution of the decrees and rules of those laws which shall remain in force; and the collection of taxes; the administration of justice, the execution of judgments; the approbation or the alteration of the sentences in the councils of war; the commutation of punishments, with the advice of the council of state, and upon the proposal of the courts, or on having previously heard them; the granting of amnesty or pardon for public or private offences, always with the advice of the council of state; the delivery of commissions or *lettres de marque*. The exercise of the natural power as chief of the general administration of the republic in all its branches, and in virtue of being entrusted with the supreme power of the state; finally, the presidency of the council of state, when he thinks proper.

"Art. 2d. The supreme council will be assisted in the exercise of the executive power with the advice of a council of ministers."

This famous decree explains so much, that I may safely appeal to it, in support of what I have said of its author. I have adverted to the difficulty of tracing the character of this individual, arising from his being so much the creature of circumstances. He has not sufficient vigour of spirit, nor courage of heart, nor talent, to escape from a critical situation, or to rise from a fall, without help from abroad. His good fortune in receiving such help has been almost uninterrupted since 1813. But the great secret of his power lies in the character of the people over whom he rules.

Lieutenant-Colonel Simón Bolívar, whilst he was governor of the fortress of Puerto Cabello, in June 1812, left the fortress and embarked clandestinely with some officers, in the night, without giving any previous notice to the garrison, without any order, without any capitulation, armistice, or previous treaty with the enemy. He embarked for fear of the prisoners of war, who had revolted, and taken possession of the citadel. An old soldier might admit the place to be no longer tenable. But here the garrison, finding that their commander had deserted, without leaving them any order or advice, actually retired in good order, and reached Valencia by land without losing a man; and without any attack from the prisoners in the citadel. It is an invariable rule that the commander of a place, in time of war and danger, should never leave those who have been committed to his care.

Secondly, Simón Bolívar, the dictator, liberator of the West of Venezuela, embarked in the greatest haste in the night of the 25th August, 1814, at Cumana, and fled with Santiago Mariño, from the field of war. He so completely lost his presence of mind, that, in spite of the warmest representations of his cousin Ribas and many others, he would hear nothing, and remained on board Commodore Bianchi's vessel. He sent various messages to Mariño, urging him to embark, and as soon as Mariño arrived, he ordered the commander to cut his cables and sail. Ribas, and a thousand other brave men, remained and fought for their independence and freedom. We have seen how Arismendi and Bermudes forced them to leave the ports of Juan Griego and Ocumare, treating them as fugitives and cowards, and threatening to shoot them if they set foot on shore.

Thirdly. General Bolívar came suddenly to the height of power, and was named captain-general of the armies of New Venezuela and New Granada, because the congress of the latter country was in great need of some authority to subject the province of Cundinamarca, and to occupy Santa Marta; (1814, and beginning of 1815). He felt a second time his absolute inability, and, after his ill-fated siege of Cartagena, embarked for Jamaica, whilst General Palacios, with the remainder of the army, fought bravely, and gained advantages over the Spaniards.

Fourthly. The occupation of Cartagena and Boca Chica by the patriots offered a new occasion to distinguish himself. He left Aux Cayes for Margarita, and in the naval combat (May 2d), chose his place in the long boat of Commodore Brión's vessel (the only vessel engaged, and which took the Spanish royal brig Intrépida), leaving to another the command of the officers and volunteers in his stead. In consequence of this action, General Arismendi ignorant of the part Bolívar had taken in it, not only became reconciled to the latter, but placed himself again under his orders. If Arismendi had been made acquainted with Bolívar's conduct in this action, it would have been the destruction of the projected expedition against Venezuela.

Fifthly. At the action of Ocumare (July 10th, 1816), the supreme chief left the field, and rode full speed (he is always careful to have the best runners) two leagues; jumped from his horse, and embarked on board the fast sailing privateer, Diana, Captain Debouille. As soon as he was on board, he ordered the captain to cut his cables; and arrived at the little Dutch island Bonair. General M'Gregor assembled the remainder of the troops left by Bolívar, and with them, joined General Piar at Barcelona. When Admiral Brión arrived at Bonair from Curaçao, he was astonished to hear of the flight of the supreme chief, and reproached him severely. Bolívar received his reproaches with great docility, feeling at this time his entire dependence upon the admiral. Brión, who was quick tempered, becoming cooler, succeeded at last in persuading Bolívar that his honour absolutely required him to return to the Main and rejoin his troops; and he ordered Captain Debouille to put himself at the disposal of the supreme chief. Bolívar directed his course towards the coast of Cumana. On his landing, Mariño and Piar, who had left him at Carupano, reproached him with his cowardly flight from Ocumare, and told him that if he did not embark immediately, they would arrest and try him before a court-martial. He embarked speedily, and arrived at Jaquemel, whence he passed to Port au Prince. Brión now employed all his influence to procure Bolívar's recall to the Main. After long and great exertions, he succeeded, chiefly by giving his word that Bolívar would assemble a congress, and establish a republican government, to which the latter most readily consented. In consequence of this stipulation, he was recalled, and arrived at Barcelona in the latter part of 1816. As soon as he was again at the head of the troops he disregarded his promise, resumed his title of supreme chief, and proceeded as he had done before.

Sixthly. The supreme chief, on the night of the 5th and 6th April, 1817, fled from the fortified place of Barcelona, abandoning his aide-de-camp, chamberlain, and more than 1000 men. The latter, perceiving that the Spaniards had gained the walls, killed his wife and himself. All the rest were murdered by the Spaniards. At this time, the supreme chief hid himself in the remotest part of the plains of Cumana, where he remained about seven weeks.

Seventhly. The supreme chief left the scene of war, in 1818, after his unsuccessful campaign in Venezuela. The details of this campaign are alone sufficient to give a correct idea of his military talents. He went for shelter to the strong place of Angostura, in Guayana.

These facts (and many more might be adduced) sufficiently prove that Bolívar frequently lost his presence of mind, whilst the most propitious circumstances concurred to restore his fortune. I have said enough of his talents for administration, and his mode of proceeding in civil matters, in the course of these memoirs.

But how is it possible (the question naturally arises) that General Bolívar should have liberated his country, and preserved to himself the supreme power, without superior talent?

If, by "liberating his country," it be meant that he has given his country a free government, I answer, that he has not done so. If it be meant, that he has driven out the Spaniards, I answer, that he has done little towards this; far less, certainly, than the meanest of the subordinate chieftains. To the question, how he can have retained his power without superior talent? I answer, in the first place, that the *reputation* of superior talent goes a great way. But I shall not desire the reader to be satisfied with this answer. Before the revolution of Caracas, April 19th, 1810, and ever since that time, the Spaniards themselves have constantly and powerfully contributed to assist the patriots in all their enterprises; by forcing the inhabitants to withdraw themselves from an onerous and base submission; by leaving them no alternative but to resist oppression, cruelty, and death, by force of arms, or submit to them. Without any disposition to disparage the bravery, the constancy of the Colombian people, I say that the policy, and the whole behaviour of the Spanish chieftains, during the war on the Main, has operated powerfully towards the freedom and independence of the people. It has been a stimulus applied with very little respite. Their obstinacy, their hypocrisy, their barbarous cruelties, their entire want of moderation, of even the semblance of liberal policy, of talents, and of courage, have contributed effectually to alienate from them the confidence and favourable opinion of the people. These naturally chose to be under the dominion of their native chieftains, rather than to perish under the cruelties and vexations of the Spaniards. If these latter had adopted a liberal system for administering the provinces of Venezuela and New Granada, I venture to pronounce, that, as soon as the Americans perceived the precarious situation of the mother country, none of them would have thought of separating from Spain. This opinion is supported by the well-known fact, that not one of the patriotic juntas, in 1810, had dreamed of detaching itself from the adored King Ferdinand. The stupid management of the Spanish authorities has facilitated all the operations of the patriots. The grievous faults of Bolívar and some of his generals, have been exceeded by those of his adversaries. It is not strange, therefore, that Bolívar should have been able to do all he has done with very limited talents. It has been said, long since, that oppression cannot be exercised upon any people beyond a certain point; that passing this point certainly produces resistance, and at length revolution.

The territory of Colombia has a vast extent of coast. It was impossible that it should be guarded by the Spanish troops that were sent out. Bolívar, when beaten and driven from one place, had only to go to another. The advantage in point of numbers was vastly against the Spaniards. Their greatest number of troops never exceeded twenty thousand; whereas, on the part of the patriots, there was a great majority of the people of the country, who consisted of about two millions of souls. Quiroxa's revolution, in favour of the constitution of 1812, occupied Spain at home, and prevented her sending powerful aid to [General Pablo] Morillo. The Spaniards generally, and Morillo among the rest, became tired and worn out; their troops deserted by hundreds. If Morillo, moreover, had sought to aid Bolívar, he could not have done it more effectually, than by appointing [Field Marshal Miguel de] La Torre his successor: for the drooping and sickly state of the Spaniards at that time, La Torre was but a poor physician. A powerful moral cause stood also in aid of Bolívar; I mean public opinion; which, if not unanimously in his favour, was certainly so against the cruel deeds of the Spaniards; and the Colombians, in their choice between two evils, very naturally took that which appeared to be the least.

By examining the conduct of the Spanish chieftains, both in Venezuela and New Granada, we shall find that they afforded great assistance to the limited talents of the supreme chief and liberator.

In Venezuela, the captain-general, Don Juan de Casas, as early as 1808, began to irritate the minds of the inhabitants of Caracas, by arresting, in a very arbitrary and impolitic manner, a great many inhabitants belonging to the first and most respectable families (mantuanos) in that province. There was no other motive for his arrest than ill-founded suspicion; and he was compelled to set them at liberty. But the impression remained, and stirred up many enemies to his government.

Captain-General Don Vicente Emparan, his successor, was the victim of his own obstinacy. Without regard to the disposition, or feelings, or opinions of the inhabitants, he blindly followed the orders of the regency at Cádiz, which continued to dictate and maintain laws made in the time of Ferdinand the Catholic and Philip II. Emparan, by refusing to be advised, lost himself and the Spanish cause. His great security, and the idea of his power, joined with his obstinacy, gave occasion to the revolution of the 19th April, 1810, in Caracas. The junta, which succeeded him, took the title of Provisional Junta of Venezuela, conservators of the rights of his catholic majesty, Ferdinand VII, which proved that this junta and its constituents had no idea of detaching themselves from Spain. Its detailed official report explained this very clearly, and concluded by offering the Spanish government money and support of every description, to maintain the war into which it was driven against Napoleon. The regency of Cádiz answered their kind offers by a vehement decree, dated August 3d, 1810, by which the province of Venezuela was declared to be in a state of blockade thus treating its inhabitants like enemies of the nation! The regency ordered every means to be employed to turn out a junta sincerely attached to their king; and to punish them as rebels.

The mission of Don Francisco Cortavaria, by the regency and cortés of Spain, to the island of Puerto Rico, was the consequence of the decree of August 3d. He had a commission to pacify the Main, and to force its inhabitants to receive a new captain-general from the hands of those who ruled in Spain. This mission increased the fire of civil war, instead of extinguishing it.

The weak and cowardly Captain-General Millares, who succeeded Emparan, was but an object of contempt and mockery to his subaltern, Don Domingo Monteverde, who treated him like an instrument that is laid aside, when it becomes useless to our purpose. The latter audaciously put himself in place of the other, and violated the treaty of Vitoria, made July 12, 1812, with Miranda.

Monteverde's government was the reign of Isleños friars, monks, priests, and intriguers of various descriptions. Boves, Morales, Suasola, Antoñazas, Puy, Rosette, and other Spanish chieftains of this sort, had the upper hand. His administration was a series of perfidies, cruelties, and persecutions; one of the most complete and horrid anarchy.

Simón Bolívar, with a respectable force, approached the limits of Venezuela, announced its deliverance, and promised the inhabitants relief and freedom. These wretched people, reduced to despair, flocked by thousands to his standard for refuge from misery and death. Desertion became general in the royal army; and these troops, united with many thousands of volunteers, augmented with Bolívar's legions, and reduced the forces of the enemy to so small and weak a number, that the former had nothing to do but to march forward, assured of success and victory. The confidence of the country in the Spanish troops, and the dread of them, declined in proportion as confidence in the patriot troops increased. Thus he advanced into the interior of Venezuela, supported by a series of successes which cost him very little; and thus he entered the capital, Caracas, whence the enemy had fled. Men, money, arms, munitions of every description, were offered him from every corner, and, united with the zeal of about a million of people, desirous of assisting him to destroy the feeble remnant of the enemy, very ordinary talents only were necessary to direct this powerful mass of forces and means to the utter extermination of Spanish despotism and cruelty. But Bolívar was so elated with his unexpected success, that, at the height of his fortune, he lost all reflection, and imagined that everything was accomplished. His gross faults were the only cause of his ruin. They brought on the subsequent misery of his countrymen, and the downfall of the cause of freedom in Venezuela.

The year 1813 saw him at the summit of human grandeur and glory. The next year saw him a fugitive, in danger of being shot for desertion like the meanest soldier, and forced to seek shelter in a sister republic, Cartagena, whom he afterwards treated as a foe; laying siege to her capital in 1815.

General Monteverde being wounded, left Puerto Cabello for Curaçao, where he lived in high style, from the plunder and vexations carried on against the inhabitants of Venezuela. He left the command of the remaining royal troops to Colonel Salomon, whose conduct we have noticed.

After Bolívar's flight from Cumana, in August 1814, military despotism began again to direct the reins of the royal government. The captain-general, Cagigal, had the nominal power, but Boves, Morales, Cevallos, and other Spanish chieftains, acted, throughout Venezuela, wherever they came, as masters and conquerors. The best proof of this is the massacre of the most respectable inhabitants of Valencia, which took place in presence of Cagigal, and went unpunished. Similar excesses were committed, unpunished, in all the other provinces of Venezuela; and, throughout its whole territory, persecutions and the most barbarous cruelties were multiplied. The only man who had character and firmness enough to preserve the city of Caracas itself from pillage was the Marquis of León. And this he did, by overawing a mulatto lieutenant-colonel (Muchado), who had been a slave of the Count De La Grange. But the marquis was not a military man; his authority was personal, limited, and momentary. He was probably the only man at that time on the Main qualified by character to re-establish the royal authority. But instead of giving him full powers for that purpose, the King of Spain sent ten thousand bayonets, with a chieftain more capricious, hypocritical, despotic, and sanguinary, than any of his predecessors. Such was Don Pablo Morillo, who imagined, that to overawe every one, he had only to present himself. He took the title of "Pacificator of the New World," and arrived on the Main with the philanthropic principles which characterize him in many of his letters. He wrote to King Ferdinand, that it was necessary to regenerate Spanish America, and to exterminate, by fire and sword, "the present population, and create a new one." He began by grossly oppressing the only man capable of rendering him great service, the Marquis of San León. Him he arrested and took with him as a prisoner on his journey, because the marquis could not, or would not pay him, an extraordinary tax of twenty thousand dollars.

Admiral Marquis De Euriles, the friend and counsellor of Morillo, greatly assisted Bolívar by the advice he gave Morillo, after he knew it was impossible for him ever to reconquer the Main.

General Morales, who succeeded La Torre, was better qualified to raise the royal party; but his barbarous cruelty, his ignorance of policy, and his despotic principles, alienated from him the good opinion of both parties. Such was the general state of affairs in Venezuela, from 1810 to 1824, when the last of the Spaniards were driven from the Main by the capitulation of Puerto Cabello. Let us now look at New Granada.

The viceroy, Don Antonio Amar, was an honest man, and desired the welfare of the country, but he was too old and too weak to hold the reins of government in a time of revolution and trouble. He hesitated, and then gave way. Don Antonio Sorio succeeded him, and did worse. From that time there was no viceroy worthy of notice. Every province had its junta, and its governor or president; and these had no union, no understanding among themselves. They died away, one after another.

The reader may perhaps be acquainted with the atrocious deeds of the Bishop of Cuenca and his army of death, filled with friars and priests. He was another Peter the Hermit, with his fanatical brethren the Crusaders.

In Cartagena, Santa Marta, Puerto Bello, &c. the Spanish chieftains, after having pillaged the places, left them to their subalterns and fled.

In the eight provinces of Venezuela and the twenty-two of New Granada, the viceroys, captain-generals, governors, and Spanish leaders, have made every effort to alienate the affections of the Americans by their tyranny, cruelty, duplicity, and their general conduct, as impolitic as it was barbarous. The king, the regency, the cortes, and the juntas of Spain, have, in reality, powerfully seconded the patriots. Ever since 1810, the Spaniards have involuntarily done all they could do in favour of the patriots. Besides, the conduct of the Spanish chieftains has undoubtedly favoured the enterprises of General Bolívar, and assisted his feeble efforts. His generals and subalterns, and all the inhabitants of Colombia have powerfully supported him. Many of his generals have done far more than he has to free the country from the Spaniards. Amongst them Luis Brión was distinguished; as were also Generals Ribas, Villapol, Páez, Zarasa, Piar, Palacios, Arismendi, Gómez, Francisco de Paula Santander, Padilla, and others. None of these generals have ever abandoned their posts, or in any respect behaved so meanly as Bolívar has done. To these brave men Colombia, and Bolívar himself, owe the expulsion of the Spaniards and the salvation of the country; if their present expulsion may be called so. Of these men, Brión, Ribas, Villapol, Piar, and Palacios, no longer are living.

The brightest deeds of all these generals were performed in the absence of Bolívar. Abroad, they were attributed to his military skill and heroism, while in fact he was a fugitive, a thousand miles from the scenes of their bravery, and never dreaming of their successes. What has he done in Peru? He has destroyed freedom and independence there, as in Colombia.* His protectorate there answers exactly to his dictatorship in Colombia; a despotic military anarchy, which has driven the best inhabitants from both countries, or rendered them slaves, and which, for many years to come, will be felt as the pernicious effect of his incapacity and despotism.

General Bolívar, moreover, has never in person commanded a regiment; he has never made a charge of cavalry, nor with a bayonet; on the contrary, he has ever been careful to keep himself out of danger. He has always taken the precaution to provide himself with excellent horses and good guides, and whenever the fire approached him, has made use of both. The plain narration of facts composing these memoirs proves this assertion.

General Bolívar's expedition, in 1813, against Monteverde, and its complete success, has made him famous abroad. I have shown how easy, in his situation, success was, and that he had only to go forward. The merit, such as it may be, of consenting to go forward with a handful of men after the defection of Colonel Castillo, is General Bolívar's. The expedition was conceived and planned not so much by Bolívar as by his cousin Ribas, who was the soul and the friend of Bolívar. He and Colonel Briceño persuaded Bolívar to persevere and go forward, when, as respectable eyewitnesses have assured me, Bolívar himself wished, upon the defection of Castillo, to return to Cartagena.

The entry into Venezuela was the most brilliant epoch in the military career of General Bolívar. I have shown how easily it was made. Very little talent, surely, was requisite to drive a handful of Spaniards out of the country, and by so doing, to give liberty to the Venezuelans. He did neither, but fled for shelter to New Granada; but the memory of his grandeur remained, and having been the tyrant of his country, he was regarded as her *Liberator*. His fame procured him a good reception at Tunja, in November, 1814; and the congress of New Granada named him captain-general of the armies of Venezuela and New Granada, the highest military charge in the Spanish American armies. But this was trifling when compared with his dictatorship in Venezuela.

Congress, and all true friends of liberty, now entertained sanguine hopes that Bolívar had acquired wisdom by experiencing adversity, and that he felt an ardent desire to retrieve his faults and deserve their confidence. These hopes were founded upon his verbal promises made to his

---

*The two battles fought in Peru were gained in his absence: in the one he was a hundred miles from the field of action; in the second, at Ayachuco, where he was ill. General Antonio José de Sucre gained both, and Bolívar had the honour and the name.

friends in Tunja, and upon his numerous proclamations, and solemn promises, to give freedom, liberty, and welfare, to the Granadans. But he had acquired the habit of acting as master, and of following the impulses of his vain and haughty disposition. He entirely disregarded the confidence placed in him, and the obligation he was under to the congress of New Granada, which placed him at the head of a strong army, that he might be enabled to fulfil the important and double commission given him. He took, with perfect ease, the open and undefended capital of Bogotá, but suffered his troops to plunder it during forty-eight hours. The most important task assigned him was the conquest of Santa Marta, which, at the time, could have been easily completed; but he preferred the gratification of his own revenge, in besieging Cartagena, which had received him within her walls with distinguished hospitality whilst he was a fugitive, and proscribed by Arismendi and Bermudes. His principal aim in besieging, and endeavouring to take Cartagena, was to avenge himself upon Castillo, who commanded in the place. The dreadful consequences of this siege have been detailed already.

In the assembly of patriots, held in the beginning of 1816, in the city of Aux Cayes [Haiti], its members named General Bolívar as their commander-in-chief, because Commodore Brión, upon whom the expedition depended, had formally and openly declared, that if Bolívar should not be appointed the commander-in-chief of the projected expedition, he would not advance a single dollar. Brión was, at that time, the principal supporter of the patriots; Commodore Aury was the next; but the former had more money, and a more extensive credit than the latter, and was animated by the great promises of Bolívar to act in his favour. The president of Haiti, Alexander Petion, was also in favour of General Bolívar, and assisted him powerfully in the projected expedition. Besides all this, Bolívar had sacrificed his fortune in favour of the cause, and had been the most elevated chieftain, in rank, since 1813.

Commander Aury was the only member of this assembly who opposed, not the nomination of Bolívar, but his assuming the civil and military power alone. He proposed a council of government of three or five members, over which Bolívar should preside. The latter rose and spoke vehemently against a division of power, and concluded by saying, that he would rather resign than consent to Aury's proposal. Bolívar was well aware that Brión and Petion would do little or nothing if any other chieftains were elected, and therefore ventured to speak of resignation. Not a voice was heard in support of Aury; and Bolívar proposed a loud and individual vote, which was given for his being commander-in-chief of the projected expedition. The proceedings were reduced to writing beforehand, and were signed by every member except Aury, upon whom Bolívar avenged himself as we have seen.

From the time when Aury expressed himself so strongly against the absolute and undivided power of Bolívar, the latter began to fear that others might follow that example. Since 1813, Bolívar had been accustomed to have all around him acknowledge and submit to his authority, and obey implicitly all his orders, however arbitrary or despotic. When the dictator ordered the execution of the 1,200 Spaniards, in February, 1814, more than a thousand inhabitants of Caracas and La Guaira murmured deeply against this cruel and sanguinary deed; but no one dared to oppose, or even to speak openly against it.

When Bolívar heard from me that General Santiago Mariño had given a secret commission to Captain Bouille, a man of colour, to recruit three hundred choice soldiers from Haiti, he became very uneasy, and said to me that Piar had certainly advised Mariño to do so. He added, that Piar, being a man of colour, was a very dangerous one, and that he had the greatest influence over Mariño, and that Piar's object was to enable Mariño again to become his rival, as he had been in 1813 and 14. He then requested me to find some means of defeating Mariño's object, without having it known that he, Bolívar, cared about it. This was done as I have already related.

As soon as the supreme chief arrived at Carupano from the Island of Margarita, his body-guard was organized. Twenty-five men, with an officer, were daily placed before his head-quarters, and relieved every twenty-four hours.

In December, 1817, when Bolívar arrived at Barcelona, he again organized a body-guard. This was repeated at Angostura; and since that time this corps has been augmented so much, that he appointed the general of division, Rafael Urdaneta, the commander-in-chief of it. He had various generals of brigade under his orders; but principally General Anzoatigui, who was always blindly devoted to him. Since that time this body-guard has accompanied him everywhere.

There can be no doubt that the institution of this body-guard has been the ruin of liberty in Colombia; because the bayonets have supplied the place of both military and administrative skill ever since the Spaniards were driven from the territory. These alone have kept the weight of argument and opinion on his side. In imitation of the famous motto, "*Ultima Ratio Regum*," engraved upon the cannon of Frederick II, of Prussia, Bolívar should engrave upon the muskets of his body-guard, "*Ultima Ratio Dictatorum*." Their bayonets, supported by the money supplied by English stock-jobbers, have given him a supremacy over the congress, who, in the latter times of his presidency, have been the slaves of his will. I may ask, has any one of the distinguished patriots ever opposed the least hint to his known will? These patriots, having nothing to oppose to the bayonets of Bolívar, have always the majority of members against them.

Bolívar has several times offered his resignation, but never unless he knew beforehand that no one would dare to appear in favour of accepting it. He has a great many enemies, but the bayonets are all on his side.

In order to preserve his usurped power, he is careful to treat all his guards well, and to attach their officers to him by paying great attention to them, and making them large presents. He took his Colombian bodyguard to Peru, and when he left Peru, in 1826, he brought back as a bodyguard along with his Colombian troops, 1,500 Peruvians, under the plausible pretext of having troops sufficient to march against the rebels at Valencia.

His simply being in power attaches many to him. A great source of his influence is his having the disposal of all the offices of Colombia, in the civil and military departments; and those who flatter and please him best, get the best offices, without the least regard to their qualifications. He is a great dissembler, and possesses such ease of manners, that he charms those whom he wishes to gain to his purpose, seldom refusing their requests, and never meeting them with rebuke. The most common actions of men in power, under whatever name they may rule, are generally regarded as generous and extraordinary deeds, while far nobler deeds of private men pass unnoticed. This is the case with Bolívar. He spends 20 or 100,000 dollars without hesitation, when he can immediately have what sum he pleases. He knows well that so long as he reigns he shall not want money.

The great mass of the Colombian people are ignorant, bigoted, and rude, to a degree not easily conceived by one educated in almost any protestant country, particularly in the North American states. Hence it is, that Bolívar's speeches, proclamations, promises, conversations, are thought of so highly. These people, once getting a notion into their heads, keep it fast. They think Bolívar a great man, and believe that his monstrous faults are in fact the faults of others, because he tells them so. Besides, he generally shows only the fair side of any event whatever.*

Whenever he is about to appear, on solemn occasions, before the public, he is careful to prepare his friends and creatures, by informing them what he intends to do, and how they are to act. He then goes, surrounded by a numerous body of officers, all devoted to him, and a large number of troops, who remain without, under arms. Surrounded by this force, he is always sure of the strongest party. This military show imposes upon all, and so overawes his boldest and most decided enemies, that they are forced to be silent, knowing his vain, vindictive, and treacherous character, and being sure that if they opposed him they should, sooner or later, become

---

*See his justificatory memoir, published at Cartagena, in Sept. 1814; his proclamation before he embarked for Jamaica, in May, 1815; that published after the execution of General Piar, in 1817, &c.

the victims of his vengeance. A more striking proof of his vindictive spirit, need not surely be required than his siege of Cartagena, carried on for the purpose of taking vengeance on Castillo for an insult received two years before, and to avenge Pineres' defeat (and his own) in his effort to be elected president of the government of that province. What senator or representative could be rash enough to oppose him? He could not be opposed, with any chance of success, but by some military chieftain, who should have at command a force equal, at least, to his own. All the present chieftains are in favour of Bolívar, and all hold offices of a high grade under him. The power and the wealth of the country are in the hands of those who are interested deeply in supporting his power.

It is by means of all these advantages united, that General Bolívar has preserved his power since 1813. His security is now so great that he feels himself above dissembling any longer. He has thrown off the mask, and acts the part and speaks the language of an independent and powerful sovereign. He will preserve his power, as long as those who surround him remain attached to him, probably as long as he lives. His removal, whether it should happen by his death or otherwise, would produce a civil war.

All well informed men, who are acquainted with the different manners and habits of thinking, and with the heterogeneous character of the provinces, and of the chieftains now composing this colossal mass called a republic, will agree with me that it is impossible so to unite these parts that the body may enjoy that liberty which is necessary to the existence of a republic. If, therefore, Bolívar should be suddenly removed, these ambitious chieftains, each of whom has his partisans and admirers, would place themselves at the head of armed men and march one against another. The hatred of which I have spoken in my introduction as existing in a very high degree between the Caraguin [Caracas] and Granadan government, and the jealousy existing among all the chieftains, would soon overturn the state. Colombia would be the theatre of a desperate and bloody war. The strongest would reign just so long as he continued to be so.

I speak freely of the characters of the principal chieftains in Colombia; and I have a right to do so, for I know them well. My acquaintance with them has been sufficient to give me a knowledge of the degree to which their minds have been cultivated and enlightened, as well as of their distinctive characters, and their actual worth. It is absurd to suppose that a people kept in ignorance, slavery, bigotry, and superstition, for three centuries, can be raised at once to the degree of enlightenment, knowledge, and virtue, possessed (for example) by the people of the United States, who perhaps are the only people ripe for the blessings of true liberty, grounded upon wise laws, and supported by a liberal and virtuous population. Time alone, and that well improved, by giving the Colombians good institutions, and affording them good examples, and a frequent intercourse with enlightened strangers, can, by degrees, introduce among them the elements of knowledge, and raise them to that high state of mind which is capable of appreciating freedom.

Who, in Colombia, is able to prescribe wise laws? Who is able to make the people see their use, or to persuade or compel them to obey them? Who can be found there to support such laws in opposition to his own individual interest? Bolívar's example, had he been capable, would have gone a great way toward producing the happiest results. But, unfortunately for Colombia, and indeed for all the other Spanish republics, Bolívar has neither virtue, firmness, nor talent sufficient to raise himself above his own sphere of mediocrity, passion, ambition, and vanity. He is far from being competent to lay a foundation for good laws, schools, useful institutions, and a flourishing commerce. Had he been fit for these things, he would long since have invited and protected strangers, and encouraged agriculture, in a country where soil and climate combine to lighten the labour of man, and to multiply the comforts of life. He would have encouraged commerce, instead of depressing it. He would have made it the interest of the clergy to inspire the people, who are devoted to them, with the principles of morality, union, and patriotism. He would have insisted upon the freedom of religious opinion, and protected the people in the use of all the means necessary for the enjoyment of it. He would have consulted men of experience and virtue; and surrounded himself with men of talents and probity.

But what has this man done during the last four years, that is, since 1824, when Colombia was cleared of the last Spanish troops? Instead of remaining in his native country and employing all the means in his power to establish a solid government, we see him, even as early as 1822, seeking a new field for his ambition, a new scene of what he deems glory. He goes to the south, overruns a new country, destroys the congress in Peru, and places himself there, at the head of a despotic military government, renewing the dictatorial excesses of 1813 and 14 in Venezuela. By force of arms he detaches a portion of Peru, calls it the republic of Bolivia, and gives it a monarchical constitution, of which he is the president and protector. When he saw that his protectorship was going the wrong way, he thought of no remedy but a timely retreat; the expedient he had always been accustomed to resort to. He retired to Guayaquil, whence, as I have been well informed, he secretly sent out emissaries to Valencia, Caracas, Puerto Cabello, and Cartagena. Páez having openly raised the standard of revolt against the existing constitutional form of government, Bolívar adroitly seized this pretext to name himself dictator, annulled all congressional forms, assumed all the powers to himself; and passing over to Valencia, held secret conferences with Páez, and his old and intimate friend, Dr. Miguel Peña, and not only left Páez unpunished, but confirmed him in his post.

Bolívar is suddenly struck with conviction of the necessity of a reform and a change in the constitution of Colombia! The national convention assembles at Ocaña. During their session, Bolívar, some leagues off, surveys their operations with an anxious and jealous eye. The result is too well known. The convention expires, and Bolívar, become its substitute, is compensated for all his restless nights and his sorrow; and sits upon his throne, with the title of "Supreme Chief, President Liberator!"

Such is the political life of the cunning Simón Bolívar. His favourite rule is, to do every thing by himself; and he has acted upon it,—overturning or transforming every thing. At the head of the twelve departments, he placed, under the name of intendants, military chieftains, the greatest part of whom were totally unacquainted with any kind of administration whatever. He made Soublette intendant of Caracas; Mariño, of Maturin, and so on. He has destroyed the little commerce of the country by heavy imposts, by his famous decree on patents, by his not admitting of the Colombian *vales* in the public treasury, by imposing arbitrary taxes upon merchants, and incarcerating foreigners, (which he did at La Guaira and Caracas in the beginning of 1816,) and refusing to hear their just representations. Agriculture and national industry have been destroyed by his campaigns in Peru, and by the numerous levies recently made, by way of preparation against a new attack of the Spanish, expected from Cuba, against Colombia.

The finances are so ruined that Bolívar knows not how, any longer, to pay the interest of the English loan, and keep the national credit even up to its present sunken state. Thus has he destroyed the welfare of Colombia, and ruined Peru; and should he appear elsewhere, his appearance would produce the same result.

But the worst of Bolívar's acts is the last, where he has thrown off his flimsy mask, and declared that "bayonets are the best, the only rulers of nations." This pernicious example, it is to be feared, will be followed by other chieftains in the new Spanish republics.

9

Pablo Morillo, the War, and the Riego Revolt

Stephen K. Stoan

In 1815, General Pablo Morillo arrived in Venezuela with an expeditionary force of 10,500 well-equipped Spanish troops and the mission to reconquer the provinces of Nueva Granada. With Fernando VII returned to the throne in Madrid and Napoleon defeated and a captive, large numbers of Spanish troops were available for duty in the Americas. Owing to the campaigns of the savage José Tomás Boves, who led the cavalry forces of the pardo llaneros, *Venezuela was already more or less under royalist control. Boves died in battle just prior to the arrival of the Spanish expeditionary army. Needless to say, there were frictions between the haughty European Spanish officers and* pardo *commanders, who fought for land and recognition of their status as full citizens. Some Spanish officers were liberals who did not want to fight to suppress Americanos, and many soldiers were the refuse of the metropolitan regiments. By mid-1816, Morillo's army and the royalist forces of Nueva Granada had reconquered Cartagena after a siege of 106 days and the loss of 3,000 of Morillo's troops to disease and desertion. The insurgents moved into rugged marginal areas where they fought a guerrilla war against royalist patrols and outposts.*

As was the case throughout the Americas, effective counterinsurgency required a constant inflow of fresh officers and soldiers. Morillo's force suffered terribly from tropical diseases, bad diet, lack of pay, and desertion. By the end of 1817 the Spanish army had lost many of its units to disease, desertion, and small dispersed garrisons that could not be used by the army of operations. With morale destroyed and mistrust a major factor among pardo royalists, *Morillo's army ceased to be an effective force. Many of the* pardos *and even some white criollos recognized that there was little future for them with the royalists and added their significant cavalry strength to the patriot cause.*

From Stephen K. Stoan, "Pablo Morillo, the War, and the Riego Revolt," in *Pablo Morillo and Venezuela, 1815–1820* (Columbus: Ohio State University Press, 1974), 203–36. Reprinted by permission of Stephen K. Stoan.

Morillo lost hope about reconquering Nueva Granada and sought to salvage his own career by many requests for a transfer to Spain. The restoration of the Spanish constitution in 1820 pulled any remaining teeth from the royalist counterinsurgency. Although Bolívar's forces were successful, Stoan criticizes the military skills of the Liberator as a field commander. Caracas fell definitively to the patriot forces on May 14, 1821, and Cartagena a few months later on October 10.

Stephen Stoan is chief librarian at Drury College, Springfield, Missouri.

It cannot be said that the fighting in Venezuela stopped after 1810, not even with the arrival of the Expeditionary Army. Although Margarita was the principal bastion of patriot resistance at that point, its surrender by no means brought peace to the captaincy general. Some rebels fled to nearby islands or to New Granada, and others, having rejected the proffered amnesty, continued operations in the llanos with the Orinoco River at their backs.

The pardos who made up the royalist armies of [Francisco Tomás] Morales posed a particularly delicate problem for Morillo. Armed, they were a menace to domestic order. Disarmed, many would join republican ranks. Morillo's instructions, foreseeing this difficulty, had enjoined him to disarm the most tractable of the pardos and take the remainder to New Granada, where their acclimatization and martial qualities might be put to good use. This policy was only partially successful. Although some five thousand of Morales's troops were selected to accompany the expedition, more than three thousand had deserted before the day of embarkation. Many enlisted thereafter under patriot banners. To bring his own army up to necessary strength, Morillo was forced to resort to recruitment.[1] When the expedition sailed for Cartagena in 1815, the military situation of Venezuela was no less dangerous than when it had arrived.

The deterioration of the military position of the royalists in the captaincy general during Morillo's absence in New Granada obliged him to return to Venezuela in late 1816. The campaign of 1817, due largely to the brilliance of Manuel Piar, weakened the royalist position. Although the Expeditionary Army won several brilliant victories during the campaign of 1818, particularly against Bolívar, the work of José Antonio Páez served to strengthen the strategic posture of the patriot forces even further. Bolívar's victory at Boyacá in New Granada in 1819, soon followed by the Riego Rebellion in Cádiz, left royalist forces in Venezuela in a near-impossible situation. The constitutionalist government in Spain made no effort to supply the army, relieved Morillo of his command, and ordered an immediate truce. In late 1820 Morillo and Bolívar signed a six months' armistice and a treaty to regularize the war. Morillo departed Venezuela in December 1820.

The Nature of the Warfare

From the time of Bolívar's declaration of war to the death in 1813 until Morillo's arrival, the fighting in Venezuela was carried on without regard for the humanitarian rules devised to mitigate the brutality of warfare. Bolívar proposed to put to death every peninsular Spaniard captured, and Boves responded by declaring war to the death against creole whites. The resulting carnage in the year 1814 staggers the imagination, and one of Morillo's primary concerns on reaching Venezuela was to put an end to such indiscriminate slaughter.

Some precision in definition is in order here, since it is often stated that the war to the death continued until the treaties signed in 1820. This is only partially true. Although the patriots, as will be seen, continued at least sporadically and perhaps consistently to murder captured Spaniards, Morillo ordered, on 2 May 1815, that any royalist soldier who killed a prisoner on the field of battle would be executed.[2] He attempted thereafter to wage war in accordance with the laws accepted in Europe at that time. However, the Spanish government continued to consider the principal *leaders* of the revolution to be traitors subject to punishment following a formal indictment. Also, the government was prepared to try those who committed common crimes such as arson or robbery, or who, in violation of the rules of warfare, had murdered captured royalist soldiers.

There is considerable documentation demonstrating Morillo's procedures in these matters. Though he was not personally involved in fighting in Venezuela upon his arrival, he dispatched troops to the interior to liquidate the pockets of insurgency that remained. He instructed these units first to do whatever was possible to win the patriots over peacefully with pardons, as he had done on Margarita.[3] Once in New Granada, Morillo's policies become more evident. Even though the Colombians several times declared war to the death, murdering every Spanish soldier they captured, Morillo continued pardoning nearly all captured troops. He even extended an amnesty to José Fernández Madrid, president of the patriot government, because the man approached him to that effect.[4]

One letter sent by Morillo to Spain after the capture of Cartagena reveals the criteria he applied in determining who should be tried. He included the names of twenty-two persons executed by the war councils following a trial. Five had murdered Spanish prisoners in the dungeons, two were arsonists, three were murderers of Spanish prisoners, arsonists, and infidentes (traitors), and the remainder were infidentes.[5] The eyewitness observer Rafael Sevilla, a relative of Morillo's, claimed that the general's decision to try the principal leaders was motivated primarily by the recently arrived news that Margarita had rebelled again.[6] Colombian historians have listed one hundred and one victims of execution.

It must be insisted, however, that though Morillo's policies represented a vast improvement over the war to the death proclaimed by Bolívar, they still reflected a certain intransigence on the part of the Spanish government. Without really compromising her moral position, Spain could have ruled out the concept "traitor" altogether, as England had done in 1776 and as the Union would do in 1861. Although Morillo's personal sentiments opposed this line, he nonetheless would have obeyed orders religiously.

Besides, his attempts to end the slaughter of the year 1814, Morillo also made every effort to maintain rigid discipline among his troops. The documentary evidence on this point is overwhelming. Morillo ordered on numerous occasions that civilians be well treated, that the troops leave women alone, and that legal procedures be followed when seeking supplies.[7] His principal disciplinary problems were with former guerrilla leaders such as Francisco Tomás Morales, Sebastián de la Calzada, and Pascual Real, and with the Venezuelan troops that he gradually recruited from among Boves's former solders. Enrile noted in a representation to the Spanish government that "continual punishment" of Venezuelan troops had been necessary in New Granada.[8]

In dealing with the former guerrilla commanders, Morillo attempted at first to use tact rather than severity in his efforts to curb their undisciplined and illegal conduct.[9] From a pragmatic point of view, Morales, Real, and Calzada were invaluable because of the great influence they had among the Venezuelan troops, which they largely recruited on their own. But in April 1817 Morillo found it necessary to arrest and indict both Morales and Real for their conduct since returning to Venezuela in 1816. By November, however, because of the outcry from extreme royalists, who virtually idolized Morales, Morillo released the Canarian from confinement and brought him to the general staff, though the indictment still stood and Morales was not given a new command.[10] Morillo released Real at the same time. In early March 1818, as a result of Bolívar's invasion and the desperate need for experienced commanders, Morillo restored both men to their former commands, though he refused to quash the indictments.[11] The Spanish officer Ramón Hernández de Armas, in attacking certain claims made by Calzada after the war, insisted that Salvador Moxó, Morales, Real, and Calzada had been responsible for whatever breaches of discipline had existed in the Expeditionary Army.[12] Though he had written to defend Miguel de la Torre, not Morillo, Hernández de Armas noted in passing that Morillo had been in no way responsible for any excesses committed by the army.

Morillo, therefore, was trapped between his recognition that campaign armies can easily commit depredations that alienate civilians and his realization that Morales and others had invaluable rapport with many of Boves's former soldiers, who, if not used in royalists armies, might be enlisted by the patriots. In February 1819, when asking for more troops, he insisted that they be "good," since some of the leaders who had been in command earlier in the revolution "caused by their horrible conduct transcendent evils that still weigh upon us." He also mentioned that some American companies as well as the regiment of Granada had deserted to the enemy. "With these kinds of pacifiers," he continued, "Your Excellency must know that the rebellious provinces of America will never be reduced to their duties."[13]

Indeed, everything seemed to undermine the royalist forces. The regiment of Granada was from Spain and had been dissolved after many of its soldiers had deserted. As mentioned earlier, discontent was present among many of the peninsulars at the time of their departure, and vigilance was necessary to avoid their fleeing. It appears too that Ferdinand had deliberately sent known liberals, especially among the officers, to America, and many of these men were unwilling to fight for the preservation of the empire. Morillo's lot was unenviable from whatever viewpoint, and it is easy enough to understand his desire to be relieved of his command. It should be observed, however, that for the most part his soldiers adored him, not only for his leadership but also for the humility with which he shared their suffering. He had himself been a common soldier accustomed to physical deprivation and personal exposure during battle. He never balked at eating unsalted meat, conceding his horse to the wounded while he went on foot, or risking his life on the field.

It should not be thought, on the other hand, that the patriots had people flocking to their banners. As in most wars, the masses would have preferred to be left in peace, but found themselves dragooned into fighting for causes they scarcely understood. In preparing for the campaign of 1818, for instance, Bolívar issued a decree of martial law in republican territory. It ordered that every male between the ages of fourteen and sixty report for military duty within eight days. Those who did not would be reputed "traitors" and executed "irremissibly." Any individual who aided, protected, or concealed those included in the decree would be shot. Any officer who for "whatever reason or pretext" left a single man "without being enlisted" would be shot.[14] Royalist efforts to raise troops could not have been more drastic.

The War: 1815–1817

The arrival of the Expeditionary Army and the surrender of Margarita left Bolívar in a pessimistic mood. Although he believed that Morillo was bringing only 4,000 or 5,000 troops, he was convinced that American opinion was still favorable to the royalists. Bolívar predicted that the Spanish army would increase rather than diminish, "because the people, being accustomed to the old dominion, obey these inhuman tyrants without repugnance." Public opinion, in Bolívar's view, was still not "decided," and although "the men who think are all, all advocates of independence, the majority are still ignorant of their rights and do not know their own interests."[15]

Morillo was not so sure. His decision to create a dictatorship was inspired partially by the rebelliousness of the pardos, although he appears to have believed that the forces he left behind would be adequate to deal with the situation if wisely used. It appears too that he foresaw no great difficulty in reconquering New Granada, for he sent 1,600 men to Peru and 600 to Puerto Rico while he engaged in the siege of Cartagena.[16] In this he was correct. Within six months after the fall of the fortified city, his Spanish-Venezuelan army had reoccupied a kingdom more than twice the size of France. The desertion of the llaneros, on the other hand, and the appearance of José Antonio Páez to lead them so altered the military situation in Venezuela that by September 1815 Bolívar was gloating over the reversal of republican fortunes.[17] In November, Margarita rose again under Arismendi.

Morillo lost what optimism he may have had on hearing of the latter event, for the strategic situation of the island, to be discussed later, was of such a nature that its loss seriously compromised Spanish arms. Besides, Morillo had come to believe that public opinion in both New Granada and Venezuela was decidedly in favor of independence. Although unable to tell Spain frankly that he had no stomach for fighting a repressive war, he intimated as much. On 18 February 1816, before the campaign in the viceroyalty had terminated, he asked that Moxó replace him as captain general of Venezuela and that he be relieved of his command.[18] Spain refused the latter request and the other ten that followed it.

Morillo explained his analysis of the military situation in March 1816. He noted, essentially, that as the royalist army reoccupied rebel territory, it became weaker through "dissemination," aggravated by sicknesses and losses of every kind. In view of the territory the army had to cover and the enemy it had to face in Venezuela, it was really little more than a "skeleton." The patriots had waited for the royalist forces to spread themselves thin before taking the offensive again by revolutionizing Margarita, Cumaná, and Guayana. Morillo explained that "His Majesty will understand that if the rebels lose territory, they reconcentrate and are stronger at the point they attack, while we are really weaker."[19]

On the matter of public opinion, Morillo informed Madrid that only Cartagena in all New Granada could be considered faithful. The remainder were only awaiting an opportunity to rebel again, "especially the priests, of whom not a one is good." He could not take the Venezuelan soldiers back to their country lest they desert to the patriot side. Under the circumstances he was forced to leave them as garrison troops in New Granada, together with a few Europeans stationed in Cartagena. It was natural, then, that he should ask Madrid to shift the Venezuelans to Peru, where they would pose no threat. Morillo continued to explain that although in Spain it was widely believed that "only four leaders" had caused the rebellion, such was not the case in Venezuela, where, "the clergy and all classes" were partisans of independence. Morillo ventured to say that if a leader were to appear who could unite the numerous patriot factions in Venezuela, "I see nothing flattering for the King's arms." On 21 May, 31 August, and 9 November 1816, Morillo repeated his request to be relieved.

The geography of Venezuela and its relationship to New Granada must be understood in order to comprehend the nature of the strategic problem. The land is relatively flat along the extensive coast but almost immediately gives way to a stretch of mountains and highlands to the south. In these regions lie most of the principal population centers. Along the coast, from west to east, are, respectively, the cities of Maracaibo, Coro, Puerto Cabello, La Guaira, Barcelona, and Cumaná. Valencia lies just south of Puerto Cabello, the major fortified city, and Caracas lies south of La Guaira. The island of Margarita is located near the eastern end of the coast to the north of Cumaná. At the extreme eastern end of the country is the mouth of the Orinoco river and the island of Trinidad, Spanish until 1797 and English thereafter. The river system itself has its origins in New Granada. One of its most important tributaries, the Meta, rises near Bogotá. It flows from the west to the east, traversing the vast llanos of Venezuela which lie to the south of the mountainous region mentioned above. The river formed the southern boundary of the old provinces of Barinas, Caracas, and Cumaná, from west to east respectively, and the northern boundary of Guayana. The towns of Barinas, San Fernando de Apure, and Calabozo lie in the llanos near the river, and the capital of Guayana is situated at the delta.

Rebel bands were still at large in the plains when Morillo arrived and when he departed. The loss of Margarita gave the patriots an excellent base near the mainland and not far from the mouth of the Orinoco. As they progressively built up their naval power with the aid of the Dutch admiral from Curaçao, Luis Brión, and as Spanish naval power declined for lack of financing, it was necessary for the patriots only to capture the city of Guayana and several important towns upriver to be able to dominate both the llanos and the entire course of the Orinoco. Control over the plains would give them access to the vast numbers of horses and cattle in the region, which could be used for trading purposes, and, above all, a direct approach to Bogotá should they decide to use it. This was Morillo's greatest fear. The 4,000 Venezuelan troops left in the viceroyalty could be expected to be easily won over by an army of their compatriots coming up the Orinoco toward the capital. The only European troops in New Granada were in Cartagena, too few in numbers and too distant to be of value.[20] Morillo repeatedly asked, from early 1816 on, that an expedition of 4,000 peninsulars replace the Venezuelans, who should then be sent to Peru. Spain never acted on this proposal, and in 1819 the patriots succeeded in doing precisely what Morillo had so clearly foreseen in 1816.

Morillo's other fear, that a leader would appear to unite the rebel bands, was verified more quickly. By February 1816 Bolívar was in Haiti acquiring aid from Alexandre Pétion for an expedition to Venezuela. In early May he landed in Margarita and proceeded thence to the mainland. Moxó's apparently inept military dispositions gave the patriots considerable advantages, and throughout 1816 they made steady progress in Barinas, the llanos of Caracas and Cumaná, and Guayana. Bolívar, however, was unable during that year to establish himself as commander over the other chieftains. This was partially because they were operating in scattered and distant locales with little direct communication, and partially because Bolívar had not demonstrated maturity as a field commander. In one of the first major engagements he personally directed, near Ocumare, his forces were badly beaten by Francisco Tomás Morales. That redoubtable veteran of the war to the death, about whom many a royalist legend grew, had been sent back to Venezuela by Morillo to raise an army of pardos. Gathering some of his men from the jails, he routed Bolívar with a force half the size of his opponent's.[21]

Nonetheless, the royalist position was not reassuring when Morillo reentered the country in December 1816. Urdaneta and Zaraza had joined forces in the llanos of Caracas. Páez was operating along the Apure river, Monagas was attacking Barcelona, Mariño was besieging Cumaná, and Piar was moving against Guayana. Bolívar himself was managing to enforce his will over the others. To make matters worse, confusion in intelligence led Morillo to make a poor decision. Moxó had earlier given him deceptive reports of enemy progress. Then, claiming that enemy forces were too strong, Moxó changed his mind and opposed the campaign that Morillo devised on the basis of the earlier reports. Morillo chose to stick to his original plan.

Essentially, the royalists had to reconquer Margarita but also secure the province of Guayana in order to block the mouth of the Orinoco to patriot forces operating in the llanos. Morillo decided to initiate operations against Margarita first and leave smaller forces on the mainland to hold the line there for the time being. He himself planned to move along the coast, lifting the sieges of Barcelona and Cumaná as he advanced, and to assault Margarita. At the same time Miguel de la Torre was to enter Guayana to relieve the province of pressure from Manuel Piar. This plan would have been adequate had Morillo not underestimated the strength of enemy forces on the mainland. As it was, he would not now listen to Moxó, and seemed obsessed by the desire to punish Margarita for what he saw as her treachery.

By late June 1817, after numerous bouts with Cambreleng for supplies and with a newly arrived expedition from Spain of 2,700 men under José Canterac, Morillo was ready to sail to Margarita. The fighting on the island was bitter, but by the middle of August only Asunción and the *fortaleza del norte* remained in patriot hands. At this point news arrived that Guayana had been attacked by numerically superior patriot forces. On 18 July Piar had captured the city of Guayana and on 3 August had occupied Baja Guayana. La Torre's army was nearly decimated, and Captain General Pardo notified Morillo that Caracas itself was in danger. Morillo decided to abandon Margarita without completing the reconquest in order to salvage the situation on the mainland.[22]

Whatever the reasons for Morillo's serious misjudgment in undertaking the campaign of 1817, it is certain that the results were as Moxó had predicted. José Antonio Páez also believed that Morillo should have concentrated first on Guayana, then attacked Margarita.[23] Some argued that Pardo's exaggeration of the dangers on the mainland was the reason for the failure. Had Morillo remained on the island a few more weeks, he could have completed its subjugation, then moved against Guayana.[24] As it was, the royalist position was worse at the close of the campaign than at the outset. Both Guayana and Margarita were lost, Morillo's forces diminished, and the economic situation had worsened.

Simón Bolívar, meanwhile, was finally getting his authority recognized. Perhaps the most serious threat he faced was a suspected pardo conspiracy to destroy the creole officer corps and convert the independence movement into a nonwhite affair. The supposed leader was Manuel Piar, the excellent mulatto general who had routed La Torre and conquered Guayana. Since Piar refused to recognize Bolívar as supreme commander of the patriot forces, he was tricked by the Liberator into entering his camp alone. Bolívar then had him arrested, tried by a consejo de guerra for "insubordination," and shot on 16 October 1817.[25] Morillo's intelligence had intercepted several letters from Alexandre Pétion, dictator of Haiti, to Piar that seem to bear out the theory of a black conspiracy to destroy the white ruling class throughout the Caribbean and create a series of Negro republics.[26] If this was so, it is a historical point that merits investigation.

By all odds, the racial problem had not been laid to rest. Morillo expressed constant fear because of the diminution of the white class and the growing preponderance of the peoples of color. In the interior of Venezuela, he noted, one scarcely saw a white face by 1817. In November he discovered in his own army a minor conspiracy led by a pardo captain named Alejo Mirabal. Sending Mirabal to the peninsula, Morillo asked Madrid to reward him for his services but under no circumstances to return him to Venezuela.[27]

These pardo plots were perhaps enough to keep the whites unnerved, but they seem not to have presented a serious threat to the now reentrenched white class. In preparation for the campaign of 1818, Morillo began drafting those veterans of Boves still available for service, for his forces had gone on dwindling. He gathered them, as he said, "insensibly," so that the old troubles would not arise.[28] He even proposed to the real acuerdo to create a battalion of slaves recompensing them with their freedom. He noted to the Audiencia that this measure was necessary to forestall the patriots, who were recruiting largely from among the slaves. Moreover, the blacks were subject to discipline, made excellent soldiers, and fought well in the climate. Some two thousand were already serving in the royalist army. Lastly, Morillo was interested in gaining their loyalty to the whites in case of trouble from the more intractable pardos. The Audiencia rejected Morillo's proposal on the grounds that to arm the slaves might be dangerous.[29]

The Campaign of 1818

The fighting in 1817 had resulted in the capture of Guayana by the patriots and their retention of control over Margarita. They now dominated most, but not all, of the Orinoco valley with attendant access to the sea and foreign aid. Bolívar had succeeded in establishing himself as commander in chief of the patriot forces and had, for whatever reasons, rid himself of Piar. Morillo, however, appears to have been unimpressed with Bolívar's ability, for he never once singled him out as being a good leader. The only patriot chieftain for whom he expressed great respect, and this on several occasions, was José Antonio Páez. He called Páez the most "dangerous" of his adversaries and noted that the llanero leader was "not lacking in intelligence and bravery."[30]

The setting for the campaign of 1818 was essentially as follows. The patriots controlled all but the western end of the Orinoco valley and the llanos. This meant two things to the royalists. First, if the enemy conquered San Fernando de Apure and a few other towns, they would be able to dominate the entire valley and have direct access to the heart of New Granada, whose Venezuelan garrisons might easily be won over. Second, their supremacy in the llanos gave them control of most of the country's cattle and horses, vital to the royalists for food and for cavalry. In general terms, the patriots were strong in cavalry and weak in infantry, which made them invincible on the plains. The royalists had splendid infantry but insufficient cavalry, rendering them virtually unbeatable in the hill country between the llanos and the coast, where most of the population lived.

Morillo, lacking a fleet and much else, could not now renew his attack on Margarita. Rather he was concerned with securing the western end of the Orinoco in order to seal New Granada off from the enemy. In early February 1818 he was in Calabozo in the heart of the llanos with 1,800 men. His intelligence was faulty, and on 12 February a patriot army of some three thousand cavalry and two thousand infantry under Bolívar and Páez succeeded in surrounding him. Some small royalist detachments caught outside the town were trapped and annihilated.[31] The situation could not have been more desperate. Morillo was greatly outnumbered, overwhelmed in cavalry, and more than twenty leagues from the mountains and safety. Furthermore, the population of Calabozo, some seven thousand to eight thousand, was strongly royalist and anxious to leave with him.[32] It was this predicament that produced consternation in Caracas, and had Páez rather than Bolívar been in command of the patriots, it is likely that the royalist cause would have been damaged beyond repair.

But the Liberator violated nearly every elementary rule of warfare. With Morillo in the palm of his hands, he decided, against the advice of Páez, to move the bulk of his troops to the town of Rastro, some three leagues away on a river. He left only a small guard to observe the royalists. The rotation of the surveillance troops was so regular that Morillo was able to predict their movements almost to the minute. This gave him his opportunity. At 11:00 P.M. on 13 February the entire civilian population of Calabozo, surrounded by the troops, slipped out of the town in silence. Morillo and his officers, conceding their horses to the sick and wounded, led the way on foot. By dawn, when the patriots discovered they were guarding a ghost town, the royalists had long since disappeared over the horizon. By noon of the next day they had covered fifteen kilometers.

The situation was still not beyond redemption for the patriots, for Morillo was necessarily moving slowly because of the several thousand civilians. It was necessary only to catch him in the llanos before he reached the mountains. Páez observed that the royalists were obviously making straight for the town of Sombrero in the foothills, and suggested that the patriots strike out in that direction. But Bolívar, contending that one must always pursue an army by following its tracks, insisted on marching the troops to Calabozo first, a distance of three leagues.[33]

Bolívar's principal defender, Vicente Lecuna, insists that the patriot general wanted to march north but deferred to the wishes of his subordinates.[34] This defense is as incriminating as what was probably the truth, for a good officer acts decisively when he knows he is right. If indeed Bolívar did act so indecisively, it would seem to indicate that he was as inexperienced and confused as the rest of his officer corps. Lecuna also claims that Morillo made so much commotion leaving that his movements were not unknown to the patriots. Again, if this is true, Bolívar's decisions become even more incomprehensible. It would have been unforgivable to permit the royalists to march all night without having initiated pursuit.

In any case, Bolívar's dalliance permitted Morillo to proceed unmolested until 4:00 P.M. on 14 February, when advance units of the patriot cavalry caught up with him. The Spanish infantry kept the enemy at a distance with a killing fire, and, having rested only two hours during the night, the royalists reached the mountains by daybreak of 15 February. The two hundred men lost by Morillo because they could not keep up the pace were butchered by the llaneros when captured. Vergara has calculated that it took Bolívar's army, mostly cavalry, longer to cover the twenty leagues between Calabozo and Sombrero than it had taken Morillo to do so with thousands of civilians, including women and children, mostly on foot. By not alternating his troops for marching and resting, Bolívar arrived at Sombrero with his whole force exhausted and thirsty. The royalist infantry, now strongly fortified in the highlands, decimated the patriots as they attempted to approach a nearby river for water. Morillo continued his orderly retreat northward. By 18 February he had entered Comatagua, to be joined by five hundred fresh troops, and on 23 February was in Villa de Cura, where more reinforcements arrived. There he remained for the rest of the month.

Following the disaster at Sombrero, Bolívar withdrew to Calabozo. The morale of his men plummeted to such depths that desertions became widespread. The Liberator wrote Páez that the army was "nearly dissolved," and he feared sending his remaining troops in search of the deserters lest they also abandon the cause.[35] Páez, who after Sombrero had left to lay siege to San Fernando de Apure, returned with his men to Calabozo, but he and Bolívar quickly had another falling out. Páez observed that in the mountains the Spanish infantry was redoubtable against the patriot cavalry, which made up the bulk of the army. He advised that the republicans first capture San Fernando. In this way they could secure the llanos and the Orinoco valley up to the borders of New Granada and deprive the royalists of what few cattle and horses remained at their disposal. But Bolívar was mesmerized by the idea of conquering Caracas. Páez stated in his memoirs that this enchantment with the capital city was what had led Bolívar to withdraw from Calabozo initially, for he was considering leaving Morillo to march north, a plan revealing an abysmal ignorance of strategy. In this latest dispute between the two men, Bolívar finally permitted Páez to take some troops to besiege San Fernando, but he insisted on moving the bulk of the army northward toward Caracas.[36]

Morillo deployed his forces in early March in preparation for Bolívar's invasion.[37] He had some four thousand infantry and one thousand cavalry, in comparison to an unknown number of patriot troops, which cannot have been too inferior to Morillo's forces. Some of Bolívar's defenders, in attempting to explain away his ultimate defeat, claim he had only 2,200 soldiers. This seems highly unlikely, for no responsible commander would have taken the offensive against Morillo outnumbered more than two to one. Bolívar began his advance on 6 March, and Morillo withdrew up the Aragua valley, permitting the patriots to occupy Villa de Cura, Victoria, and Maracay. By 12 March, the main rebel force was near El Consejo.

The Spanish commander had withdrawn with his main army to Valencia, a short distance to the west of El Consejo. He left only 900 men under Miguel de la Torre to guard the approaches to Caracas, which lay to the east of the patriot army. This was the logical deployment to make, for in Valencia, Morillo had Puerto Cabello, the principal fortification, to his back, while Caracas was militarily indefensible. To explain Bolívar's position another way, he was between two royalist forces only twenty leagues apart, the stronger, under Morillo, to the west, and the weaker, under La Torre, to the east.

Having placed himself in such a dangerous position, Bolívar ought to have done two things. First, he should have acted quickly to destroy either one or the other of the Spanish forces. Instead, he tarried for three days creating a "government," naming civil officials for the newly "conquered" region, recruiting soldiers for whom he had no weapons, and riding around exploring the area. Second, he should have selected Morillo's force as the one to be attacked. Morillo was on relatively flat land near Valencia where the Liberator could have put his cavalry to good use. And the prime rule of warfare in a situation such as this one is to destroy the enemy's main force first. The rest will come in the order of things. But having dallied, Bolívar decided to attack La Torre and his 900. Again the fascination with Caracas prevailed over hardheaded strategic thinking. Even if he took the capital, he could not hold it; and the main Spanish army would remain intact. To make the decision even more foolish, the approach to Caracas was rough terrain where La Torre's infantry could obstruct his cavalry for days while Morillo moved in to close the trap.

Morillo had analyzed the situation properly. On 5 March he wrote La Torre stating that he did not believe that Bolívar would advance farther north but to be on guard nonetheless. He added that if Bolívar attacked, the obvious place would be in Valencia, where the terrain was good for cavalry.[38] On 8 March he wrote La Torre again that he was convinced that, if Bolívar advanced, he would not move toward Caracas because of an insufficiency of infantry and because of the extreme unsuitability of the area for cavalry operations.[39]

A fortuitous circumstance stayed Bolívar's plan of attack. On 14 March his reconnaissance intercepted a dispatch from Morillo to La Torre ordering the latter to attack the patriots at El Consejo. Morillo, hoping to catch Bolívar in a pincers and cut off his retreat to the llanos, had already begun advancing eastward, rolling back Monagas as he went. Since Morillo was only one day's distance by then, the Liberator made the decision to withdraw toward the south. By 15 March, he, Zaraza, and Monagas had regrouped in Villa de Cura.

After wasting the better part of the day in discussion, they determined to continue their southward retreat, for Morillo's advance guard of 1,500 men under Francisco Tomás Morales was fast approaching. By 16 March the patriots had reached the "gorge of Semen" (*quebrada de Semen*) near La Puerta, where Boves had defeated both Campo Elías and Bolívar in 1814. But the Liberator and his general staff nevertheless resolved to give battle there. This was but the last of numerous errors. As Vergara noted, "to accept combat on broken ground against an infantry as disciplined and maneuverable as that of Morillo is a sin which has no absolution before history."[40]

When the battle commenced at 6:00 A.M. on 16 March, the royalist forces had not yet all arrived. Morales and the vanguard, 1,000 infantry and 500 cavalry, initiated the attack. The main army under Morillo was still at two leagues distance, and La Torre's 900, bringing up the rear, were too far away to be a factor. Morales, though greatly outnumbered, sustained the attack bitterly for three hours. The impetuosity of his assault was such that Rafael Urdaneta, one of the patriot officers, insisted even when writing his memoirs that the insurgents were facing Morillo's main army. He affirmed that the Spanish general was personally directing one of the columns, and that the reinforcements that arrived at 9:00 A.M. were those of La Torre.[41] By the latter hour, Morales's line had broken and his men were retreating in disorder, while the patriots, having lost most of their officers, were advancing largely without direction.

Morillo rode up considerably in advance of his troops at the moment of the royalist retreat, and quickly succeeded in restoring order to the dispersing vanguard. By ordering the advance units of the army to throw away their knapsacks and run to the battlefield, he brought about 1,500 fresh troops into play. Hastily assuming battle formation, the royalist infantry unleashed a withering fire that drew the advancing patriots up short. Morillo turned their momentary hesitation to good advantage. With drawn sword, he led the squadron of flying artillery in a frontal assault on republican ranks. The lines joined momentarily, then the patriots broke.

Bolívar, wrote Bartolomé Mitre, "lost even his papers in this battle, and it appears he had lost his head too. Furious and desperate, he squandered his person in the bitterest part of the combat, as if he were seeking death. . . ." The Argentine reasoned that the Liberator understood "the enormous responsibility that weighed upon him for the immense errors committed in pursuing a foolish course of action, without taking any measure to avoid a catastrophe."[42] Bolívar abandoned the field near noon, and by dawn of the following day was seventeen leagues away in Hato del Caimán.

The third battle of La Puerta was, like the first two, a disaster for the republicans. Over half of Bolívar's infantry was lost, and only 400 later rejoined him in the llanos. Morillo lost 300 killed and 300 wounded, but he himself suffered a near mortal lance wound as he led his troops against enemy lines. Although the weapon passed through his body and later had to be pushed out from behind, he had managed to remain in the saddle several minutes, seize a patriot banner, and tear it to shreds as an inspiration to his troops. Morillo received a second title on this occasion: he had already been named conde de Cartagena, and he now became marqués de la Puerta.

Besides the disaster at La Puerta, the patriots lost a number of other engagements during 1818 at Ortiz, San Carlos, Cojedes, and Rincón de los Toros.[43] But these royalist victories must be put in perspective. They were mostly defensive actions that gained Morillo nothing beyond a momentary respite while Bolívar recruited a new army. The Venezuelan debt reached staggering proportions, supplies and provisions were in shorter supply, and José Antonio Páez had managed to do what Bolívar should have done initially—capture San Fernando de Apure and secure the llanos for the patriots. Morillo was under no illusions as to his position. Without cavalry he could never reconquer the plains from Páez, "the rebel chief of most knowledge and fortune," as Morillo put it.[44] Using the excuse of his wound, which was serious enough and troubled him for the rest of his life, he sought to be relieved for the seventh and eighth times on 18 March and 20 September. Spain again turned a deaf ear to this request.

In the patriot camp Bolívar's mismanagement of the campaign of 1818, combined with the fact that his army was still murdering captured soldiers indiscriminately, produced a serious crisis between the Liberator and a number of recently arrived British volunteers. Gustavus Hippisley, John Brown, George L. Chesterton, James Hackett, and Henry Wilson were the principal officers who became disgusted with the quality of the patriot leadership and with the nature of the fighting. Even some English officers who stayed on and fought for the republicans, such as J. H. Robinson and Francis Burdett O'Connor, expressed dismay at the murder of prisoners or at the undisciplined and haughty comportment of the creole officers, who resisted taking any advice whatever.[45]

Alfred Hasbrouck claims that the Englishmen who left or were forced by Bolívar to leave all had personal reasons for turning against the Liberator and writing "libels" about him,[46] but there is no reason to doubt the sincerity of their disgust with the conduct of the war. Hackett stated that he felt he could not honorably fight for the patriots when they cold-bloodedly put all prisoners to death and even scoured the battlefields in search of wounded to finish off.[47] Hippisley described in his memoirs the merciless massacre of unarmed prisoners, sanctioned by Bolívar, and was further disenchanted because of the Liberator's lack of military abilities.[48] "Tactics, movements, and manoeuvre," wrote Hippisley, "are as unknown to him as to the lowest of his troops. All idea of regularity, system, or the common routine of an army, or even a regiment, he is totally unacquainted with."[49] Another English officer had told Hippisley after the battle of Ortiz that an inferior number of Spaniards had defeated Bolívar because of their superior discipline and generalship. The Liberator "had so puzzled matters, and so confounded the line, that the infantry were beaten, and nearly destroyed before Bolívar could collect himself, which extorted some sharp rebukes from Páez to the chief in person."[50]

Hippisley's discontent with the conduct of the campaign of 1818 caused him and Colonel Henry Wilson to lead a movement to try to install Páez as head of the patriot movement. The Liberator got wind of the conspiracy and had both men expelled. Hasbrouck accepts, on the basis of two patriot sources and an English newspaper report, that Wilson was a spy sent by the Spanish minister in London to stir up trouble against Bolívar.[51] There is no reason to accept such a far-fetched explanation. Páez definitely showed himself to have a better grasp of strategy and tactics than Bolívar, and the British officers no doubt noticed this. In trying to make Páez head of the movement, they were probably hoping to strengthen the patriots militarily. A British officer who continued fighting for the patriots reported that when Bolívar left for Angostura in mid-1818, he gave foreigners the choice of accompanying him or remaining with Páez. Virtually all of the Englishmen chose to remain behind with the llanero leader and, in Bolívar's absence, contrived to procure for Páez the title captain general, a title already held by Bolívar, Santiago Mariño, and Gregor MacGregor.[52] Bolívar quashed the movement and exiled Wilson, the commander of the British contingent.

The Liberator thus retained control of the patriot army and by early 1819 was getting foreign aid, in both men and matériel, in increasing quantities. In February, Morillo described the overwhelming evidence of foreign influence. The patriot forces were decked out in British uniforms, and even the llaneros had English saddles and helmets. More soldiers of fortune had arrived to form the British Legion, which was to be of considerable importance to Bolívar in the campaign of 1819. Foreign merchants, anxious to crack the Spanish trade monopoly, were supplying the republicans with what they needed.[53] When Morillo sought naval forces, an investigation in Madrid revealed that only one corvette, and that one in need of repairs, was available.[54] By that time there remained but 3,000 Europeans in the now 13,000-man fighting force. Warfare, disease, and desertion had annihilated the Expeditionary Army.

When Morillo learned in July 1819 that Bolívar, advised by British officers, was moving up the Orinoco toward Bogotá, his pessimism was complete. He dispatched La Torre to attempt to reach New Granada before the Liberator and take command of the troops there. His principal concern, as he put it, was "the little confidence I have in the loyalty of the Venezuelan troops, who are the best in the viceroyalty; not being sustained by Europeans, they can be readily seduced with any reverse they might suffer." In all of New Granada the only peninsulars were stationed in Cartagena.[55]

Morillo's every prediction since 1816 had come to pass. On 7 August two Venezuelan armies clashed in Boyacá to decide the fate of the viceroyalty. One was led by Bolívar, the other by Lieutenant Colonel José Barreiro, an inexperienced commander who through confusion in New Granada found himself directing the royalist army. La Torre had failed to arrive in time. Twelve provinces of the viceroyalty fell to the republicans in a single battle, "because," as Morillo afterward noted, "of the disposition, sentiments, and general opinion of the inhabitants."[56]

Although Cartagena and the coast remained in Spanish hands, Morillo predicted that 8,000 men could not reconquer what was lost. And if Cartagena fell too, 30,000 troops would not suffice.[57] It was the old story of attempting to keep a disaffected population under control by force. It is doubtful that the 20,000-man army that Ferdinand was then assembling in Cádiz could have done more than prolong the struggle a few more years. But it never sailed. On 1 January 1820 Rafael Riego began the revolt that brought the constitutionalists back to power in Spain. A new and no less futile approach was in the offing.

The Revolution of 1820: Political Aspects

Whatever Morillo's view of the change of government in Spain, he greeted the application of the new system to Venezuela with misgivings, for he still believed that the war could only be waged with some success under a form of martial law. With the reextension of the Constitution of 1812 to America, Morillo's *mando absoluto* ceased. Since the military and political commands were separated, civil officials were enabled to obstruct seriously the operations of the army. Also, some confusion arose in the transition from one constitutional set-up to another, especially as it bore upon officeholding. And the lifting of press and other forms of censorship bared personal and ideological squabbles among loyalists and gave to patriot sympathizers the freedom to propagate their views with relative impunity. A related problem was that Madrid ordered the negotiation of a truce under the supposition that the rebels were "liberals" fighting against an absolutist Spain. The problem of the cease-fire, however, will best be discussed in a different context.

The most immediate difficulty Morillo faced was to assure a smooth transition to the new system without a major alteration in personnel. Since Madrid had ordered the constitution to be effected without designating which officials were to assume which positions under the new system, there was room for disagreement in some important cases, and Morillo was determined to prevent certain individuals like Andrés Level de Goda from increasing their influence. Before proceeding to discuss the activities of the fiscal, however, it is first necessary to understand the legal points involved.

In simple terms the restored Constitution of 1812 provided, on the one hand, that executive, legislative, and judicial powers be separated, and, on the other, that the civil and military spheres be divorced. A jefe político appointed by Madrid was to exercise the executive power and a captain general the military. The Cortes, in which the Indies were to be represented, were to legislate for the entire realm, and the audiencias were to restrict themselves to purely judicial functions. Or to put it another way, the tribunals could no longer function as the real acuerdo. Two other points were also important. The constitution provided that in the absence of the jefe político the intendant was to act as his substitute. And if a field army were operating within a province, its commander might assume the captaincy general. Under the old system of course, Morillo was acting both as governor and captain general, although he had delegated these offices to Ramón Correa while he directed the army.

Morillo and the Audiencia, on 7 June, became involved in a dispute over how the jefatura política was to be filled in the absence of a royal appointment. The tribunal, still dominated by Level, proposed that the electors who were to name representatives to the Cortes also select a jefe político. Morillo, anxious to avoid a major change, proposed that since the constitution provided for appointment, not election, of the jefe político, the man then exercising the governorship with royal approval should automatically assume the office. In other words, Morillo wanted Correa to remain in political command, and he, as commander of the army, would assume the captaincy general.[58]

Under prodding from Level, the Audiencia asked for time to study Morillo's suggestion. The fiscal, seeing that the cabildo and the archbishop agreed with Morillo's interpretation, then persuaded the tribunal to swear the new constitution immediately. By this legal artifice the Audiencia ceased to act as the real acuerdo, leaving Morillo in the position of having to make his decision without advice and forcing him to take the oath without delay.[59] On the same day, 7 June, Correa became jefe político and Morillo captain general. Shortly thereafter Morillo delegated his position to Francisco del Pino in order to be with the army in the field.

In this way, no major change in personnel occurred, although the faculties of the new officials were different from what they had been under the old system. But the possibilities for legal dispute had not yet been exhausted. The commandant of La Guaira, José Caturla, complained that Morillo's dispositions were illegal. According to his interpretation, the governorship under the old regime went united to the captaincy general, not the other way around, and the offices were inseparable. If Morillo reassumed the captaincy general, he had also reassumed the governorship, leaving Correa with no political character. Caturla reasoned further that the jefatura politica should then be filled by the substitute designated by the new constitution, i.e., the intendant. He consequently informed Madrid that by right Francisco Javier de Arambarri should have become jefe político.[60] Madrid, deciding that under the old regime the military and civil powers were separable and that the former went united to the latter, approved Morillo's dispositions and authorized him further, if he thought it necessary, to assume the jefatura política as well.[61]

The plottings of Level de Goda are not altogether clear, for the documents do not reveal the politicking within the Audiencia. One must consult the fiscal's memoirs and those of the creole royalist José Domingo Díaz to get an inkling of what was occurring. Díaz, who remained a staunch defender of Morillo and seems to have shared his confidences, claimed that Level hoped to have himself elected jefe político. He noted that whereas previously Level had scarcely deigned to permit the highest dignitary to enter his office, he suddenly became, with the publication of the new constitution, "the least of citizens, always surrounded by zambos and Negroes."[62] Díaz, in rehashing Level's unsavory past, supplied details that Arambarri had not. Supposedly Level was barred from the Colegio de Abogados for stealing 600 pesos from its funds and for his "scandalous and criminal conduct" in Trinidad, where he had once accepted fees from both parties to a dispute by defending one and advising the other.[63]

Level is a complex person to analyze. Politically liberal and humanitarian in some measure, he also seems to have been opportunistic, contentious, and power-hungry. He did not mention in his memoirs, which is to be expected, that he himself aspired to the jefatura política. Rather, he accused Morillo of having cheated his father-in-law José Duarte out of the position. In other words, he adopted Caturla's thesis but would have had the interim superintendent occupy the post. Curiously, Level accused Morillo of the very game of which he himself had been accused by Díaz, i.e., hoping to ride to power with the support of the peoples of color. In one writing he stated that he would disregard "the very valid rumor that Morillo . . . attempted to become lord of the territory of Venezuela." In another he frankly claimed that Morillo hoped to make himself dictator of the country with the support of the pardos.[64]

The basis for these allegations was a decree issued by Morillo in June granting rights of citizenship to those blacks who would serve in the army. Level claimed that the measure was illegal, since the constitution set limits on such rights for Americans of African origin.[65] The opposition of the Audiencia, dominated by Level, forced Morillo to withdraw the decree. It is unthinkable to conclude, knowing Morillo's character, that he even considered the possibility of becoming head of an independent Venezuela. He obviously issued the decree to forestall the loss of the blacks to the patriot side. The truce, the ease of moving from one zone to another, and press freedom made it inevitable that the republicans would capitalize on their more liberal program regarding Afro-Americans. Peninsular liberals, anxious to maintain Spanish ascendance within the Cortes, had deliberately restricted citizenship rights in the more populous Indies. Hoping to nullify the effects of this shortsighted disposition, Morillo, while he technically retained the mando absoluto, had issued the above-mentioned decree but had backed down under pressure from the letrados.

Level seems also to have been involved in some way in a dispute between Duarte and Alustiza over control of the superintendency. Alustiza claimed that since the new constitution had made the asesoría of the superintendency an honorary position, Duarte could no longer act as a substitute for Arambarri, the proprietor. In this eventuality Alustiza himself, as senior auditor of the Tribunal of Accounts, should succeed to the post. Morillo, no letrado himself, at first agreed to recognize Alustiza until there should be a resolution of the dispute by Madrid. Alustiza, however, backed down to avoid a "scandal," and Spain later ruled that Duarte had been in the right.[66]

Level, without revealing his own role in the tiff, claimed that Morillo had given the superintendency to Alustiza, then agreed to return it to Duarte on the condition that the latter bind himself not to claim the jefatura política from Correa.[67] This version is difficult to square with the documents, including Duarte's letter of complaint and the dossier apparently sent by Alustiza. Moreover, the dispute occurred in early October, some four months after the new constitution had been put into effect. Possibly Level had prodded his father-in-law to claim the jefatura política, but there is no evidence that the latter did so. With the exception of the Audiencia, which Level dominated, no one else in Venezuela or in Spain seemed to doubt that Correa should assume the position. Since Level did not protest formally to Spain, but only made these accusations against Morillo in his memoirs, it must be concluded that his personal animosity toward the general was what prompted the venomous and frequently ludicrous charges he made.

In early October, at the time of the Alustiza-Duarte affair, the long-smoldering resentments between Level and Morillo erupted to such an extent that the fiscal sought and received a license to leave Venezuela. Morillo had already complained in August that certain ultraliberal elements, taking advantage of the unlimited freedom of the press, were fomenting discord by their incendiary writings and selecting him as their special target. Some military men in La Guaira had hoisted the green and yellow cockade of the patriots in place of the Spanish colors. When Morillo forbade it, some of the press criticized him as a "coward and traitor."[68] A few days after the Alustiza-Duarte affair, he complained of similar libelous statements appearing in the press. This time he mentioned Level by name. Morillo charged that Level was directing toward the pardos propaganda so inflammatory as to undermine discipline within the army. On this occasion, as in August, Morillo asked again to be relieved. He insisted that his continued presence under prevailing conditions was disruptive, and that his departure would "calm spirits."[69]

Level claimed that at this point Morillo, Correa, and del Pino conspired to assassinate him. Supposedly, Morillo's black aide-de-camp attacked Level one evening with a saber but failed even to wound him.[70] The truth of this allegation, as with so many of Level's charges, is difficult to come by. It must be surmised, on the basis of a general estimate of the characters of the individuals involved, that, though the aide-de-camp might have menaced or even attempted to kill Level, Morillo was not a party to it. Moreover, to include the jefe político and captain general of Venezuela in the plot seems even more fanciful. Possibly the aide had heard Morillo's private rantings against Level and took it upon himself to dispatch the fiscal. At any rate, Level asked Morillo for a passport, received it, and was in Cádiz by 8 November.

The change of government in Madrid, all things considered, did nothing to improve the royalist position in Venezuela. The personnel of the administration remained the same. The constitution did not better the juridical position of much of the population, since persons of African origin could only be recognized as citizens by special dispensation of the Cortes. Commercial policy relative to Venezuela remained as restrictive as ever. Home rule for the American provinces was not seriously considered. The provisions restricting voting rights in the Indies did not offer Americans any foreseeable possibility of improving their condition within the new constitutional framework, for peninsulars retained a voting majority in the Cortes. And many creole conservatives were now alienated from the mother country, which had become liberal and anticlerical. The Constitution of 1812, in short, had fewer adherents in America than the old regime had had. In the last analysis, the constitutionalists in Spain were as blind to the motive forces of the rebellion, or as intransigent toward the kind of changes demanded by the creoles, as they had been between 1810 and 1814. The reforms sought by Morillo in 1815 went unheeded by both factions in the peninsula, with predictable results.

The Revolution of 1820: Military Aspects

The restoration of the liberal constitution would have been disastrous for the royalist army even had Spain not simultaneously ordered the negotiation of a six months' truce. Morillo, who was shortly to affiliate himself with the moderate constitutionalists now in control of the government, called their policies "crazy," for they did not know "the country, nor the enemy, nor the events, nor the circumstances."[71] José Domingo Díaz noted that under the new charter "the most miserable constitutional alcalde" could obstruct the operations of the army by withholding supplies. Judicial power in financial matters passed from the intendants to elected provincial deputations.[72] The decentralization of power in many hands paralyzed the economy further and increased the privations of the army, while the patriots were functioning under dictatorial rule.[73]

Operating under the mistaken assumption that the constitution had removed the cause for the fighting in America, the government made no effort to arrange for economic aid for the army. Morillo attempted to explain that the insurgents were fighting because "they do not want to be Spanish," but his opinions went unheeded.[74] Spain ordered that a truce be negotiated with the patriots and that the war be "regularized," i.e., fought under the rules of international law. The last measure was certainly long overdue.

After June 1820, with the arrival of the constitution, Morillo's new instructions, and another general pardon, the royalist position deteriorated rapidly. Morillo released indicted or convicted rebels from prison.[75] On 6 May he unilaterally announced a forty-day armistice to which the patriots, seeing that it could only work to their advantage, agreed. The cease-fire was extended until late in the year, when a six months' truce on land and sea was arranged. Throughout the latter half of the year desertions from the royalist army mounted. Press freedom and the right to pass without hindrance from royalist to republican zones enabled the patriots to propagandize among their compatriots serving in the Spanish army, a task made easier by the deteriorating economic situation on the royalist side. Between June and the end of August some eight hundred Venezuelans deserted. These losses forced Morillo to shorten his lines and abandon territory and population to the patriots. He lamented that "there is not a single inhabitant who is thinking of following the government of the nation, some because they oppose it, and the majority out of expediency [*conveniencia*]."[76] War-weariness must be accounted an important factor. The Venezuelan troops, as Morillo observed, were not like the peninsulars, fighting for their preservation in a foreign land.[77] Many deserted not to join the other side but simply to go home. In September, Morillo reported an occurrence that was becoming more frequent. Captain Juan Manuel Silva stirred up a considerable area to revolt, went over to the patriots, and was rewarded with the rank of lieutenant colonel.[78] Morillo no doubt had been right in 1816 when he reported that Venezuelan sentiment favored independence. The dictatorship had suffocated much of the opposition, which was now becoming evident in the relaxed atmosphere of the constitution.

Morillo did not wish to undergo the "humiliation" of negotiating with the men against whom he had fought for so many years. On 4 July, 6 August, and 8 October, he asked to be relieved for the tenth, eleventh, and twelfth times since 1816. The picture he painted of the army was not encouraging. Less than one-third of the peninsulars who had come over in

1815 were still alive.[79] He insisted to Madrid that a man who had appeared with the "apparatus of war" could not play the role of conciliator, "because he is singled out by the ill will of passions, and because it is not possible to keep many friends after six years of command with arms in hands." He repeated that he had "little aptitude as a politician," and that the work of pacification could best be carried out by men "whose knowledge and understanding are rarely found on battlefields or amid the sound of arms."[80] The government agreed to transfer him, but ordered that he first negotiate with the patriots for the truce and for regularization of the war.

Venezuela's leading royalists were seized by near panic when it became known that Morillo had been conceded his transfer. Within a day of the arrival of the news, José de Alustiza convoked in his home a junta of the principal civil, ecclesiastical, and military authorities, including the deputies elected to the Cortes. They determined to beseech Morillo to suspend the use of his royal license and remain in the country until peace was restored. They informed him that they were "convinced of the almost inevitable consequences of the fulfillment of the royal resolution." His knowledge and leadership were desperately needed "at the head of an army which respects and adores him."[81]

Within a few days, other letters arrived pleading with Morillo to remain. The cabildos of Ocumare, San Francisco de Yare, San Antonio, Maiquetía, La Guaira, and numerous other cities and towns made known similar sentiments. The officers of the plazas of Caracas and La Guaira wrote in a similar vein on 6 November. The colegio de abogados noted that Morillo's departure would so damage morale that the economy itself would falter, and that "the majority of the merchants are thinking of leaving this place and are abandoning their establishments."[82] The Real Consulado wrote that it regarded "the loss of a considerable part of the monarchy" as the "inevitable result" of his departure.[83] The magistrates of the Royal Audiencia, without Level de Goda, were persuaded that "their security and public tranquility" were "inextricably" linked to his presence in the country.[84]

The entreaties of Venezuela's leading officials were to no avail. Morillo realized the near hopelessness of the royalist position under any circumstances, and the program of the constitutionalist government left no hope whatever. Nevertheless, he arranged for negotiations with the patriots as instructed.[85] On 22 November 1820 his emissaries met with those of Bolívar in the city of Trujillo, where the Liberator had proclaimed the war to the death seven years earlier. By 26 November the accords had been completed, one for a truce, the other for regularization of the war. Although disagreeing with a few provisions, Morillo ratified them on 26 November and 27 November and had an amicable personal interview with Bolívar.

The first of the documents, a *Tratado de Armisticio*, arranged for a truce of six months' duration. The lines were to be stabilized where they were, and hostilities at sea should terminate within thirty days in American waters and ninety days in European. Freedom of movement and communication between the two zones was guaranteed. Neither side was to resume warfare without a forty-day advance notice. The second accord, a *Tratado de Regularización de Guerra*, arranged for the regular exchange of captured soldiers, who would be considered prisoners of war. Spies and reconnoiterers, and this was the article Morillo opposed, were also to be treated as prisoners. The bodies of the dead were to be interred or cremated by the side that had won a battle.[86]

Morillo turned his command over to Miguel de la Torre on 3 December and left Venezuela within a few weeks. La Torre reported that the army consisted of 9,961 effectives, a striking contrast to the 18,000 under arms in 1818.[87] The cease-fire did not last long. Patriot corsairs continued attacking Spanish shipping by flying the flag of Buenos Aires rather than Colombia. On 11 December, Bolívar moved an extra battalion into Barinas because of "supply difficulties." He informed La Torre that this was an "insignificant" infringement of the armistice. Under protest from the new Spanish commander, the Liberator eventually removed the troops to a point just outside the city, still a violation.[88] But it was in Maracaibo that the truce dissolved into meaninglessness.

As early as 15 December a citizen of Maracaibo, which had been strongly royalist throughout the revolution, complained to Morillo of the actions of the cabildo, which had control of the police forces. Numerous persons were speaking openly in the streets of independence, as if it were already recognized, and the cabildo did nothing to restrain them. Seeing this, a group of pardos turned out one Sunday morning shouting, "Long live the king and death to the insurgents." The alcaldes immediately imprisoned and indicted the men as conspirators. Meanwhile, the regidores were nightly leading civilian vigilante committees to arrest those who publicized their antirepublican sentiments.[89] On 18 January 1821 two influential leaders of the city had a meeting with Rafael Urdaneta, a patriot general. Following this conference, Urdaneta, by closing off the lagoon and impounding the vessels on it, deprived the city of supplies. On 26 January he moved a battalion of troops to the banks of the lagoon, and on the evening of 28 January the troops moved toward the city because of a "revolution" that had occurred that morning. On the following day, patriot forces occupied Maracaibo.[90]

La Torre insisted that the republicans had violated the armistice within two months of its signing and certainly without giving an advance notice of forty days. Bolívar claimed that Maracaibo had joined the republicans of its own volition, which was not an infringement of the truce. Although both versions are in some measure true, it would seem that the republicans must be charged with bad faith. They violated the accord by sealing the lagoon, confiscating the ships on it, and moving troops to within a few hours' march of the city. These provocative military dispositions were clearly designed to aid the "revolution" by placing royalists in an indefensible position.

The resumption of warfare hastened the collapse of Spanish power. The patriots now commanded larger forces, superior economic resources, and considerable foreign aid of every kind. The policy of the Spanish constitutionalists had played completely into their hands. Bolívar and Páez began an advance from the southwest while Bermúdez invaded from the east. In May the latter occupied the capital, and on 24 June 1821 the patriots under Bolívar won an important victory at Carabobo against a smaller royalist force under La Torre, a battle in which the British Legion proved to be of decisive importance. For the Spanish, Venezuela was lost. Until 1823 they clung to some of the coastal towns, including Puerto Cabello, besieged and suffering great privations.

As for Pablo Morillo, he was named captain general of Madrid upon his return to Spain in early 1821. There he put down risings by absolutists and radicals during the next year and a half. In 1823, following the invasion of the 100,000 Sons of Saint Louis, he fled to France and was not permitted to return to Spain while the absolutists remained in power. With the ascendance of the liberals early in the following decade he returned, was made captain general of Galicia, and there fought the Carlists after 1833. He died in 1837 after an agonizing intestinal ailment caused by the lance wound he had received in the battle of La Puerta.

Notes

1. Juan Manuel de Cagigal, *Memorias del Mariscal de Campo Don Juan Manuel de Cagigal sobre la revolución de Venezuela* (Caracas, 1960), pp. 168–69.

2. Antonio Rodríguez Villa, *El teniente general don Pablo Morillo, primer conde de Cartagena, y marqués de la Puerta*, 4 vols. (Madrid, 1908–10), 1: 142.

3. Rough draft of a letter to Pablo Morillo, Caracas, 21 June 1815, Archivo General de la Nación, La Colonia: Gobernación y Capitanía General, Tomo CCLIV, f. 279 (archive hereafter cited as AGN).

4. Representación de Antonio Van-Halen y Sarti al Rey, Madrid, 14 January 1818, Archivo Histórico Nacional, Estado, Archivo Torrepando, Leg. 10 (archive hereafter cited as AHN).

5. Morillo to the Ministry of War, Cartagena, 16 February 1816, Rodríguez Villa, 3: 130–32. For other data on this matter, see Ministry of War to Morillo, Madrid, 16 August 1816, ibid., p. 101; Morillo to Ministry of War, Santa Fe, 31 May 1816, ibid., p. 159.

6. Rafael Sevilla, *Memorias de un oficial del ejército español* (Madrid, 1916), pp. 88–95. An excellent example of Morillo's attitude is found in one of his letters to Miguel de la Torre, Santa Fe, 24 July 1816, AHN, Estado, Archivo Torrepando, Leg. 15: "Our main objective must be to attract the guerrilla bands by treating everyone with the greatest humaneness and gentleness so that they will

be persuaded to put down their arms and return peacefully to their homes. For rigor must only be used with the principal leaders, not with those who have succumbed to the blandishments of the deceivers and who have acted blindly without knowing good from bad. For these reasons you should avoid accustoming to gunfire the guerrilla bands you find, but rather try to break them up by whatever means seem politic in the light of what you know of the character of the inhabitants. Remember that guerrilla bands are not destroyed with rigor or with force, but with tact and good treatment. . . ."

7. Morillo to La Torre, Valencia, 21 March 1818, AHN, Estado, Archivo Torrepando, Leg. 2; Morillo to La Torre, Achagua, 15 March 1819, ibid.; Morillo to La Torre, Hato de San Andrés, 28 January 1819, ibid.; "Instrucciones para la Marcha de los Cuerpos," Caracas, 30 May 1815, AHN, Estado, Torrepando, Leg. 3; Morillo to La Torre, Valencia, 28 April 1820, ibid. A good example of Morillo's rigor in these matters is in Morillo to La Torre, Valencia, 28 October 1817, ibid.: "In order to avoid these disturbances that cause so many evils, you will order that the troops in this division observe the most rigorous discipline and follow their marching instructions to the letter. Otherwise, they should never march." See also "Orden general de 9 al 10 de Septiembre de 1816, dada por el Brigadier Enrile," Rodríguez Villa, 3: 102–3, in which Enrile reported sentencing a second lieutenant to six years in prison for mistreating prisoners, a soldier to four years for robbery, and another soldier to death for having raped two women.

8. Enrile to the Ministry of War, Madrid, 19 June 1817, Rodríguez Villa, 3: 299.

9. See, for example, Morillo to La Torre, Ocaña, 25 March 1816, AHN, Estado, Torrepando, Leg. 2: "You should not be at all surprised that Calzada's troops are guilty of some excesses, for you must consider them little more than undisciplined guerrillas. In spite of everything, however, they have not ceased to toil and suffer considerable privations. You should nevertheless try, as you pass through the villages, to use tact in mollifying them and in getting the residents to return to their homes."

10. Morillo to the Ministry of War, Calabozo, 19 November 1817, Rodríguez Villa, 3: 461– 63.

11. Morillo to the Ministry of War, Valencia, 11 March 1818, ibid., pp. 520–21.

12. Ramón Hernández de Armas, *Defensa é impugnación contra el papel intitulado Idea sucinta que del carácter y disposición militar del mariscal de campo Don Miguel de la Torre ha dado a la prensa el coronel Don Sebastián de la Calzada* (Puerto Rico, 1823), pp. 13–32.

13. Morillo to the Ministry of War, Headquarters of Caño de Atamayca, near Arauca, 28 February 1819, Rodríguez Villa, 4: 13.

14. Proclamation of Martial Law by Simón Bolívar, 11 December 1817, Archivo General de Indias, Estado, Leg. 71 (archive hereafter cited as AGI).

15. Bolívar to Maxwell Hyslop, Kingston, Jamaica, 19 May 1815, *Cartas del Libertador*, ed. Vicente Lecuna, 11 vols. (Caracas, 1929–48), 1: 146. It was while Bolívar was in Jamaica that two persons bribed the Liberator's black servant, Pio, to kill his master. Bolívar let it be rumored that Morillo had ordered the assassination, which, as Madariaga points out, is unlikely. Tomás Cipriano de Mosquera, a friend of Bolívar, stated in his memoirs that the Liberator definitely discovered the names of the two men who hired Pio. Then, the two somehow managed to "escape." If Bolívar had had definitive evidence from the two that Morillo was involved, he would certainly have publicized the proof. Rather, he had an article printed in the Kingston newspaper stating that he did not know the names of the two men who had bribed Pio. At the same time, he permitted the rumor to circulate that Morillo had personally ordered the assassination. O'Leary believed that

Morillo was in no way implicated, and Bolívar never openly made the accusation himself (see Salvador de Madariaga, *Bolívar*, 2 vols. [México, 1951], 1: 516–20, and Tomás Cipriano de Mosquera, *Memoria sobre la vida del General Bolívar* [Bogotá, 1954], pp. 169–70). It should be noted that Morillo, in accordance with instructions, had placed a price on Bolívar's head, but this is a different matter from ordering an assassination.

16. Morillo to the Ministry of War, Santa Fe, 31 May 1816, Rodríguez Villa, 3: 162.

17. Bolívar to the Gaceta Real de Jamaica, Kingston, (n.d.) September 1815, *Cartas del Libertador*, 1: 214.

18. Ministry of War to Morillo, Madrid, 15 July 1816, Rodríguez Villa, 3: 80–81.

19. Morillo to the Ministry of War, Mompox, 7 March 1816, ibid., pp. 134–35.

20. Morillo to the Ministry of War, Santa Fe, 9 November 1816, ibid., pp. 228–29.

21. Morales to Morillo, Ocumare, 15 July 1816, ibid., p. 82.

22. Morillo to the Ministry of War, Cumaná, 28 August 1817, ibid., p. 43–49; Bolívar to Leandro Palacios, 7 August 1817, *Cartas del Libertador*, 1: 295–96; Administrador Principal de Caracas a los Directores Generales de la Real Renta de Correos, Caracas, 28 August 1817, AGI, Estado, Leg. 64.

23. José Antonio Páez, *Memorias*, 2 vols. (New York, 1878), 1: 235.

24. José Domingo Díaz, *Recuerdos sobre la rebelión de Caracas* (Madrid, 1829), pp. 211–13.

25. José Gil Fourtoul, *Historia constitucional de Venezuela*, 2 vols. (Berlin, 1907), 1: 250–60.

26. Morillo to the Ministry of War, Chaguarama, 8 May 1817, Rodríguez Villa, 3: 379–85.

27. Morillo to the Ministry of War, Calabozo, 20 November 1817, ibid., pp. 464–65.

28. León de Ortega to the King, Madrid, 3 February 1820, AGI, Estado, Leg. 57.

29. Morillo to the Ministry of War, Valencia, 25 January 1818, Rodríguez Villa, 3: 493–98.

30. Morillo to the Ministry of War, Calabozo, 22 December 1817, ibid., pp. 478–82; Morillo to the Ministry of War, Villa de Cura, 26 February 1818, ibid., p. 512.

31. Páez, *Memorias*, 1:184. Páez could not conceal his admiration for the Spanish infantry: "Our guard charged six or eight times without being able to break the square formed by the royalist infantry. Finally, after dismounting and with lances in hand, they advanced together with the chasseurs and destroyed that entire force, which defended itself with equal bravery." In a footnote Páez remarked that his llaneros were equally impressed; they said that "cuando quedaban cuatro, se defendían c— con c—, es decir, que hasta solo cuatro formaban cuadro. Certísimo; no se rendían y era menester matarlos."

32. Francisco Javier Vergara y Velasco, *1818*, 2d. ed. (Bogotá, 1960), pp. 119–50. This work by a Colombian general is the most exhaustive and competent study of the campaign of 1818 and will be followed here unless otherwise indicated. It should be noted that Morillo's version of the campaign, which Vergara could not have seen while writing his, is in substantial agreement (Morillo to the Ministry of War, Valencia, 2 April 1818, Rodríguez Villa, 3: 525–31). The official bulletin of the royalist army, also in general agreement with the above two works, is in Estado Mayor General. Ejército Expedicionario. Del Resumen Histórico de las Operaciones de este Ejército que comprende la Campaña de 1818 y últimas

ocurrencias del año 1817, AGI, Cuba, Leg. 901-B. Legajos 898 through 901 include the entire official bulletin of all operations of the Expeditionary Army.

33. Páez, *Memorias*, 1: 185–86.

34. Vicente Lecuna, *Crónica razonada de las guerras de Bolívar*, 3 vols. (New York, 1950), 2: 149.

35. Bolívar to Páez, Calabozo, 24 February 1818, *Memorias del general O'Leary*, by Daniel Florenciano O'Leary, 28 vols. (Caracas, 1883–1914), 15: 600.

36. Páez, *Memorias*, 1: 189–90.

37. The succeeding section, as the previous one, will be taken from Vergara y Velasco, *1818*, pp. 173–212, unless otherwise indicated.

38. Morillo to La Torre, Valencia, 5 March 1818, AHN, Estado, Torrepando, Leg. 2.

39. Morillo to La Torre, Valencia, 8 March 1818, ibid. Morillo wrote: "I am firmly convinced that if the enemy advances into the interior of these provinces they will never do so in that direction. For it is evident to you that they do not have sufficient infantry, that there is a long and difficult rocky pass up to the town, and that there is no pasture or subsistence for the horses. If by good luck they were to attempt it, they would arrive in such a deplorable condition that we could not ask for a better chance to destroy them."

40. Vergara y Velasco, *1818*, p. 193.

41. Rafael Urdaneta, *Memorias* (Madrid, 1916), pp. 132–38.

42. Bartolomé Mitre, *Historia de San Martín y de la emancipación sudamericana*, 3 vols. (Buenos Aires, 1968), 3: 206.

43. Morillo to various ambassadors, Valencia, 5 May 1818, Rodríguez Villa, 3: 653–54; Morillo to the Ministry of War, Valencia, 22 April 1818, ibid., pp. 546–48.

44. Ibid., pp. 564–65.

45. J. H. Robinson, *Journal of an Expedition 1400 miles up the Orinoco and 300 up the Arauca* (London, 1822), pp. 101, 160–63, 84–87; Francisco Burdett O'Connor, *Independencia americana* (Madrid, 1916), p. 51.

46. Alfred Hasbrouck, *Foreign Legionaries in the Liberation of Spanish South America* (New York, 1928), p. 100.

47. James Hackett, *Narrative of the Expedition which sailed from England in 1817* (London, 1818), pp. 56, 121–22.

48. Gustavus Hippisley, *A Narrative of the Expedition to the Rivers Orinoco and Apure in South America* (London, 1819), pp. 378–79, 464.

49. Ibid., pp. 462–63.

50. Ibid., pp. 418–19.

51. Hasbrouck, *Foreign Legionaries*, pp. 76–78. Latin American historians naturally accept this thesis. See Luis Cuervo Márquez, *Participación de la Gran Bretaña y de los Estados Unidos en la independencia de las colonias hispanoamericanas*, 2 vols. (Bogotá, 1938), 1: 262–67; Guillermo Ruiz Rivas, *Simón Bolívar: más allá del mito*, 2 vols. (Bogotá, 1970), 1: 450–53.

52. William D. Mahoney, *Memorias de un oficial de la Legión Británica* (Madrid, 1916), pp. 123–24.

53. Morillo to the Ministry of War, Headquarters in Caño de Atamayca, near Arauca, 28 February 1819, Rodríguez Villa, 4: 10–14.

54. Secretary of the Navy to the Secretary of State, 1 January 1819, AGI, Estado, Leg. 64.

55. Morillo to the Ministry of War, Calabozo, 2 July 1819, Rodríguez Villa, 4: 43.

56. Morillo to the Ministry of War, Valencia, 12 September 1819, ibid., p. 50.

57. Ibid., pp. 51–55.

58. Letter and expediente from Pablo Morillo to the Ministro de Gobernación de Ultramar, Valencia, 23 June 1820, included in "Correspondencia con el Exmo. Señor Secretario de Estado y del Despacho de la Gobernación de Ultramar, de 23 de Junio a 31 de Octubre de 1820," AHN, Estado, Torrepando, Leg. 6.

59. Andrés Level de Goda, "Memorias de Level de Goda," *Boletín de la Academia Nacional de la Historia* 15 (1932): 203–12.

60. Letter and expediente from José Caturla to the King, Puerto Cabello, 9 July 1820, AGI, Caracas, Leg. 175.

61. Gobernación de Ultramar to Morillo, Madrid, 9 September 1820, AHN, Estado, Torrepando, Leg. 1.

62. José Domingo Díaz, "Epítome de la vida pública de Don Andrés Level de Goda, fiscal de la hacienda pública de Venezuela," *BANH* 15 (1932): 143.

63. Ibid., pp. 140–45.

64. Level de Goda, "Memorias," pp. 203–12; Andrés Level de Goda, "Antapadosis," *BANH* 15 (1932): 620.

65. Level de Goda, "Memorias," pp. 203–12.

66. Letter and expediente from José Duarte to the Ministry of Finance, Caracas, 8 October 1820, AGI, Caracas, Leg. 830; expediente without accompanying letter, 6 October 1820, ibid.; rough draft of a dictamen of the Contaduría General to the Ministry of Finance, 24 December, 1820, ibid., Leg. 467.

67. Level de Goda, "Antapadosis," pp. 631–32.

68. Morillo to the Ministry of War, Valencia, 6 August 1820, AHN, Estado, Torrepando, Leg. 6.

69. Morillo to the Ministry of War, Caracas, 8 October 1820, ibid., Leg. 3.

70. Level de Goda, "Antapadosis," pp. 631–32.

71. Díaz, *Recuerdos*, p. 238.

72. Ibid., pp. 241–42.

73. Morillo to the Secretary of State, Valencia, 6 August 1820, AHN, Estado, Torrepando, Leg. 6.

74. Morillo to the Gobernación de Ultramar, Valencia, 26 July 1820, Rodríguez Villa, 4: 207– 8; Morillo to La Torre, Valencia, 19 August 1820, AHN, Estado, Torrepando, Leg. 2.

75. Morillo to La Torre, Valencia, 20 June 1820, AHN, Estado, Torrepando, Leg. 3.

76. Morillo to the Ministry of War, Valencia, 28 August 1820, Rodríguez Villa, 4: 225–26.

77. Morillo to the Ministry of War, Valencia, 4 July 1820, AHN, Estado, Torrepando, Leg. 6.

78. Morillo to the Ministry of War, Valencia, 8 September 1820, ibid.

79. Morillo to the Ministry of War, Valencia, 4 July 1820, ibid.

80. Ibid.

81. Extract of a letter from Jefe Político of Venezuela, 27 November 1820, AGI, Caracas, Leg. 175; Pablo Morillo y Morillo, *Mémoires du général Morillo, comte de Carthagène, marquis de la Puerta, rélatifs aux principaux événements de ses campagnes en Amérique de 1815 à 1821* (Paris, 1826), pp. 279–82.

82. Ibid., p. 293.

83. Ibid., p. 283.

84. Ibid., p. 285.

85. Virtually all the correspondence between Morillo and the patriot leaders has been compiled by Pedro Grases and Manuel Pérez Vila in *El Amor a la Paz*, published by the Presidencia de la República (Caracas, 1970).

86. Morillo to the Ministry of War, Puerto Cabello, 16 December 1820, AHN, Estado, Torrepando, Leg. 6.

87. La Torre to the Ministry of War, 21 December 1820, ibid.

88. *Manifiesto de la correspondencia que ha mediado entre los Generales Conde de Cartagena y Don Miguel de la Torre, jefes del ejército de Costa Firme, con el de los disidentes Don Simón Bolívar, desde el restablecimiento de la constitución hasta la escandalosa ruptura del armisticio por Bolívar* (Madrid, 1821), pp. 54–57, 61–63.

89. Martín de Urdaneta to Morillo, Maracaibo, 15 December 1820, AHN, Estado, Torrepando, Leg. 83.

90. *Manifiesto de la correspondencia*, pp. 63–66.

10

The Guayaquil Conference and Bolívar's Relations with Peru, 1822

General Daniel Florencio O'Leary

The rivalries between northern and southern South America commenced when General José de San Martín's Argentine and Chilean troops occupied coastal Peru and Simón Bolívar's Colombian forces headed south to eliminate royalist support in Pasto and to occupy Quito and Guayaquil. Rather than fight San Martín's army, the remaining Spanish royalist forces abandoned the Peruvian capital and coastline to develop almost impenetrable bases in the Andes. Bolívar sent General Antonio José de Sucre to occupy Quito and Cuenca in Ecuador. As president of Colombia, Bolívar occupied Guayaquil on July 11, 1822, and used his army to annex a city that did not appear anxious to join the Colombian confederation.

San Martín lacked the power to finish off the royalists in Peru, and he traveled to Guayaquil to meet with Bolívar. While memoirist General Daniel Florencio O'Leary, the Liberator's aide-de-camp, adopted a pro-Bolívar interpretation, no records were kept of the San Martín-Bolívar meetings, which has given rise to a great deal of speculation by historians and to some apocryphal accounts by San Martín's would-be supporters representing the Argentine view. In addition to requesting troops and arms to bolster the Peruvian campaigns against the royalists, San Martín may have wished to discuss the future of Guayaquil. Receiving nothing in the way of aid from Bolívar, San Martín returned to Lima, resigned his position, and then went to Chile and into exile in Europe.

The unexpected arrival of San Martín at the Guayaquil estuary on July 25, 1822, not only occasioned surprise but also made everybody forget for the moment the excitement of recent days. When the Liberator learned of his arrival, he sent his aides to welcome him and commissioned Colonel Ignacio Torres to deliver to him a letter in which he

From *Bolívar and the War of Independence: Memorias del General Daniel Florencio O'Leary: Narración*, translated and edited by Robert F. McNerney, Jr. (Austin: University of Texas Press, 1970), 220–35. © 1970 by the University of Texas Press. Reprinted by permission of the University of Texas Press.

expressed his pleasure over the surprising news and deplored the fact that there was not enough time to prepare an adequate welcome. He added that he was extremely anxious to meet the father of Chile and Peru. When San Martín's ship, the schooner *Macedonia*, approached the harbor on the morning of the twenty-sixth, Bolívar went on board and had the pleasure of embracing his most distinguished collaborator in the fight for South American independence.

General San Martín was received by the people of Guayaquil in a manner befitting his high rank and his great contribution to the American cause. During his two days' stay in the city he divided his time between important official business and the festivities improvised by the hospitable people to celebrate the happy occasion. He spent the morning in conferences with the Liberator; after dinner in Bolívar's house, they both attended the balls given in San Martín's honor. The subjects of his conversations with the Liberator were the state of America and the best way to bring the war to a successful conclusion. A short time previously, plenipotentiaries from Colombia and Peru had agreed upon a treaty that bound both republics to render each other mutual assistance until the end of the war with Spain. Since the war in Colombia had already ended, San Martín had come to ask the Liberator for aid in order to bring the war in Peru to a close.

This was the apparent object of his visit, but the current rumor was that the Protector's motives were not as friendly and sincere as they appeared to be. It was said that his aim was to reach Guayaquil at the time of the arrival of the division of Santa Cruz, while the Liberator was still occupied in Quito, in order to encourage the Peruvian party with his presence and obtain, perhaps, the annexation of the province to Peru. San Martín's character might have given grounds for this suspicion, which became stronger during his short stay in Guayaquil when it was noticed that he looked rather displeased and preoccupied.[1]

It would be difficult to find two individuals less alike in character than Bolívar and San Martín. Bolívar was frank, candid, passionately devoted to his friends, and generous to his enemies; San Martín was cold, reserved, and incapable of pardoning offenses or of bestowing favors that did not work to his own advantage. Both of them achieved the goals they had in mind, but by means as different as the routes they followed to their meeting place in Ecuador. The Argentine, after being rewarded for his services to Peru, abandoned her cause; the Venezuelan, after being banished by his compatriots, returned to Colombia and gave them liberty. The former was born and grew up in poverty and acquired a fortune. The latter inherited a large fortune and died almost in poverty. San Martín accepted the title of Protector of Peru; Bolívar rejected the crown offered to him in Colombia. Both were benefactors of their countries, and both were victims of the ingratitude and the persecution of the peoples whom their genius and their courage had redeemed. My references to San Martín are based solely on what I have heard about him from people who knew him. On the other hand, I speak of Bolívar from my intimate knowledge of his character. But I should be committing an injustice if I did not mention the glories of Chacabuco and Maipú.

San Martín spent the greater part of his youth in Spain and served with distinction in the Spanish army as a cavalry officer. Having returned to Buenos Aires in 1812, he achieved renown in the battle of San Lorenzo and was given command of the Army of the Andes. He skillfully executed the crossing of the cordillera that separates Mendoza from Chile, and the battle of Chacabuco was the reward for his daring. On the glorious battlefield of Maipú he gave manifest proof of his genius by gaining independence for Chile. Inasmuch as he was convinced that Chile would never be able to enjoy the blessings of peace while Peru had sufficient means to cause trouble, he made plans to rescue Peru from Spanish domination. His undertaking was crowned with the most surprising success in the beginning. The best veteran unit of the royalist army transferred its allegiance to his forces. José de la Mar, Andrés Santa Cruz, Antonio Gutiérrez de la Fuente, and other leaders also joined his army. The gates of the capital were opened to him, and Callao delivered itself into his hands.

In Lima, San Martín encountered what Hannibal had encountered in Capua: the luxury that begets soft living and the seduction that produces the vices that soon demoralize an army. But the Argentine was very inferior to the African and was not able to conquer these great evils. The soldiers from Chile succumbed to the effects of the climate, and the veterans who had followed him from the banks of the Río de la Plata were seeking an opportunity to throw off the weight of an authority that they could not tolerate, either because of envy or because they resented his arrogance as Protector of Peru. Plots and conspiracies followed each other in rapid succession and threatened to destroy San Martín's authority. The defeat at Ica broke the magic spell that seemed to bring him success.

His enemies took advantage of his absence in Guayaquil to punish the insolent haughtiness of his prime minister, Don Bernardo Monteagudo. After causing a popular uprising, they deposed him and drove him into exile. This was the welcome they gave San Martín upon his return. Although he assumed the supreme command again, he remained in power for only a month. After installing the Congress he had convoked, he presented his resignation, which was accepted immediately. Then he embarked secretly, leaving Peru in a state of anarchy and subject to the selfish desires of a few impudent demagogues. The country was, in addition, threatened by the royalist army, which had regained its superiority.

The Liberator, who was accustomed to solving almost impossible problems, overcame the few difficulties that arose in Guayaquil. When the electoral college met on July 31, a heated debate took place, and anger was beginning to rise to a high pitch when the Liberator made known his desire to have the meeting ended, since its only object was to proclaim the annexation of the province to the territory of Colombia. The electoral college thereupon declared that thereafter the province was forever to be a part of the Republic of Colombia. The few dissatisfied members made a protest, which they later published in Peru. The members of the junta made it a point of honor to leave the country. The local troops were either discharged or redistributed among the units of the Republic, but the Liberator gave the officers complete freedom to do as they pleased. All the officers and officials who left the country were well received in Peru, where they obtained posts. Before long they forgot their pretended wrongs. Olmedo sang the praises of Bolívar, Jimena served him faithfully, and Roca became one of his admirers.

The annexation of Guayaquil to Colombia awakened the jealousy of the southern republics, which claimed that it was an act of usurpation and viewed as despotic the measures adopted by the Liberator to effect the union. In reality, the Liberator was only performing his duty in obedience to the sovereign will of the people of Colombia, whose fundamental law included Guayaquil in Colombia's territory. If the uti possidetis was the rule observed by Mexico and Chile, Colombia had a right to act in the same way. If each province were permitted to establish its sovereignty, South America would soon fall into a most frightful state of anarchy. The Liberator established the framework of society on a firm foundation by getting rid of this source of trouble.

Only a captious critic would condemn the means employed to effect the annexation. The Liberator could not, without failing to do his duty, recognize the Guayaquil junta as anything other than a de facto government. Congress had given him authority to subjugate the southern provinces. The separation of Guayaquil from the rest of the Republic would have established a dangerous precedent. Any other province had the same right to seek independence and constitute itself into a sovereign state. If Guayaquil had opposed annexation, the Liberator would have been justified in having used coercive measures. His conduct on the occasion was extremely considerate. He had made his plans known well in advance, and he carried them out without cruelty or bloodshed. The factions disappeared quickly, and there was more peace and quiet in the city than had been known since the year 1820. Guayaquil was declared a department of Colombia, and a school and a court of commerce were established in the capital. These and other benefits conferred upon it by the Liberator won for him the affection and the blessings of a grateful people.

The division commanded by Santa Cruz returned to Peru after receiving replacements for the casualties it had suffered in the campaign. Two thousand Colombian soldiers requested by General San Martín also embarked for Peru. The Liberator offered him a larger number, but he did not believe that more were needed or that the country could maintain a larger force than the one it had under arms. In his interview with San Martín, the Liberator asked him insistently if it would not be better to march to the interior of Peru with all available forces rather than to divide them and thus expose the army to the risk of being defeated in piecemeal fashion. The Protector answered with the objection that the independent provinces of Peru did not have sufficient resources to move a large force across the Andes. The governments that succeeded San Martín in power made the same mistake, with unfortunate consequences for the country. Finally, the Liberator, although without control of the vast territory they had possessed, other than the department of Trujillo, and although the royalists occupied the rest of the country, convinced the Peruvians of the serious mistake they had made and showed them the superiority of his genius in the brilliant campaign that he directed in Peru.

On September 1, 1822, the Liberator departed from Guayaquil to visit the provinces of Cuenca and Loja, leaving General Salom in charge of the administration of the new department, a happy choice that satisfied everybody and resulted in many useful improvements. The fact that he had established the independence of his country did not satisfy the Liberator, for the task would not be complete until he had made that independence permanently secure. The picture of the state of Peru given him by San Martín was not really satisfactory. Bolívar did not find San Martín very sincere, but neither his own frankness nor the offers he made enabled him to break down the Protector's reserve. A mistaken sense of pride, Bolívar thought, had prevented him from describing the real state of the country he had planned to liberate. When Bolívar later consulted men who had an intimate knowledge of Peru's resources and the ability of the royalist generals who commanded the army there, his suspicions regarding San Martín were confirmed, and he immediately decided to renew the offers he had made to him. The opinions of the members of the new political government of Peru are apparent in the imprudent and discourteous answer made to his proposals by the governing junta.

After having accepted San Martín's resignation, the Congress entrusted the executive power to a three-man junta made up of General José de la Mar, Don Felipe Antonio Alvarado, and the Count of Vista Florida, the first two of whom were foreigners. Olmedo and others of the group who had left Guayaquil managed to obtain seats in Congress, where they showed evidence of their injured pride and their desire for vengeance. The machinations did real harm to the reputation of the Liberator. Le Mar himself, the president of the junta, was not above the petty jealousy that dishonored some of his colleagues. Herein must lie the explanation of the resolution of Congress with respect to the Liberator's generous offer and the rude manner in which the governing junta transmitted it to him. Everything indicated a need for the help offered them in support of the wavering state of independence, which was threatened by civil strife and by a foreign enemy who was energetic and daring.

The imprudent conduct of the government and its supporters did not stop there. The auxiliaries from Colombia were also slandered for no good reason in the libels that appeared daily, being singled out as false friends and dangerous allies despite their irreproachable conduct. The junta regarded with indifference the frequent protests submitted by the Colombian general. It soon became apparent that there was need for a treaty that would guarantee the subsistence, clothing, and pay of the Colombian troops. Colonel Juan Paz del Castillo was consequently given instructions to propose such a treaty, but the governing junta of Lima rejected it. The Colombian troops thereupon withdrew and returned to their country with the consent of the junta, whose conduct on this occasion gave rise to dishonorable charges that I believe to be unfounded.

The decision of the Colombian general was a fatal blow for the junta. The moment could not have been more inopportune, because everything seemed to conspire to multiply the misfortunes of the country. The fiscal measures adopted by Congress increased rather than relieved the general uneasiness. The issuance of paper money brought an end to credit and paralyzed commerce. The government consoled itself with the hope that victory by the republican forces in the South would re-establish confidence and produce a favorable reaction; but near Moquegua in January, 1823, the Spanish General Jerónimo Valdés finally routed the large, well-organized division comprising the troops brought by San Martín from Chile and the Río de la Plata. General Rudecindo Alvarado, a brother of the member of the junta with the same name, was barely able to save five hundred of the four thousand men with whom he had landed at Iquique two months previously.

While preparations were being made for the proposed expedition to Peru before news came of the rejection of his offer, the Liberator busied himself with the organization of the civil government of the departments. He visited the provinces and the capital of Cuenca, and then the capital of Loja, which borders on Peru. In all the municipalities and villages along his route he made as many improvements as he could. But he was able to devote only a short space of time to this peaceful work in the South, for it was interrupted by the Pasto rebellion in the North.

The stupid inhabitants of these provinces allowed themselves to be seduced by a Spanish officer who had escaped from among the group that had surrendered in Quito. A nephew on his mother's side of the devastator of Venezuela, he took the name of Boves rather than his father's name. Though he lacked talent and courage, that terrible name was sufficient recommendation for the people of Pasto. The area between the Guáitara and Juanambú rivers quickly became a vast center of rebellion and disorder. The Liberator immediately ordered General Sucre to march there with troops from the garrison in quito and the surrounding towns. Sucre was repulsed on November 24 when he attacked the natives of Pasto on the almost inaccessible ridge of Taindala, overlooking the Guáitara River, but after he received reinforcements, he made a strategic move that fooled the rebel leader and completely upset his defense. The capture of the Taindala position marked the completion of the major part of the campaign.

Sucre advanced immediately and overtook Boves at Yacuanquer. The valor of Colonels Córdova and Sandes and the aggressiveness of their troops decided the battle, and the rebels were completely routed. On the following day Sucre demanded the surrender of the city, but his demand was ignored. Though twice defeated, the natives of Pasto regrouped in the outskirts of the city. There, for more than an hour, they stood their ground with characteristic courage before finally giving way. In the horrible slaughter that followed, soldiers and civilians, men and women were indiscriminately sacrificed. Boves, seeking safety in flight, went through the mountains leading to the headwaters of the Marañón River, descended the river, and reached the coast of Brazil. The people of Pasto received the punishment that their crimes and stupidity merited.

During the course of these events the Liberator retired to a country house near Ibarra, a city between Quito and Pasto, where he seemed to forget the cares of the war and of government, dividing his time between study and hunting. Ever since the year 1820 his varied and constant activity had left him almost no time for rest. During this period of seclusion he was visited by Colonel Don Bernardo Monteagudo, who had been deposed and exiled from Peru in the absence of the Protector. Bolívar received him with courteous hospitality, even though Monteagudo had stood out as a vehement critic of his administration. Monteagudo was a talented man of great learning and experience whose political ideas went from one extreme to another when he finally occupied positions of great responsibility. After San Martín appointed him secretary of state, he incurred the hatred of the inhabitants of the capital with his decree of proscription. Nonetheless, the short period of his administration revealed his great gifts as a statesman and the vigor of his resolute character, as seen in the impetus he gave not only to military affairs but also to the whole complex mechanism of government. His policy may have been unwise, but it shows him to be a man who was superior to his contemporaries. After his fall he was charged with having accumulated great wealth during his administration. I take pleasure in stating that these charges are not only unjust but also slanderous. The best proof of his integrity is that he died poor. During his visit with the Liberator he delighted the group gathered there with his pleasant conversation and his vast store of knowledge. Bolívar, who knew how to profit from the experience of others, obtained from him a complete knowledge of the character of the Argentines.

Near the end of December the Liberator left Ibarra for Pasto, where he arrived January 2, 1823. Convinced that generosity was wasted on a people who were incapable of appreciating it, he decided to punish them severely. Since, however, he always adhered to the principles of justice, he first tried to find out what reasons they had to offer in justification of their crime, but they maintained an obstinate silence. He thereupon ordered General Salom to enroll in the army all the citizens of Pasto who had taken up arms against the Republic. After making other provisions and appointing Colonel Juan José Flores governor of the province of Pasto, he returned to Quito.

Salom carried out his assignment in a manner that did little honor to him or to the government. The inhabitants assembled in the public square of the city in answer to a summons from Salom, and they had read to them the law stating the duties of the magistrate and the rights of the citizens. Then, however, a picket of soldiers entered the square and seized about a thousand of the men, who were immediately sent to Quito. Many of them perished on the way or at a later date after declaring in unmistakable terms their hatred for the laws and the name of Colombia. None of the men taken from Pasto proved useful to the Republic, for nothing could ever reconcile them to military service in the cause of independence.

While on the way from Ibarra to Pasto, the Liberator had received alarming dispatches from the government in Bogotá informing him that the municipal government of Caracas had accompanied its oath to observe the constitution with a formal protest against it. The government unwisely ordered the prosecution of those who had protested, but the courts declared that there was no ground for action. This incident did implant the seed of discord, and during this period there was born an opposition party that bitterly attacked the executive power in the press. The vice-president reported all these events to the Liberator with the exaggeration that comes from injured pride. He also conveyed the suspicion that all the members of Congress were imbued with the ideas that prevailed in the Caracas faction, as he called the opposition. The Liberator, whose own painful experience had made him more hostile toward the federal system than was perhaps wise, obeyed on this occasion, as on others, the dictates of sincere patriotism. In a communication to the vice-president he categorically expressed his disapproval of the innovators and urged the executive power to do its utmost to prevent the legislators from making any changes in Colombia's fundamental code of laws, which he had sworn to uphold.

In a communication addressed to the Congress on the same subject, he offered the representatives the brilliant victories won by the liberating army. Then he declared: "The Constitution of Colombia is sacred for ten years and shall not be violated with impunity while I have any blood running through my veins and the liberators are under my orders." Contrary to the expectations of many people, who did not consider proper the use of such plain and unambiguous language, Congress gave him a most sincere vote of thanks for the sentiments he had expressed. This frank declaration produced the effect desired. All thoughts of innovation were abandoned, and the government, with the Liberator's support, won a victory. Bolívar's influence in Colombia was so great during that period that it was limited only by his moderation. He could have had anything he wanted then.

Upon his return to Quito near the end of January, after the pacification of Pasto, the Liberator learned that the Peruvian government had discharged the Colombian auxiliary troops and that the troops had arrived on the coast during the season when its climate is most unhealthy. Despite the torrential rains, he started for Guayaquil immediately, and on his arrival he found the troops dreadfully ravaged by disease. His presence helped to encourage the subordinate authorities to do everything possible for the sick, who, thanks to their care, soon regained their health. A few days after his arrival, when he was hoping for a rest, he received news of a disaster in the northern part of the Republic and an appeal for help from the Colombian government. In all its conflicts it confidently turned to the Liberator, for it felt sure that his advice would bring a solution.

After the battle of Carabobo the general staff and the remnants of the royalist army took refuge in Puerto Cabello, from where, with a superior naval force, they could easily move their troops along the coast. The province of Coro, like Pasto loyal to the King, served them as a base of operations. La Torre met with stiff resistance in his efforts to regain territory, but his successor, General Morales, succeeded in occupying the city and province of Maracaibo and then invaded the provinces of Trujillo and Mérida. The government of Colombia proclaimed martial law and had it enforced with excessive rigor. When informed of this alarming state of affairs, the Liberator immediately left Guayaquil for Bogotá, but he decided to turn back after five days' travel when two messengers brought news of Morales' withdrawal and the government's energetic action. The defeat of Alvarado's army at Moquegua made his presence in the South indispensable.

Once aware of the extent of the danger, the Liberator promptly ordered the various units stationed in the South to make ready to march. The terrible disaster of Moquegua filled the inhabitants of the free provinces of Peru with sorrow and consternation, but the governing junta appeared to be more apathetic than ever. Though La Mar, its president, was a brave soldier, he was hesitant about making decisions. The army units quartered in the environs of Lima demanded that Congress appoint Don José de la Riva-Agüero chief executive of the nation, and he was so appointed on February 27, 1823, after a second demand from the army. The first act of the new president was to send General Mariano Portocarrero to Guayaquil to apologize to the Liberator for the conduct of the junta and to request the aid he had offered.

The Liberator assured General Portocarrero that Colombia would do her duty in Peru, sending her soldiers as far as Potosí. He told him to tell the Peruvian government that Colombian soldiers were already hurrying toward Peru on board the ships of the Republic. Bolívar was not exaggerating matters when he said this, for the ships carrying two thousand men were already on their way down the river. Furthermore, two thousand more men set out for the same destination two days later. The Peruvian general, who was accustomed to the listless manner in which all governmental action was taken in his country, was filled with admiration and astonishment when he saw the ease with which the Liberator handled the large number of affairs under his charge and supervised everything of any consequence. While busy with these preparations, the Liberator decided that it would be wiser to protect the Colombian troops in Peru by compelling that government, through a treaty, to fulfill its promises. On March 18 the plenipotentiaries of the two nations subscribed to a formal pact, according to which Colombia was to send six thousand men to the aid of Peru. In return, Peru was to pay all expenses and adequate compensation to officers and men, as well as supply necessary ammunition and mounts and replace the army losses numerically with men from her own territory. This pact gave rise in later years to disputes between the two negotiating parties.

After the Peruvian envoy expressed his gratitude to Bolívar for taking such prompt and generous action, he went on to say that his mission would not be complete unless he obtained the Liberator's promise to go to Peru to direct the campaign. The Liberator replied that he was ready to go provided the General Congress of Colombia was not opposed to his absence. When General Portocarrero returned to Peru with the most promising news, the joy of the Lima patriots exceeded all bounds, for they had feared that the Liberator would treat them with the scorn they deserved in view of the insults hurled at him by the Lima newspapers and the government suspicion of his motives.

The Liberator thought that it would be better to carry the war to Peru and use the resources of her free provinces against the royalists rather than to maintain a defensive position and eventually endanger the entire Republic of Colombia. It was, however, only after serious and mature deliberation that he decided to risk his reputation on what was then believed, with reason, to be a reckless undertaking—that of rescuing Peru from the domination of Spain, thus wresting from Spain the last of her richest possessions. The undertaking was, indeed, to be even more daring than Bolívar with his keen insight judged it would be.

While awaiting a reply from the Congress of Colombia to his request for permission to go to Peru, he devoted himself more earnestly than ever to making the necessary preparations. He had conferred the command of the troops sent to Lima upon General Manuel Valdés, but he appointed General Sucre to the post of minister plenipotentiary to the Lima government, with sufficient authority to intervene whenever necessary. General Salom succeeded Sucre in the civil and military command of the southern department. The second division of the expeditionary army embarked at Guayaquil during the course of the following month, and it was necessary to make really extraordinary efforts to complete the complement of six thousand men.

The president of Peru sent a second deputation to urge the Liberator to come to Peru to direct operations. They believed that without his presence there all efforts to destroy the Spanish army would be of no avail. The Peruvian Congress, grateful for the timely assistance he had sent them, gave him a solemn vote of thanks. Despite Bolívar's ardent desire to satisfy the eager wishes of the Peruvians, his respect for the fundamental institutions of his country hindered him from doing so. He decided to wait in Guayaquil for the permission he had requested from Congress. Aside from this consideration, new disturbances in Pasto required his presence in that area.

When the inhabitants of that turbulent province observed that most of the troops had gone to Peru, they conceived the idea of re-establishing the authority of the King in the provinces of Quito. A large number of those who had hidden in the woods banded together with other malcontents and marched on the city of Pasto on June 12. The attack was so violent that the veteran troops under Colonel Flores could not resist it. Flores was defeated and barely managed to retreat to Popayán with a few officers and a small cavalry unit. The leader of this revolt was Agustín Agualongo, an astute Indian of exceptional courage. Informed of the defenseless state of Quito, he marched on the capital after organizing his increased forces. When Salom received news of Flores' fate, he sent a courier to inform the Liberator and left with the few troops in the city to check the advance of the rebels. He had to withdraw before Agualongo's superior forces, leaving the road to Ibarra open to him.

It did not take Bolívar long to come to a decision. He immediately ordered all the convalescents in the hospitals to march to Quito, and he himself hurried to that city and called the militia into active service. Convinced that deception was the only means of compensating for the lack of adequate forces, the Liberator feigned a withdrawal, thus leading the rebels to believe that they could take possession of Quito. At noon on July 17, while the rebels were making merry in the streets of Ibarra, the Liberator himself, accompanied by his staff and an escort of lancers, surprised their outposts and put them to the sword. When advised of this unexpected attack, Agualongo made a hurried departure from the city with his troops and proceeded to take up a position on the Pasto road. Before he was able to arrange his men on the height overlooking this road, he was attacked again and completely routed. Some six hundred of his fifteen hundred men perished within half a mile of the city, and the rest scattered in all directions. Agualongo himself succeeded in escaping with about fifty cavalrymen to the mountains, where some of his scattered men joined him later. Not even in the midst of defeat did the rebels lose their indomitable courage, and they rejected the pardon offered to them if they would lay down their arms. The Liberator personally pursued the fugitives until very late at night. On the following day he had Colonel Salom advance to occupy Pasto, which he did without opposition. The night before the engagement at Ibarra the Liberator had dictated to an amanuensis one of the best and most eloquent articles he ever composed, on the American confederation. This was the way he used his time to help the common cause, despite the most distressing circumstances.

Upon his return to Quito, the Liberator found the third deputation from Peru waiting for him, this time from the representatives of the people, which must have made it more pleasing to him. Olmedo, who had a seat in the Peruvian Congress, was the principal member of the commission. This circumstance was very gratifying to the Liberator, who gave him a hearty welcome that did honor to both of them. When Olmedo informed the Liberator of the object of his mission, the latter replied that permission had not reached him yet, but that he was eagerly awaiting the opportunity to go to Peru. Olmedo was accompanied by Don José Sánchez Carrión, also a representative and a very talented and scholarly patriot.

The Liberator left for Guayaquil as soon as he had restored peace and quiet to Quito. Upon his arrival on August 2 he found waiting for him an aide of the Marqués de Torre Tagle, who had replaced Riva-Agüero in the government of Peru and was requesting the immediate presence of the Liberator in Lima, where recent events made it more necessary. At six o'clock on the morning of the seventh, the Liberator received the decree in which Congress granted him the permission he had so urgently requested. This decree arrived just after he had signed and sealed a letter to General Francisco de Paula Santander telling him that he had decided to go to Peru without awaiting the decision of Congress, because the safety of Colombia depended on his presence in that country.[2] He tore up the letter and embarked an hour later for Callao in the government brig *Chimborazo*. "Today is the anniversary of Boyacá," said a member of his staff upon embarking, "a good omen for the future campaign."[3]

Notes

1. Though we have no written account by San Martín about the much-discussed meeting between these two great leaders, most historians agree that San Martín was deeply disappointed to find that Bolívar had assumed control of Guayaquil. The definite information we do have consists of three letters dictated by Bolívar the day after San Martín's departure. According to Bolívar, San Martín stated that he did not wish to become involved in Guayaquil's affairs, that his forces in Peru were stronger than those of the Spaniards, that he intended to retire to Mendoza, Argentina, after strengthening the government of Peru but without waiting until the end of the war, and that he favored a constitutional monarchy for Peru. In other letters written shortly thereafter, Bolívar spoke favorably of San Martín.—Ed.

2. Even though O'Leary was an eyewitness, he is wrong when he says that the Liberator had decided to embark for Peru without receiving the permission of the Congress of Colombia. See the truth of the matter in Vicente Lecuna, *Crónica razonada de las guerras de Bolívar*, III, 302–303. The antecedents are on pages 272–273.—Vicente Lecuna.

Lecuna states that a communication from Bolívar's secretary, José Gabriel Pérez, to the secretary of foreign affairs of Colombia, dated August 3, 1823, proves conclusively that the permission from Congress had arrived in Guayaquil by August 3.—Ed.

3. The date for the Liberator's departure does not agree with what is said in the communication found in *Memorias*, XX, 265. But we do not believe that O'Leary was mistaken, for he was one of the group that accompanied Bolívar—Simón Bolívar O'Leary.

In the communication referred to above, dated August 6, 1823, Bolívar's secretary stated that Bolívar was embarking right away. But in a letter to General Salom dated August 7, 1823, Bolívar said: "I am embarking right now."—Ed.

IV

The Defeat of Spain in the Americas

11

Chaos and the Military Solution: The Fall of Royalist Peru

Timothy E. Anna

Very much like pincers, the independence movements of the northern and southern countries intruded upon a Peruvian population divided both on the issue of republicanism versus monarchy and on the question of independence. The move of royalist military forces into the Andes left San Martín as Protector and then Bolívar with some difficult military and political questions. Many Peruvians wanted the foreigners from La Plata, Chile, and Colombia simply to disappear. They questioned Bolívar's motivations in Peru. Governments in Lima negotiated with the royalists in Cuzco with both sides fragmented into factions and able to agree only that outside intervention by Colombians and Argentines was not wanted. When General Antonio José de Sucre crushed the royalists at Ayacucho in December 1824, only Callao and a few isolated Spanish posts in Upper Peru remained in Spanish control.

The reticence that prevented a Peruvian decision for independence was not unique. In many other areas such as Puerto Cabello, Pasto, and in parts of Central America New Spain, the traditional ties with Madrid attracted significant support. In New Spain, the Peruvian indecisiveness (and near anarchy) was avoided because the royalist defense system collapsed when Agustín de Iturbide and his supporters crafted a formula under the Plan de Iguala and created slogans that appealed to broad segments of the populace. However, in Peru the royalists were effective against the patriots on the battlefield until they gambled and lost at Ayacucho. Like New Spain, which obtained its independence with the fortress of San Juan de Ulúa at Veracruz remaining for a time in Spanish hands and threats of reconquest attempts poisoning future relations between Mexico and Spain into the 1830s, the quixotic last stand of General José Ramón Rodil at Callao foreshadowed future difficulties for Peru.

From Timothy E. Anna, "Chaos and the Military Solution," in *The Fall of the Royal Government in Peru* (Lincoln: University of Nebraska Press, 1979), 214–38, 268–71. © 1979 by the University of Nebraska Press. Reprinted by permission of the University of Nebraska Press.

Timothy Anna is Distinguished Professor of History at the University of Manitoba in Winnipeg, Manitoba, Canada.

In the two years after San Martín's withdrawal, the independent part of Peru lapsed into chaos so intense that even the incomparable Bolívar at first despaired. When the government passed into the hands of Peruvian leaders, the state was crippled by internal factionalism, bankruptcy, and treason. By late 1823 Peruvian independence presented to the world a truly pathetic picture. Separate armies existed of Peruvians, Chileans, Colombians, and Argentinians. The political state was leaderless, with two different men claiming to be president of the republic. Congress collapsed under the pressure. The arrival of Bolívar in September 1823—a full year after San Martín's departure—added a new element to the mixture, one that many Peruvian leaders feared and tried to subvert. As Bolívar himself testified: "Peruvian affairs have reached a peak of anarchy. Only the enemy army is well organized, united, strong, energetic, and capable."[1] Bolívar's assessment was correct, for the royalist army under [Viceroy José de] La Serna and his commanders had kept itself intact in the highlands and, making use of the considerable support for the royal cause that existed among the Indians, the mestizos, and the few whites of the interior and south, offered an ever-present threat to the cause of independence. Indeed, for several months in 1824—during the period when Lima was again in royal hands and while Bolívar lay sick at Pativilca—the royalists actually regained control of all except one province of Peru. They came very close to winning the war and smashing the independent regime. Only the leadership of Bolívar—unflinching and sometimes brutal—eventually stopped the rot and organized an effective patriot fighting force. Even so, independence came only as the result of a military contest, and the long siege of the royalist forces and their supporters at Callao throughout 1825 and into January 1826 proved once again that many Peruvians—including some of the most important leaders of the independent government—had still not committed themselves to independence. Peruvians never did decide. The independent regime had been founded at Lima in 1821 by default, it came close to being utterly eliminated in 1824, and by 1825 it had won a military campaign and had defeated the royal army; but true commitment had never been present.

Every author writing on Peruvian independence has commented, in one form or another, upon the essential phenomenon of Peru's inability to support independence. [Gerhard] Masur ascribed it to the treason of the creole upper class: "When circumstances seemed to favor the cause of freedom they followed it; when the barometer of the new cause dropped, they quickly turned and, elusive as mercury, followed the Spaniards." [John] Lynch pointed to the same factor: "The creoles were committed to neither cause; seeking only to preserve their own position, they awaited the victory of the strongest." [Jorge] Basadre ascribed it to the conflict between the continentalism of Bolívar and the nationalism of Peruvians, making a strong case to show that many Peruvian leaders viewed Bolívar as a new Napoleon, combined with the "anguish and the disillusion of the aristocracy facing a war that seemed a continuous carnage accompanied by endless exactions and permanent anarchy." [Mariano] Paz Soldán, with the outspoken fervor of a man who was witnessing the subsequent turmoils of the Peruvian state, blamed it on the treason and ignorance of the nobles. [Ruben] Vargas Ugarte attributed it, fundamentally, to the inability of Peru to support two contending armies and to the material devastation caused by the war from 1821 to 1824.[2]

From September 1822, when San Martín retired from Peru, to September 1823, when Bolívar arrived, the government of the independent regime was in the hands of the Peruvian aristocrats who had so long desired to hold power. They established three separate administrations, all three of which failed to hold the government together or to strengthen independence. Congress, to which San Martín surrendered power, created an executive, the Governing Junta, which consisted of three undistinguished men—José de La Mar, a former royalist officer; Felipe Antonio Alvarado, noted only as the brother of General Rudesindo Alvarado, general-in-chief of the patriot army of the south; and Manuel Salazar y Baquíjano, the conde de Vista Florida. The junta could do nothing, for its powers were too limited and the times needed energetic and active leadership. General conditions remained very bad. The government had no money, troops and civil employees were not paid, criminals infested Lima and its outskirts, the army of the center remained inactive, desertion was endemic, the navy was insubordinate and mutinous. Forced loans could be collected only with threats of confiscation and exile.[3] Writing in November 1822, the English Protestant minister James Thomson, who came to Lima to set up a Lancastrian school system and to distribute copies of the Bible, reported: "At the moment there exists a great anxiety in the government for lack of money. . . . This seems to be the principal obstacle impeding the general independence of Peru."[4] Finally, on 21 January 1823, the Congress's major military offensive collapsed with the defeat at Moquegua of the first Intermedios expedition. A royalist army encamped at Jauja, within easy reach of the capital. Parliamentary rule could not stand the pressure. The patriot army urged Congress to appoint a stronger executive and enforced its demands with threatening troop movements. On 27 February 1823, therefore, Congress did away with the Governing Junta and appointed José de la Riva Agüero as first president of the republic.[5]

Riva Agüero's administration lasted less than four months. Yet in that short period its accomplishments were more than those of either its predecessor or its successor. Riva Agüero, a long-time supporter of independence and a dedicated nationalist, concentrated on restoring the fast-disappearing military order of the republic. He immediately invited Bolívar to send a Colombian army to aid in the cause of independence, despite his intense fears of the impact of Bolívar's involvement in Peruvian affairs. An army of 4,000 Colombian troops arrived under command of Bolívar's chief lieutenant, Antonio José de Sucre, but Bolívar himself as yet forbore to enter the maelstrom of Peruvian affairs. Within Peru itself Riva Agüero created and dispatched the second Intermedios expedition, composed of 5,000 troops. He reorganized the decadent navy, placing it under command of Jorge Guise. He created new battalions in several parts of the country and founded the Academia Militar. To help rescue the government from total bankruptcy, Riva Agüero presided over the first of the loans from London, negotiated by Juan García del Río and Diego Paroissien, who had originally been sent to Europe by San Martín. The first loan was for 1.2 million pounds. Riva Agüero also sent agents to Chile and to Buenos Aires in search of loans, but with little result.[6] The president even offered Viceroy La Serna a two-month armistice and treaty of peace, but the viceroy, certain of the imminent disintegration of the republic, rebuffed the suggestion.

Well might the viceroy bide his time, for the collapse of the republic was well advanced. Riva Agüero, who had been imposed by military pressure, did not even have the support of all the Congress. When the second Intermedios expedition departed from Lima, the capital itself was left with few defenses. Sucre, already on hand to send eyewitness reports to Bolívar, told his leader:

> The army has no chiefs; the country is as divided as the troops of the different states; Congress and the Executive are in discord and this will not have a happy result; there are no supplies for the troops and the little that can be acquired is poorly used. . . . In short, a thousand evils show themselves to presage that all will be destroyed and in the disintegration the Colombian division will be part of the ruins.[7]

Seeing his opportunity, royalist General [José] Canterac immediately moved down upon Lima. Unwilling to risk the newly arrived Colombian division in a futile defense of the city, on 17 June 1823 Sucre withdrew his forces to Callao, where he joined Riva Agüero, Congress, and the other civil political authorities who had already taken refuge there. The next day Canterac reoccupied Lima.

The civilian population of Lima responded to the royal reoccupation with what the cabildo called a "general emigration." This is confirmed by other sources. James Thomson said 10,000 persons fled Lima, and the British business agent Robert Proctor said that the only residents who stayed in Lima were those who were in no way identified with the patriot cause. Well might the civilians flee, for the royalists imposed a forced contribution of 300,000 pesos upon the city.[8] Nonetheless, not all the capital's residents resisted the Spaniards. A number of officials remained at their posts—for which they were later removed from office—and when the royalists departed a number of Limeños went with them.

Canterac, discovering once more that Lima was not defensible, abandoned it again in less than a month, on 16 July. When his army left the city it took what silver it could find from the churches, together with the machinery in the Casa de Moneda and many of the books and documents in the National Library—a total booty valued, according to Thomson, at more than 2 million pesos. When the royalists withdrew toward Cuzco, a number of Limeños threw themselves on royal protection and fled with them.[9] This was the second time Canterac proved he could come and go from Lima as he liked, and the second time the royalists voluntarily abandoned the capital on the grounds that it was a military liability.

While the patriots were taking refuge in Callao, Congress formally deposed Riva Agüero as president. Sucre was made supreme commander of the combined armies, and on 17 July Congress made the marqués de Torre Tagle chief executive. On 16 August he was formally created president of the republic by the part of Congress that continued to meet in Lima, but after Bolívar's arrival in Peru the next month Torre Tagle functioned merely as a figurehead in charge of the civilian government. Riva Agüero, meanwhile, transferred to Trujillo together with his supporters in the Congress, where he steadfastly refused to give up the presidential office or to recognize Torre Tagle. Torre Tagle replied by declaring Riva Agüero an outlaw and then by offering a reward to anyone who captured the tyrant dead or alive.[10] Peru now had two presidents, each of whom refused to recognize the legitimacy of the other. Torre Tagle proceeded to order the suspension or removal from office of all government employees who had remained in Lima during the month of Canterac's occupation, including the president of the High Court of Justice and several judges and departmental directors. This only guaranteed the further deterioration of civil government in Lima, already greatly disrupted. The interim president of the department of Lima, the regidor José Freyre, had fled to join his benefactor Riva Agüero; he was replaced as president of the department by the alcalde Juan de Echeverría y Ulloa.[11]

In the outlying vicinity of Lima the situation had reached a new low of confusion and disruption. The patriot government, while it was located in Callao, had ordered the killing of two oxen from every hacienda in the region of the capital to provide meat. The hacendados and the Lima city council begged for relief, charging that this policy would destroy not only the output of the farms but its occupants as well. There was no help for the hacendados, however. Before another six months had passed the majority of them had been totally ruined. In January 1824 a hacendado from Miraflores, near Lima, reported that the army's extortions had left him without slaves, cattle, mules, or seed. An outside witness estimated that the losses to this one hacienda in only one year amounted to 34,400 pesos. The hacendado asked to have a debt he owed the government excused. The fiscal of the Ministry of Finance replied that the problem of the supplicant was no different from that of a hundred other hacendados; his request should not be allowed or else the others would clamor for the same relief.[12] [Gustavo] Vergara Arias cites many other cases of haciendas that were destroyed by patriot montoneros who preyed on outlying farms to the point that it was often impossible to distinguish patriot guerrilla forces from bands of looters and common criminals. Proctor testified that the Spaniards took so many mules from Lima after their brief occupation in 1823 "that it cost more to carry merchandise from Callao to Lima than to bring it from England."[13]

Torre Tagle proceeded to organize a government, and he appointed as ministers Francisco Valdivieso for Foreign Affairs, Juan de Berindoaga for War and Navy, and Dionisio Vizcarra for Finance.[14] But as the time for Bolívar's arrival drew near it was clear that the independent state was absolutely bankrupt. All the fundamental sources of wealth had been exhausted. Special contributions continued to be decreed, of course, but they were simply not collected. Bolívar himself, shortly after his arrival, noted: "Lima is a large pleasant city which once was rich."[15] Robbery and civil unrest were uncontrolled. Major charitable agencies verged on collapse. The Lima public orphanage announced that it was unable to buy milk for the children and was about to close its doors. In November 1823 the dean of the archdiocese reported that the cathedral had no money left for salaries, music, or sacred rites. Even the Colombian auxiliary troops suffered from lack of arms, clothes, and equipment. As a result, they joined the other undisciplined forces in robbery and assault.[16]

All pretense to government credit or orderly borrowing by a sovereign power was abandoned. A forced loan for 150,000 pesos decreed against the merchants in August had to be reduced to 80,000 pesos later in the month, and even that sum caused considerable vexation for the people. In November, Torre Tagle negotiated another loan from a number of merchants that proved the government's desperation. The contract with the group of private merchants called for them to grant the government 50,000 pesos in cash and 150,000 pesos in goods, in return for a 300,000 peso lien against future customs. This effectively absorbed all future customs revenue, and the man who held the contract, José Ignacio Palacios, was even given the right to appoint his own customs officers. In September, Torre Tagle asked Chile for a new loan of 2 million pesos against the London loan. Chile refused, having already lent Peru 1.5 million pesos. The government had already drawn more than 1.5 million pesos against the London loan, while in the Riva Agüero period alone it had issued new contracts for supplies and arms to a value of 2.5 million pesos.[17]

Peru now entered a sort of nether world. Words are inadequate to describe the gravity of the situation or the extent of the anarchy.[18] From July 1823 until December 1824, the patriot cause seemed close to defeat. After the second Intermedios expedition was defeated and destroyed, the rump government of Riva Agüero in Trujillo made this clear by opening negotiations for settlement with Viceroy La Serna. Riva Agüero at first proposed the celebration of an armistice of eighteen months, during which time the definite peace with Spain would be arranged and joint Spanish-Peruvian forces would break up the rebel forces of the Lima government. Viceroy La Serna, encouraged by the collapse of the rebels and not able to decide which of the two presidents was the legitimate one with whom to negotiate, decided not to accept Riva Agüero's offer but appointed a representative to go to Trujillo to talk with him. In November 1823 Riva Agüero proposed a complete sellout, offering to establish a kingdom in Peru under a Spanish prince chosen by Ferdinand VII, with a provisional regency under La Serna, and based on the Spanish constitution. It would have been a type of independence—there is no question of that—but La Serna had no chance to reply to the proposal.

In the midst of the confusion one thing had become undeniable: the presence of Simón Bolívar himself was now required to prevent the total collapse of independence. Responding to the frequent appeals from the Peruvians, Bolívar sailed for Lima, arriving on 1 September 1823, more than a year after San Martín had made way for him. Despite the intense suspicion many Peruvians felt toward him—many of them viewed the Colombian president as a Napoleonic usurper—all the civil and ecclesiastical authorities turned out to greet him.[19] Bolívar allowed Congress to make him military dictator and commander of all the various armies in Peru. He immediately encountered the frustration of trying to deal with Peruvian suspicion of his motives, and he wrote: "I shall always be the foreigner to most people and I shall always arouse jealousy and distrust in these gentlemen. . . . I have already regretted that I came here."[20] Indeed, when Bolívar tried to initiate talks with Riva Agüero in Trujillo his approach was rejected by the rebellious ex-president, who viewed Bolívar as a tyrant and usurper. Torre Tagle was no less suspicious but depended too much on the Colombian forces to act freely.

Shortly after Bolívar's arrival the Peruvian army of the south disintegrated. Determined to secure the north if possible, the Liberator traveled toward Trujillo to try to effect a reconciliation with Riva Agüero. Before he could arrive there, however, Riva Agüero was overthrown, on 25 November 1823, by one of his own military aides, Antonio Gutiérrez de la Fuente. Convinced that Riva Agüero's negotiations with the royalists constituted open treason, de la Fuente marched to Trujillo and deposed him. The former president was imprisoned in Guayaquil, where he was eventually freed by

Vice-Admiral Guise, commander of the Peruvian navy. He then went into exile in Europe.

After the disappearance of Riva Agüero, Bolívar returned to Lima. Finding it impossible to improve the military and supply situation there, he determined in late 1823 to move to the north, where he could regroup an army free of the pestilential anarchy of Lima. He wrote: "Providence only . . . can create order out of this chaos."[21] Traveling north by sea, Bolívar fell gravely ill. On 1 January 1824 he was carried from his ship to the little harbor of Pativilca, thirty miles north of Lima. There he lay for two months, fighting for his life against the first attack of the tuberculosis that eventually killed him. From his sickbed on 12 January he informed Torre Tagle that he would resign and return to Bogotá if fresh supplies and money were not sent to his Colombian army of the north within one month.[22]

And now, in the first months of 1824, the inevitable collapse of the patriot cause occurred. With the armies deserting, with the Liberator desperately trying to recover his health, the final straw came when Torre Tagle emulated his erstwhile opponent Riva Agüero in committing treason. Torre Tagle sent his minister of war, [Juan de] Berindoaga, to negotiate a settlement with the royalists. Bolívar was not opposed to a truce, which would allow time for the 8,000 Colombian reinforcements he had ordered to arrive. Torre Tagle, however, apparently contemplated more than a mere cease-fire. Berindoaga went to Jauja to talk with the royalists. The talks came to nothing, however, and Berindoaga returned to Lima, where Torre Tagle informed him that he and the vice-president, Diego de Aliaga, had opened negotiations of their own with the royalists, this time without Bolívar's knowledge or consent.[23] Torre Tagle's representative traveled to Yca to confer with the royalists who had recently taken the town, saying that the president desired to unite with the Spaniards in order to resist the Colombian usurper Bolívar. Whether an actual conspiracy for the royal seizure of Lima with Torre Tagle's connivance was formulated is not clear. At any rate, General Canterac, leading the royal forces that were advancing toward Lima, understood he would have Torre Tagle's support. Bolívar, still at Pativilca, understood the same, and he ordered Torre Tagle, Aliaga, and Berindoaga—the president, vice-president, and minister of war of the republic—to be arrested and sent to him. Torre Tagle interpreted this as an order for his execution, and he panicked. What was he to do now?

The answer came quickly. In the midst of these Machiavellian negotiations the patriot troops in Callao—now the only usable forces on hand in the capital—had been ignored by the civil authorities. Motivated by their lack of pay and unwilling to transfer to the north as ordered by Bolívar, the Argentinian and Chilean forces garrisoning Callao's forts mutinied on 5 February 1824, under the leadership of a sergeant named Dámaso

Moyano. Unable to attract any attention to their privation, on 10 February the mutineers released all the royalist prisoners in the jails at Callao, and one of them, Colonel José de Casariego, assumed command of the place, raising the Spanish flag. Meantime, in preparation for the expected advance of royalist forces, Bolívar had ordered General Enrique Martínez to retire from the capital, leaving it undefended, and taking with him anything that might be useful to the enemy, including the horses and clothes of the civilians. Bolívar appointed General Mariano Necochea, an Argentinian, to command the capital. On 10 February Congress went into recess; on 17 February Torre Tagle turned his command over to Necochea; on 27 February—again motivated by the impossibility of defending the capital—Necochea abandoned Lima. Two days later the royalists, under General Juan Antonio Monet, occupied the city. This time the republic was in complete collapse. The civilians, with Callao denied them as a refuge, were unable to flee the Spaniards.

The disorder and chaos of that last week of February 1824 was on a scale Lima had never before experienced. Robert Proctor left a detailed account of the terror provoked by the mutiny at Callao. A few days before the mutiny, Proctor and his wife had traveled to Chorrillos—the "Brighton of Lima," as he described it—to take their oldest child to the pure air of that seaside resort. Hearing in the meantime that their newborn infant, left behind in Lima, had been taken critically ill, he and his wife rushed back to Lima on 27 February. It took them many hours to travel the few miles' distance, dodging royalist troops, mutinous patriots, bandits, and guerrillas. At the walls of Lima a band of patriot soldiers tried to force them to detour to royalist-held Callao. After bribing the soldiers, they entered the city and found to their horror that it was already in the hands of the mutinous Callao garrison, Necochea having retreated only that morning. Proctor's landladies, royalists like so many other propertied persons, were "overwhelmed by pleasure at the entry of their royalist friends," and only with effort could they be restrained from walking out into the streets to greet their liberators. The mutineers, however, were not rescuers but looters. As night fell, Lima embarked on a nightmare. Proctor stood on his balcony and watched the fighting swirl about him as rampaging soldiers from Callao sacked houses and shops at will. Mounted grenadiers smashed down the doors of neighboring houses and stripped them bare. "We saw much of what went on. . . . It was a horrible night for Lima." The next morning he ventured into the plaza, where he watched the officers of the mutineers shooting the looters without hearing or trial, and he noted that among those executed was the innocent servant of an English friend of his. "Everyone fervently prayed now for the entry of some respectable force, even though it be the enemy, for protection." That same night Proctor's house in Chorrillos was looted by Callao troops, and his child and the nursemaid were forced at gunpoint to reveal the hiding place of the valuables that had been transferred there for safekeeping. The robbers carried off the plate and valuables in bags made from the family's clothing. After smashing all the furniture in the house, the looters fled. The child and servant returned to Lima and reported that the highway was filled with bandit montoneros who insulted the servant girl and threw lighted matches at them through the carriage windows. Two days later the royal army of 3,500 well-disciplined men—Spaniards, creoles, Indians, and blacks—entered Lima, and the distracted and terrified population, forgetting all politics and politicians, silently watched their arrival.[24] The main body of royal forces marched on to Callao but left 200 soldiers behind to patrol the city.

The royalist General Monet offered amnesty to any inhabitant of Lima who would support the restored royalists. In the heat of the moment, and in a mad dash to save their own necks, almost the entire leadership of the republic went over. Since the royalists had refused Torre Tagle's request to regard him as a prisoner of war, he went over to their side instead. Following the lead of the president of the republic, others rushed to save themselves. They included the vice-president, Diego de Aliaga; Carlos Pedemonte, president of Congress and bishop of Trujillo, the patriots' choice for archbishop of Lima; Juan de Berindoaga, minister of war; the president of the department of Lima; various congressmen; many civil employees; and more than 240 military chiefs, together with many distinguished citizens.[25] The conde de Villar de Fuente—former head of the Consulado in royalist days—became governor of the city. There was no patriot army left; the royalists surrounded the city and were taking the provinces. Independence appeared lost.

Basadre makes a good case that the creole aristocrats who went over to the royalists were motivated chiefly by their exhaustion with the war and by the apparent impossibility of winning it. When Bolívar arrived and took leadership from them, they began to speak of the Liberator's regime in terms of "slavery," "tyranny," and "despotism." Viewing the War of Independence as nothing more than a civil war between Spaniards and Colombians, they determined that they were, after all, more closely aligned spiritually and culturally with the Spaniards. Their class prejudices led them to view the rough Colombian soldiers as their enemies, the cultivated royalists as their peers. Torre Tagle wrote Berindoaga: "I have resolved myself in my heart to be more a Spaniard than Don Fernando."[26] At Pativilca, Bolívar—faced with the defection of the entire leadership of the patriot cause—poured out his anger toward the Peruvians. "On all sides I hear the sounds of disaster. My era is that of catastrophe. Everything comes to life and perishes before my eyes as though struck by lightning."[27]

The extent of the turnabout in Lima was far greater than a mere temporary reoccupation by the royalists. The Spaniards held Lima from Feb-

ruary until December 1824, with occasional retreats to Callao when patriot forces drew near. Callao was the bastion, and it remained in royalist
hands without interruption until January 1826. General José Ramón Rodil
held Callao and was governor and intendant. In Lima life returned to something resembling normality in the good old days of the viceroyalty. It is
true that Viceroy La Serna remained in Cuzco, but in Lima life was much
the same as before. The Consulado was reorganized under its former con-
suls Francisco Xavier Izcue and Manuel Exhelme and pledged its support
to Rodil and the "legitimate cause." The cabildo met (though its acts have
disappeared; probably they were later lost in Callao) and, most important,
it consisted of many of the same members as in 1820. Such stalwart "republicans" as Juan de Echeverría (Torre Tagle's president of the department of Lima), Francisco Moreyra (the liberal of the 1812–14 period),
the marqués de Montemira (son of the field marshal La Serna had left in
command of Lima in 1821), and even the firebrand young radical of the
1810s the conde de la Vega del Ren sat placidly on the cabildo and col-
laborated with the royalists. The cabildo publicly thanked Rodil for creating a mobile column under Colonel Mateo Ramírez to defend the city
from the rebel guerrilla bands that terrorized the vicinity. The royalist
propaganda sheet *Triunfo del Callao* announced that perfect harmony
reigned between the military authorities and the civil authorities of Lima
and its environs.[28] Even the Protestant Thomson was allowed to keep open
his Lancastrian school. It had 230 students and was housed in the former
Dominican college.[29]

And in the most extraordinary act of all, on 6 March Torre Tagle issued a public manifesto, edited by Berindoaga, calling on the citizens to
support the royalists:

> The tyrant Bolívar and his indecent satellites have wanted to enslave
> Peru and make this opulent territory a subject of Colombia.
> Peruvians: Bolívar is the greatest monster that has existed in this
> land. He is the enemy of all honorable men, of all those who oppose his
> ambitions. The national army offers you constant security, it has been
> joined by the leading authorities, the most distinguished men of the
> country.
> Men of all classes who live in Peru, unite and come to the salvation
> of the land that Bolívar wants to convert into a desert.[30]

In response to this plea, so many deserters came to join the royalists that
they were able to create a volunteer Cuerpo de Cívicos of 600 men to keep
order in the city.[31]

During the year of royal administration of Lima, several forced donations and loans were taken among the citizens, the 5 percent tax on urban
real estate was reestablished, the customs was reopened, and various other
sources of revenue were found. The royalists collected at Lima 511,644
pesos—all in silver—during the year. That was not, of course, on a par

with revenues before 1820, but it was not bad in the circumstances. Lima spent almost all that sum on its own military expenses and pledged a further 238,000 pesos to the royalist army of the north. The naval headquarters at Callao spent 334,000 pesos more on the royal naval squadron that was now gathered. The squadron consisted of one ship of the line, one heavily armed corvette, three brigantines, and several transport and support ships, a total of ten vessels.[32] This force was sufficient to protect Callao but not to face open encounters with the combined naval forces of Peru, Chile, and Colombia that on the whole continued to command the coast. The Spanish fleet remained under the protection of Callao's forts until the Battle of Ayacucho, whereupon it abandoned American waters. The Peruvian squadron under Guise had established a blockade of Callao, but apparently it was not possible to hold it firm at all times. At any rate, the land forces thrown up by Bolívar under Colonel Luis Urdaneta to prevent communications between Lima and the royalists in the highlands were not successful. The royalists in Callao were able to come out of the forts to provision themselves, twice undertaking sallies into the Valley of Chancay, where the patriot militia and montoneros abandoned the field. Similarly, the outguards of the occupation forces in Lima ventured into the countryside in May and July without being stopped by the patriots.[33]

Even the Lima Casa de Moneda churned back into action under the royalists. Its new director was none other than the former vice-president Diego de Aliaga. He reported to Rodil in April that the mint was completely ruined but that he could make it serviceable again after some repairs. Incredible as it may seem—given that the mint was the first target of each of Lima's occupiers—Aliaga actually got it producing again. In May General Canterac in Huancayo sent Viceroy La Serna two pesos newly minted in Lima. Nonetheless, in June Viceroy La Serna decreed the creation of a new Casa de Moneda in Cuzco, because as long as Bolívar remained on Peruvian soil he did not wish to depend entirely on the reactivated mint in Lima. Furthermore, the mines at Cerro de Pasco, which supplied Lima, were not producing, whereas mines were active in the provinces of Cuzco and Puno, under royal control and closer to Cuzco. In recognition of what it apparently perceived as its increased status, in April the cabildo of Cuzco formally asked Spain to declare Cuzco the capital of Peru. The financial affairs of the royal forces were sufficiently stable that Rodil began granting permissions in Callao for the export of cash on foreign merchant ships, whereas in March Bolívar ordered a complete ban on the export of gold and silver from the territory under his control.[34]

By the end of March 1824 the powers of the patriots were at their lowest ebb. In that month Bolívar established his headquarters in Trujillo and watched more or less helplessly as royal forces took most of the rest of the country. Bolívar actually controlled only one province, though to be sure it was the one best situated for his purpose, which was to keep his army intact until the expected reinforcements could arrive from Colombia. For the time being he was forced to order his Peruvian troops to pitch their camps in the north of the province and the Colombians to camp in the south, thus preventing the Peruvians from going over to the enemy and the Colombians from deserting back home. His only immediate purpose was to wait, to survive, and to keep the army from disintegrating like the Chilean army in the south of Peru. He wrote: "I expect much of time. . . . What matters to us after all is to keep intact at any cost."[35]

La Serna, meanwhile, did not let down his guard. At no time was he prepared to predict success. But there was a certain air of cautious optimism about his letter to Spain in March 1824. Ferdinand VII had been restored to full absolutist powers in December 1823. La Serna now wrote to say that of all the dangerous elements he had faced in his command in Peru the most divisive had been the Constitution. Declaring that in the past he had not let his real feelings be known, he said that he had nonetheless abolished the constitutional system in every location that fell under his control during the campaign of 1823. He issued a formal decree on 11 March 1824 in Cuzco, abolishing all the acts of the constitutional government. Tadeo Gárate, royal intendant of Puno, reported that twelve provinces had now been reduced to royal control and that in abolishing the Constitution Peru had undergone a "happy transition from democracy or anarchy to a legitimate Government recognized by all the world."[36] In the first months of 1824, therefore, the royalist commanders had considerable grounds for self-congratulation; they appeared to be on the verge of complete success. Like Bolívar, they had consciously aimed at riding out the storm with their forces intact so as to be able to retake Peru as soon as the rebels had destroyed themselves through internal dissension.

Bolívar, however, did not give up. Dedicated to the proposition that, as he wrote Sucre, "We are the executors of South America," he turned his attention to rebuilding his forces in Trujillo. Perhaps at no other point in his career did his genius for organizing and commanding men and his commitment to the cause effect such a significant change in patriot fortunes. In only three months he drew together an army of almost 10,000 men, consisting of the Colombian forces and what survivors there were from earlier patriot forces. The army's training was entrusted to a polyglot group of officers—Colombian, Argentinian, Peruvian, and English. The civilian population of Trujillo was marshaled to sew uniforms, cloth was commandeered from the residents, tin and other metals collected. Windows were stripped of their iron grills, and even house keys were melted down. To keep his soldiers paid and loyal, Bolívar first reduced their pay to one-fourth, then confiscated the church silver in the province of Trujillo to pay them. He also ordered the temporary confiscation of all private property of anyone living in the territory controlled by the Spaniards, even if they were themselves patriot sympathizers.[37] To free himself and his commanders from civilian political turmoil—the downfall of each of the patriot leaders before him—he turned all government affairs over to one person, the Peruvian José Faustino Sánchez Carrión, a man of noted ability and patriotism. It was Sánchez Carrión, indeed, who was most responsible for provisioning the new army and for creating its revenue and supply networks. In March 1824 Bolívar created him "minister general of the affairs of the Peruvian republic." After the patriot victory, Sánchez Carrión continued as minister of government and foreign affairs until his death shortly after on 2 June 1825.[38]

In short, the great key to Bolívar's success was that he concentrated his attention exclusively on the creation and support of an army whose only job was to carry the war into the highlands that stretched from Jauja to Cuzco, where the royalists had their stronghold. With Colombia at his back to supply horses, mules, and manpower, Bolívar virtually ignored coastal Peru and most of all Lima. Indeed, retaking Lima was not even a serious objective. That would come in time, but it would be of value only if the main body of royal forces had been defeated in the mountains. Bolívar set his troops to work training in the mountains to help acclimate them to the altitude. He acquired 10,000 cattle as a reserve meat supply. The cavalrymen were given mules to carry their arms and supplies so that their service horses could be kept fresh. To bivouac the troops in their journey to the highlands, Bolívar ordered shelters stocked with food and water. If the royalists were to be defeated it could only be by military strength, and that was his objective. On 15 June Bolívar ordered his troops to begin their march to the highlands. He wrote, "I am possessed by the demon of war and am about to end this fight one way or another."[39]

Early in 1824 the patriots received an unexpected but critical assist through the defection of the royal commander of the army in Upper Peru since 1820, General Pedro Antonio Olañeta. General Olañeta despised Viceroy La Serna, General Canterac, and General Jerónimo Valdés, the three chief royal officers who had themselves once been his superiors in Upper Peru. In January 1824, having been informed via Buenos Aires of the fall of the liberal regime in Spain before La Serna himself knew of it, Olañeta openly mutinied against the viceroy, overthrowing the constitutionalist government in Upper Peru and replacing it with an absolutist regime of his own. Faced with virtual civil war within his own ranks, viceroy La Serna sent General Valdés, commander of the royal army of the south, to deal with the revolt. On 11 February 1824 Olañeta entered Chuquisaca, where he proclaimed absolute monarchy and the abolition of the constitutional system. He appointed his followers to the audiencia and declared himself commander of the "Provinces of the Río de la Plata."

Valdés realized he was unable to depose the entrenched Olañeta, who was surrounded by his own followers and family and widely supported by the conservative Upper Peruvian elite. On 9 March 1824 the two commanders signed an agreement by which Olañeta was permitted to remain commander in Upper Peru in return for recognizing La Serna's authority, furnishing troops to the royalists in Lower Peru, and submitting to Valdés's commands. When Valdés withdrew, however, Olañeta broke his agreement and assumed direct political command of Upper Peru.[40] It should be noted that Olañeta's treason occurred only a month before La Serna himself abolished the Constitution, which shows that it was more an attempt to seize power than a crusade to restore a particular political system.

The most damaging impact of the Olañeta rebellion was that it deprived La Serna of the security of a friendly Upper Peru, while it absorbed the attention of Valdés's army of the south at the very moment (March 1824) that Bolívar in the north was at his weakest and most vulnerable to a combined assault. In June 1824 Olañeta rejected an ultimatum from Viceroy La Serna ordering him to submit to his command. After the royalist defeat at Junín, General Valdés left Upper Peru to join the main viceregal army, leaving Olañeta in command of what would shortly become Bolivia. Bolívar, of course, rejoiced at this turn of events. He declared: "The Spanish now also suffer the influence of the evil star of Peru. The Pizarros and Almagros fought each other. La Serna fought Pezuela . . . now Olañeta is fighting with La Serna."[41] Recognizing that nothing more advantageous could possibly happen to him, Bolívar wrote Olañeta assuring him of his friendship, and the Upper Peruvian rebel replied in kind. A few months later the victorious army of Sucre defeated Olañeta in battle and mortally wounded him, thereby winning the independence of Bolivia.

The Spanish royalists in Peru were stunned by Olañeta's treason. In a long and bitter memorial, La Serna's representatives in Spain wrote to the peninsular government to survey the multitude of glories La Serna and his officers had achieved since they took power in January 1821. Reviewing the great royal campaign of 1822 and 1823, they concluded that the insurgents had lost nearly 18,000 men, mostly from desertion, in the same period that the viceroy had kept his armies intact and in fighting form. All of this campaign was now being risked by the treason of Olañeta. La Serna had saved Peru, he had saved the army, he was on the verge of victory, when suddenly the insubordination of one man wrecked his chance to recover all of Peru. They urged that Olañeta be called to court to answer for his conduct. The king, however, proved that he was unworthy of the loyalty of La Serna and his men by subsequently appointing Olañeta viceroy of Buenos Aires, on Olañeta's claim that he could reconquer the La Plata region. In an incredible Council of Indies consultation, the councilors voted to overrule the strong objections of La Serna, Canterac, and Valdés and allow Olañeta's appointment to stand, for Olañeta was the king's kind of man.[42]

Bolívar's army, which had set out from Trujillo on 15 June ascended into the Andes in a month. By 15 July the army crossed the Andes and reached Pasco. On 6 August, outside Canterac's headquarters of Jauja, the patriot army confronted the royalists in the battle of Junín. The royalists were defeated, breaking formation and fleeing from the field. La Serna's northern supply lines were cut, although Canterac managed to retreat to Cuzco with most of his army intact.

Four months passed quietly, as both La Serna and Bolívar collected their forces in preparation for what was now viewed as the decisive test. The Spanish highland bastion had been breached at last. Far away from Lima and the turbulent coastal desert the future of Peru would be decided, in the clear, cold air where Spain had first won Peru three centuries before. In the interim, Bolívar departed for the coast to organize his government throughout the districts that now fell into patriot hands. General Sucre was left in charge of the army in the mountains, with full authority to determine its future course of action. In September a blockade was established at Callao, and Lima began to undergo daily harassment from patriot guerrilla bands.

As Bolívar approached the capital, the royalist defense there fell apart. A series of skirmishes occurred, chiefly between unimportant guerrilla or montonero groups of both sides. The suffering of the Limeños during this period was great, not only from privation but from fear. Too many of them had deserted the patriot side to be content with the prospect of Bolívar bearing down upon them. Guerrilla forces from both sides entered and left the city at any hour, committing robberies and spreading terror. Thomson testified, "As a consequence of all this the anguish that existed in the city was very great, and it was aggravated by the increase in forced contributions. . . . This was, perhaps, in former times . . . the richest city in the world, but now, it can be said with all certainty, it is the poorest."[43] On 2 November the patriot vanguard was repulsed from outside Callao but took refuge in Lima. The patriots occupied Lima temporarily, and Colonel José María Eqúsquiza was named governor, but they had to abandon it quickly on 4 December owing to an attack from the defenders of the Real Felipe of Callao who entered the capital with two pieces of artillery. The royalists then retired to the castles, and the patriot forces again returned to take Lima.[44] On 7 December 1824, Bolívar entered the now patriot-held city and proceeded to organize its defense. Callao, however, remained securely in royalist hands, and thousands of civilian collaborators fled to the protection of the impregnable fortresses.

In November, Viceroy La Serna united all the highland royalist forces, some 9,300 men, and marched out of Cuzco in a concerted offensive in search of Sucre. For a month Sucre retreated while La Serna exhausted his men in a rapid march in search of the patriots. By 1 December the two armies were marching parallel to each other. La Serna mistakenly believed Sucre was becoming entrapped, but Sucre had received orders from Bolívar authorizing him to take the offensive whenever he chose. On 8 December Sucre stopped his retreat and faced La Serna across a series of deep ditches. Aware that defeat would mean certain destruction—the patriot army consisted of only 5,780 men and proroyalist Indians in the area had been armed to pick off any retreating patriots—Sucre counted on his army's fighting with extra valor. The royalist army, on the other hand, was exhausted, not only from the last month's forced march but, perhaps, from the last four years of resistance. The great battle of Ayacucho began on the morning of 9 December. After hours of fierce fighting the royalist lines collapsed under the enthusiastic charge of the Colombian infantry. Viceroy La Serna was taken prisoner, and the royalist army was defeated. Shortly thereafter, General Canterac appeared before Sucre with an offer of surrender. The capitulation was signed that same day. It consisted of eighteen articles, mainly allowing the royalist troops and officers to leave Peru in honor if they chose or to remain in their positions if they took an oath of allegiance to independence. The patriots renewed their pledge to recognize nonmilitary debts inherited from the viceroyalty. One clause called for royalist-held Callao to surrender within twenty days.

The battle of Ayacucho was a total patriot victory and the most decisive encounter in all the American wars of independence. Spanish power in Peru was broken. More than that, Spanish power was ended on the entire continent, for La Serna's army was the last major royal force still intact. For the first time the royalists had no backup, no territory into which they could retreat, no other army to call upon. Having thrown his combined forces into the battle, La Serna lost everything in a single blow. Sucre, now bearing the title marshal of Ayacucho, swept on to final victory over the rebel Olañeta in Upper Peru in April 1825, thus establishing the independence of Bolivia. The future of Abascal's great viceroyalty was decided on the battlefield.

Peru was now independent. On 21 December 1824 Bolívar called for the reinstallation of Congress. Still vested with the title of dictator, he turned his attention to organizing and governing a devastated country. Most of the leading Spanish officers left the country on various foreign merchantmen. La Serna and three of his generals sailed on a French ship.[45] On his arrival home, La Serna was given the noble title conde de los Andes, although in a way his higher honor might well have been the deference and respect paid to him and to Canterac and Valdés by marshal Sucre in the days immediately after Ayacucho, for it was the respect the victor owed the vanquished for his long years of defending the king's patrimony. The story of the extinction of royal power in Peru should end there, but it does not. There is a final tragic footnote that shows the extent to which the decision of Ayacucho was a purely military solution.

The capitulation of Ayacucho called for the royal defenders of Callao to surrender as well. No one imagined that General José Ramón Rodil, Spanish governor of Callao, would refuse. Yet when Bolívar informed Rodil of the royal army's defeat, the commander refused even to receive a patriot representative. When Viceroy La Serna sent his own commissioner to order Rodil to give up the forts, he again refused to surrender. Rodil possessed two battalions and a brigade of artillery, a total of more than 2,500 soldiers, commanded by competent officers. The forts were well provided with livestock and other necessities, the towers and ramparts had been reinforced, and the commander expected help to arrive from Spain.[46] Furthermore, when Lima fell to the patriots in early December, at least 3,800 civilian refugees had sought protection with the royal forces in the forts. Among them were former president Torre Tagle and his family, former vice-president Aliaga and his family, former minister of war Berindoaga, nobles, merchants, members of Congress, and collaborators of the royalists. Though Rodil obviously felt no obligation toward the civilians, he was determined to restore the honor of the royal flag by holding on to the strongest fortification on the entire Pacific coast. Thus Callao came to play the role for which it was destined. Never conquered, never breached, it now became the last bastion of Spain in Peru. The year-long siege of Callao began. It was the final death watch not only of Spanish power but of the more self-serving members of the old Lima elite as well.

The patriots, distracted by the liberation of Bolivia and exhausted by their exertions, instituted an unenthusiastic siege. The naval blockade, which began in December 1824 with the Chilean fleet, ultimately came to include Peruvian and Colombian ships as well. To supply Lima, Bolívar had to declare Chorrillos the official port city. The land siege was established at Bellavista, a mile from the forts. In the midst of constant skirmishes, the patriots were able to deny the castles any further livestock or supplies. They did not, however, attempt a general assault.

In the castles, Rodil—who by most accounts was obsessed with the essentially pointless defense of the forts—imposed a regimen of espionage and terror. The occupants included not only Spanish and Peruvian veteran soldiers but patriot prisoners from the earlier rebellion of Moyanos, as well as civilian nobles, commoners, wives, and children. As many as 200 persons were executed by Rodil for conspiracy. A special espionage system was created, and the slightest sign of protest was cause for execution. When a priest named Marieluz refused to divulge to Rodil the secrets of the confessional, he was shot. Food supplies slowly ran out. Mariano Torrente says chickens sold among the refugees for 25 to 30 pesos each. As food supplies disappeared, Rodil determined that those civilians who had not brought six months' supplies with them were to be expelled. Little by little, 2,380 civilian refugees were forced out into the no-man's-land separating the forts from the patriot army. In the first weeks the patriots received the expelled civilians, but when they realized that the object of sending them out was to preserve supplies for the royalist soldiers, the patriots decided not to admit the civilians behind their lines. Many starved to death in the mile of land separating the two sides. In May, for example, twenty women were expelled from the castles but not allowed behind patriot lines. When they tried to gain readmittance to the forts Rodil ordered volleys fired over their heads. Ultimately the patriots relented and received them.[47] Rodil did release some patriot prisoners left over from Moyanos's mutiny the year before, not out of humanity, but to save precious stores and because he feared conspiracy. At one point, however, he executed thirty-six of these patriots after a riot.

After May 1825 Rodil ordered rations only for civil employees, soldiers, and collaborators. The refugees and soldiers ate horses, mules, cats, dogs, and even rats. When they were gone, the people began to die of starvation. An epidemic of scurvy and typhus swept the fort, adding considerably to the death toll. There is no consensus on the total number of deaths, and Rodil himself gave no figure for the civilians. Torrente says that 6,000 persons died of starvation and disease and 767 more died in actual military combat defending the forts. Mendiburu says that in the main fort, the Real Felipe, there were 7,000 persons, of whom only 2,300 survived. Vargas Ugarte says more than 5,000 died in the castles, not counting the 200 Rodil executed. When the forts finally surrendered in January 1826, only about 400 defenders remained alive among the soldiers, and of these only 94 chose to go to Spain, implying that the rest were Peruvians. When he returned to Spain, Rodil gave the death toll among the veteran soldiers as 2,095, with 444 survivors.[48]

Subtracting the military deaths from the total leaves anywhere from 2,700 to about 4,000 civilians who died. The lower figure is probably more accurate. These civilians included several of the foremost Peruvian leaders of the independent state. Former president Torre Tagle, who insisted till the end that he was actually a prisoner of the Spaniards, died after nine months of siege, as did his wife and son. Diego de Aliaga, the vice-president, also died, as did his brother Juan de Aliaga, conde de San Juan Lurigancho. Others included the conde de Villar de Fuente, former prior of the Consulado and governor of Lima during the Spanish occupation of 1824, and Isidro Cortazar, conde de San Isidro, the director of San Martín's paper money bank. Gaspar Rico, the royalists' most faithful propagandist, left Callao alive but died a few days later from the effects of the siege. Torre Tagle's minister of war, Berindoaga, attempted to escape on 2 October, disguised as a fisherman, but his boat was captured by a patriot patrol. He was sent to Lima for trial on charges of treason, found guilty, and executed in the main plaza on 15 April 1826. The fate of these representatives of the old-line creole elite puts the final capstone on their whole history of indecision and self-aggrandizement. Buried in unmarked graves, their names not even recorded, the last resisters of independence, like the viceroyalty of Peru itself, died a lingering, agonizing death.

On 11 January 1826 Rodil agreed to receive patriot negotiators, and an agreement for the surrender of the forts was signed on 22 January. Of the surviving defenders, most returned to Lima, while a few went to the dockside in Callao to try to get passage on the English frigate *Briton* then in port. Rodil and some other officers sailed on that ship. They arrived in Spain in August 1826, and before he could even disembark Rodil was granted the distinction of a commander's cross in the Order of Isabel La Católica.[49] So high was Ferdinand's estimation of him that in the future Rodil became captain general of Cuba and of the Philippines, minister of war, and president of the Council of Ministers. He received the noble title marqués de Rodil, and upon Ferdinand's death he was made guardian of the king's two daughters.

To Spain it appeared that Rodil had upheld the honor of the flag in the face of universal defeat. Spain did not accept Peru's independence and continued for several years, partly inspired by last-ditch stands like Rodil's, to plan the reconquest of the "rebellious overseas provinces." Spaniards, of course, had a different perspective on Peruvian independence. What Spaniards saw was that the independence of Peru—which in itself constituted a mere separation, not a social or political revolution within the country—had been achieved in only two battles, in a decision of arms.

The image that lingers in the mind, at any rate, is the one provided by Torre Tagle, Aliaga, Perindoaga, and the other 3,800 or more civilian refugees in Callao. No matter how unedifying it may be, their conversion back to the royal side suggests that many politically active citizens had not yet chosen independence. Three thousand eight hundred persons was a considerable portion of the total population of Lima—three hundred more than the total number who had signed the Declaration of Independence in 1821. No matter how mixed their motives might have been, these people were still voting against independence with their feet. Even though the royal government had collapsed and its leaders had already fled the country, they preferred to cling to the belief that Spanish power might reassert itself. Submitting their destinies, and their lives, to the control of a fanatic megalomaniac was preferable to residing peacefully under the command of Bolívar and his Colombian army. Ayacucho—the glory of America—did not constitute a referendum for these Peruvians. Whether they were right or wrong, whether they misunderstood the motives of the victor and the purposes of the vanquished, across a century and a half they still bear stark witness that as late as 1825 the vigorous sentiment expressed in the 1821 Declaration of Independence—"That the general will is decided in favor of the Independence of Peru from Spanish domination"—was not unequivocally true.

Manuel Vidaurre—that troubled royal oidor of Cuzco who eventually supported independence and returned to Peru in 1824—wrote about this inability to give up the heritage of three centuries in his *Cartas Americanas* (1823). His words assume an immensely tragic significance when viewed in the light of the refugees in Callao, for their duality was his. He wrote:

> I love the Spanish nation like a grandmother, and the American like a mother. I weep to see these beloved persons destroyed. The one, old but inexperienced and with bad habits that impel it . . . to domination and conquest. The other, young, weak, without resources, going from desperation to faint-heartedness, from heroism to barbarity, with signs of virtue and with many vices.[50]

This was the Peruvians' dilemma. To give up the old empire, with all its ancient grievances of disrespect for American pretensions, monopoly, absolute monarchy, arbitrariness, and frustration meant throwing themselves blindly into a future that threatened many evils, social destruction, militarism, and possible foreign domination by their northern neighbors. No, Peru was not dragged kicking and screaming into independence. Neither did it embrace the new day of independence with joy and anticipation of good fortune. It staggered on, impelled by forces it could not control, afraid of the future but burdened by the past. None of the other Spanish American independence movements is so profoundly troubling. A considerable portion of the population of Lima resisted independence to the very end, and many paid with their lives. The event was accomplished, the deed was done, and Peruvians still had not decided.

Notes

1. Quoted in Gerhard Masur, *Simón Bolívar* (Albuquerque:University of New Mexico Press, 1948), p. 358.

2. Ibid., p. 360; John Lynch, *The Spanish American Revolutions, 1808–1826* (New York: W.W. Norton, 1973), p. 266; Jorge Basadre, *Historia de la república del Péru*. 10 vols. 6th ed., aug. (Lima: Editorial Universitaria, 1968–70), 1:75; Mariano Felipe Paz Soldán, *Historia del Perú independiente*. 2 parts, 2 vols. each. Lima, 1868–74, Facsimile reproduction (Buenos Aires, Instituto Nacional Sanmartiniano, 1962), part 2, 1:44; Ruben Vargas Ugarte, *Historia general del Perú*. 6 vols. (Barcelona: I.G. Seix y Barral Hnos., 1966), 6:302.

3. Francisco Valdivieso to Rafael Menendez, Lima, 20 January 1823, Archivo Nacional del Perú, Archivo Histórico de Hacienda (hereafter cited as ANP, AHH), OL 70–31.

4. James Thomson, "Impresiones de Lima entre 1822 y 1824," in Estuardo Núñez, ed., *Relaciones de Viajeros*, 4 vols. Tome 27 of *Colección documental de la independencia del Perú* (hereafter cited as CDIP) (Lima: Comisión Nacional del Sesquicentenario de la Independencia del Perú, 1971), 2:15.

5. Basadre, *Historia de la república*, 1:24–28; Vargas Ugarte, *Historia general del Perú*, 6:241–50.

6. Basadre, *Historia de la república*, 1:31–34; Vargas Ugarte, *Historia general del Perú*, 6:252–54; for a study on the long-term effect of the British loans subsequently taken by Peru see W.M. Mathew, "The Imperialism of Free Trade: Peru, 1820–1870," *Economic History Review* 21 (1968): 562–79; and for the history of this first loan see Mathew, "The First Anglo-Peruvian Debt and Its Settlement, 1822–49," *Journal of Latin American Studies* 2, no. 1 (May 1970): 81–98.

7. Quoted in Basadre, *Historia de la república*, 1:35.

8. Biblioteca Municipal de Lima (hereafter cited as BML), Actas de Cabildo, book 45, 5 and 9 September 1823; Thomson, "Impresiones de Lima entre 1822 y 1824," in Núñez, ed., *Relaciones de Viajeros*, CDIP, tome 27, 2:36; and Robert Proctor, "El Perú entre 1823 y 1824," in ibid., 3:206.

9. Thomson, "Impresiones de Lima entre 1822 y 1824," in Núñez, ed., *Relaciones de Viajeros*, CDIP, tome 27, 2:38–39; Vargas Ugarte, *Historia general del Perú*, 6:277–79.

10. Decrees of Congress (Torre Tagle's supporters), Callao, 21 June 1823; Lima, 16 August 1823; and Lima, 19 August 1823, respectively, ANP, AHH, OL 70–80, OL 66–18, and OL 66–19; Order of Congress (Riva Agüero's supporters), Callao, 23 June 1823, ANP, AHH, OL 70–78.

11. Decree of Torre Tagle, Lima, 23 July 1823, ANP, AHH, OL 66–8; BML, Actas de Cabildo, book 45, 2 September 1823.

12. Cabildo of Lima to Torre Tagle, Lima, 30 July 1823, ANP, AHH, OL 85–13; Angel de Alfaro to Minister of Finance, Lima, 20 January 1824, ANP, AHH, OL 4–9.

13. Gustavo Vergara Arias, *Montoneras y guerrillas en la etapa de la emancipación del Perú (1820–1825)* (Lima: Editorial Salesiana, 1973), pp. 49–60; Proctor, "El Perú entre 1823 y 1824," in Núñez, ed., *Relaciones de Viajeros*, CDIP, tome 27, 2:250.

14. Decree of Torre Tagle, Lima, 18 August 1823, ANP, AHH, OL 66–20.

15. Quoted in Masur, *Bolívar*, p. 360.

16. BML, Actas de Cabildo, book 45, 6 June 1823; Francisco de Echagüe to Berindoaga, Lima, 12 November 1823, ANP, AHH, OL70–142a; Vargas Ugarte, *Historia general del Perú*, 6:302.

17. Paz Soldán, *Historia del Perú independiente*, part 2, 1:216–17.

18. Reinforcing the sense of absolute anarchy is the absence of documents relating to several key events. A large body of collected reports and correspondence from Viceroy La Serna, being carried to Spain by his commissioners Antonio Seoane and the marqués de Valleumbroso, was thrown overboard when the commissioners were seized by Buenos Aires corsairs off the coast of Brazil; Unsigned note to Secretary of War, Madrid, 5 October 1822, Archivo General de Indias, Seville (hereafter cited as AGI), Ultramar 812. Torre Tagle lost many of his papers in two fires in the palace—one on the night of 13 July 1822, and one set by the Spaniards in July 1823: *Gaceta del Gobierno*, 2 October 1822; Paz Soldán, *Historia del Perú independiente*, part 1, 1:313; Proctor, "El Perú entre 1823 y 1824," in Núñez, ed., *Relaciones de Viajeros*, CDIP, tome 27, 2:248. The Acts of the Lima cabildo also have significant gaps. There are no records from 10 June to 22 July 1823—during the first royalist occupation, BML, Actas de Cabildo, book 45, 22 July 1823. More seriously, the Acts of the cabildo ceased altogether on 27 January 1824—a few days before the second Spanish occupation. Book 45 is the last Libro de Actas in the Biblioteca Municipal de Lima. Finally, the newly founded National Library, containing San Martín's personal collection of books, was looted by the royalists in 1823 and 1824.

19. Berindoaga to Minister of Hacienda, Lima, 2 September 1823, ANP, AHH, OL 70–83.

20. Quoted in Masur, *Bolívar*, p. 360.

21. Quoted in ibid., p. 364.

22. Bolívar to Berindoaga, Pativilca, 12 January 1824, ANP, AHH, OL 99–4.

23. Basadre, *Historia de la república*, 1:77–78.

24. Proctor, "El Perú entre 1823 y 1824," in Núñez, ed., *Relaciones de Viajeros*, CDIP, tome 27, 2:324–28. At the end of March 1824 Proctor and his family fled Lima, without passports, on a British warship.

25. Basadre, *Historia de la república*, 1:82.

26. Quoted in ibid., 1:84.

27. Quoted in Masur, *Bolívar*, pp. 366–67.

28. Cabildo to General Rodil, Lima, 17 March 1824, AGI, Estado 75; *Triunfo del Callao, Extraordinario*, Lima, 20 March 1824.

29. Thomson, "Impresiones de Lima entre 1822 y 1823," in Núñez, ed., *Relaciones de Viajeros*, CDIP, tome 27, 2:57–58.

30. "El Marqués de Torre Tagle a sus compatriotas," Lima, March 1824, AGI, Estado 75.

31. Vargas Ugarte, *Historia general del Perú*, 6:317.

32. "Estado que manifiesta las cantidades de Plata que ingresado en esta Tesorería," Callao, 31 December 1824, ANP, AHH, OL 112–95; Estados, Lima, 31 December 1824, ANP, AHH, OL 112–96; "Estado . . . de los gastos causados por los Buques de guerra," Callao, 31 December 1824, ANP, AHH, OL 112–97.

33. Vargas Ugarte, *Historia general del Perú*, 6:330.

34. Aliaga to Rodil, Lima, 4 April 1824, AGI, Lima 1270; La Serna to Minister of Finance, Cuzco, 30 June 1824, AGI, Lima 1270; Council of Indies summary, 1824, AGI, Lima 1024; Requests from merchants to Rodil for export licenses, 1824, ANP, AHH, OL 112–14; Decree of Bolívar, Trujillo, 11 March 1824, ANP, AHH, OL 96–4.

35. Quoted in Masur, *Bolívar*, p. 370.

36. La Serna to Minister of Grace and Justice, Cuzco, 15 March 1824, AGI, Lima 762; Gárate to King, Puno, 18 April 1824, AGI, Indiferente 1325.

37. Masur, *Bolívar*, p. 370; Decree of Bolívar, Trujillo, 11 April 1824, ANP, AHH, OL 96–5.

38. August Tamayo Vargas and César Pacheco Vélez, eds., *José Faustino Sánchez Carrión*, vol. 9 of *Los Ideólogos*, tome 1 of CDIP.

39. Masur, *Bolívar*, pp. 369–73.

40. Lynch, *Spanish American Revolutions*, pp. 279, 281. See the testimony of Valdés in his "Exposición," dated Vitoria, 12 July 1827, in Horacio Villanueva Urteaga, ed., *Documentación oficial española*, 3 vols., tome 22 of CDIP, 3:315–84.

41. Quoted in Masur, *Bolívar*, pp. 372–73.

42. Domingo Ximenez and others to ministers of government, Madrid, 28 December 1824, AGI, Estado 74; Council of Indies Consulta, Madrid, 6 July 1825, Lima 604. Olañeta was already dead by this time.

43. Thomson, "Impresiones de Lima entre 1822 y 1824," in Núñez, ed., *Relaciones de Viajeros*, CDIP, tome 27, 2:80–81.

44. Vargas Ugarte, *Historia general del Perú*, 6:348–49.

45. Ibid., p. 366.

46. Paz Soldán, *Historia del Perú independiente*, part 2, 1:294.

47. Nestor Gambetta, *El "Real Felipe" del Callao* (Lima: Imprenta del Ministerio de Guerra, 1945), p. 59; Mariano Torrente, *Historia de la revolución de la independencia del Perú* (edited version of his *Historia de la revolución Hispano-Americana*, Madrid, 1829–30), in Felix Denegri Luna, ed., *Memorias, Diarios y Crónicas*, tome 26 of CDIP, 4:319–28.

48. Summary of other secondary sources in Vargas Ugarte, *Historia general del Perú*, 6:387; Marqués de Zambrano to Secretary of Hacienda, Madrid, 12 August 1826, AGI, Lima 1480.

49. Zambrano to Secretary of Hacienda, 12 August 1826, AGI, Lima 1480.

50. Quoted in Basadre, *Historia de la república*, 1:261.

12

"A Grave for Europeans"?
Disease, Death, and the Spanish-
American Revolutions

Rebecca Earle

The problems with health and hygiene in the independence wars of Spanish America would try the health-care systems of the most modern army today, let alone the primitive medicine of the early nineteenth century. As Rebecca Earle indicates, about the only solution to reduce the impact of vomito negro *(yellow fever) and malaria was to employ local troops who resisted these diseases. Spanish military and naval doctors recognized the role of swampy areas in proximity to garrisons and knew that mosquitoes might be involved in sickness. However, they accepted the theory of the times that exhalations from stagnant water and swamps—and not the mosquitoes—were the cause. Many European soldiers fell ill in tropical ports only a few days after disembarking. Despite many so-called cures, the best remedy was to get them to temperate climates as soon as possible. In strategically significant ports, such as Cartagena, Veracruz, and Callao, the death rates were horrendous. In New Spain the rebels under José María Morelos adopted an old but effective defensive tactic: to hold European invaders at Veracruz on the tropical Gulf Coast where they would contract yellow fever. By this means, in 1814 well over 50 percent of the troops arriving with a battalion of the Regimiento de Tiradores (sharpshooters) de Castilla died, and many more were left useless for combat duty.*

Venereal diseases also maimed and killed thousands of soldiers as well as officers who sought popular remedies and evaded the mercury cure that probably poisoned them anyway. Altitude sickness, or soroche, *as well as cold weather debilitated many European soldiers who were sent to the highlands of Peru, Upper Peru or Bolivia, and New Spain. Moreover, skin diseases such as mange and infections caused by insect*

From Rebecca Earle, " 'A Grave for Europeans'? Disease, Death, and the Spanish-American Revolutions," *War in History* 3 (1996): 371–83. Reprinted by permission of Edward Arnold (Publishers) Limited, London, England.

bites and poor hygiene drove many soldiers on both sides to distraction. In addition, as described by Earle, the military- and Church-operated hospitals that treated military personnel were often terrible places more suitable for dying than for effecting cures. Indeed, soldiers feared hospitalization more than disease and deserted in large numbers when there was an epidemic. Simply by witnessing the withering away of their companies and battalions, many men sought to escape what appeared to be certain death if they continued in their posts.

Rebecca Earle teaches at the University of Warwick, Coventry, United Kingdom, from which she also received her Ph.D. Her research concerns the social and political history of late colonial and early national Colombia.

> The millions who perish in the fleets and armies of contending nations are swept away in greater multitudes by the secret malignancy of [febrile infection], than by all the destructive implements of war.[1]

W hy do soldiers die? It has been claimed that for European soldiers of past centuries, the most common cause of death was disease, not battle.[2] Certainly there are many striking examples of the fatal impact of disease on military ventures. During Cuba's war of independence in the 1890s, five times as many Spanish soldiers died from illness as were killed in battle.[3] A century earlier, British troops fighting in the Caribbean against American and French revolutionaries had suffered appalling losses to disease. Tens of thousands of British soldiers succumbed to yellow fever, dysentery, and other tropical ailments.[4] Clearly, ill health could be a formidable opponent. Yet the effect of disease on war has often been overlooked by historians. Few accounts, for example, consider the influence of disease on Europe's other military campaign in the Americas during the Age of Revolution: the Spanish-American wars of independence. Between 1811 and 1818, Spain dispatched over 40,000 troops to its American colonies, in an attempt to halt the spread of revolution. Very few of these soldiers survived to return to Spain; many, perhaps most, died of disease. This essay will explore the fate of the largest contingent of Spanish troops sent to the Americas during this period. This was the Spanish Expeditionary Army, which in 1815 arrived in Venezuela to defeat the republican troops of Simón Bolívar. The impact of disease on this army forms the first half of the paper. The second half will consider the responses of soldiers and officers to the health crisis that confronted them.

The Spanish Expeditionary Army

Before proceeding, it will be useful to trace, in the most summary terms, the contours of the Spanish-American revolutions. These wars of independence, which began in 1808 and continued until the mid-1820s, constitute a major revolutionary process, separate from, yet comparable to, the American and French Revolutions which preceded them. By 1826 Spain had lost the entirety of its overseas empire, with the exception of Cuba, Puerto Rico, and the Philippines; Spanish authority had been rejected across all of mainland Spanish America.[5]

Following Napoleon's invasion of the Iberian peninsula in 1808, most of Spain's American colonies had separated themselves from the remnant of Spanish government and began to function as autonomous states or statelets. In some regions this was accomplished with relative ease. The Viceroyalty of Río de la Plata, for example, freed itself from meaningful Spanish control in 1810, and from then on most of its provinces remained outside the Spanish sphere. In other regions the period from 1810 to 1815 was a time of bloodshed. The Viceroyalty of New Spain in particular experienced a violent attempt at social revolution. In yet other areas, the customary order was less disturbed. The government in Lima, although threatened on all sides by revolution, remained loyal to the crown until the 1820s. In the Viceroyalty of New Granada, on which this paper will focus, events followed a still different course.[6]

The Creoles in the Viceroyalty of New Granada at first responded to the French invasion of Spain with concern. Within a year, however, the surface unity had shattered. The major cities formed separate juntas intended to govern the viceroyalty in the absence of the Spanish monarch. These bodies, although ostensibly loyal to the imprisoned Ferdinand VII, were immediately perceived as revolutionary, and by 1812 most had indeed declared independence from Spain. The unifying role played by Spain was not, however, occupied by any other entity. Efforts to create a central government in the capital, Santa Fe de Bogotá, failed. The viceroyalty instead acquired several competing governments, which soon declared war on each other. Thus, when Ferdinand VII returned to the throne in 1814, there was no independent 'New Granada', but rather a disunited collection of smaller states.

The rebellions in New Granada and the other American colonies had attracted the concern of successive governments in Spain itself, although only very inadequate responses had been essayed prior to the defeat of the French. In 1814, however, Spain determined to stamp out the spark of overseas revolution. A considerable military force was assembled, and the Viceroyalty of New Granada was chosen as the destination.[7] This Expeditionary Army, commanded by General Pablo Morillo, a veteran of the Peninsular War, arrived in Venezuela in April 1815. Finding the Captaincy-General already virtually restored to royal control, Morillo moved his army to Cartagena, perhaps the most important city in New Granada. After a siege of 106 days Cartagena surrendered to the Spanish, and the army soon recaptured the remainder of the country, thereby completing the

'Reconquest' of New Granada. Thus by mid-1816 the situation of the Spanish in the Viceroyalty looked promising. The interior of the country had been recaptured with only derisory resistance, and Spanish officials appeared to be well on the way to re-establishing the colonial government. Within a few years, however, the state of affairs had altered considerably. General Morillo's army proved incapable of resisting the advances of insurgent troops led by Simón Bolívar, and growing opposition to the royalist military was making life difficult for the Spanish. By 1818 General Morillo was predicting catastrophe. In 1819 republican troops routed royalist forces north of the capital, and within a year Spanish control was confined to the northern and southern margins of the country. In 1822 the last Spanish troops withdrew from the viceroyalty, now christened the Republic of Colombia. Spain's defeat, I will here argue, was due not only to a confluence of errors, both military and political, but also to the microbe. Indeed, the military historian Julio Albi has calculated that from 1810 to 1824, Spanish troops fighting in Venezuela and New Granada suffered an overall fatality rate of between 90% and 96%. This astonishingly high figure is attributed by Albi rather casually to 'the climate, disease, insufficient food, and primitive health care'.[8] While Albi provides little evidence, his assessment is, as we shall see, very accurate.

Sickness and Disease

General Morillo's army arrived in Venezuela in April 1815. After a brief sojourn in Caracas he moved his troops westward, into New Granada, where they laid siege to the fortified city of Cartagena, on the Caribbean coast. They were soon to experience problems. Cartagena, with its tropical climate, had long been a grave for soldiers; in 1764, for example, a full 30% of the city's military garrison were ill.[9] General Morillo's troops too soon faced the consequences of campaigning near Cartagena. In December 1815 General Morillo reported that, in six months, nearly half the 7,000-odd men laying siege to Cartagena had either died or deserted.[10] As the royalist army's only military engagement during this period had been a handful of skirmishes outside the city's walls, it is clear that large numbers of soldiers were falling victim to the region's notorious climate. Reports of the terrifying death rate from disease in the Spanish camps spread; the *Royal Gazette and Bahama Advertizer*, for example, stated that vast numbers of Spanish soldiers had died, not from battle-wounds, but from disease. The *Gazette* blamed 'the excessive rain, and . . . the excessive heat' of New Granada's Caribbean coast.[11] Throughout the war, the Caribbean coast was the region most afflicted by disease, and it was there that Spanish troops suffered the greatest losses.

The effect on Morillo's army of the loss of so many soldiers to disease was difficult to counteract. After the capture of Cartagena in December 1815, Morillo complained that the army had been reduced to 'a very small number' of troops, because of 'the many terrible diseases' suffered during the blockade.[12] The royalist army indeed grew progressively smaller, despite the efforts of its commanders to recruit replacements in New Granada and Venezuela itself. As early as May 1816 General Morillo noted that since he left Spain he had been unable to recruit enough new soldiers to replace those dead from disease.[13] The Spanish never succeeded in finding enough new recruits to fill the vacancies left by sickness. Military service was, as always, unpopular, and the Spanish troops died faster than new recruits could be found. Losses were such that by November 1816 there remained only one regiment composed entirely of European soldiers. By late 1817 there were no European troops remaining in New Granada at all, with the exception of one unit stationed in Cartagena.[14]

The mortality rate from disease continued to grow throughout the remainder of the war, particularly in the area of the Caribbean coast. Already in early 1816, nearly 14% of the men in the Second Battalion of Albuera, an important unit stationed near the coast, in Mompós, were sick.[15] In Cartagena during 1818 and 1819, nearly one in ten officers, to say nothing of the troops, appears to have been ill at any given moment.[16] By 1820 the situation was even worse. In the coastal city of Ríohacha, officers estimated that only one-third of the troops were in even 'indifferent health'. Commanding officer Vicente Sánchez Lima lamented that 'nakedness, hunger, and the fearful spectacle of fever now constitute the sad and melancholy lot of the soldier'.[17] By the start of the republican siege of Cartagena in 1820, over two-thirds of the city's royalist garrison were in hospital. Blame again fell on the 'very hot and damp weather'.[18]

Despite the particular risks associated with the Caribbean coast, illness afflicted troops across the Viceroyalty. In January 1816 half the troops stationed in the Neogranadan interior, in Zaragosa, were ill, and in late 1817 outbreaks of smallpox struck troops stationed in a number of different regions. In the eastern plains of Casanare, where some 1,000 royalist troops were on campaign, soldiers were being sent to hospital at the rate of about one a day.[19] From Venezuela, Morillo wrote in 1817 to the Spanish Minister of War that, in the two years since it had arrived in the Americas, the army had lost one-third of its force to disease. 'The mere bite of a mosquito', he wrote,

> often deprives a man of his life, or causes an ulcer that first incapacitates him for a long time, and then leaves him an invalid. A multitude of men in the division of Brigadier [José] Canterac have recently gone blind as a result of having slept outdoors [rather than in barracks]. The local diet causes every type of illness in Europeans, and very few are able to resist its fatal influence. The immense wildernesses in which the war is conducted, the lack of any sort of assistance, the contaminated water which it is often necessary to drink, and the extraordinary fatigue

suffered by the soldiers, who are obliged to march over such considerable distances through such diverse climates: all this contributes to our
destruction, and to the annihilation of the troops.[20]

Illness clearly had a disastrous effect on the Expeditionary Army. Did
the republican armies under the command of Simón Bolívar suffer equal
losses? Although Bolívar's troops were by no means immune from disease, he himself affirmed that the royalists were stricken more severely.[21]
Bolívar suggested that troops coming from Europe were more susceptible
to tropical ailments. More importantly, the royalists were far less successful than the republicans in recruiting replacements for soldiers dead
from disease. Local conscripts were essential for the royalist army to
maintain its strength, as Spain sent no peninsular troops to New Granada
after 1815. As we have seen, local recruits never proved sufficient to
counter losses to disease.

Health Care

Many different diseases afflicted the Spanish troops. The most common
seem to have been dysentery, smallpox, scurvy, and a variety of tropical
'fevers', particularly yellow fever. Sexually transmitted diseases were also
a problem, at least among officers.[22] Soldiers, of course, suffered from
other types of infirmity as well. For example, troops stationed in the eastern plains of Casanare in 1817 were struck with some sort of haemor-
rhaging disease (perhaps tuberculosis) that left them spitting blood.[23] In-
jury also took a terrible toll, as infections were difficult to cure. Ulcer-
ated wounds of all kinds tormented officers and troops alike; wounds in
the feet were notoriously fatal. (In this context it is worth recalling that
soldiers often lacked adequate footwear. One unit, for example, shared 32
pairs of shoes between over 300 soldiers.)[24]

Soldiers tried various remedies for the diseases that attacked them.
One of the most common illnesses was *calentura*, a general term for feverish, heat-related illnesses, including malaria. Rafael Sevilla, who fought
with General Morillo during most of the campaign, recorded in his memoirs several different ways of treating *calentura*. These remedies give some
indication of the level of medical care available to sick soldiers. Sevilla
detailed several relatively straightforward cures, such as eating a particular fruit, and also other, more prolonged, treatments. One such consisted
in drinking a cup of rum, then, one hour later, a cup of orangeade boiled
with spirit of nitrate, then, an hour after that, another cup of rum, etc.,
combined with a cup of broth every four hours. Another possible treatment, invented by Sevilla himself, was to go on a long and vigorous walk
as soon as the fever began. After this, one rested and drank a cup of tea.
(Sevilla devised this remedy while in the British Caribbean.) This would
bring on a 48-hour attack of high fever, followed by a complete cure.

Sevilla found all of these methods effective. On one occasion, however, he was given quinine, which had no positive effect at all. Indeed, the effectiveness of quinine in treating even malaria was uneven. The amount of actual quinine in the cinchona bark-based remedies varied to such an extent that it could not be relied upon to effect a cure.[25] Sevilla also fell ill with a disease locally known as *el bicho*, which caused nausea and fever, as well as headache and an ache in the bones. He was cured of this by a reportedly very unpleasant treatment involving lemons, the details of which were not spelled out in his memoirs.[26] Aside from his unsatisfactory encounter with quinine, Sevilla does not appear to have tried any of the standard European treatments for fever. In particular, he makes no mention of bloodletting or the use of purgatives. Nor did he resort to professional medical assistance.[27]

It was very common for soldiers (and indeed the public at large) to resort to folk remedies of this sort. Native medicinal products were frequently employed in ways considered deeply unorthodox by Europeans.[28] Moreover, folk healers, rather than doctors, often oversaw treatment. Throughout the eighteenth century New Granada's doctors had complained about the prevalence of *curanderos*, or folk healers, whom the public consistently favoured. Viceroy Francisco Montalvo summed up the situation in 1815: 'medicine and surgery lie in a state of utter abandon, and the inhabitants are obliged to place themselves in the hands of local healers, whom, because of their skill and local knowledge, they prefer, quite rightly, to European doctors, who are, in fact, an ignorant lot.'[29]

Not all popular treatments involved the use of folk medicine; some were matters of simple hygiene. In the preceding decades, medical practitioners in Europe had laid growing emphasis on the importance of cleanliness. Their concerns were echoed in New Granada, where officers repeatedly ordered their troops to keep clean and to wash as regularly as possible. To prevent the potentially fatal infections of the feet that were literally crippling the Spanish army, soldiers were advised to wash their feet daily in *aguardiente* (sugar-cane brandy) or, failing that, warm water. Sensibly, soldiers were frequently advised to avoid drinking water; *aguardiente* itself, or water mixed with *aguardiente*, was the preferred beverage.[30]

Moreover, as the climate, or more specifically the humidity, was felt to be responsible for much of the ill health, the royalist army took measures to construct barracks that prevented the soldiers from coming into contact with the damp ground and protected them from the warm air. Soldiers were further advised to keep out of the rain, although they were provided with few means of doing so; unsurprisingly, few military manoeuvres were called off because of heavy rain.[31] In blaming New Granada's humid and unwholesome air for their troops' ill health, royalist officers reflected both the current views on the origins of fever and European prejudices about South America's climate. In the preceding decades, influential climatic determinists such as the Abbé Raynal and the Comte de Buffon had affirmed that the region's climate was partially responsible for its perceived backwardness and lack of development.[32] Other features of Neogranadan life were considered equally insalubrious. The local diet, regarded as unsuitable for European troops, was frequently blamed for causing illness.[33]

Various more experimental methods for preserving the soldiers' health were also tried. In late 1815 General Morillo noted that few soldiers fell sick while actually out on manoeuvres: most illness struck in the barracks itself. Morillo therefore ordered that all troops under Field Marshal Miguel de la Torre's command be sent out daily on a lengthy circular march with full rucksacks. This measure, surely unpopular with the troops, was intended to improve the dismal health record of La Torre's division.[34] It is worth noting that on this occasion medical policy was made, not by a doctor, but by an officer. This was far from unusual for independence-era New Granada. Even public health measures, such as the smallpox vaccination campaign of 1816–17, were initiated and run by non-medical military officers.[35]

The metropolitan government also took an interest, of sorts, in the health of royalist troops. In December 1815 King Ferdinand VII issued a directive to government officials in the colonies, urging them to provide good care for injured soldiers.[36] As a consequence, following the arrival of General Morillo's Expeditionary Army in Venezuela, colonial officials within the viceroyalty were requested to report on the state of health care in each region, detailing in particular the availability of hospitals. A number, but by no means all, of the viceroyalty's governors reported the existence of hospitals, run by charitable institutions, which they claimed could cope with the few soldiers who sought admission. The low demand for hospital places was, Viceroy Montalvo felt, the result of the poor care provided in these hospitals, rather than an indication of the good health of the military population. The hospital in Santa Marta, for example, was described by Viceroy Montalvo as 'lacking doctors, medicine, in short, everything'.[37] There was clearly a need for more and better hospitals, and as a result a number of entirely new hospitals were built by the royalist army.[38] The most important of these were built in the area around Cartagena, which served as the royalists' headquarters for much of the war. The principal hospital was the Hospital Militar de San Carlos. This could comfortably hold 500 patients, and in extreme cases up to 500 more could be accommodated in the hospital's corridors and hallways. There were, however, only 440 beds. Patients suffering from dysentery, which, General Morillo reported, 'has afflicted this army so terribly', were held in separate accommodation.[39] The hospitals were divided into various sections, with officers and enemy prisoners housed separately. These hospitals were run at government expense, although food was provided in part by the surrounding towns and villages, which were obliged to supply food and money on a rota. Considerable amounts of both were needed; the hospital's 97 non-medical staff alone consumed 126 pounds of bread, 126 pounds of meat, and some 20 pounds of rice every day. The patients themselves were fed either ordinary rations, which consisted of meat, rice, and bananas, or, depending on their health, on half-rations, or some other variation on the basic menu.[40]

The official hospital diet created problems of public order. Although there is no evidence of actual riots breaking out as a result of the food, complaints about the poor quality of hospital food were frequent. Indeed, on 13 May 1816 an order was issued that 'any soldier who throws food at the orderlies, claiming that it is inedible, and using indecent and indecorous language inappropriate for polite society, will be punished with fifteen days in the stocks'.[41] Moreover, the food was not only unpalatable; it was also very meagre. On occasion the hospital assistants actually sold to villagers the food intended for the patients.[42] Food was evidently so scarce in the hospital of Sabanalarga that patients began slaughtering their own pigs in the patio of the hospital, 'to the detriment of their health', according to hospital staff. Attempts to outlaw this behaviour met with opposition from patients, who complained of the 'despotic and arbitrary behaviour' of the hospital staff.[43]

The ambience in these hospitals was, not surprisingly, disagreeable. Hostility reigned between the patients and the staff. The orderlies complained of continual harassment, and the patients reportedly made their frequent criticisms with excessive arrogance.[44] The overall atmosphere of an army hospital was summed up by a hospital inspecor in July 1816. He commented that in these hospitals the patient suffered from 'the pain of his ills, the loss of comfort and subsistence, . . . the horrible companionship of a moribund neighbour, and the hardship of ill-treatment . . . leaving aside the shortage of clothing and bed linen, whose absence is directly disadvantageous to the patient.'[45] Such was the lethal atmosphere of most hospitals that in 1818 a woman afflicted with leprosy pleaded not to be confined to one as, if she were, she would certainly die from melancholy.[46]

Troops of either army might be accommodated in a given hospital. As hospitals did not generally employ guards, prisoners fit enough to do so could and did escape from them with little difficulty.[47] Following the 1820 treaty regularizing the war agreed between Generals Morillo and Bolívar, the safety of troops in enemy hospitals was guaranteed, but the royalists did not always respect this agreement. Republican convalescents in the hospital of Miraflores were attacked and killed by the royalists in 1822.[48]

Despite the presence of the new military hospitals, then, health care still left a great deal to be desired, even by contemporary standards.

Furthermore, the hospitals suffered regularly from shortages of medical supplies.[49] As noted, the quality of the doctors practising in New Granada was also regarded as poor. Their lack of skills had already been causing concern before the outbreak of the war, which did nothing to improve matters.[50] Viceroy Montalvo, commenting on the high mortality suffered on the Caribbean coast, remarked that on the rare occasions, when a disease did not prove fatal, 'it is not because of the attention of "doctors" who lack both experience and scientific training, but rather because of a spontaneous physical recovery [by the patient]',[51] Of course, during this period doctors were often held in no higher esteem in Europe itself, and for good reason.[52]

The level of medical care available in New Granada, then, was in no way able to cope with the demands placed on it by the Expeditionary Army. There was thus little remedy to the steady decline in troop size brought about by illness. Thousands of soldiers died in the epidemics of dysentery, smallpox, and other illnesses, and the already small royalist army shrank irreversibly in size. Attempts at recruiting replacement troops never succeeded in filling the vacancies left by disease, nor did Spain ever send additional troops to New Granada. General Morillo complained endlessly that his understaffed and undersized army stood no chance of defeating the insurgents. 'They are just waiting for us all to die of infection and disease,' he lamented.[53]

It should be evident that disease played an important role in the defeat of General Morillo's forces. Those who survived the war returned to Spain with ruined health. General Morillo's successor as commander-in-chief, Miguel de la Torre, left office after seven years of service with his formerly robust health 'shattered'.[54] In 1818 General Morillo had compared himself to Hernán Cortés, as both he and Cortés had employed native troops in their military campaigns.[55] General Morillo could as accurately have drawn a comparison with the Aztec king Montezuma, whose own forces were destroyed by smallpox and other diseases. Inadequate health care and inept doctors did little to prevent deaths. Although the Spanish-American Revolutions did not quite achieve the terrifying death rates suffered by the British in the Caribbean two decades earlier, when whole regiments had died from disease, the Spanish, like the British before them, correctly regarded warfare in the Americas as 'fatal for Europeans'.[56]

Notes

1. Robert Robertson, 1790, quoted in William Bynum, 'Cullen and the Study of Fevers in Britain, 1760–1820,' in W.F. Bynum and V. Nutton, eds., *Theories of Fever from Antiquity to the Enlightenment, Medical History*, Supplement I (London, 1981), p. 141.

2. See e.g. John Keegan, *A History of Warfare* (London, Hutchinson, 1993), p. 361.

3. Hugh Thomas, *Cuba or the Pursuit of Freedom* (London, Eyre & Spottiswoode, 1971), p. 414.

4. Michael Duffy, *Soldiers, Sugar and Seapower: The British Expedition to the West Indies and the War against Revolutionary France* (Oxford, Oxford Univ. Press, 1987), pp. 326–67. See also Piers Mackesy, *The War for America, 1775– 1783* (London Longmans, 1964), pp. 6, 336, 526.

5. For an accessible account of the Spanish-American revolutions, see John Lynch, *The Spanish American Revolutions, 1808–1826* (New York, W.W. Norton, 1986).

6. The Viceroyalty of New Granada roughly comprised present-day Venezuela, Colombia, Panama, and northern Ecuador. I follow standard practice by using the term 'New Granada' to refer to present-day Colombia. 'The Viceroyalty' refers to the entire region.

7. For the choice of New Granada as a destination, see Edmundo Heredia, 'El destino de la expedición de Morillo', *Anuario de Estudios Americanos* XXIX (1972).

8. Julio Albi, *Banderos olvidadas: el ejército realista en América* (Madrid, Ediciones de Cultura Hispánica, 1990), pp. 403–5.

9. Juan Marchena Fernández, *Oficiales y soldados en el Ejército de America* (Seville, Escuela de Estudios Hispano-Americanos, 1983), pp. 210, 213, 214. For the effect of disease on the Spanish colonial army in Mexico, see Christon Archer, *The Army in Bourbon Mexico, 1760–1810* (Albuquerque, Univ. of New Mexico Press, 1977), pp. 38–61; and Christon Archer, 'Combating the Invisible Enemy', *New World* II (1987).

10. Antonio Rodríguez Villa, *El Teniente General Don Pablo Morillo, Primer Conde de Cartagena, Marqués de la Puerta (1778–1837)* I (Madrid, Editorial América, 1920), p. 181. (NB: Two different editions of this work are cited in this paper. The first is a four-volume edition, published between 1908 and 1910. The second, cited here, is a shorter, two-volume edition version published in 1920. All citations which include the date 1920 refer to this later edition.)

11. *Royal Gazette and Bahama Advertizer*, 27 Mar. 1816, AGI, Estado, legajo 57, doc. 32. See also Pablo Morillo to José de Abascal, Torrecillas, 21 Oct. 1815, AGI, Diversos, legajo 4, ramo I.

12. Pablo Morillo to Francisco de Montalvo, Cartagena, 5 Feb. 1816, AGI, Papeles de Cuba, legajo 707. Also see Francisco Montalvo to Juan Sámano, Cartagena, 30 Jan. 1818. *Los últimos virreyes de Nueva Granada, Relación de Mando del Virrey Don Francisco Montalvo y noticias del Virrey Sámano sobre la pérdida del Reino (1813–1819)*, in Eduardo Posada and P.M. Ibáñez, eds., Biblioteca de la Juventud Hispano-Americana, Editorial América (Madrid, n.d.), pp. 94–5.

13. Pablo Morillo to Minister of War, Santa Fe, 31 May 1816; Antonio Rodríguez Villa, *El Teniente General Don Pablo Morillo, Primer Conde de Cartagena, Marqués de la Puerta (1778–1837)* III (Madrid, Real Academia de la Historia, 1908), pp. 164–9. For military service during the eighteenth century, see Allan J. Kuethe, *Military Reform and Society in New Granada, 1773–1808* (Gainesville, Univ. of Florida Press, 1978).

14. Pablo Morillo to Minister of War, Santa Fe, 9 Nov. 1816, in Rodríguez Villa, *Pablo Morillo* III, p. 299; and Francisco Montalvo to Minister of Grace and Justice, Cartagena, 24 Sept. 1817, AGI, Audiencia de Santa Fe, legajo 631.

15. Reports on the Second Battalion of Albuera, Mompós, 1816, AGI, Papeles de Cuba, legajo 738.

16. See Vicente Villete to Subinspector General, Cartagena, 31 Dec. 1819; and also Report by Ignacio de la Ruz, Cartagena, 3 Feb. 1819, for comments about troop mortality in the coastal city of Santa Marta, both in AGI, Papeles de Cuba, legajo 738.

17. Vicente Sánchez Lima to Comandantes Militares de la Hacha, Moreno, 26 Nov. 1820, AGI, Indiferente General, legajo 1568.

18. First Declaration of Gabriel de Torres, Havana, 2 Nov. 1824, AGI, Papeles de Cuba, legajo 2136A.

19. See e.g. Vicente Sánchez Lima to Pedro Ruíz de Porras, Zaragosa, 8 Jan. 1816. AHNM, Estado, legajo 8745; Antonio Meléndez to Gabriel de Torres, Mompós, 5 Apr. 1817, AGI, Papeles de Cuba, legajo 712: Cabildo of Anserma to Francisco Montalvo, Anserma, 27 June 1817, AGI, Santa Fe, legajo 631; Diary of the Primer Batallón del Regimiento Infantería de Numancia, 15 Dec. 1817, AGI, Papeles de Cuba legajo 759A; José María Barreiro to Juan Sámano, Santa Fe, 2 Aug. 1818, *Los ejércitos del Rey, 1818–1819* I, in Alberto Lee López, ed., Biblioteca de la Presidencia de la República (Bogotá, 1989), p. 39; Rodríguez Villa, *Pablo Morillo* II (1920), p. 31; and José María Caballero, *Diario*, Biblioteca de Bogotá (Bogotá, Editores Villegas, 1990), p. 217. For a 'type of plague' in 1816, see Francisco Montalvo to Juan Sámano, Cartagena, 30 Jan. 1818, in *Los últimos virreyes*, p. 95; and Pablo Morillo, Description of the 1816 attack on the interior of New Granada, BRAH, sig. 9/7651 (legajo 8).

20. Pablo Morillo to Minister of War, La Guaira, 10 Sept. 1817, in Rodríguez Villa, *Pablo Morillo* III, pp. 442–3. Also see Miguel de La Torre to Pablo Morillo, Guayana, 4 May 1817, AHNM, Estado, legajo 8718, docs. 51–2; and Pablo Morillo to Minister of War, Caño de Atamayca, 28 Feb. 1819, in Rodríguez Villa, *Pablo Morillo* IV, pp. 10–14.

21. For illness in the republican armies, see Oscar Beaujón. 'La medicina en la Campaña del Sur', *Boletin de la Academia Nacional de la Historia* (Caracas) LVII (1974). For a comparison of the health of the two armies, see Simón Bolívar to Juan Bautista Arismendi, Carúparo, 26 June 1816, in *Escritos del Libertador* IX (Caracas, Sociedad Bolivariana de Venezuela, 1973), pp. 285–7.

22. See Pablo Morillo to Minister of War, Maracay, 1 Apr. 1817, in Rodríguez Villa, *Pablo Morillo* III, p. 369; Tomás de Heres to Ruperto Delgado, Cali, 20 May 1817, AGI, Santa Fe, legajo 631; Diary of the Primer Batallón del Regimiento Infanteria de Numancia, 13 Nov., 15 Dec. 1817, AGI, Papeles de Cuba, legajo 759A; Lists of sick officers in Venezuelan hospitals, 1820, AHNM, Estado, legajo 8728, docs. 379–408; Miguel de la Torre to Minister for Overseas, Caracas, 22 Mar. 1821, AGI, Audiencia de Caracas, legajo 55; Juan de la Cruz Mourgeon to Minister for Overseas, Panama, 28 Aug. 1821, AGI, Santa Fe, legajo 668; and Rafael Sevilla, *Memorias de un oficial del ejército español, campañas contra Bolívar y los separatistas de América* (Madrid, Editorial América, 1916), p. 124.

23. Reports of Carlos Tolrá, Chocontá, Nov. 1817, BRAH, sig. 7665 (leg. 22), fo. 512. See also Juan Sámano to Pablo Morillo, Santa Fe, 29 Aug. 1818, BRAH, sig. 7665 (Leg. 22), fos. 607–9; and Cabildo de Anserma to Francisco Montalvo, Anserma, 27 June 1817, AGI, Santa Fe, legajo 631.

24. Marchena Fernández, *Oficiales y soldados*, pp. 219–20; list of invalids in Puerto Cabello, 20 Nov. 1815, AGI, Papeles de Cuba, legajo 897; Francisco Warleta to Pablo Morillo, Remedios, 17 Mar. 1816, BRAH, sig. 9/7658 (legajo 15), fos. 38–9; Pablo Morillo to Miguel de la Torre, Santa Fe, 23 June 1816, AHNM, Estado, legajo 8717; Diary of the Primer Batallón del Regimiento Infantería de Numancia, 15 Dec. 1817, AGI, Papeles de Cuba, legajo 759A; Pablo Morillo to Minister of War, Barquisimeto, 22 July 1818, in Rodríguez Villa, *Pablo Morillo* III, p. 598;

and Antonio Van Halen to Miguel de la Torre, Caracas, Mar. 1821, AGI, Audiencia de Caracas, legajo 55. For shoes, see Relación de las prendas que se hallan, Mompós, 26 Nov. 1816, AGI, Papeles de Cuba, legajo 712.

25. Bynum, 'Cullen and the Study of Fevers', p. 147.

26. See Sevilla, *Memorias*, p. 45, 144, 166, 198. For the treatment of yellow fever in Mexico, see Archer, *The Army in Bourbon Mexico*, pp. 42–4; for altitude sickness, see Albi, *Banderas Olvidadas*, p. 162.

27. Bynum, 'Cullen and the Study of Fevers'; and Peter Mathias, 'Swords and Ploughshares: The Armed Forces, Medicine and Public Health in the Late Eighteenth Century', in J.M. Winter, ed., *War and Economic Development* (Cambridge, Cambridge Univ. Press, 1975), pp. 78–9.

28. See Francis Hall, *Colombia: su estado actual* (London, 1824), repr. in David Sowell, ed., *Santander y la opinión angloamericana* (Santafe de Bogotá, Biblioteca de la Presidencia de la República, 1991), pp. 61–71.

29. Francisco Montalvo to Juan Sámano, Cartagena, 30 Jan. 1818, in *Los últimos virreyes*, pp. 136–7. See also Memorial de Francisco Flórez Moreno, Cádiz, 10 Jan. 1811, AGI, Ultramar, legajo 811, for remarks by a Spanish doctor about the state of health care in the Americas in 1789; and Marcelo Frías Núñez, 'Enfermedad y sociedad en la crisis colonial del antiguo regimen: Nueva Granada en el tránsito del siglo XVIII al XIX. Las epidemias de viruelas' (Tesina de Licenciatura, Centro de Estudios Históricos, Madrid, 1991), p. 66. Compare Duffy, *Soldiers, Sugar and Seapower*, p. 374, for comments about British sailors' use of 'folk-medicine' (i.e., rum) in the West Indies.

30. Beaujón, 'La medicina en la Campaña del Sur', pp. 720–1; Pascual Enrile to Miguel de la Torre, Santa Fe, 10 Aug. 1816, AHNM, Estado, legajo 8724, doc. 55; and Morillo's Instrucciones para la marcha de los cuerpos, Caracas, 30 May 1815, AHNM, Estado, legajo 8717, doc. 17.

31. Pablo Morillo to Miguel de la Torre, Santa Fe, 23 June 1816, AHNM, Estado, legajo 8717, Doc. 78; Orden general del 19 de agosto 1818, AGI, Papeles de Cuba, legajo 759B; and Ejército Expedicionario, Resumen histórico de las operaciones y movimientos de las columnas y tropas . . . desde el mes de Noviembre de 1816, entry for 30 Dec. 1816, AGI, Papeles de Cuba, legajo 759B.

32. For the climate debate, see Thomas Glick, 'Science and Independence in Latin America (with special reference to New Granada)', *Hispanic American Historical Review* LXXI (1991): David Brading, *The First America, the Spanish Monarchy, Creole Patriots, and the Liberal State, 1492–1867* (Cambridge, Cambridge Univ. Press, 1991), pp. 89, 197, 428–32; and Anthony Pagden, *European Encounters with the New World* (New Haven, CT, Yale University Press, 1993).

33. See Francisco Montalvo to Juan Sámano, Cartagena, 30 Jan. 1818, in *Los últimos virreyes*, p. 40.

34. Pablo Morillo to Miguel de la Torre, Torrecilla, 4 Oct. 1815, AHNM, Estado, legajo 8717, doc. 33.

35. For the smallpox vaccine, se AGI, Papeles de Cuba, legajo 712; Juan Sámano to Pablo Morillo, Popayán, 19 Aug. 1816, and Jaime Serra to Juan Sámano, Popayán, 31 Aug. 1816, both in BRAH, sig. 7665 (leg. 22), fos. 52–3, 75. (Francisco Tamariz, who spearheaded the drive to reintroduce the vaccine, may have had some medical training.)

36. Francisco Montalvo to Juan Sámano, Cartagena, 30 Jan. 1818, in *Los últimos virreyes*, pp. 113–37.

37. *Op. cit.* P. 114. Cf., on military hospitals in the British Caribbean; Duffy, *Soldiers, Sugar and Seapower*, pp. 348–9.

38. See e.g. Antonio Meléndez to Gabriel de Torres, Mompós, 26 May 1817, AGI, Papeles de Cuba, legajo 712; and Miguel de la Torre to Pascual Enrile,

Mompós, 2 Jan. 1816, AHNM, Estado legajo 8724, doc. 4; Resúmen histórico de las operaciones y movimientos de las columnas y tropas . . . desde el mes de noviembre de 1816, AGI, Papeles de Cuba, legajo 759B; Oswaldo Díaz Díaz, *La reconquista española* II, Historia Extensa de Colombia VI (Bogotá, Academia Colombiana de Historia, Editorial Lerner, 1964), p. 285; José María Barreiro to Juan Sámano, Tunja, 16 Oct. 1818; and Juan Sámano to José María Barreiro, Santa Fe, 19 Nov. 1818, both in López, *Los ejércitos del Rey* I, pp. 68–70. 97–8.

39. Pablo Morillo to Minister of War, Santa Fe, 9 June 1816, in Rodríguez Villa, *Pablo Morillo* III, p. 174; and Pablo Morillo to Miguel de la Torre; Torrecillas, 4 Oct. 1815, AHNM, Estado, legajo 8717.

40. Strangely, in the hospital in Sabanalarga bananas were strictly forbidden, and staff who brought bananas into the hospital compound were reprimanded. See Orden no. 1 for Hospital in Sabanalarga, 13 May 1816, AGI, Papeles de Cuba, legajo 714.

41. *Op. cit.*

42. *Op. cit.*; Dictamen de Anselmo de Bierna y Maza, Cartagena, 24 Apr. 1816, AGI, Papeles de Cuba, legajo 707; and Estado de enfermos en el hospital de San Carlos, Cartagena, 31 Mar. 1816, AGI, Papeles de Cuba, legajo 715, for comments about the hardness of the bread.

43. Antonio María Díaz to Gabriel de Torres, Sabanalarga, 17 May 1816, AGI, Papeles de Cuba, legajo 714.

44. Orden no. 1 for Hospital in Sabanalarga, 13 May 1816.

45. Informe sobre hospitales militares de la Plaza de Cartagena de Indias, Cartagena, 29 July 1816, AGI, Papeles de Cuba, legajo 714.

46. Josef Alvarez to Gabriel de Torres, Mompós, 13 May 1818, AGI, Papeles de Cuba, legajo 712. See also the comments about military hospitals in colonial Mexico in Archer, *The Army in Bourbon Mexico*, pp. 261–7.

47. Josef Alvarez to Gabriel de Torres, Mompós, 27 Nov. 1817, AGI, Papeles de Cuba, legajo 712.

48. Beaujón, 'La medicina en la Campaña del Sur', p. 718–19.

49. See various documents in AGI, Papeles de Cuba, legajo 714; Antonio María Díaz to Gabriel de Torres, Sabanalarga, 27 Mar. 1816, AGI, Papeles de Cuba, legajo 714; and various letters of Francisco Morales, BRAH, sig. 9/7660 (legajo 17), fos. 561, 569, 345.

50. See Memorial de Francisco Flórez Moreno, Cádiz, 10 Jan. 1811, AGI, Ultramar, legajo 811.

51. Francisco Montalvo to Juan Sámano, Cartagena, 30 Jan. 1818, in *Los últimos virreyes*, p. 137.

52. For concise comments about the contemporary status of doctors in England, see Roy Porter, *Disease, Medicine and Society in England, 1550–1860* (London, Economic History Society, 1993).

53. Pablo Morillo to Miguel de la Torre, Guadelupe, 19 May 1816, AHNM, Estado, legajo 8717, doc. 69.

54. Hoja de Servicio of Miguel de la Torre, AHNM, Estado, legajo 8718, doc. 100. A few other examples will suffice. Lt. Col. Donato Ruíz de Santa Cruz was reportedly very ill with tuberculosis by 1818; see Juan Sámano to Pablo Morillo, Santa Fe, 29 Aug. 1818, BRAH, sig. 9/7665 (leg. 22), fos. 607–9. The long-serving Pedro Ruíz de Porras, governor of Santa Marta, was seriously ill in 1819; see Report on Pedro Ruíz de Porras, Madrid, 16 May 1819, AGI, Papeles de Cuba, legajo 739. Francisco Warleta, who had enjoyed robust health, fell sick with scurvy in 1818; see Report on Colonel Francisco Warleta, Cahudare, 14 Feb. 1818, BRAH, sig. 9/7658 (legajo 15), fo. 91. Col. Vicente Sánchez Lima, 'and almost all the officers and much of the troops', were very sick from fevers and infections in

early 1816; see Francisco Warleta to Pablo Morillo, Remedios, 17 Mar. 1816, BRAH, sig. 9/7658 (legajo 15).

55. Juan Sámano to Pablo Morillo, Santa Fe, 29 Aug. 1818, BRAH, sig. 9/7665 (leg. 22), fos. 607–9

56. See Duffy, *Soldiers, Sugar and Seapower*, pp. 326, 337–8; and Pablo Morillo to José de Abascal, Torrecillas, 21 Oct. 1815, AGI, Diversos, legajo 4, ramo 1.

13

The Spanish Army and
the Loss of America, 1810–1824

Margaret L. Woodward

*Given our knowledge of nineteenth- and twentieth-century history, Spain's
military failure to suppress the people of enormous continental territories distant from the motherland will come as no surprise. While there
were strong royalist movements in many of the American possessions, eventually these wilted up against popular struggle and entrenched guerrilla-
style warfare. Many people became exhausted and desired peace. Most
European Spanish soldiers had little stomach for permanent duty in the
brutal business of applying counterinsurgency violence against populations that wished to control their own destinies. In 1812 and 1813, toward the end of the Napoleonic intervention in Iberia, duty overseas offered
the prospect of promotions and even of glory. With recognition that these
conflicts were often dirty wars involving skirmishes fought in dangerous
rugged terrain and in mortifying tropical climates, many soldiers placed
fame second to survival. Moreover, the restoration of Ferdinand VII in
1814 made peninsular officers in the Americas accept the fact that they
were far from the circles of patronage in Madrid and elsewhere in Spain
where senior commanders advanced the careers of their more junior aco-
lytes. Well-connected officers petitioned powerful family members and
friends to obtain transfers from colonial duty back to the metropolitan
army. Moreover, most officers and soldiers viewed overseas service as a
form of involuntary servitude. Tours of duty almost never commenced with
specific terms, and most men (and their women and children) knew that
they would have to abandon their families and interests for a long time—
possibly for the rest of their lives. It was clear that Spanish soldiers who
remained healthy would serve for the duration, however long that might
turn out to be.*

From Margaret L. Woodward, "The Spanish Army and the Loss of America,
1810–1824," *Hispanic American Historical Review* 48, no. 4 (November 1968):
586–607. © 1968 by Duke University Press. Reprinted by permission of Duke
University Press.

When news reached Spain about barbarous attitudes where slaughter of prisoners replaced rules of warfare, desertions by many European Spaniards, and decimating death rates from yellow fever and other diseases, few men stepped forward for overseas service. After the disasters of the Riego Revolt in 1820 that restored the Spanish constitution of 1812 and liberalism, the senior command could no longer contemplate a policy of ordering troops to serve in the Americas. In 1821 the Consejo de Guerra at Madrid admitted that "blind obedience"—a constant in military discipline—was no longer the rule in the Spanish army: "The soldier believes that he has the right to deliberate before he obeys." Until this attitude changed, only volunteers were to be dispatched to Havana and other posts in the Americas. The Consejo concluded that without high morale, troops sent to the Americas would either be of no use or would surrender* at the first opportunity. No matter how much fanatical patriots within the army might promote attempts at reconquest, with the exception of Cuba and Puerto Rico, Spain had lost the Americas.

Margaret Woodward holds a Ph.D. in history from The University of Chicago.

S pain's loss of its Latin American empire was one of the most momentous events of the nineteenth century, with repercussions that can be felt even in the present day. Yet whatever is known of the subject has generally come from studies of the Latin American participants in the war. Popular attitudes in Spain, particularly those of the Spanish army (which was directly concerned with the war), have heretofore been neglected. A little probing into the contemporary press and into the military archives from 1810 to 1824 reveals peculiar features of the Spanish attitude hard to reconcile with the "national tragedy" then in progress.[1]

During the entire revolution Spain was beset with difficulties. In 1808, at a nod from Napoleon, both the aged Charles IV and the new king, Ferdinand VII, voluntarily turned the country over to the French and meekly removed themselves to Bayonne. The Spanish people watched with smoldering resentment as Joseph Bonaparte arrived with his court, and then, on May 2, rose in revolt and for the next six years fought the invader. A new government was formed which proclaimed its loyalty to Ferdinand, but it had to flee to Cádiz before the onrushing armies. There in 1810, besieged on several sides, a group of liberals seized the opportunity to turn Spain into a constitutional monarchy.

It was at this juncture that word arrived of insurrections in the empire, first in New Spain and Venezuela, then spreading quickly to Peru, Chile, and the Río de la Plata. Despite the truly desperate situation in Spain itself, the immediate reaction was a general outcry to send an army

---

*Report of the Consejo de Guerra, Palacio, Madrid, September 11, 1821, Archivo General Militar de Segovia, leg. 227.

to crush the revolts. Juan López Cancelada, writing in 1810, called for a mighty "expedition of peace"; and other men, also, thought that only through military action could Spain "positively secure" its control over the rebels.[2] In 1808 Spain had about 125,700 men stationed permanently from Mexico to the Río de la Plata.[3] But since many of these troops were native Americans,[4] drawn from the same populations which were now rebelling, observers in Spain felt that the regular units would not be sufficient. Although never unanimous, the demand for force finally convinced the government, and on May 14, 1812, it dispatched the Second Battalion of Albuerna to the Río de la Plata.

Criticism welled up at once in Spain. As might have been expected, the French-controlled *Gazeta de Madrid* attacked the move, in words that could have come from a Spanish pen. "Fathers," went the plea, "look at the fate which you are preparing for your sons: a certain death in remote countries, or a camp [so far away that] you will never see them again."[5] Repeated statements of this sort during the next decade suggested that nothing could be more loathsome and fearful to a Spaniard than the prospect of death on the other side of the world. The lusty spirit of the conquistadors was nowhere to be seen.

By 1813 two more expeditions of 2,000 and 3,000 men had gone from Cádiz to the Río de la Plata,[6] making 6,500 or 7,000 troops that had been sent in all. But the force was insufficient, and both British and Spanish observers estimated that at least 3,000 more troops would be required to secure Buenos Aires.[7] This was precisely the figure said to be needed at the same time to bolster Spain's defenses against the French.

Complaints began to pour into Cádiz from both sides of the Atlantic against the government's military policy. In Spain, Valentín Ortigosa complained in 1813 of the "painful evils" which sending the first troops had caused and asked how they were to procure the ships and money needed to send any more. He concluded that the entire effort would be disastrous for Spain and useless in crushing the revolutions.[8] Events in America seemed to confirm his warning. The two expeditions sent in 1813 arrived in Montevideo with over 800 men ill from scurvy and malnutrition. Conditions continued to be difficult after the landing, and discontent was rife. From New Spain came word of desertions, not only of native soldiers, but also of Europeans, some of whom had been shot "to show that they cannot use the excuse they were kidnapped."[9]

Along with desertions, both the Spanish expeditionary forces and the loyal troops already stationed in America suffered from widespread insubordination among the lower-echelon officers. In Venezuela as early as 1812 a conflict arose between the governor of that province, José Cevallos, and Captain Domingo Monteverde, who was supposed to be under the governor's command. Cevallos accused Monteverde of disobedience, and others on the scene supported the accusation.[10] News of the sorry state of affairs in Venezuela quickly began to circulate in Spain. Later, after Monte-verde had become a general, his enemies accused him of clumsiness and ignorance.[11] His demagoguery and ambition were said to have contrib-uted substantially to the resumption of hostilities in Venezuela after Miran-da's capitulation in 1812. According to an exposé of 1820, his "perfidious" and "scandalous" actions had *"conducted the province to the border of a precipice, provoking the intestinal war of Hueria and Maturín."*[12] A Spanish officer witnessing these events feared that Monteverde was causing the "paralysis of the Reconquest" and warned the Spanish government: "There is no alternative to sending respectable forces from the Peninsula or aban-doning this country."[13]

In that same year (1814) Ferdinand VII was restored to the Spanish throne. Although primarily concerned with eradicating all vestiges of lib-eralism in the country, he still found time to answer the plea for "respect-able forces" in America. To head the new expedition he selected Pablo Morillo, a modest soldier who had risen to the rank of field marshal in the war against the French. On August 14, 1814, Morillo was appointed captain-general of Venezuela and general-in-chief over an expeditionary army of 10,000 men, the largest force thus far sent to the colonies.[14] Al-though he tried to escape his deep involvement with the war in the colo-nies, he became virtually its symbol. From 1814 to 1820, when he returned to Spain, Morillo made a valiant but vain effort to lead his men to victory.

Michael Quin, a travelling Englishman, called the king "delirious" to think that he could reconquer a courageous and numerous people "with a handful of discontented soldiers,"[15] and events bore him out. Although the army was supposed to depart from Cádiz in November 1814, foul weather prevented the sailing. Despite another attempt to sail in Decem-ber, the fleet was forced to stay there until February 17, 1815. According to Rafael Sevilla, a young officer under Morillo, the soldiers were bribed to go to America by being promoted "one rank higher," but the transpar-ent scheme "disgusted the army," and "few officers" volunteered to go. All of the men were quartered and watched to avoid desertions, and every day the departure was announced for the following day.[16] One reason for the close supervision was that Cádiz was seething with secret societies modeled on Freemasonry, which hoped to restore the Constitution of 1812. Naturally the plotters tried to interest the troops in their plans. Morillo himself was initiated into one of these societies and urged to lead a revo-lution, but he refused and tried to hold the other members to their duty. With some of the soldiers he succeeded; others deserted.[17]

Though no uprising occurred among the soldiers in 1815, largely be-cause of his magnetic leadership, army morale was extremely low. Morillo felt obliged to conceal the true destination of his command, and for months, the men believed that they were sailing to Buenos Aires. Not until the expedition was well at sea was the word given out that they were really going to Costa Firme. According to Sevilla, this "accursed news" spread about his ship on February 25, causing "general consternation," because "we all knew . . . that in Costa Firme the war was fought without quarter and with savage ferocity. General Morillo, understanding the bad effect which this change of plan would cause, sent us an encouraging proclamation . . ."[18] The grumbling men acquiesced sullenly, and it is not surprising that when an accidental fire broke out on the *San Pedro* as she lay off the coast of Margarita, everyone assumed that there had been a mutiny.[19]

From the day of their arrival in America the Spanish troops were dissatisfied, despite their initial successes against the rebels. The inducements promised to them did not all materialize, and a minor revolt broke out in some companies from Extremadura.[20] Among the officers there were also rivalries, quarrels, and general bitterness.[21] Increasingly pessimistic about future success, Morillo asked to be relieved of command in June 1816. By the next year Margarita had been lost again, and the discord among the officers continued. In January 1818, Morillo once more wrote to Madrid requesting a transfer and complained of "the cowardly manner" in which the Spanish officers fled from the rebels, "seeking only their own personal safety."[22] Both times his request was ignored.

The most serious indication of low morale in the army was the problem of desertions.[23] Rafael Sevilla was sent out to track down a deserter as soon as he landed in Costa Firme,[24] and by 1816 references to large numbers of deserters were beginning to crop up in official correspondence. On January 26 the general-in-chief of the *Estado Mayor* wrote that he was looking in vain for the "prisoners and deserters of the fleet." Five weeks later he mentioned that "the roads are full of robbers from the many deserters of the . . . [Fifth] division,"[25] and in May 1816, Morillo wrote to Miguel de la Torre that in Caracas "they are deserting in flocks."[26]

The flights continued during 1817, although penalties became more severe. One soldier was arrested simply because he announced at the house of a certain Carmen Rosas, that "many soldiers" were considering defecting to the enemy.[27] A decree of 1815, which established the death penalty for anyone caught more than one-half league from the army, had no noticeable effect. In 1819 Morillo wrote to another officer demanding that the original decree be more widely publicized.[28] But a month later an entire battalion deserted, to the great consternation of the Spanish officers.[29] In 1820 (the year that Morillo's resignation was finally accepted) the situation was desperate. On July 31, he wrote to the jefe superior político for help in order to prevent the "dissolution of the army." The number of defectors had reached, "in a short time, more than 300 men from the Third Battalion of the King, and not a few from the Second of Valencey, Barina, Príncipe and the other divisions. . . ."[30] By now the king's army was in such obvious danger of losing the war that the deterioration of morale was to be expected. But in view of the fact that Morillo's entire Spanish force had numbered only 10,000 men, the numbers who deserted are impressive. On December 23, 1820, an officer reported his failure to apprehend any of the 336 men who had defected during the previous August; and on December 30, another officer listed 800 men missing.[31]

In 1821 many officers began to shirk their responsibilities and apply for transfer back to Spain, testifying that they "no longer found themselves fit to continue in service."[32] Miguel Valbuena wrote to La Torre at this time complaining that both the colonel and the lieutenant colonel had left his regiment for Spain, "in the critical circumstances of seeing this plaza blockaded by the enemy, abandoning in this way their most sacred obligations."[33] Other officers continued to complain desperately about the loss of men, lamenting that "everywhere one hears evil spoken of the king's troops and of the Spaniards."[34]

It is virtually impossible to determine the total number of Spaniards who defected, and one must also bear in mind that desertion was a common problem for all armies of the day, particularly in the tropics. Nevertheless, the evidence indicates that the Spanish forces were riddled to an unusual degree. One difficulty in keeping them together was that more than half were native American troops, many of them virtually kidnapped and forced to fight against their fellow countrymen. Although in the early years of the revolutions numerous Americans were eager to fight for the royalist cause, from 1817 on defeat cooled their allegiance to Spain. During the last several years of the wars, American recruits were provided "almost entirely" by forced levies a few days before a new campaign, as in the case of Brigadier General Mariano Osorio, who went into Chile in 1818 to battle the forces of [José de] San Martín: "The regiments were filled up, a few days previous to their embarkation, with prisoners, Negroes, and recruits of the worse description. . . ."[35] Small wonder that the men seized their first opportunity to defect. A British naval officer in 1821 reported that the entire King's Regiment of Numantia, close to 700 men, had deserted to San Martín. Out of 6,000 or 7,000 men in the royal army of Peru, he estimated that only 2,500 were Europeans. He added: "It is quite certain many of the royal troops will join San Martín the moment his army approaches Lima. . . ."[36]

In some cases all of a given group of deserters were Americans,[37] but there is no question that Europeans also were frequently involved. On September 11, 1820, Morillo wrote that the enemy was trying to enlist all the men in the area, "without distinction as to position or age, managing to bring over to their side even the soldiers of the Spanish nation."[38] Particularly convincing are the reports of British naval officers stationed off

Buenos Aires, Valparaíso, and Callao. In January 1818, Captain William Bowles of the *Amphion* wrote about the army of Peru:

> A very bad spirit pervades the whole corps: the Europeans are dissatis-
> fied and disaffected to a degree I could hardly have believed possible if
> I had not witnessed it myself; the squadron of lancers mutinied on the
> mole, and refused to embark till troops were brought up to compel them.[39]

Like many other British officers stationed there, Bowles was a shrewd and objective observer. He attributed the discontent to "the disunion which prevails amongst the Spaniards themselves—the dislike of the army to the harassing and inglorious service on which they are employed. . . . I heard many officers of rank express their earnest hope that the war might soon terminate in the acknowledgement of the independence of this country."[40]

If desertion and insubordination increasingly threatened the success of the royal forces in America, it is also true that back in Spain the people showed less and less interest in actively supporting the war. The true measure of this attitude can be seen in the government's continued difficulty in raising expeditions, a fact which had profound political connotations.

With every passing month, fewer men seemed willing to risk death in the malarial wastes of the colonies. Stragglers brought back to Spain hair-raising descriptions of dense jungles, of deserts "like petrified seas" and tales of "putrefying corpses, impenetrable forests, man-eating reptiles," and of tigers "roaring at night."[41] Even in the rigorously censored pages of the *Gazeta de Madrid* such stories had an effect. In September 1815 the Ministry of the Indies reported that the soldiers assigned to go to America were "delaying their departure in a scandalous way"; and a year later the Ministry of War complained of the "scandalous desertion" of the soldiers who were to be sent overseas as replacements.[42]

Nevertheless, the government finally answered Morillo's pleas for another expedition. He had written repeatedly for more men and supplies, and Minister of State León y Pizarro (by his own account) worked tirelessly to prod his fellow ministers into action.[43] At length, on May 21, 1818, an expedition put out from Cádiz for Peru, consisting of the *María Isabel* with thirty cannons and ten *transportes* carrying in all 2,080 men. Very shortly they met with bad weather, and the men took advantage of the opportunity to make known to the commanding officer of the expedition a long list of grievances. Their complaints were not heeded, and on July 25, the entire crew of the *Trinidad*, led by Remigio Martínez, revolted, killed six officers, and sailed to the Río de la Plata, where the people of Buenos Aires received them joyously on August 26. There they informed the government of the United Provinces that they had planned the uprising even before leaving Cádiz and revealed all the details about the expedition. They were then housed in special quarters and exposed to a continuous round of visits from curious sightseers.[44]

The Spanish government tried to conceal the news of the incident from its people, but *El Español Constitucional*, published in London by a group of émigré liberals, did not hesitate to quote the entire story as it appeared in the *Morning Chronicle*. The article related that when the men left the Canary Islands they were in a "deplorable situation," lacking clothing and sufficient supplies. "Besides," it continued, "all the soldiers knew very well the sad fate of the devotees of Morillo [sic] . . .," and did not want to share it.[45] The British, eager to start trading with the new, "independent" American republics, naturally took the incident as a sign of the growing resistance in Spain to the war and used it in propaganda.

News of this incident was virtually suppressed in Spain, but within two years fear of fighting in the colonial wars contributed to another uprising of such importance that it could not be concealed: the Revolution of 1820. Its instigators obviously acted out of political motives and did most of their scheming in the headquarters of the Freemasons at Cádiz. In fact, the man described as "the soul and expression of the Revolution of 1820," Antonio Alcalá Galiano, was a prominent Freemason.[46] An elfish little person with peculiar bulging eyes, Alcalá was best known as an orator, with a voice described as eloquent and irresistible by people who heard him. The Englishman Michael Quin saw him once at the Cortes in 1821 and reported that at the end of each speech the people would bear him on their shoulders out of the Cortes and into the street past a crowd of cheering admirers.[47]

The voice of Alcalá Galiano was first put to active use in behalf of revolution during 1817, as he began to call for the liberation of the country from the stifling absolutism of Ferdinand VII. He described himself as a "violent political fanatic," and worked in an intermediary body of the Freemasons known as the Taller Sublime to build up support for the revolt.[48] Even at this level, the military took an extremely important part in the planning;[49] but the revolt might never have been carried out, had not a new expedition been formed to sail to America.

Some contemporaries claimed that the government was aware of the revolutionary activity in the Spanish army, and hoped to banish the suspects to the colonies, where they could do no harm.[50] Even if the government were innocent of such scheming, it had undeniably picked a poor moment to send out another expedition. Fourteen battalions were gathered in Cádiz in preparation for their departure, under the command of Enrique O'Donnell, the Conde de La Bisbal, who was a Freemason.[51] Veterans from America continued to give accounts of the miserable conditions there "which gave rise to the feeling that the members of the expedition were going to their execution."[52] Particularly demoralizing were the stories told by the wounded, with haggard, feverish faces, who were recovering in a Cádiz hospital. Just back from Colombia where they had fought under Morillo, they would talk to the officers of the new expedition, and, "showing their wounds and skeletons, told of their misery and the continuous privations which they had suffered, and the death of their companions. . . ."[53]

Ramón de Santillán, La Bisbal's aide-de-camp, wrote in his memoirs that the government believed it could reconquer America "without doubt" through the new expedition. But there were only fourteen thousand men in all, including cavalry, and "the moral conditions of these troops," he wrote, "already bad in themselves, had been worsened by the secret artifices . . . which were employed . . . to corrupt them."[54] On the other hand, he admitted that the manner in which the men were selected to go was unfortunate. Almost all of the soldiers had already fought in the War of Independence against Napoleon and had completed their legal period of service. They were told that the selection would be done by lot, but as Santillán admitted, "no one doubted that partiality had a greater part in it than luck."[55] In the infantry many of the officers were given salary increases to go, but the cavalry officers either had to sail with the expedition or retire. So many requested retirement that the officers of the three regiments "were renewed four or five times."[56]

Morale was thus very low among those soldiers who "had many times already shown their fear of dying in the New World," and it was worsened by the propaganda of American agents.[57] American Freemasons had lodges in London and Lisbon and numerous connections within Spain. Carlos Pueyrredón was particularly active in dispatching money and agents to Spain, for as Supreme Director of the United Provinces, he knew that the expedition was bound for the Río de la Plata. Other active Argentines were Tomás Lezica and Andrés Argibel, merchants living in Cádiz who generously scattered money and proclamations through the city.[58] Finally, as if all the human efforts to demoralize the troops were not enough, a serious epidemic of yellow fever broke out in Cádiz, a ghoulish reminder of the deadly tropical diseases which awaited them in the Indies.

The revolutionaries made one false start in July 1819, but were thwarted by the last-minute treachery of O'Donnell. After renewed preparations on the first day of the new year the commander of the Battalion of Asturias, Rafael Riego, led an uprising in Cabezas de San Juan, proclaiming the Constitution of 1812. That same night he surprised the officers at Arcos de la Frontera. Meanwhile, Colonel Antonio Quiroga revolted in Alcalá de los Gazules and in San Fernando. Neither man succeeded in taking Cádiz, and in the face of this discouraging start Riego began an expedition across Andalucía. His effort was a disaster. Repelled in Málaga, impotent in Córdoba, he found his army of 1,500 almost completely melted away through desertions when he reached Extremadura. Had not other constitutionalist revolts broken out in La Coruña, Zaragoza, and Barcelona,

the outcome of Riego's abortive endeavor would have been quite different.[59] As Rafael Comellas points out, the initial uprising "was confined
exclusively to the expeditionary army."[60] And according to a sarcastic
contemporary, it was initiated solely to avoid the trip to the New World:
they proclaimed the Constitution only in order to "give their rebellion an
honest appearance."[61] These comments, together with Riego's failure to
lead the men beyond the first stages of the uprising, indicate that the men's
attitude toward the American wars influenced the entire proceedings. Even
the soldiers loyal to the king seemed to agree with the unfortunate members of the expedition. In a proclamation issued by Manuel Freyre at the
Cuartel General of Seville on January 20, he urged his own men to remain
loyal to Ferdinand, telling them openly what every one of them probably
already believed, that the fight which would bring them glory did not lie
in the steaming jungles of the colonies.[62] As to the new revolutionary government, within a month, the *Gaceta Patriótica del Ejército Nacional*, a
voice of the most radical rebel leaders, began to advocate dispatching commissioners to America to arrange for the recognition of independence.[63]

The Revolution of 1820 has been the subject of numerous works by
students of Spanish history, but they have never sufficiently emphasized
its almost total dependence on the whims of the dispirited *ultramar* expeditionary force. The army which provided the power for the revolutionary
leaders was not in the least committed to a constitutional regime. Although
some of the revolutionary leaders courted the indifferent troops by coming out for an end to the colonial war and for American independence, the
army did not respond. As soon as their own interests were served, the
troops abandoned the revolutionary cause, leaving a tiny minority to establish a government which had neither public support nor military force
to back it up. During the next three years there was general chaos, with
party squabbles, political assassinations, and riots in the streets. When in
1823 a French expedition was sent in to overthrow the constitutional government, its success was anticlimactic. The liberal government had never
really been established.

Likewise, very little attention has been paid to the important repercussions which the disruption of the expedition had in America. Without
exaggeration the failure of the Cádiz army to sail could be described as
the most important single factor determining the loss of the Río de la
Plata. No doubt independence would have come eventually, but the fact
remains that the years 1819–1820 were the most favorable time in the
entire decade for a Spanish reconquest. Captain Bowles stationed off
Buenos Aires reported on first hearing of the expedition: "I have never
before seen Buenos Ayres in so defenceless a situation, nor discontent
and poverty so general."[64] The new government was torn with internal
squabbling, and even the war hero San Martín was subjected to accusations and plots. Bowles wrote that the news of the expected invasion had

caused "little sensation," and that the government made virtually no preparations for defense. In short, "the present is the moment when a Spanish expedition would experience fewer difficulties than at any former period of the revolution. . . ."[65]

The lost opportunity and the negative attitude in the peninsula caused despair among the wretched soldiers already in the colonies. In 1821 a letter by a "well-known officer" to *El Espectador* expressed the misery so universally felt. The officer remarked that in the Spanish press no subject escaped discussion, "however small and negligible," except for the war in America, and the latter was treated with "the most lamentable indifference." Then with the bitterness of a condemned and forgotten man, he asked sardonically to be forgiven for his bad humor:

> Beneath the fire of the enemy cannon, one cannot speak with the calmness, or rather, with the indolence, of you in Madrid. You do not care to think either of peace, or of sending us another brig to continue the war. A more terrible situation does not exist. Our fate has been decided: we are condemned to perish in the obscurity of this campaign without even leaving the memory of our names [behind].[66]

What is the real explanation for the inferior morale of the Spanish troops, and the insubordination, doubtful loyalty, and defection of so many soldiers? And apart from the reasons for the low morale, were there other occasions than the Revolution of 1820 when it served the interests of political manipulators?

The most obvious reasons for the apathy and misery of the troops were that in the opinion of many the empire was not worth risking their lives for, and that they had a particular distaste for service in the tropics. After six years of battling against Napoleon, many of them were probably tired of war and wished to return to their own affairs. Even with special inducements these men went to America against their will. When the inducements failed to materialize, and the war turned out to be even fiercer than they had imagined, one can understand their readiness to flee.

Yet apart from this basic explanation of the events which occurred, another factor played a part in the morale and performance of the army—politics. In Cádiz during the Revolution of 1820 the army served the interests of certain political leaders, and the military malaise was also put to good use in America. There numerous events indicate that political alliances and hostilities were more important to some men than the course of the war. This is simply another manifestation of the same basic attitude exhibited by the common infantryman who was so inclined to desert; the apathy and discontent which affected him also affected his superiors. But the symptoms of his superiors were not apt to be cured by bolting into the jungle at the start of a battle. The officers would stay on the scene and loudly protest their loyalty to the cause, but jeopardize the entire war effort and at the same time reveal their indifference to it by pursuing their political rivalries. As it happened, the principal actors in these political episodes were liberals, a fact which is not difficult to explain. Back in 1811 and 1812 there had been liberals in Cádiz who advocated force to defeat the rebels in the colonies, but Ferdinand VII so expanded the policy with the mammoth (for Spain) expedition of General Morillo that force in America came to be identified as his own absolutist policy. After the restoration in 1814 the king alienated many Spaniards by his merciless repression of the liberals, particularly those involved with the Cádiz Constitution of 1812. Henceforth anyone with even lukewarm liberal sympathies would have viewed with distaste the prospect of serving with the king's troops in America. The real war to them was the one at home against royal despotism. Such men who were forced to serve in the colonies were not particularly enthusiastic about the cause, nor were they always loyal to the king's viceroys and captains-general.

The first manifestation of these political tensions appeared in 1814 and 1815 when Morillo's expedition was preparing to leave Cádiz. Contemporaries were aware that Freemasons and other secret societies were then attempting to turn the soldiers against Ferdinand and frequently succeeding. No doubt many of the rivalries which broke out among the troops after their arrival in Costa Firme were planted among them by the Masons and other liberals. There are many other striking incidents to choose from. A particularly intriguing case is that of Javier Mina, a Spaniard who led an army to fight against his own countrymen for the freedom of Mexico.

Javier Mina was the nephew and comrade-in-arms of a brilliant hero in the War for Independence, the famed guerrilla fighter from Aragón, Francisco Espoz y Mina. Both men were suspect because of their known revolutionary tendencies, but while the older of the two was treated with disdain, Javier was offered the command of a division in Mexico. This offer, incidentally, lends credence to the belief that the king was not averse to using the distant war in the colonies to rid himself of troublesome liberals. Javier refused the command indignantly and said openly what certain other Spanish liberals no doubt believed but lacked the courage to express. The Spanish government was acting, he declared, "as though the cause that the Americans defend was different from that which raised the Spanish people to glory . . . and as though I would be the executioner of an innocent people. . . ."[67] The two, working together, fomented an uprising in Pamplona against the hated king, whom Javier described bitterly as "the very one whom Spain had ransomed with rivers of blood . . . and [who had] made her bow again under . . . tyranny and fanaticism. . . ."[68] The plot failed, and Javier escaped. In exile he decided to go beyond neutrality in the fight against the Mexican revolutionaries—he would fight in their behalf. His decision no doubt owed something to a £2000 pension which the British government granted him, but it was also in large part a product of idealism. A third motive could well have been revenge against Ferdinand VII. After soliciting support in both England and the United States, and after various reversals of fortune, he finally landed on the Mexican coast in 1816 with a tiny expeditionary force of 270 men. He and his soldiers fought against overwhelming odds for about a year before he was finally captured and executed in 1816.[69] Mina's expedition so outraged the Spanish press that instead of trying to conceal it from the public, the editors gave daily accounts of the rebel's acts in extravagant and bloodcurdling detail. His capture and death were widely hailed as a fitting end to such treachery, and the men who apprehended him received generous awards and decorations.[70] The official explanation for his conduct was that he was another victim of "unbridled ambition."[71] This may have been the case. But at the same time he seemed to be rebelling in a particularly spectacular manner against the king's absolutism.

When the news arrived in America that the restored Constitution of 1812 was supposed to be promulgated there and obeyed by all authorities, the animosities of several years burst into the open. Rivalries between absolutists and constitutionalists (paralleling those in Spain itself) all too often became more important than the conduct of the war against the rebelling colonists.

In 1821 Viceroy Juan Ruiz de Apodaca of New Spain so alienated many of his officers and men that on July 5 some of the officers staged a coup and forced him to relinquish command to Field Marshal Francisco Novella. An anonymous veteran analyzed the reasons for this event in a pamphlet of 1822, citing numerous instances of incompetence on the part of the viceroy and telling of dissension among some of the officers. In one incident the Battalion of Murcia asked for reinforcements, and the viceroy sent only 700 men. These men, wrote the veteran, "undertook the march under terrible disillusionment, and although they were all Europeans the fire of discord devoured their officers. . . . Many of those soldiers were seduced by the papers which the enemy circulated . . . , as a result of which a great number passed over to the enemy, and the rest succumbed shamefully because of the inability and cowardice of the chief who commanded."[72]

While this tragic episode reveals a measure of incompetence on the part of the viceroy and disloyalty among certain officers, were these factors the sole reasons for overthrowing Apodaca? As early as 1815 the Spanish army in New Spain had suffered from desertions and poor command; yet the viceroy was not overthrown.[73] The coup occurred in 1821, one may suspect, because in that year Apodaca was known to be "horrified" at the new constitutional regime in Spain and did not want to proclaim the constitution. His vacillation angered liberal officers, for it challenged the validity of the code and led many people in New Spain to "doubt that they had to respect it." As a result, one liberal complained that "an apathetic government, instead of invigorating the law, deprived it of its force. . . ."[74] Like many liberals in Spain itself, the liberal officers in America expected the constitution to attract most of the rebels back to the mother country. Apodaca's reluctance to accept it struck them as treasonable, tantamount to giving up the last chance to save the empire.

Political differences among the soldiers led them to mutiny against the high command. Insubordination and apathy were widespread, and one doubts whether under such circumstances the army could ever have defeated an enemy. These political dissensions in America were not confined to any one province; during the same year that Apodaca was overthrown in New Spain, Viceroy Joaquín de la Pezuela was ousted from Peru under strikingly similar circumstances and probably for the same reasons.

As a general Pezuela had gained many victories for the king, but his liberal officers later maintained that upon assuming the office of viceroy in 1816, he was responsible for a series of catastrophic defeats, including the Battle of Maipú and the loss of an important ship, the *María Isabel*.[75] The situation was already serious when the advance of San Martín's army in 1820 made it intolerable. According to Jerónimo Valdés (one of these officers), when Pezuela learned of the approaching army "he acted as San Martín himself would have acted; which is to say, he diminished his troops. . . ."[76] By 1821 the Spanish army was blockaded by land and sea, and morale was so low that every day brought new desertions among both soldiers and officers, "and there existed among the loyal men the most melancholy discontentment."[77] In addition to his lethargy, the much maligned viceroy aroused further comment by a series of foolish appointments—in particular by placing suspected traitors in command of the two provinces of Trujillo and Guayaquil.[78]

The result of these circumstances was one of the most celebrated incidents of the Spanish-American wars. A group of Spanish officers, including many leading figures of the army—Jerónimo Valdés, García Camba, Francisco Narváez, Antonio Seoane, and others—forced Pezuela by a coup to resign his office.[79] It is quite possible to accept the officers' explanation that the overthrow of Pezuela was justified by the very real danger in which the army of Peru found itself or to argue that, even if a grievous act of insubordination, it was partly brought on by the viceroy's unpopularity.[80] Many accounts, both contemporary and more recent, do not attribute the incident to anything more than these two possible causes.[81] But although both undoubtedly played a part in the coup, it would be a mistake to ignore the obvious political implications of what occurred. On one hand Pezuela, like Apodaca, was distressed and disgusted by the proclamation of the constitution in 1820 and likewise delayed promulgating it.[82] On the other hand all of the officers who took part in his ouster were liberals. Some American witnesses at the time even stated openly that Pezuela fell because of "the existence in the Spanish Army of a constitutional party"; it was a fact acknowledged by all sides that some of the Spanish generals had already tried to take over power by establishing a military junta to dictate policy to the viceroy.[83]

The political significance of Pezuela's fall becomes even more apparent in the light of an incident which occurred shortly afterwards to the embarrassment of the succeeding viceroy, José de la Serna. At the end of 1823, when in Spain the constitution had once again been abolished and the king restored to his full arbitrary power, General Antonio Olañeta was defending La Paz, Cochabamba, and Osuro against the onslaught of [Simón] Bolívar. Olañeta suddenly left his post, persuaded the squadron of dragoons from Tarifa to join him, collected all the other forces from the Desaguadero river to Potosí, and took over the entire latter province. Next, he attacked General Rafael Maroto, the Spaniard in command of Charcas, and took over that province as well.[84]

How is one to explain such a seemingly treacherous action? Among the reasons advanced are the well-known "hatred" between Olañeta and Maroto; the influence of Olañeta's nephew, Casimirio; and perhaps even concern for the shaky commercial holdings which Olañeta had been promoting in Peru since 1810 (to the disgust of the military there).[85] But the general himself and most of his contemporaries cited a different reason. By a quirk of fate Olañeta learned about the overthrow of the Constitution in Spain and the restoration of King Ferdinand before the main body of the royal army became aware of it; and he apparently hoped to ingratiate himself with the king by pretending that he, of all the officers in Peru, was the only one who had been loyal during the past three years. Thus he attacked La Serna and all the officers under him for being constitutionalists, Jews, and heretics (the latter two points thrown in to please the Catholic king) and set himself up as the only true representative of Spanish interests. Olañeta's position was untenable, for in 1820 he had written to the viceroy that he had "celebrated the new constitutional institutions with supreme rejoicing. . . ."[86] Olañeta's celebration of the constitution was short-lived; and equally precipitous was the change in his attitude toward the enemy. Espartero maintained that at this same time he saw in the possession of the American generals Arenales and Las Heras, communications from Olañeta "which left no doubt as to his close union with the rebels. . . ."[87] Other contemporaries also accepted as fact that he was "in accord with the insurgents" and that he enjoyed "a close and shameful union with the enemies."[88] Throughout 1824, Olañeta harassed the Spanish forces, supposedly communicated with Bolívar, Antonio José de Sucre, and Arenales, and incorporated some of his erstwhile prisoners-of-war into his own ranks. He also made his own contribution to the final, climactic Battle of Ayacucho of December 9, 1824, when Spain in effect lost the empire. In that battle the Spanish army was faced not by one but by two enemies—the American army of General Sucre, and 3,000 soldiers led by Olañeta. Bolívar so appreciated the services of the Spanish general that he published a proclamation urging Peruvians to honor him as "one of their liberators."[89]

Olañeta's record of having once supported the constitution and his later dealings with the enemy prove him to have been an opportunist of the first water.[90] In any case, however, it is significant that he based his entire appeal on a political issue, absolutism versus constitutionalism.[91] In this he provides evidence that the downfall of Pezuela had involved the same issue. Olañeta pointedly refused to recognize Pezuela's successor, La Serna, on the grounds that he was usurping royal authority, and Olañeta appealed to all of Pezuela's supporters to flock to the new army of absolutism.[92] Presumably many of them did. The only really unusual feature of this royalist escapade is that the general was not a liberal—practically the only exception to the usual pattern.[93]

The Spanish army is a useful instrument by which to measure some of the attitudes current in Spain toward the wars being fought to save the colonies. We can conclude that the troops during the entire period were reluctant to take part in the colonial campaigns. They rebelled before embarking, on the voyage over, and once they reached America. So casual were they toward the fate of the empire that they not only deserted, but frequently joined the ranks of the enemy. In 1820 they prevented the departure of an entire expedition by joining in a liberal revolt against the king, and significantly, they participated in the revolt only until the expedition was dispersed, then quietly slipped out of Riego's army. It was not to establish the constitution that these troops followed Riego; it was only to escape being sent to America.

In all probability these soldiers were not acting solely out of fear. They were responding also to the apathy of the Spanish public and to a conviction that their sacrifices would be in vain and their death unmourned. They were distressed at the prevalent apathy and especially at the way that political protaganists of both sides—but especially the liberals—exploited the fears and tensions of the war for their own ends.

These were not normal times. One suspects that had Spain been faced by revolts of this magnitude in its empire fifty years earlier, the public would have enthusiastically supported any effort to put them down. On the other hand, one could argue that fifty years earlier it had mattered considerably less what the public thought, for since that time even the rigid absolutism of Spain had suffered severe and irreparable cracks. By 1814, men who formerly had been content to criticize Manuel Godoy in the safe confines of literary salons had now had a taste of power. For six years they had governed the country in a time of great national crisis— for which they were rightly proud—and at the same time they had written into the Constitution of 1812 all of the rights and freedoms which they so avidly espoused. Yet in 1814, not only were their services ignored or ridiculed; all that they had done was totally and ruthlessly abolished, and they themselves were hunted down like criminals. Thereafter, many of them had but one goal: revenge against Ferdinand VII. On the surface this dedication of theirs had nothing to do with the revolts in the colonies, but in fact it had a considerable bearing on them.

From the madcap escapade of Javier Mina to the wrecking of the 1820 expedition, the liberals as a whole severely impeded the king's recovery of his empire. They began to play on the fears of the soldiers as early as 1814, and their propaganda intended more than merely frightening the men against the expedition: it was also aimed at embarrassing the king. How else can one explain why the mutineers of the *Trinidad* sailed, not to a neutral country, but to the port of Buenos Aires where they gave information to the enemy? The most spectacular example, the seduction of the 1820 expedition, identified the liberals with an attitude of leniency if not indifference towards the colonies. This position was to prove embarrassing between 1820 and 1823 (when they again fell from power).

In the New World also, political battles begun in the peninsula were pursued with fervor, regardless of whether they disrupted military campaigns. Particularly after the revolution of 1820, liberals and conservatives fought for power at the expense of the war effort, with the liberals winning the most important positions. After the overthrow of Pezuela, the army of Peru was identified as a hotbed of leftists, especially after the same officers were defeated in the great battle at Ayacucho in 1824. With each passing year the ouster of the viceroy was attributed more to political than military reasons, and was even held as the cause for losing the battle and the empire.[94] Olañeta, who also sought power at the expense of the war, has been regarded as a hero by conservatives ever since. From Mariano Torrente to Enrique Gandía, his intercourse with the enemy and other dubious activities have been passed over, and he has emerged as a great patriot.[95] Ayacucho was not even important, asserts Gandía, for it defeated only the constitutionalist branch of the army. "Spanish domination continued to be powerful in Upper Peru, and could have recovered all that was lost if a misplaced bullet had not killed . . . Pedro Antonio de Olañeta, . . . champion of monarchical absolutism in the New World!"[96] The posthumous glory of Olañeta reveals the incredible degree to which the political views of the Spanish officers obscured and undermined the real objective in Peru, as in all Latin America—the reconquest of the colonies.

Notes

1. Research for this article was made possible by grants from Samuel Kunstadter and the American Association of University Women.

2. Juan López Cancelada, quoted in Jaime Delgado, *La independencia de América en la prensa española* (Madrid, 1949), 102; "¡Seremos al fin franceses!" *El Robespierre español*, April 3, 1811, 28.

3. Alexandre Moreau de Jonnes, *Statistique de l'Espagne* (Paris, 1834), 235.

4. It is very difficult indeed to estimate what percentage of the total army in the colonies consisted of Americans. Some regiments were entirely American, such as the Regimiento de Voluntarios de Fernando VII de Veracruz, created in 1810 of local Veracruz businessmen. A list of all the regiments can be found in the *Estado Militar de España*, in the *Guia oficial de España* (Madrid, 1816). But unfortunately there is not a breakdown of the troops. According to Laura Ullrick, 2,000 men in Venezuela were Spanish, or about a fifth of the total force there. "Spanish Administration in Venezuela, 1808-1820," (Ph.D. dissertation, Northwestern University, 1921). For the sake of convenience I use the term "American" throughout this paper to refer to Latin Americans.

5. *Gazeta de Madrid*, June 23, 1812, 709.

6. According to Captain William Bowles, in Gerald Graham and R. A. Humphreys, *The Navy and South America, 1807–23* (London, 1962), 106, 116.

7. *Ibid.*, 117. See also report of Comisión de Reemplazos, *El Universal*, April 11, 1814, 402 and April 12, 1814, 407.

8. Quoted in Anon., *Reflexiones en contestación al artículo comunicado inserto en el Universal número 169. . . .* (Madrid, 1821).

9. *El Amigo de las Leyes*, April 12, 1813, 134.

10. José Cevallos, Representación hecha por . . . , September 15, 1812. Biblioteca Nacional, Madrid (hereafter cited as BN), MS 18632.

11. *Diario de Juan Verdades*, February 4, 1814, 105.

12. Pedro de Urquinaona y Pardo, *Relación documentada del origen y progresos del trastorno de las provincias de Venezuela . . .* (Madrid, 1820), 131, 133. His italics.

13. José Mariano Aloy to Excemo, Sr. Ingen. Gral. De los Rs. Extos, Puerto Cabello, August 4, 1814. Madrid, Servicio Histórico Militar (hereafter cited as SHM), Ms 1–1–7–26.

14. Laura Ullrick, "Morillo's Attempt to Pacify Venezuela," HAHR, III (November 1920), 535. Between 1810 and 1826, the total number sent, according to one contemporary, was 30,000. José Presas, *Pintura de los males que ha causado á la España el gobierno absoluto . . .* (Burdeos, 1827), 101.

15. Michael Quin, *Memorias históricas sobre Fernando VII*, trans. by Joaquín García Jiminéz (Valencia, 1840), I, 171.

16. Rafael Sevilla, *Memorias de un oficial del ejército español . . .* (Madrid, [1916]), 22.

17. Ullrick, "Morillo's Attempt," 536.

18. Sevilla, *Memorias*, 24.

19. *Ibid.*, 41. The Americans tried to make propaganda of the incident, claiming that American prisoners had been left in the hold, an accusation hotly denied by the Spaniards. George Flinter, *A History of the Revolution of Caracas . . .* (London, 1819), 184.

20. Andrés García Camba, *Memorias para la historia de las armas expañolas en el Perú* (Madrid, 1846), I, 178.

21. Ullrick, "Morillo's Attempt," 546. The only major officer who gave Morillo his complete devotion, according to Ullrick, was Miguel de la Torre (who succeeded him).

22. Quoted in *ibid.*, 554.

23. Desertions were so well known in Spain that they entered the literature of the period. See, for example, Idelfonso Bermejo's novel, *Espartero. Novela contemporánea . . .* (Madrid, 1845), I, 266 ff.

24. Sevilla, *Memorias*, 50.

25. Correspondence of D. Pascual En——(!), letters No. 19, 29, and 36. Archivo Histórico Nacional, Madrid, Torrepando Collection (hereafter cited as TP, AHN), Leg. 6, capeta 13.

26. *Ibid.*, June 30, Leg. 3, No. 87.

27. *Ibid.*, Leg. 10, capeta 26, No. 4.

28. *Ibid.*, June 30, Leg. 3, No. 87.

29. *Ibid.*, Antonio Tovar to Miguel de la Torre, Leg. 6, Capeta 12, No. 28.

30. "Correspondencia . . . sobre reemplazos y desertores del Ejército," *ibid.*, Leg. 6, Capeta 12, No. 28.

31. Pedro Mayoz to José Casata, *ibid.*, Leg. 4, no number; and M. de Casa to General-in-Chief, *ibid.*, Leg. 4, no number.

32. This quotation is taken from a petition of fourteen officers, July 3, 1820, for release from service. *Ibid.*, Leg. 10, Capeta 27, No. 114.

33. This was Cartagena de las Indias. *Ibid.*, January 8, 1821, Leg. 4, no number.

34. *Ibid.*, March 31, 1821, Leg. 4, No. 51.

35. Captain William Bowles to Secretary of Admiralty Croker, *Amphion* at sea, January 4, 1818, in Graham and Humphrey, *The Navy and South America*, 218. For British comments on Spanish desertion see *The Correspondence of Lord Burghersh, 1808–40* (London, 1912), 26, 31, 37.

36. Captain William H. Sheriff, Callao, February 5, 1821, in *ibid.*, 326.

37. As in the defection of Col. D. Arana and 1,000 men in October 1820, since his battalion was known to have only natives in it. Morillo to Secretario del Estado y del Despacho Universal de la Guerra, October 11, 1820, TP, AHN, Leg. 3, No. 70.

38. *Ibid.*, Leg. 6, Capeta 12, No. 32.

39. Bowles to Croker, January 4, 1818 in Graham and Humphreys, *The Navy and South America*, 218.

40. *Ibid.*, 219.

41. See Sevilla, *Memorias*, 79, 106, 125, and 208.

42. *La Gazeta de Madrid*, September 7, 1815, 1045 and April 4, 1816, 344.

43. José García de León y Pizarro, *Memorias* (2 vols., Madrid, 1953), I. 265 ff.

44. Carlos Calvo, *Anales Históricos de la Revolución de la América Latina* (5 vols., Paris, 1864–1867), IV, 4–6. Calvo credits them with the loss of the *María Isabel*, for they revealed the ship's destination. The liberal officers in Peru blamed the loss on Viceroy Pezuela.

45. *El Español Constitucional*, December, 1818, 305.

46. Marqués de Villa Urrutia, *Fernando VII, Rey absoluto* (Madrid, 1931), 165.

47. Michael Quin, *A Visit to Spain* . . . (London, 1823), 158. Other contemporaries did not admire him. See Carlos LeBrun, *Retratos políticos de la Revolución de España* (Philadelphia, 1826), 127; and Anon., *Galería en miniatura de los más célebres periodistas* . . . (Madrid, 1822), 26. For a recent biography, see Felipe Ximénez de Sandoval, *Antonio Alcalá Galiano, el hombre que no llegó* (Madrid, 1948).

48. The group usually met at the house of Francisco de Isturiz in Cádiz. Antonio Alcalá Galiano (trans. and partial author), *Historia de España* . . . by S. A. Dunham (7 vols., Madrid, 1844–1846), VII, 65.

49. See the discussion of José Luis Comellas, *Los primeros pronunciamientos en España, 1814–1820* (Madrid, 1958), 305 ff.

50. See *ibid.*, 308.

51. Alcalá Galiano, *Historia*, VII, 64.

52. Ullrick, "Morillo's Attempt," 561.

53. Alcalá Galiano, *Historia*, VII, 65.

54. Ramón de Santillán, *Memorias (1815–1856)* (2 vols., Pamplona, 1960), I, 9.

55. *Ibid.* This was a far cry from the rumors which reached America that the expedition would have 26,000 men, or twice as many as it in fact had. See Bowles to Croker, August 13, 1819, in Graham and Humphreys, *The Navy and South America*, 273.

56. Ramón de Santillán, *Memorias*, I, 9.

57. C. Laumier, *Histoire de la Révolution d'Espagne en 1820; précédés d'un aperçu du Regne de Ferdinand VII* (Paris, 1820), 152.

58. Antonio Ballesteros y Beretta, *Historia de España y su influencia en la historia universal* (7 vols., Barcelona, 1918–1941), VII, 167.

59. Ferran Soldevila, *Historia de España* (3 vols., Barcelona, 1957), VI, 375–376. The number of works written on the revolt is quite large. See, for example, Eugenia Astur, *Riego y la revolución del año veinte* (Oviedo, 1933); and of course, Comellas, *Los primeros pronunciamientos*, 303–353. For further bibliography, see Ballesteros y Beretta, *Historia*, VII, 165–166.

60. Comellas, *Los primeros pronunciamientos*, 332.

61. José Presas, quoted in *ibid.*, 309

62. Quoted in *Diario de Barcelona*, February 9, 1820, 314.

63. *Gaceta Patriótica del Ejército Nacional*, February 29, 1820, 85.

64. Bowles to Croker, February 13, 1819, in Graham and Humphreys, *The Navy and South America*, 260.

65. Bowles to Croker, April 3, 1819, in *ibid.*, 267.

66. *Espectador*, September 7, 1821, 582.

67. As translated and quoted by Harris Gaylord Warren, "The Origin of General Mina's Invasion of Mexico," *The Southwestern Historical Quarterly*, XLII (1938), 3.

68. Translated and quoted in *ibid.*, 2. By "ransom" he is referring to the fact that the Spanish public believed that in 1808 King Ferdinand was kidnapped by Napoleon. Napoleon insisted that the Spanish king go to Bayonne, but the latter did so voluntarily and was not "kidnapped."

69. See William Davis Robinson, *Memoirs of the Mexican Revolution; including a narrative of the expedition of General Xavier Mina* (London, 1821), I, 81–102; and H.G. Warren, "Xavier Mina's Invasion of Mexico," HAHR, XXIII (February 1943), 52–76. For a personal account of the expedition, see the report of J. M. Hebb of April 30, 1819, Archivo General de Indias, Seville, Papeles de Estado, Audiencia de México, Leg. 14, No. 3, 14–52, located in the Ayer Collection of the Newberry Library (Chicago). Mexico was a temptation to other international expeditions also. See V. Vital-Hawell, "El aspecto internacional de las usurpaciones americanas en las provincias españoles . . . de 1810 a 1814," *Revista de Indias*, XXV (January-June 1965), 115–154.

70. Robinson, *Memoirs*, II, 119. Apodaca, for example, received the title of Condo de Venadito. See *Gazeta de Madrid*, January 27, 1818, 96–97; March 3, 1818, 228–231; August 4, 1817, 861–863.

71. See Mariano Torrente, *Historia de la revolución hispano-americana* (3 vols., Madrid, 1829–1830), I, 373.

72. Anon., *Compendio de los acontecimientos de Nueva España desde el año 1810, hasta la pérdida de aquella parte de la monarquía española* (La Coruña, 1822), 6.

73. D. Juan Comargo, Memorias sobre el Reyno de Nueva España, Provincias internas y Californias . . . , Veracruz, October 24, 1815. MS at SHM, 46.

74. Anon., *Compendio de los acontecimientos*, 5.

75. Jerónimo Valdés, *Exposición que dirige al rey don Fernando VII, sobre las causas que motivaron la pérdida del Perú* (Madrid, 1894), 28. Pezuela's responsibility for Maipú has been denied by his defenders. There is more evidence to charge him with the loss of the *Maria Isabel*. Significantly, the anonymous sympathetic author of *Personajes célebres del siglo XIX . . .* (3 vols., Madrid, 1843), III, 13, makes a point of ignoring the subject.

76. Valdés, *Exposición*, 32.

77. García Camba, *Memorias*, I, 369.

78. Valdés, *Exposición*, 37–39.

79. See José Canterac, et al., *Copia del oficio que los gefes del ejército nacional pasaron al Excelentísimo señor virrey del Perú don Joaquín de la Pezuela* (Madrid, 1821), 1.

80. From the time he replaced the "affable and benevolent" Viceroy Abascal in 1816, Pezuela suffered from unpopularity. See Juan Larrange, Noticias sobre el Perú, MS 2005425, BN.

81. In the *Diario de Barcelona* very little was said except that Pezuela had resigned for reasons of health, "heeding the general vote of the troops." La Serna was widely praised. See June 27, 1821, 1282.

82. Torrente, *Historia*, III, 29.

83. Quoted by Valdés, *Exposición*, 11; García Camba, *Memorias*, I, 369; Anon., *Personages célèbres*, 15ff; and see also, John Miller, *Memoirs of General Miller . . .* (2 vols., London, 1828), I, 282.

84. Valdés, *Exposición*, 65ff. See also García Camba, *Memorias*, II, *passim*.

85. Valdés, *Exposición*, 63. On Casimirio and the commercial holdings, see Torrente, *Historia*, III, 450ff.

86. Valdés, *Exposición*, Appendix 31, 158–159.

87. *Ibid.*, 66.

88. Pedro Chamorro y Baquerizo, *Biografía del ecselentísmo [sic.] Sr. . . D. José Santos de la Hera . . .* (Madrid, 1853), 27. Of course, a biographer of La Hera would be expected to take a critical view of his enemy, Olañeta.

89. Valdés, *Exposición*, Appendix 50, 194.

90. According to Valdés (*ibid.*, 7) Olañeta was trying to establish himself in a position of power so that he might take over as viceroy of Buenos Aires.

91. Ballesteros y Beretta, *Historia*, VII, 413.

92. Anon., *Personages célèbres*, 23; Valdés (*Exposición*, 7) calls them "Pezuelistas."

93. In 1821, Miguel Valbuena complained to La Torre of a colonel of the Cazadores de León, whose company was suffering from his "blind obstinacy in opposing the constitutional system" which all of his men had "happily accepted." Cartagena de las Indias, January 8, 1821, TP AHN, Leg. 4, no number.

94. Fifteen years later Espartero was popularly known in Spain as the head of the "ayacuchos," a leftist political clique, comprised mainly of liberals who had fought together in Peru. The career of this clique is further evidence of the effects, both direct and indirect, which the war in the colonies had on Spanish politics. See Margaret L. Woodward, "Spanish Apathy and American Independence (1810–1843)" (Ph.D. dissertation, University of Chicago, 1964), Chapter VII.

95. Torrente, *Historia*, III, 510. Torrente admits, however, that the discord within the Spanish forces was the main cause of the defeat (p. 503).

96. Enrique Gandía, "Las guerras de los absolutistas y liberales en América," *Revista de Indias*, XIV (July-December 1954), 408. Olañeta was murdered by his own men in February 1825.

Suggested Readings

As might be expected, considering the importance of the subject of national independence, historians of each Spanish American nation have written numerous major works and published multivolume document series. Much of this work commenced in the nineteenth century, and there was an outpouring of studies to commemorate the centennial of independence around 1910 with another for the sesquicentennial in the 1960s. Early works and memoirs by participants are still valuable as are the enormous studies by subsequent generations. Unfortunately, few of these works are available in English. One exception is the abridged section from General Daniel Florencio O'Leary's *Memorias*, which was translated by Robert F. McNerney, Jr., *Bolívar and the War of Independence* (Austin: University of Texas Press, 1970). Another useful collection of Simón Bolívar's writings, compiled by Vicente Lecuna and edited by Harold A. Bierck, *Selected Writings of Bolívar*, 2 vols. (New York: Colonial Press, 1951), makes available such documents as the famous proclamation of "War to the Death," the Jamaica Letter, and correspondence with many major figures including Francisco de Paula Santander, José de San Martín, Pablo Morillo, Bernardo O'Higgins, and Antonio José de Sucre. Some of the memoirs by English-speaking participants in the wars are valuable for their descriptions and insights while other observers wrote with political agendas or the desire to gain vengeance. One of the best studies is John Miller, *Memoirs of General Miller in the Service of the Republic of Peru*, 2 vols. (London: Longman, Rees Orme, Brown, and Green, 1829), reprinted in 1973 by the AMS Press in New York.

There are a number of comprehensive studies that provide excellent starting points for additional research. John Lynch has published many books and articles on Spanish American independence. His major survey, first issued in 1973, *The Spanish American Revolutions, 1808–1826: A Unified Account of the Revolutions that Swept over South and Central America in the Early Nineteenth Century* (New York: Norton, 1986), is in print in the second edition. Although somewhat dated now because of the flood of new works, Lynch offers a clear overview of the different movements. His recent edited study, *Latin American Revolutions, 1808–1826: Old and New World Origins* (Norman: University of Oklahoma Press, 1994), contains some translated documents as well as the work of major scholars today. Finally, Lynch's *Caudillos in Spanish America, 1800–1850* (Oxford: Clarendon Press, 1992), examines many important themes.

Other comprehensive overviews include Jay Kinsbruner, *Independence in Spanish America: Civil Wars, Revolutions, and Underdevelopment* (Albuquerque: University of New Mexico Press, 1994), which is the revised and enlarged edition of his 1973 book; and Richard Graham, *Independence in Latin America: A Comparative Approach* (New York: McGraw-Hill, 1994), another updated study first published in 1972. Still useful although out of print is the edited work by R. A. Humphries and John Lynch, *The Origins of the Latin American Revolutions, 1808–1826* (New York: Alfred A. Knopf, 1966). For scholarly chapters on the different regions as well as broad overviews on the independence movements see Leslie Bethell, ed., *The Cambridge History of Latin America*, vol. 3 (Cambridge, Eng.: Cambridge University Press, 1987). Also see Barbara A. Tenenbaum, ed., *Encyclopedia of Latin American History and Culture*, 5 vols. (New York: Charles Scribner's Sons, 1996). Jaime E. Rodríguez O.'s most recent work, *The Independence of Spanish America* (New York: Cambridge University Press, 1998), stresses political processes.

The background to the independence era particularly concerning the Bourbon reforms has been an area of considerable interest to historians. On administrative reform see the pioneering and still useful study by Herbert I. Priestley, *José de Gálvez, Visitor General of New Spain, 1765–1771* (Berkeley: University of California Press, 1916). Also see John Lynch, *Spanish Colonial Administration, 1782–1810: The Intendant System in the Viceroyalty of the Río de la Plata* (London: Athlone Press, 1958); John R. Fisher, *Government and Society in Colonial Peru: The Intendant System, 1784–1814* (London: Athlone Press, 1970); and Kendall W. Brown, *Bourbons and Brandy: Imperial Reform in Eighteenth-Century Arequipa* (Albuquerque: University of New Mexico Press, 1986). To examine different aspects of Bourbon reformism see David A. Brading, *Miners and Merchants in Bourbon Mexico, 1763–1810* (Cambridge, Eng.: Cambridge University Press, 1971); Brian R. Hamnett, *Politics and Trade in Southern Mexico, 1750–1821* (Cambridge, Eng.: Cambridge University Press, 1971); Nancy M. Farriss, *Crown and Clergy in Colonial Mexico: The Crisis of Ecclesiastical Privilege, 1759–1821* (London: Athlone Press, 1968); Susan Deans-Smith, *Bureaucrats, Planters, and Workers: The Making of the Tobacco Monopoly in Bourbon Mexico* (Austin: University of Texas Press, 1992); John Preston Moore, *The Cabildo in Peru under the Bourbons, 1700–1824* (Durham: Duke University Press, 1966); Mark A. Burkholder, *Politics of a Colonial Career: José Baquíjano and the Audiencia of Lima* (Albuquerque: University of New Mexico Press, 1980); Linda Arnold, *Bureaucracy and Bureaucrats in Mexico City, 1742–1835* (Tucson: University of Arizona Press, 1988); Luz María Hernández Sáenz, *Learning to Heal: The Medical Profession in Colonial Mexico, 1767–1831* (New York: Peter Lang, 1997); John E. Kicza, *Colonial Entrepreneurs: Families and Business in Bourbon Mexico City* (Albuquerque: University of New Mexico Press, 1983); William B. Taylor, *Magistrates of the Sacred: Priests and Parishioners in Eighteenth-Century Mexico* (Stanford: Stanford University Press, 1996); and Doris M. Ladd, *The Mexican Nobility at Independence, 1780–1826* (Austin: Institute of Latin American Studies, 1976).

Concerning precursor revolts and foreign influences see William B. Taylor, *Drinking, Homicide, and Rebellion in Colonial Mexican Villages* (Stanford: Stanford University Press, 1979); John Rydjord, *Foreign Interests in the Independence of New Spain: An Introduction to the War of Independence* (Durham: Duke University Press, 1935); Scarlett O'Phelan Godoy, *Rebellions and Revolts in Eighteenth-Century Peru and Upper Peru* (Cologne: Bühlau Verlag, 1985); John L. Phelan, *The People and the King: The Comunero Revolution in Colombia, 1781* (Madison: University of Wisconsin Press, 1978); Anthony McFarlane, *Colombia before Independence: Economy, Society, and Politics under Bourbon Rule* (New York: Cambridge University Press, 1993); and P. Michael McKinley, *Pre-Revolutionary Caracas: Politics, Economy, and Society, 1777–1811* (New York: Cambridge University Press, 1985).

For studies on the Bourbon army see Lyle N. McAlister, *The "Fuero Militar" in New Spain, 1764–1800* (Gainesville: University of Florida Press, 1957); Leon G. Campbell, *The Military and Society in Colonial Peru, 1750–1810* (Philadelphia: American Philosophical Society, 1978); Allan J. Kuethe, *Military Reform and Society in New Granada, 1773–1808* (Gainesville: University Presses of Florida, 1978); idem, *Cuba, 1753–1815: Crown, Military, and Society* (Knoxville: University of Tennessee Press, 1986); and Christon I. Archer, *The Army in Bourbon Mexico, 1760–1810* (Albuquerque: University of New Mexico Press, 1977).

On the nature of the rebellions and the reaction of Spain, there is much more published research on New Spain than on the other viceroyalties. Beginning with the Hidalgo Revolt see Hugh M. Hamill, *The Hidalgo Revolt: Prelude to Mexican Independence* (Gainesville: University Presses of Florida, 1966). On José María Morelos see Wilbert H. Timmons, *Morelos of Mexico: Priest, Soldier, Statesman* (El Paso: Texas Western College Press, 1963). There are two studies on Agustín de Iturbide: William Spence Robertson, *Iturbide of Mexico* (Durham: Duke University Press, 1952); and Timothy E. Anna, *The Mexican Empire of Iturbide* (Lincoln: University of Nebraska Press, 1990).

On the nature of the war and its impact on the life and institutions of New Spain see Brian R. Hamnett, *Roots of Insurgency: Mexican Regions, 1750–1824* (Cambridge, Eng.: Cambridge University Press, 1986); idem, "Mexico's Royalist Coalition: The Response to Revolution, 1808–1821," *Journal of Latin American Studies* 12:1 (May 1980): 55–86; John Tutino, *From Insurrection to Revolution in Mexico: Social Bases of Agrarian Violence, 1750–1940* (Princeton: Princeton University Press, 1986); Eric Van

Young, *Hacienda and Market in Eighteenth-Century Mexico: The Rural Economy of the Guadalajara Region, 1675–1820* (Berkeley: University of California Press, 1981); Peter F. Guardino, *Peasants, Politics, and the Formation of Mexico's National State: Guerrero, 1800–1857* (Stanford: Stanford University Press, 1996); Eric Van Young, "Islands in the Storm: Quiet Cities and Violent Countrysides in the Mexican Independence Era," *Past and Present* 118 (February 1988): 13–55; Christon I. Archer, "Bite of the Hydra: The Rebellion of Cura Miguel Hidalgo, 1810–1811," in Jaime E. Rodríguez O., ed., *Patterns of Contention in Mexican History* (Wilmington, DE: Scholarly Resources, 1992), 69–93; Archer, "The Indian Insurgents of Mezcala Island on the Lake Chapala Front, 1812–1816," in Susan Schroeder, ed., *Native Resistance and the Pax Colonial in New Spain* (Lincoln: University of Nebraska Press, 1998); Archer, "The Royalist Army in New Spain: Civil-Military Relationships, 1810–1821," *Journal of Latin American Studies* 13:1 (May 1981): 57–82; idem, "The Army of New Spain and the Wars of Independence, 1760–1821," *Hispanic American Historical Review* 61:4 (November 1981): 705–714; idem, "Insurrection-Reaction-Revolution-Fragmentation: Reconstructing the Choreography of Meltdown in New Spain during the Independence Era," *Mexican Studies/Estudios Mexicanos* 10:1 (Winter 1994): 63–98; idem, "New Wars and Old: Félix Calleja and the Independence War of Mexico, 1810–1816," in B. J. C. McKercher and A. Hamish Ion, eds., *Military Heretics: The Unorthodox in Policy and Strategy* (Westport, CT: Praeger, 1994), 33–56; Archer, "The Cutting Edge: The Historical Relationship between Insurgency, Counterinsurgency, and Terrorism during Mexican Independence, 1810–1821," in Lawrence Howard, ed., *Terrorism: Roots, Impact, Responses* (Westport, CT: Praeger, 1992), 13–28; Timothy E. Anna, *The Fall of the Royal Government in Mexico City* (Lincoln: University of Nebraska Press, 1978); Nettie L. Benson, *Mexico and the Spanish Cortés, 1810–1822* (Austin: University of Texas Press, 1966); Jaime E. Rodríguez O., ed., *The Independence of Mexico and the Creation of the New Nation* (Los Angeles: UCLA Latin American Center, 1989); idem, ed., *Patterns of Contention in Mexican History* (Wilmington, DE: Scholarly Resources, 1992); idem, ed., *The Evolution of the Mexican Political System* (Wilmington, DE: Scholarly Resources, 1993); idem, ed., *Mexico in the Age of Democratic Revolutions, 1750–1850* (Boulder: Lynne Rienner, 1994); and idem, ed., *The Mexican and Mexican-American Experience in the Nineteenth Century* (Tempe: Bilingual Press/Editorial Bilingüe, 1989). Rodríguez's edited volumes are especially useful because they contain essays by Mexican as well as foreign historians of Mexico. To trace the events of districts and regions see Peter Gerhard, *A Guide to the Historical Geography of New Spain* (New York: Cambridge University Press, 1972).

Although the situation is changing, the historical literature on the South American revolutions of independence is not as extensive as that on New Spain. There are several works in English on Bolívar but not as many as one might expect considering the vast output of Spanish-speaking historians, nor is there a good study of José de San Martín in English to match the output of Argentine scholars in Spanish. On Bolívar see Gerhard Masur, *Simón Bolívar* (Albuquerque: University of New Mexico Press, 1969); idem, "The Conference at Guayaquil," *Hispanic American Historical Review* 31:2 (May 1951): 189–229; Salvador de Madariaga, *Bolívar* (New York: Pelligrini and Cudahy, 1952); and John J. Johnson, *Simón Bolivar and Spanish American Independence, 1783–1830* (Princeton: D. Van Nostrand, 1968).

On the revolutions see Charles W. Arnade, *The Emergence of the Republic of Bolivia* (Gainesville: University Presses of Florida, 1957); Donald E. Worcester, *Sea Power and Chilean Independence* (Gainesville: University Presses of Florida, 1962); Timothy E. Anna, *The Fall of the Royal Government in Peru* (Lincoln: University of Nebraska Press, 1979); Alfred Hasbrouck, *Foreign Legionaries in the Liberation of Spanish South America* (New York: Columbia University Press, 1928); Stephen K. Stoan, *Pablo Morillo and Venezuela, 1815–1820* (Columbus: Ohio State University Press, 1974); Tulio Halperín-Donghi, *Politics, Economics, and Society in Argentina in the Revolutionary Period* (Cambridge: Cambridge University Press, 1975); and Jaime E. Rodríguez O., *The Emergence of Spanish America: Vicente Rocafuerte and Spanish Americanism, 1808–1832* (Berkeley: University of California Press, 1975). For Spain's reaction to the independence wars see Timothy E. Anna, *Spain and the Loss of America* (Lincoln: University of Nebraska Press, 1983); and Michael P. Costeloe, *Response to Revolution: Imperial Spain and the Spanish American Revolutions, 1810–1840* (Cambridge: Cambridge University Press, 1986).